This Small Army of Women

"V.A.D."

There's an angel in our ward as keeps a-flittin' to and fro,
With fifty eyes upon 'er wherever she may go;
She's as pretty as a picture and as bright as mercury,
And she wears the cap and apron of a V.A.D.

The Matron she is gracious and the Sister she is kind,
But they wasn't born just yesterday and lets you know their mind;
The M.O. and the Padre is as thoughtful as can be,
But they ain't so good to look at as our V.A.D.

She's a honourable miss because 'er father is a dook,
But, Lord, you'd never guess it and it ain't no good to look,
For 'er portrait in the illustrated papers for you see
She ain't an advertiser, not *our* V.A.D.

Not like them that wash a tea-cup in an orficer's canteen
And then "Engaged in War Work" in the weekly press is seen;
She's on the trot from morn to night and busy as a bee,
And there's 'eaps of wounded Tommies bless that V.A.D.

She's the lightest 'and at dressin's and she polishes the floor,
She feeds Bill Smith who'll never never use 'is 'ands no more;
And we're all of us supporters of the harristocracy
'Cos our weary days are lightened by that V.A.D.

And when the War is over, some knight or belted earl,
What's survived from killin' Germans, will take 'er for 'is girl;
They'll go and see the pictures and then 'ave shrimps and tea;
"E's a lucky man as gets 'er — and don't I wish 'twas me!

Poem discovered among the papers of Canadian Voluntary Aid Detachment nurse (VAD) Louisa Johnson and also published in E.R. Jaquet, *These Were the Men: Poems of the War, 1914–1918*.

THIS SMALL ARMY OF WOMEN

Canadian Volunteer Nurses
and the First World War

Linda J. Quiney

UBCPress · Vancouver · Toronto

26 25 24 23 22 21 20 19 18 17   5 4 3 2 1

Printed in Canada on FSC-certified ancient-forest-free paper
(100% post-consumer recycled) that is processed chlorine- and acid-free.

Library and Archives Canada Cataloguing in Publication

Quiney, Linda J., author
This small army of women : Canadian volunteer nurses and the First World War /
Linda J. Quiney.

Includes bibliographical references and index.
Issued in print and electronic formats.
ISBN 978-0-7748-3071-3 (hardcover). – ISBN 978-0-7748-3074-4 (EPUB). –
ISBN 978-0-7748-3075-1 (Kindle). – ISBN 978-0-7748-3073-7 (PDF)

1. Military nursing – Canada – History – 20th century. 2. Military nursing – Newfoundland
and Labrador – History – 20th century. 3. Nurses – Canada – History – 20th century.
4. Nurses – Newfoundland and Labrador – History – 20th century. 5. Voluntary aid detachments
– Canada. 6. Voluntary aid detachments – Newfoundland and Labrador. 7. World War,
1914-1918 – Medical care – Canada. 8. World War, 1914-1918 – Women – Canada. I. Title.

D629.C2Q56 2017   940.4'7571   C2017-901575-3
                                                     C2017-901576-1

Canada

UBC Press gratefully acknowledges the financial support for our publishing program
of the Government of Canada (through the Canada Book Fund),
the Canada Council for the Arts, and the British Columbia Arts Council.

This book has been published with the help of grants from the British Columbia History of
Nursing Society and the St. John Ambulance Association of Canada, and with the help of the
University of British Columbia through the K.D. Srivastava Fund.

Printed and bound in Canada by Friesens
Set in Fournier by Artegraphica Design Co. Ltd.
Copy editor: Deborah Kerr
Indexer: Noeline Bridge
Cover designer: George Kirkpatrick

UBC Press
The University of British Columbia
2029 West Mall
Vancouver, BC V6T 1Z2
www.ubcpress.ca

CONTENTS

Figures and Tables / vi

Acknowledgments / ix

Abbreviations / xii

Introduction / *3*

1 This Ardent Band of Ladies: Birth of the Canadian VAD Movement / *15*

2 Enthusiastic and Anxious: Mobilizing the Voluntary Nursing Service / *42*

3 Every Woman Is a Nurse: Framing the Image of the VAD / *80*

4 No Time for Sentiment: Making a Useful Contribution / *117*

5 Saying Goodbye: Forgetting, Remembering, and Moving On / *161*

Appendices / 190

Notes / 194

Bibliography / 235

Index / 252

FIGURES AND TABLES

Figures

Central Nursing Division No. 1 Toronto Corps, 1913 / *19*

Members of the St. John Ambulance Brigade, Newfoundland District, who cared for SS *Newfoundland* survivors, March 1914 / *20*

Frances Cluett in Europe, n.d. / *23*

Voluntary Aid Detachment, St. John Ambulance Association, Ottawa Nursing Division No. 32, 1917 / *25*

St. John Ambulance Association first aid certificate issued to Alice Bray, September 1915 / *29*

St. John Ambulance Association home nursing certificate issued to Alice Bray, April 1916 / *29*

Annie Wynne-Roberts, VAD, c. 1917 / *34*

Sybil Johnson, VAD, c. 1916 / *38*

Gwen Powys, SJAB Fort Rouge No. 6 Nursing Division, Winnipeg, c. 1918 / *43*

The Three Shining Lights of the Pine Hill Military Convalescent Hospital / *49*

Amelia Earhart, VAD, 1918 / *57*

Nursing Sister Ruby Gordon Peterkin, c. 1916 / *60*

Louise de Salaberry, VAD, c. 1917 / *60*

British Red Cross VAD recruitment poster / *62*

Western Group in Toronto, July 1918 / *69*

3rd London General Hospital, Wandsworth, 1915 / *73*

The Greatest Mother in the World, 1917 / *86*

Age distribution of Canadian VADs / *87*

Alice Houston, VAD, c. 1916 / *93*

Annie Gosling with a British Red Cross ambulance in France, c. 1918 / *105*

Grace MacPherson, VAD ambulance driver, May 1917 / *105*

Princess Mary, Countess of Harewood / *108*

New Brunswick ward, Duchess of Connaught Canadian Red Cross
    Hospital, c. 1916 / *112*

Grace MacPherson, VAD ambulance driver, BRCS Étaples motor convoy,
    May 1917 / *113*

Nesta the VAD, 1917 / *114*

Second Aid! / *115*

Elizabeth (Bessie) Hall, c. 1916 / *119*

VAD overseas postings by month / *131*

Jill Johnson, VAD, c. 1916 / *141*

"Don'ts for V.A.Ds" / *149*

Muriel Wainwright, VAD, c. 1917 / *149*

Milly Perley, Canadian Imperial VAD commandant / *165*

Ethel Gordon-Brown and VAD staff of the Canadian Red Cross Nurses'
    Rest House, Boulogne, July 1918 / *167*

Ethel Gertrude Dickinson, c. 1914 / *181*

Dorothy Twist / *181*

Headstone of Dorothy Twist, Aldershot Military Cemetery / *182*

Tables

2.1 Canadian and Newfoundland VADs who served overseas during the
    First World War / *50*

2.2 St. John Ambulance Brigade nursing divisions, Canada and Newfoundland,
    1912-18 / *52*

2.3 Prince Edward Island VADs overseas, Nursing Division No. 41 / *54*

2.4 St. John Ambulance Brigade, Canadian VAD contingents selected for
    overseas service / *66*

3.1 Fathers of Canadian and Newfoundland VADs, by occupation / *84*

3.2 Occupations of Canadian and Newfoundland VADs / *89*

3.3 VADs identified as university graduates / *90*

3.4 Canadian and Newfoundland VAD ambulance drivers / *100*

5.1 VAD deaths at home and overseas / *178*

5.2 Canadian VADs Mentioned-in-Dispatches / *180*

ACKNOWLEDGMENTS

FOR DECADES, CANADIAN AND Newfoundland Voluntary Aid Detachment (VAD) nurses have remained in the shadows of First World War histories. Although no Canadian or Newfoundland VAD published her own account of the war, some did leave traces of their experiences either tucked into archival collections or stored in the family attic. With the anniversary of the war, it is time to bring the history of these VADs into the light.

This book began at the University of Ottawa in the 1990s, when historian Ruby Heap discovered a photograph of a woman in a VAD uniform. The image led me to the headquarters of the St. John Ambulance Association in Ottawa, which generously opened its archive collection and library to initiate my research. What appeared to be a small organization of fewer than a hundred women was gradually revealed to include well over a thousand individuals whose uncharted history ran parallel to that of Canadian military nurses. It has been my privilege to uncover the unique experience of the Canadian and Newfoundland VADs and to restore their place in the history of Canada's war.

There are many people and organizations to acknowledge for their generous support and interest in this project. First, of course, I must thank Ruby Heap, a friend and colleague, for her invaluable mentoring. My sincere appreciation also goes to the St. John Ambulance for generously helping to fund the publication of this book. In particular, I must thank Gerry Beament, archivist, for opening their records; Dawn Roach, former priory secretary, for championing the support of this volume; and Irene Brady, her successor, for her continued support. My sincere thanks also go to the members of the Canadian St. John Ambulance Association for their unwavering enthusiasm for this project.

My deepest gratitude also extends to the members of the British Columbia History of Nursing Society (BCHNS) for generously helping to fund the publication of this book and to the president of the BCHNS, Kathleen Murphy, for her enthusiasm and support in making this possible. This was a legacy project for BCHNS, commemorating its twenty-fifth anniversary in 2015, and I am most grateful and honoured that this book was the society's first such endeavour. Thanks to nursing historian and BCHNS member Glennis Zilm for putting me in contact with the family of VAD Gwen Powys and for her own invaluable research into the history of nursing. Sincere thanks to Geertje Boschma, of the University of British Columbia School of Nursing, for her invaluable help and encouragement and for including me as an affiliate of the Consortium for Nursing History Inquiry, despite my lack of nursing credentials.

I am particularly indebted to the archivists of the British Red Cross Society Museum and Archives, in Barnett Hill and London, for allowing access to the Personnel Record Indexes of the First World War VADs, which enabled me to recover the identities of some five hundred Canadian and Newfoundland VADs who worked overseas during the war, and for their help with several of the images that appear in this book. Thanks also to the Imperial War Museum, London, for assistance with the diary of Canadian VAD Marjorie Starr, the memoir of VAD ambulance driver Jean Harstone, and images in the book.

Much of my travel across Canada and to England was funded by a Hannah Scholarship through Associated Medical Services, and this support was much appreciated. Many archivists contributed to my research in numerous institutions across Canada. The Centre for Newfoundland Studies at Memorial University provided tremendous help with the records of VADs Fanny Cluett, Sybil Johnson, Janet Miller, and several others in its wonderful collection of VAD diaries and correspondence. I am particularly indebted to retired archivist Bert Riggs and Linda White (now with Archives and Special Collections, Queen Elizabeth II Library at Memorial University) for their assistance. Linda and Joan Ritcey of the Centre for Newfoundland Studies have also been a great help with locating the images of Newfoundland VADs. The archivists of the Canadian War Museum in Ottawa assisted with the diary and records of VAD ambulance driver Grace MacPherson. The City of Ottawa Archives, the Canadian Red Cross National Archive in Ottawa, the Archives of Ontario in Toronto, and the CIBC Archives in Toronto, all supplied research assistance with various aspects of VAD history. I am indebted to many other individuals and institutions, including the Archives of Manitoba, City of Edmonton Archives, Dalhousie University Archives, McGill University Archives, Nova Scotia Archives, Provincial Archives of Alberta, and the Provincial Archives of Saskatchewan. In British Columbia, I was assisted by the Cowichan Valley Museum and Archives, by the Shawnigan Lake Museum, and by John Orr and Tom Paterson, for their research into VAD Dorothy Twist.

I am also grateful to those VAD family members, independent researchers, and genealogists who generously shared photographs, documents, and mementoes. Among them, the family of VAD Gwen Powys (Frances MacNeil, Marjorie North, and Debra North); the late E.G. Finley, son of VAD Eugenie Marjorie Ross; William Forrest, nephew of VAD Louise de Salaberry; Randy Carey, former pupil of VAD Ruby Pinfold; and Joan Rigby, for insights into the life of VAD Alice Lighthall.

This book would not have been completed without the critical advice of peer reviewers and the tremendous patience and invaluable assistance of Emily Andrew and Lesley Erickson at UBC Press, who guided it through to the conclusion, and the invaluable advice and insightful comments of Jillian Shoichet.

Finally, daughters Christina and Vanessa were always enthusiastic and supportive, and without the support and assistance of Rod there would be no book.

ABBREVIATIONS

BRCS	British Red Cross Society
CAMC	Canadian Army Medical Corps
CNATN	Canadian National Association of Trained Nurses
CRCS	Canadian Red Cross Society
FANY	First Aid Nursing Yeomanry
IODE	Imperial Order Daughters of the Empire
MHC	Military Hospitals Commission
MO	Medical officer
NS	Nursing sister
OMFC	Overseas Military Forces of Canada
RAMC	Royal Army Medical Corps
SJAA	St. John Ambulance Association
SJAB	St. John Ambulance Brigade
VAD	Voluntary Aid Detachment
WAD	Women's Aid Department

This Small Army of Women

INTRODUCTION

WITH HER SOFT LINEN head scarf and white apron emblazoned with a red cross, the Voluntary Aid Detachment nurse, or VAD, has become a romantic emblem of the First World War. Although VADs have long been idealized as a British phenomenon, there were two thousand members of Voluntary Aid Detachments from Canada and Newfoundland as of Armistice Day, November 11, 1918.[1] Most performed their war work in military convalescent hospitals across Canada and Newfoundland, but some five hundred were posted overseas as "active service" VADs. When hostilities ended, these women quietly slipped back into their civilian lives, leaving behind little tangible evidence of their unique work and experience. They were not the heroes of the conflict, and there was little public recognition of their service or of the value of their work. Whatever records or mementoes remained of their experiences were soon packed away with their well-worn St. John Ambulance uniforms – a grey dress with white collar and cuffs, a crisp white apron, and a black armband with a white Maltese cross.[2]

Instead, from the early 1930s, the published memoir of British VAD Vera Brittain, *Testament of Youth*, represented all VAD experience until the post-humous publication of her diary in 1981. A more nuanced record of Brittain's service than *Testament*, the diary stimulated a resurgence of interest from a new generation of second-wave feminist scholars.[3] In this post-1960s feminist interpretation of British women's experience of the war, scholars examined VAD memoirs, diaries, novels, and poetry through the lens of social history, sociology, and literary analysis.[4] The wartime experiences of Canadian and Newfoundland women are now benefitting from a long overdue analysis as a parallel to the masculine military experience of the war and the broader context of the civilians, including children, who remained on the home front.[5] The Canadian Army Medical Corps (CAMC) nurses of the First World War, long a footnote in the history of the soldier, have finally found a rich new voice due to recent scholarship.[6] Yet the full history of the Canadian and Newfoundland volunteer army of nursing assistants and support workers has remained all but invisible in the larger analysis of the First World War experience.[7] Who were these women? What was their role? In answering these questions, I hope to draw the Canadian and Newfoundland VADs out of the margins of the war, giving shape to their contribution at home and overseas.

The purpose of this book is to uncover the work and experience of both the Canadian and Newfoundland VAD volunteers and to explore their work as nursing assistants in Canadian military hospitals at home and in the British military hospitals overseas. Sarah Glassford and Amy Shaw's *A Sisterhood of Suffering and Service* establishes an important precedent in juxtaposing the wartime work experience of women in both dominions, significantly broadening the scope of the historical discussion. Canada and Newfoundland were independent dominions during the war years, separated not only by the Gulf of St. Lawrence but also by diverse political, economic, and social dynamics. In their historical relation to Britain, however, they shared similar imperialist patriotic sensibilities, distance from the fields of battle, and common expectations regarding women's participation.[8] Their mutual alliance to Britain in a time of crisis suggests that the experiences of Canadian and Newfoundland VADs cannot be considered in isolation. Also, these North American VADs shared perceptions regarding their demanding work, psychological adjustments, and sensitivity to the needs of the sick and wounded soldiers in their care.

In the Western world, military nursing dates from as early as the Crusades, with the Order of St. John of Jerusalem, but it was broadened and formalized during the industrial era. With the reconstitution of the Order of St. John as an ambulance association in 1858 and the subsequent creation of the International Red Cross Society (IRCS) in 1863, voluntary medical services were being organized specifically for the needs of the military in war. Historian John Hutchinson argues that the IRCS furthered the growth of international conflict by providing armies with mobile medical and nursing care.[9]

In the same period, nursing became one of the most critical contributions of women in wartime, and the image of the nurse came to be associated with middle-class womanhood. The contemporary image of the military nurse evolved out of Florence Nightingale's legacy in the Crimea in the 1850s. A romanticized mythology idealized Nightingale as the "angel of mercy" who comforted the wounded on the battlefield. As the "lady with the lamp," she popularized the military nurse as inherently maternal, feminine, and refined, and she was held up in contrast to the unkempt, untrained, and working-class nursing attendant, immortalized by Dickens's disreputable Sarah Gamp.[10] Nightingale's influence as both a nurse and a reformer helped to legitimize the middle-class volunteer as an appropriate model for wartime nursing.[11] During the second half of the nineteenth century, Nightingale schools were established, and nursing leaders worked hard to erase the image of the hired, working-class nursing attendant, replacing it with the late Victorian ideal of a a respectable, knowledgable, middle-class, and trained nurse.[12] Women's role in military nursing had also expanded, becoming more standardized and sophisticated.[13]

Canadian nurses were first recognized as part of an active military force when twelve of them, both secular and religious, were informally recruited to assist the Canadian Militia in the 1885 North West Rebellion. A small contingent of twelve military nurses subsequently served in the South African War at the close of the century, establishing a precedent for continued Canadian military nursing support in war.[14] Britain's St. John Ambulance VADs were rejected for war service because of their minimal qualifications, but within a decade the British War Office was reconsidering the value of these casually trained nursing volunteers in anticipation of conflict in Europe.[15]

The tensions between VADs and qualified career nurses are central to understanding the VAD experience. This book examines the boundaries that defined the VADs' place in the contested space of hospital wards and the challenges they presented to the authority of nursing professionals. As a second level of nursing-care provider, they complicated prevailing debates about who was a nurse. Unlike the working-class nursing attendants of an earlier era, VADs were educated and middle class, ostensibly ideal candidates for nurses' training.

In *Bedside Matters,* historian Kathryn McPherson documents the evolution of Canadian nursing in the First World War era, a period when nursing gradually transformed into a service provided by a recognized community of trained practitioners.[16] At the start of the war, nurses' training was entirely hospital-based, and the provincial legislation needed to regulate the standards and requirements of entry into nursing had yet to pass. The struggle for professional recognition was to prove far more complex and arduous than anticipated.[17]

However, with the inception of the Canadian National Association of Trained Nurses in 1908, nursing took a first significant step toward professional status. The completion of nursing registration across Canada nevertheless proved to be a slow and unsatisfactory process that continued into the postwar era. The standardization of nursing qualifications and the elevation of training to the university level were still under discussion as the first contingent of CAMC nursing sisters embarked for service overseas.[18] However, just as nurses were stepping into the spotlight, and just as nursing leaders hoped to showcase their professionalism, enhancing the status of both military and civilian nursing, the VAD movement arose, resurrecting the notions of nursing as work that any woman could do and that all women instinctively undertook.[19]

With the onset of the First World War, young women's anticipation of patriotic nursing work was also complicated by the regularizing of military nursing, which was open only to those who possessed recognized training and skills. Professionalism now framed the requirements for modern military nursing.[20] As a result, the juxtaposition of the qualified military nurse alongside the casually trained volunteer at the bedside created a complex dynamic.

Female participation in paid and unpaid labour was also evolving in the late nineteenth and early twentieth centuries, and these changes influenced the types of jobs that women could take up during the war. Before the war, middle-class women continued their tradition of unpaid community service, but they increasingly entered paid professional occupations, particularly teaching, social work, and nursing.[21] Women's paid wartime labour, however, continued to be regulated by prevailing gender and class expectations, which deemed paid work in industry and munitions as only appropriate for working-class women. As men began to enlist and were sent abroad, working-class women replaced them in the war-time industries, in farming, and in various non-traditional jobs, at higher pay than they normally received.[22] Middle- and upper-class women who hoped to serve their country were limited to patriotic fundraising, Red Cross work, and volunteer nursing.

VAD work offered Canadian and Newfoundland women a unique opportunity to make a patriotic contribution to the state as part of an organized auxiliary medical support service. Although they were not sent to the battlefields, their public service was redirected from the domestic front to meet the needs of "the boys" overseas. The community service of middle-class women was transformed into voluntary patriotic work. In Canada and Newfoundland alike, service organizations, such as the Suffrage War Auxiliary and the Women's Patriotic Association, helped to fill the gaps in materials, manpower, and finances in the state support for the war.[23] This outpouring of enthusiasm was powered by the same maternal ideologies driving the suffrage movement and middle-class women's demands for the vote on the grounds that they would then help "clean up" society. Women were regarded as the natural caregivers to soldiers in the trenches, work that was promoted as the obvious counterpart to masculine military patriotism in the field.[24] As historian Janet Watson contends, the line between women's wartime work and their service was often blurred, and considering the distinctions between them "helps move the history of the war beyond the divide between home front and combat."[25]

The expectations for female patriotic service employed the same militarist rhetoric that defined men's call to arms. Women were exhorted to "rally to the call" and to make "heroic sacrifices of time and money" in support of the war effort. Rather than be labelled as "slackers," they could "stand and be counted" by working with groups such as the Canadian Red Cross.[26] The traditional identity of middle-class women as unpaid caregivers for the family and those in need laid the groundwork for the advent of the VAD. Janet Watson argues that "the wards were their trenches," rendering the VADs as the feminine equivalent of fighting men.[27] The names on the honour rolls illustrated the risks they undertook, although more often from infection and disease than from enemy action.[28] In stepping out of her civilian role as daughter, sister, or fiancée to join the sisterhood of the "voluntary nursing army," the VAD on overseas service was characterized by a former British VAD, Olive Dent, as having satisfied "her nearest approach to being a soldier."[29] Despite her uniform and brief training, the VAD was more closely related to the middle-class volunteer worker than to the qualified military nurse. Instead of pursuing mission outreach, temperance campaigns, or rescue work during the war, she redirected her volunteer efforts to the care of wounded soldiers.

Gender norms legitimized the venture of young, unmarried, middle-class women into patriotic volunteer nursing. Like nurses, VADs wore a military-styled uniform whose long skirt masked their sexuality but whose starched white apron and saintly linen head scarf declared their abilities and dedication. Like soldiers, VADs had a brief training period, and their service lasted only as long as the war did. A temporary "warrior on the wards," a VAD could project a patriotic aura of soldiering while securing respect for her femininity as a nurse.[30]

Class expectations and ethnicity played a role as well, defining the VAD as predominantly middle-class, Anglo-Protestant, English-speaking, and white. In the First World War era, women of colour or non-European ethnicity, including Indigenous women, were not regarded as suitable candidates for nursing. As Kathryn McPherson confirms, nursing "relied on an image of feminine respectability" for its legitimacy at the bedside. As McPherson makes clear,

> respectability was constructed in a racial and national context. Nurses' respectability and definition of gentility were European in origin. White Canadian born women were expected to bring their superior sense of sexual and social behaviour to the bedside ... and to serve as role models for their social "inferiors," such as immigrants and non-whites. Visible minorities were not trusted to attend the needs of ailing white Canadians.[31]

All VADs, including ambulance drivers, recreation directors, and rest station workers, were expected to conform to the "construction of respectability" that was based on an Anglo-European model of "whiteness."

In Canada, although there were no stated racial or ethnic barriers, white, middle-class women were the preferred applicants, recruited through the St. John Ambulance Anglo-imperialist framework. Under the "Terms of Service with the Voluntary Aid Detachments of the British Red Cross Society and the Order of St. John," which applied to all colonial VAD organizations, the only stated limit referred to an applicant's age.[32] Under the British VAD program, a salaried General Service Division was established later in the war. This handled basic housekeeping work, cleaning, and cooking; the salary was intended to attract working-class women, enabling them to relinquish paid employment to take on these duties. In the case of VADs, Canadian or Newfoundlander, class and ethnicity were the socio-economic criteria for membership in the program.[33]

Yet under the direction of its matron-in-chief, Major Margaret Macdonald, the Canadian Army Medical Corps refused to take on VADs as part of the overseas military nursing establishment. Macdonald perceived a tremendous risk in accepting untrained nursing volunteers. They had no rank and received no salary, so they could not be controlled by the diminishment of either, and they lacked the nursing probationer's experience with hierarchical hospital protocol that demanded deference and unquestioned obedience. She feared that VADs might undermine the efficiency and status of the regular nursing staff. She had learned from the recent experience of the South African War, during which she had been a member of the Canadian nursing contingent. The elite women who served as nursing volunteers had challenged the authority of British military nurses, disrupting efficiency in the British military hospitals.[34] By the end of the war, though, despite her reservations, the CAMC was increasingly pressured to ease its objections to VAD nurses in the interest of government cost saving. Although VADs ultimately proved uninterested in postwar nursing, the perceived threat of their ongoing involvement motivated nursing activists to push for the completion of the provincial registration process and to consider options for university accreditation.

VAD Narratives and Personal Writings

Examining the personal writing and recorded narratives of the VADs' wartime experience allows a deep understanding of their attitudes toward work and their relationships with the military nurses, their patients, and their VAD sisters. Although modest in number as compared to the copious store of material available for the British VADs, the documents left by Canadian and Newfoundland VADs nonetheless constitute a rich resource. Most of the texts and recordings are held in local, provincial, or national archive collections across Canada and Newfoundland, with a small selection in England. None of these accounts, whether in letter, diary, or memoir form, were published by their writers, although some were obviously created with this possibility in mind.

The letters reflect a moment in time, a photograph captured in words, but despite the value of their immediacy, they present several problems. They are addressed to a specific reader, and consciously or not, the writer has shaped her message to suit her correspondent's understanding. A letter to one's mother may be quite different in tone from a letter to one's close friend or fiancé. Much depended on the closeness of the relationship and the sensibilities of the recipient. This self-censorship can be found in any written message, but during wartime it was compounded by the official censorship that restricted the contents of letters. In addition, hospital convention imposed its own censorship, well understood by the nurses and impressed upon the VADs, that they were not to discuss the private details of the patients or procedures. The result was often a cheery letter home to family or friends describing the delights of an afternoon outing with colleagues or the beauty of the French countryside, with no mention of the stresses and tensions of the hospital ward.

Diaries pose a different set of interpretive challenges. Very few have been recovered for Canadian and Newfoundland VADs. Although the official censor was not privy to their contents, they often convey a sense of expected readership, resembling notes for a novel, particularly in the case of typescript diary notes. Both Sybil Johnson from St. John's and Montreal's Marjorie Starr left typescript diaries that were undoubtedly redrafted from the original handwritten notes and thus subject to the author's reflective self-editing. Neither diary was ever published, but the possibility of publication probably influenced what was recorded – and what was left unsaid. Despite this caveat, diaries are valuable documents, containing vivid, detailed, and often highly critical accounts of hospital experiences in England and France. Not all diaries were transcribed from their original handwritten script. Most seem to have been private records, a safe place to confide the daily upheavals and frustrations to a trusted confidant who would neither criticize nor reveal the writer's innermost secrets and impressions. Emotion may have coloured her observations, but they are often the more accurate and honest for not being constructed with a readership in mind.

These are in contrast to the memoirs, which are fully intended for an audience. Canadian and Newfoundland VADs left a few brief memoirs in the form of published articles, essays, or a subtext in the chapter of an autobiography. These reminiscences were compiled at times and places that were distant from the First World War, whether by a few years or several decades. With the passage of time, the selective vagaries of memory and other interpretations have worked to colour the reality of experience. Although they must be interpreted with some caution, they too are a valuable resource, lacking only the proximity that the spoken reminiscence can provide. The archive of recorded Canadian and Newfoundland VAD voices cannot compare to the Imperial War Museum's large dedicated collection of British VAD interviews, but the small sample is important nonetheless. Years after the war, various researchers and journalists sought out veteran VADs to record their experiences for a range of projects. Despite the passage of time, they recount their wartime experiences in a lively and emphatic style. In one fortunate case, a film crew also captured memories of three Canadian VADs, all well into their nineties when the interviews were filmed for a documentary on women and the war.[35] The obvious limitations of the producer's selective editing cannot be discounted: we cannot know whether the material that ended up on the cutting room floor was of more value than what was saved. Each of these women, Elsie Chatwin, Doreen Gery, and Eva Morgan, offered a brief sampling of her particular VAD experience, providing a wealth of material and giving both a face and a voice to this history.

Sources and Records Relating to the VADs

All historical sources are problematic to a greater or lesser degree for various reasons, but the relative scarcity of materials about women who are not prominent in the historical record compounds the interpretive challenges of researching the VAD movement. The central agencies in the Canadian and Newfoundland VAD history, the St. John Ambulance and the Red Cross, have limited archival holdings for this topic. Yet they offer the critical keys to the identity of the VADs who served in British military hospitals in England and the European theatres of war. The St. John Ambulance Association records in Ottawa provide a list of more than three hundred VAD nursing members who were sent overseas under its auspices at varied intervals between 1916 and 1918. The British Red Cross Society Museum and Archives in London, England, complements this critical source with its own record of identity for all of its registered British and colonial VADs. Including nurses, ambulance drivers, and general service workers, this invaluable repository of fifty thousand VAD Personnel Record Indexes was created by members of the Joint Women's VAD Committee. These handwritten three-by-five-inch standard index cards identify most of the five hundred Canadian and Newfoundland VADs who worked in British hospitals.[36] The index provides their names, addresses, and length and location of service; some cards even include comments from the hospital matron, although the British Red Cross restricts publication of these, positive or otherwise, in the interest of privacy.

The great majority of VADs, more than 1,500, worked full- or part-time in home-front military convalescent hospitals at some point during the war. Uncovering their identities and experience is problematic, as they left few letters, and no diaries have yet emerged.[37] These VADs are cited most often through contemporary newspaper items, often in small publications that lacked a national circulation. Local St. John nursing divisions left few individual records of their membership; otherwise, they are sometimes found in the pages of the association's annual reports and monthly bulletins. If records of enrollment did exist, they have vanished from the archives.

My entry point into the history of the Canadian and Newfoundland VAD movement was the discovery of a list of more than three hundred names and addresses of Canadian VADs who were sent overseas by the St. John Ambulance between 1916 and 1918. The VAD Personnel Record Indexes in the British Red Cross Society Museum and Archives contributed significantly to the identification of an additional two hundred North American VADs who served in British hospitals.[38] Records for the VADs who worked in the home-front hospitals are more widely distributed among numerous local, provincial, and national sources. One of the most useful is the city directories of the war era, published for both Canadian and Newfoundland urban areas. These reference books provide a wealth of details concerning household composition, occupations, and socio-economic patterns, which can be traced over time for various family members. Though not statistically conclusive, they contributed to the development of a national occupational profile for several hundred VADs and allowed the Canadian and Newfoundland VAD profile to be compared with earlier assumptions established by the British VAD model alone.

All of these records contributed to a database that includes every identified Canadian and Newfoundland VAD. The objective in creating the database was to assemble a profile for a community of women whose existence had thus far been largely obscured. Material was gleaned from a range of primary and secondary sources on both sides of the Atlantic, both archival and private. These included institutional and government records, contemporary publications, personal documents, and contributions from family and others. Canadian government records for the Department of Militia and Defence and the CAMC helped to establish the federal policies on recruiting VADs for work in Canadian military hospitals at home and overseas. Particularly helpful were the records of Major Margaret Macdonald, matron-in-chief of the CAMC nursing service, establishing her response to the issue of overseas VAD assistance. The records of the St. John Ambulance in Canada and the Canadian Red Cross, both internal documents and published literature, frame the context for their support of the VAD program. Many of these records are distributed among civic and provincial archives throughout Canada.

In London, the Imperial War Museum's Women at Work Collection preserves the records of the Joint Women's VAD Committee. Headquartered at Devonshire House in Piccadilly, the committee governed the recruiting and deployment of all British and colonial VADs to Royal Army Medical Corps (RAMC) hospitals in Britain and the various theatres of war. This vast and invaluable archive of Allied women's First World War activities in all fields contains a large British Red Cross subsection, which provides a store of official reports, committee minutes, letters, and other diverse materials relating to VADs. It also includes the papers of Dame Katharine Furse, founder and first commandant of the Joint Women's VAD Committee.

The Canadian and Newfoundland VAD Experience

When the St. John Ambulance in Canada launched the VAD program in 1914, the response was not expected to match that of aspiring British VADs, who had demonstrated overwhelming enthusiasm even before war had been declared. However, Canadian women did respond with eagerness, and St. John initially struggled to contain and direct the impatient energies of VADs who wanted to serve but who had nowhere to go. The steady growth in Canadian and Newfoundland VAD reserves at home and overseas in the British military hospitals reflected the increasing reliance of the military medical services on the ready availability of VAD assistance. The evolving perception of the VADs as an essential component in the war effort is fundamental to the analysis of their work and influence, particularly in relation to the gendering of patriotic service for both women and men.

Most VADs remained on the home front, working in the expanding network of convalescent hospitals, as their aid became increasingly necessary to the care and rehabilitation of veterans. Their work was less demanding than in the war zone, but they demonstrated both stamina and courage during the crises of the Halifax explosion and the influenza epidemic. For VADs who went abroad, the demands of the job could be overwhelming, causing emotional distress and even physical debilitation, often leading to an early discharge. There were also casualties, with many nurses and VADs inevitably succumbing to the ever-present infection and illness; some suffered lifelong infirmity due to injury or disease.

In an era when women were campaigning for the vote and redefining their role in the workplace, VADs were situated somewhere between the "new woman" and the traditional middle-class community volunteer.[39] The war offered them unexpected independence during a crisis point in the early twentieth century. Many willingly left offices, classrooms, and even government jobs to take up volunteer nursing for some portion of the conflict. Although nursing was an acceptable female role, their presence as women in uniform who were working away from home challenged many preconceptions of femininity and appropriate behaviour for respectable unmarried women. As a result, society's view of the VADs was mixed: the public was often uncertain whether to applaud them as "angels of mercy" or to censure them for questionable mores.

At home or overseas, VADs saw their work as a patriotic gesture, a direct and useful contribution to the war. They were fully aware of their limitations, lacking the training and skill of graduate nurses. At times, during periods of intense demand, the line between professional and volunteer could become far less distinct, prompting nursing leaders to recognize that VAD and nurse differed little beyond the level of training.

Not all Canadian and Newfoundland VADs were nurses. As ever more able-bodied men were needed to continue the fight, new portals for women's entry into the military medical services opened up, enlarging the scope of VAD service beyond the bedside. Increasing numbers of female volunteers moved

into the hospitals, performing tasks that resembled the paid clerical and domestic work they had done during peacetime. New roles also developed for
dieticians and physical therapists in the effort to restore and rehabilitate men
to civilian independence, or back to the trenches. One task, however, was
notably outside the usual realm of middle-class women's work: that of ambulance driver.

When hostilities ceased, the VADs, like the soldiers, returned to civilian
life, often to their previous jobs in offices and schools. In their personal accounts, many lamented the quiet sameness of their postwar lives. Few benefitted directly from their wartime reputation, and the public memory of their
contribution soon faded.

This book brings the work and experience of a "small army" of Canadian
and Newfoundland women out of the shadows to claim their rightful place in
the mainstream histories of the war.[40]

Chapter One

THIS ARDENT BAND OF LADIES
Birth of the Canadian VAD Movement

CANADA'S CLOSE TIES TO Britain encouraged the steady growth and popularity of the St. John Ambulance, but the outbreak of hostilities in the summer of 1914 brought strong competition from the burgeoning International Red Cross Society (IRCS) movement, which was established to provide services for the sick and wounded in war.[1] Limited to Britain and its dominions, the Order of St. John lacked the broader international scope of the Red Cross, although it had an advantage as an ongoing peacetime emergency medical service agency. Canada's relatively small military-medical elite of the era saw Dr. George Sterling Ryerson holding the positions of general secretary for St. John Ambulance and commissioner for the Canadian Red Cross. When the South African War erupted in 1899, he sailed for South Africa to represent the Canadian Red Cross, leaving St. John in Canada all but defunct. Lacking a peacetime mandate in Canada, the Canadian Red Cross slipped into relative dormancy when the war ended in 1901.[2]

Creating an army of volunteer nurses was not in the plan when the St. John Ambulance established a Canadian branch in 1883. During the early years of its development in Canada and Newfoundland, it worked to mitigate the perils of Newfoundland's sealing and fishing industries and the increasing dangers of Canada's expanding rail industries. At this time, women played a minimal role in the association, involving little more than preparing materials for the men's first-aid classes.[3] Despite the limited opportunities, they persevered, progressively taking a fuller part in activities. With its incorporation in Canada in 1910, the women of the St. John Ambulance established their own parallel programs in first aid and home nursing.

At the same time, with war looming in Europe, the British parent organization had already begun to construct a far more active role for women as Voluntary Aid Detachment nursing members. In 1909, the British government enacted a "Scheme for the Organization of Voluntary Aid in England and Wales," which enjoyed almost instant popular approval, gaining momentum as war approached.[4] Novelist and veteran VAD Agatha Christie later recounted the popular joke that women's enthusiastic preparation for VAD work put any man who suffered an accident "in mortal terror of ministering women closing in on him," causing him to cry out in alarm, "Don't let those First Aiders come near me. Don't touch me girls. Don't touch me!"[5]

At the time, the concept of a VAD nursing organization held scant interest for St. John Ambulance organizers in Canada. The possibility of war in Europe was of little concern to Canadians who were endeavouring to build a secure and prosperous future for their families. Nevertheless, there was a need to encourage women's interest in the work of the association, to broaden its influence in Canada. Britain's new Voluntary Aid Scheme offered a practical framework for engaging women in the health and welfare of the family and community through volunteer nursing. Unlike in Britain, the proposal for VAD nursing programs initially encountered a lukewarm reception from English-speaking middle-class women, who were the preferred recruits. In this pre-war period, they were more concerned with the realities of daily life. Married women had the responsibilities of home and family. At the same time, many unmarried middle-class women were exploring new employment opportunities during their years between school and marriage, and the more elite were occupied with charity and club work, or just having fun.[6] Veteran VAD Violet Wilson later described the sense of carefree abandon and lack of urgency that many young, middle-class Canadians felt just prior to the war: "It seems unbelievable, on looking back at that long summer, that we did not realize anything of the threatening situation in Europe. The gay and thoughtless summer months passed quickly, and then suddenly war was upon us."[7]

When Britain entered the war on August 4, 1914, the lives of young Canadian men and women changed dramatically. For men, the next step was obvious, whereas the women began to seek out a useful contribution to the war effort. Working-class women would soon enjoy a multitude of better-paid job opportunities. For the rest, the St. John Ambulance now proposed the challenge of nursing, galvanizing thousands of young, middle-class Canadian women to contemplate taking this entirely new path. In this era, assuming the mantle of the nurse was not out of line with the expectations of gender and class, but carrying it into the military hospitals was a much bolder step. The first major test would be to acquire the necessary training and preparation to meet both the public and professional standards for the work of a volunteer nurse.

Creating a VAD Scheme

Following the declaration of war, the Canadian government quickly established a National Relief Committee to co-ordinate all wartime voluntary medical assistance and fundraising. This umbrella committee brought together the Department of Militia and Defence, the Canadian Red Cross Society (CRCS), and the St. John Ambulance to avoid duplicating personnel and resources. The Militia Department was to identify the requirements for assistance, whereas the CRCS was to fund, collect, and transport all materials and voluntary personnel needed for military medical aid. The St. John Ambulance was to concentrate on training and organizing its Voluntary Aid Detachments, both ambulance and nursing members.[8] The CRCS set to work, mounting a massive, well-regulated volunteer program and providing the essential funds, materials, and services for the support of sick and wounded Canadian men in military hospitals abroad.[9] These volunteer efforts consumed countless hours of women's time and energy, but despite the scope and variety of the work, it could not offer younger women an active involvement in the war effort. Instead, it fell to St. John to develop a unique opportunity for wartime "active service," for a singular community of volunteer women in Canada and Newfoundland.

   In pre-war Britain, the VAD nursing program had caught women's interest by linking the nursing programs to prevailing ideas about middle-class responsibility for the moral and physical health of society, and the future health and security of both nation and empire.[10] However, little in the way of a similar challenge, excitement, or glamour was offered to Canadian women. Church organizations were appealed to as suitable recruiting centres for the foundation of St. John Ambulance Brigade (SJAB) nursing divisions, where women of the appropriate class and demeanour were most likely to produce the preferred membership. Femininity and a good family, particularly if the would-be recruit could boast a British heritage, plus connections to the military, medical, or clerical communities, were the ideal requirements for a VAD nursing candidate. Educated, middle- and upper-class women were actively encouraged, compensating for their lack of nursing qualifications with impeccable social credentials.

These qualities would distinguish the St. John Ambulance VAD nurses from the untrained paid "nurses" of the past.

Rather than highlighting the potential for wartime nursing, the "Annual Report for 1913 of the St. John Ambulance Brigade Overseas within the Dominion of Canada" had presented a less than enticing rationale for training as a VAD nursing member:

> Have you ever stopped to think of the position of the average working man when one of his family, especially if it be the housekeeper, is taken sick. Perhaps not sufficiently sick to be taken to the hospital, she is left to lie at the mercy of the amateur nurse, since the cost of a graduate nurse is often more than the salary of the man. Could your church auxiliaries do some good if they were trained and regularly drilled in Home Nursing, in such cases? Here is the argument for establishment of a Nursing Division.[11]

The report included a photograph of Central Nursing Division No. 1, Toronto, the first in Canada. The twenty-three members, most in their twenties, were elegantly posed in the style of a nursing graduation photograph. They wore the grey uniform dress of the St. John Ambulance VAD, largely concealed by a white bibbed apron, and cuffs. The decorative bonnet, tied with a bow under the chin, was similar in style to a model frequently adopted by British nurses of the era. The costume evoked an association with the work of graduate nurses, as well as their femininity and respectability. As an inducement to join, however, the accompanying description of the division's prewar activities was perhaps less enticing. These involved attending "all of the duties undertaken by the men" of the ambulance division, being "very active amongst the sick poor in Toronto," and taking "hundreds of poor children on Fresh-Air Outings" to enjoy "dainties and sports." Beyond the possible attraction of wearing a uniform, these tasks offered little glamour or glory to stir the imagination of energetic young women who wanted a more stimulating public service role.[12]

Distanced as they were from the threat of war in Europe, Canadian women saw little opportunity for active patriotic service as VAD nurses. In November 1911, the Militia Council developed a volunteer medical services support scheme, the "Organization of Voluntary Medical Aid in Canada," that included both men and women.[13] Based on the 1909 "Scheme for the Organization of Voluntary Aid in England and Wales," it was not approved by government until March 1914, and even then it accorded the leading role to the men of the ambulance divisions.[14] When the war began, the St. John Ambulance could

Central Nursing Division No. 1, Toronto Corps, 1913. *Courtesy St. John Ambulance*

boast only three nursing divisions at the ready "to render organized aid in time of public emergency," as compared to twenty-four men's ambulance divisions.[15] Although the work of the pre-war Canadian SJAB nursing divisions was linked to social welfare, public health, and national service, it lacked the novelty and glamour of that undertaken by the British VAD program. Greater scope for leadership and autonomy lay in women's organizations, such as the Imperial Order Daughters of the Empire (IODE), the Young Women's Christian Association, and Local Councils of Women. Designed to attract the wives and daughters of the St. John Ambulance business and professional membership, the Canadian VAD program still mirrored traditional community health and social welfare projects.[16] From the perspective of younger women, it lacked a clearly defined purpose to distinguish it from other conventional women's voluntary work. At the same time, the Order of St. John in Britain was constructing a framework for wartime VAD work, presenting the appealing prospect of a clearly defined role for women as auxiliary nurses in the event of war.[17]

Although a smaller organization than its Canadian counterpart, the Newfoundland St. John Ambulance Association (SJAA) enjoyed a more enthusiastic

Members of the St. John Ambulance Brigade (Overseas), Newfoundland District,
who cared for the SS *Newfoundland* survivors, March 1914. *Courtesy of the Centre
for Newfoundland Studies, Memorial University Libraries*

response from women, and grew quickly after the colony achieved dominion
status in 1907. In March 1914, when a disaster claimed 251 sealers aboard three
ships, including the SS *Newfoundland,* a brigade was ready to assist. Of the 89
men rescued, only 11 survived to be cared for by brigade members in a hastily
organized emergency hospital at St. John's.[18] Following the declaration of war,
Newfoundland's first brigade nursing division was established in St. John's by
September 1914, with classes in home nursing and first aid provided to some
five hundred men and women by December. The value of this training had
been proven in the recent disaster, but Newfoundland women were eager to
take a greater part in the war effort, and thousands had already enlisted in the
Women's Patriotic Association. The lady superintendent of the SJAB, Adeline
Browning, stressed that the two courses were essential for any woman who
wished to join a VAD division. As Browning explained, the Joint Women's
VAD Committee at Devonshire House required the completion of the two
SJAB courses "before they will undertake to place her as probationer in one of
their hospitals."[19] Browning also cautioned that membership in a division was
no guarantee of overseas nursing work, but about forty Newfoundland VADs
eventually worked abroad as nurses or ambulance drivers during the war.[20]

Following the South African War, the British government determined to
reorganize its system of voluntary medical military aid, as the British military's
experience of volunteer nursing during the conflict had at times been chaotic.[21]
The St. John Ambulance and the British Red Cross maintained an uneasy relationship during this time, disagreeing over recruitment qualifications when

the new "Scheme for the Organization of Voluntary Aid in England and Wales" was instituted in 1909. As a result, the St. John Ambulance was granted permission to organize its own detachments. The overwhelming majority of VAD detachments remained under BRCS jurisdiction, about five-sixths of the total, but the outcome resulted in a lack of uniformity in the training and experience of the British VAD movement.[22] The discord once again bubbled to the surface in October 1914, when the British War Office initiated the Joint War Committee, assigning authority for the deployment of all VADs in the military hospitals to the Red Cross. In his exhaustive history of the Red Cross, John Hutchinson argues that the rancour was driven equally by class and jurisdictional disputes. In his view, the British social elites regarded the Order of St. John as more upper class in tone, having "probably erroneously" perceived the BRCS to be more democratic in its structure.[23]

Such disagreements did not affect the relationship between the two service agencies in Canada. Under the 1914 Voluntary Medical Aid scheme, St. John was given sole responsibility for training and organizing the VADs, whereas the collecting and distribution of funds was left to the CRCS. There was no obvious animosity or resentment between the two groups regarding control of the purse strings. Both operated under the wartime umbrella of the National Relief Committee. With a far less entrenched class system in Canada, and only a borrowed aristocracy, they enjoyed considerable overlap in their administration and membership. Perhaps in response to some muttered undercurrents, the Duke of Connaught, governor general and grand prior of the order in Canada, later discounted any "real friction" between the two agencies during the war. He defended the arrangement, acknowledging that "the Red Cross had the right to step forward and we took second place." The two organizations certainly shared common imperial and patriotic interests, and the Red Cross proved both generous and prompt in funding requests from St. John for the Canadian VAD program. The arrangement left St. John free to concentrate on recruiting and training candidates for the Voluntary Aid Detachments.[24]

Developing a Voluntary Nursing Program

Frances Cluett, more familiarly known as Fanny, was thirty-three when she took her first steps toward becoming a VAD. A teacher from the small fishing community of Belleoram on Newfoundland's south coast, she travelled first to St. John's for training and then to hospitals overseas. An animated correspondent, she wrote a wealth of letters during her four years of VAD service in England, France, and finally Constantinople, vividly recounting her time abroad. The letters demonstrate her humour, the depth of her response to the suffering of her patients, and her calm, pragmatic approach to VAD nursing. In one of them, she left a brief account of her intense period of training:

> At 8 p.m. Mrs. Browning took me down to the British Hall to the lecture room. I was just a little late. There were seven girls already there. Dr. Reeves lectured to us, we had to apply bandages ourselves. I got an introduction to Miss Janes; so I applied bandages to her. Mrs. Browning and the Dr. looking on. The first bandage went around the arm and body. Second fracture we had to splint the arm, and bandage also put in slings. The third bandage was around the elbow, fourth bandage was around the forearm, the last one around the hand.
>
> Miss Janes is going to call for me at 3 p.m. this evening. We are going to practice bandaging again. Monday night at 8 p.m. another lecture ...
>
> We are rushed with training, and will I am afraid be sent across quicker than I thought.
>
> Of course I can't say for sure: but Mrs. Browning told me last night that perhaps we would be through in five weeks![25]

This passage provides a unique glimpse of VAD training, as other Canadian and Newfoundland VADs seldom mentioned it in their letters or diaries. Perhaps it seemed too mundane to record or too distant from real hospital work. If a trainee were still living at home, letters to family were unnecessary, and diaries usually began when VAD work did. As a consequence, what we know about the training program comes more from St. John literature than from the students who were enrolled in it.

Seemingly unaware of the enthusiasm for VAD training in Britain during the five years prior to 1914, the St. John Ambulance in Canada was unprepared for a similar response from Canadian women once hostilities were declared.[26] Newfoundlanders like Fanny Cluett and Clare Janes were equally ready to do their bit for King and Country in 1914. With the British Red Cross and the St. John Ambulance both recruiting in the new dominion, some Newfoundland VADs were sent overseas much earlier than the Canadians.[27] The "Organization of Voluntary Medical Aid in Canada" anticipated that VADs would work as nurses only in the event of invasion and then solely as a support for the men in the brigade ambulance division.[28] More surprising, perhaps, than the keen response of Canadian women was the rapid absorption of the St. John Ambulance men into the military medical services overseas. This development left an unexpected gap in the manpower reserves of the brigade detachments at home, a problem that was compounded by the lack of interest shown by civilian

Frances Cluett in Europe, n.d.
*Courtesy of Archives and Special
Collections, Queen Elizabeth II
Library, Memorial University*

men. Many were well suited for work in an ambulance division, but most apparently opted to apply for more lucrative employment opportunities.[29] The secretary of the SJAA in Ottawa characterized this attitude as both short-sighted and deficient in patriotic spirit. Referring to the women's response, he declared, "I regret to say that the same interest is not taken by the men in this work. Some way should be found of presenting forcibly to every one of us who may be liable sooner or later for military service the necessity of having as complete a knowledge as possible of First Aid."[30] Exactly how a mandatory conscription of ambulance trainees could be achieved was not made clear.

Men in Britain were also uninterested in ambulance work, a contrast to Canadian and British women, who were eager to undertake VAD nursing. Their response underscores Anne Summers's description of VAD service in Britain as "a women's movement," a label that applies equally to their colonial sisters, even though men ultimately administered the VAD program.[31] Through almost four years of war, some sixty-one thousand men and women in Canada received SJAB first aid instruction, and "at least 75% took the home nursing course in addition ... thereby qualifying for V.A.D. work either at home or abroad."[32] These numbers indicate that some forty-five thousand Canadian women overall were certified to join a VAD nursing division during the war, though only a fraction did so. In the initial preparation for invasion, St. John created six Voluntary Aid Detachments to serve each of the Militia Department's six military districts across the country, situated in Halifax, Quebec City, Montreal, and Ottawa, and later in Saint John and Victoria. By the end of the war, there were thirty-six nursing divisions nationally.[33]

Despite the assertions of a postwar review of the program, the training and preparation of Canada's VAD nurses was far from clearly defined when the conflict began. The Ottawa Nursing Division formally enrolled some thirty members in January 1915, and over the next few months it secured and furnished a suitable teaching space. Its resourceful commandant, Hazel Todd, had prevailed on the federal Public Works Department for the use of "a good sized room" for instruction. She then invited the public "to assist in furnishing the room, complete with kitchen, bathroom, beds and all the other requisites for practising the work required."[34] Her account of the division's steady progress allows a rare glance into the transformation of untrained volunteers into certified VAD nursing members:

> As soon as the room was ready for use, a course of lectures was given to members of the V.A.D. by prominent doctors; all through the summer weekly classes were held by graduate nurses, for instruction and practice in practical ward work. The Girl Guides volunteered to act as model patients, and so enabled the young ladies to become familiar with the handling of patients, and the making of beds with the patients in them, etc.[35]

Hazel Todd left little to chance in preparing "the young ladies" for their anticipated war service once the organizational framework of the Ottawa detachment was finalized in early January 1915. Its officers were elected, and a report written by Todd clarified its "Aims and Objects":

1) To be able to put to practical use the knowledge acquired in St. John Ambulance lectures on First Aid and Home Nursing, by continual practise in making of beds, poultices, dressings, preparing of invalid diets, and the practical application of roller bandages, triangular bandages and splints.

2) In a time of calamity or public distress, caused by fire, earthquake, war, etc., to be able, within a few hours, to turn any suitable large room or building into an emergency hospital, and to assist graduate nurses in the care of the sick and wounded.

3) To be able to act as probationers under graduate nurses in convalescent homes which may be established by the Militia in Ottawa or vicinity.[36]

Voluntary Aid Detachment, St. John Ambulance Association, Ottawa Nursing Division No. 32, 1917. Hazel Todd, lady superintendent, is second row centre. *Photo by Pittaway, courtesy City of Ottawa Archives, MG042–18–378/CA020071*

Todd's report refers to ongoing weekly lectures, interspersed with instruction in the preparation of invalid diets and classes in the study of Braille. These skills proved invaluable for many VADs who worked in hospital kitchens or in hospitals and wards that treated blinded veterans, whether at home or overseas. Enrollment in the Ottawa Nursing Division had risen to seventy as of November 1915, "all enthusiastic and anxious to do all they can to help in any way." Through the autumn of 1915, Hazel Todd involved her students in various Ottawa activities to practise and demonstrate their new skills. The VADs set up a display tent at the Central Canada Exhibition to advertise the program. They collected fruit, jam, and books to distribute to the 77th Battalion and Engineers, which were camped at the local Rockcliffe base, and they prepared rail-side meals for troops passing through Ottawa en route to Quebec. Pleased as they were to be useful, these women and hundreds of others enrolled in VAD divisions across Canada had hoped for more than expanded community service with a military theme. Todd's news that a military convalescent hospital was to open in Ottawa early in the new year was suffused with understated gratification that the VADs would "be able to serve in relays as probationers under graduate nurses."[37]

Membership in the St. John Ambulance Brigade ambulance division was drawn primarily from men who worked in trades and industries where safety was of special concern. In 1914, these typically included shipyards, rail yards, mines, and mills, as well as public services such as the police and fire brigades. By contrast, the women of the nursing divisions frequently came from the Anglo-Protestant middle classes. Many were recruited from women's service organizations or from groups affiliated with the Protestant churches. Women from respectable white-collar occupations, mainly teaching and clerical work, were also welcomed into St. John nursing programs. In the pre-war era, it was hoped that they would serve as role models and would enable the benefits of home nursing and hygiene to be "spread throughout the country" for poor and working families.[38] St. John VAD nursing candidates were expected to be well educated, having achieved the equivalent of a high school diploma, a qualification that was also required of nursing probationers. St. John knew that to legitimize its VADs to care for civilians and soldiers, their training program must include modern developments in nurses' education. Neither the VAD nurses nor the ambulance assistants would lay claim to professional authority: the association's stated goal was to provide all of its students with the ability "to render first aid to a victim in a scientific prompt way."[39]

In Canada, the St. John Ambulance had sole jurisdiction over the preparation of VAD candidates, which facilitated country-wide standardization of training. Regardless, the training was necessarily dependent on local interpretation of the requirements and on the availability of instructors and facilities. The *British Red Cross Society Nursing Manual,* the official text for VAD training, was written by a British authority on emergency ambulance organization, Dr. James Cantlie. In content and organization, it closely paralleled contemporary nursing textbooks, although the actual course of instruction gave only a brief overview of the expertise and practical skills expected of a fully qualified nurse (see Appendix 1).[40] However, certification as a VAD nurse required two courses of instruction, which was not the case for the men who joined the ambulance division.

Nursing candidates had to complete a course in first aid, just like the men in the St. John Ambulance division (see Appendix 2). Their course was the same in almost all respects, covering the treatment of various emergency conditions such as fractures, hemorrhage, or poisoning.[41] St. John reinforced the value of its training procedures by engaging only qualified medical and nursing personnel to teach the courses and conduct the exams. Retired graduate nurses often taught the home nursing course, and several prominent female physicians also offered their services. Dr. Ellen Douglass in Winnipeg and Dr. Margaret

Patterson in Toronto both established their own VAD nursing divisions during the war. Douglass also escorted several VAD graduates to England in January 1918, to be taken on by the British military hospitals.[42]

St. John established strict protocols for instruction and examinations, underlining the standards of VAD certification and the quality of its nursing members. As a further demonstration of meticulousness, course instructors were not permitted to examine their own students, though as Fanny Cluett discovered when she took her own exams, some of these directives could be flexible. In her case, speed was of the essence, as both she and her VAD training partner Clare Janes were slated for imminent transfer to a British military hospital. Their examiner in St. John's followed the spirit of the guidelines, if not the exact procedures.[43] Apparently accustomed to a tight schedule, he combined the VAD first aid and home nursing exams, and dispensed with the written component. As the protocols stipulated, the exam was not conducted by Dr. Reeves, who had instructed both Cluett and Janes. Instead, Dr. Burden took on the task, ensuring the impartiality required for a fair examination.[44]

Their few weeks of training and study may not have occasioned the same level of stress as three years of intense graduate nurse's instruction culminating in a final exam. Regardless, for Fanny and Clare the prospect of missing a guaranteed placement in a British war hospital was a significant fear. Never one to complain or over-dramatize, Cluett was genuinely relieved to learn that she had passed the exam, a sentiment probably experienced by countless other aspiring VADs. In a letter to her mother, she described their ordeal:

> Miss Janes and I went to Dr Burden's last Tuesday night to be examined on First Aid and Home Nursing. The both of us passed. He asked us quite a few questions. Miss Janes was supposed to have a broken collar bone and a severe bleeding from the palm of the hand which could not be stopped, I of course had to treat it. He then asked me how I would change an undersheet for a person who was very ill. He then asked me what I would do in a case of Diphtheria, what disinfectants I would use, and how strong to use them. I had to read the clinical thermometer and treat a case of poisoning. He asked me to make a linseed meal poultice, etc. He asked a good many questions.
>
> After he told us we passed you can imagine how light we felt, as I have been one whole week studying night and day, I was getting sick of it: but thank goodness that part of it is over.[45]

Fanny's letter shows that Dr. Burden had not followed the SJAB suggestion to employ "demonstration models." The regulations were originally designed for larger groups taking their exams in less pressured conditions. The use of "model" patients, typically two Boy Scouts for every ten candidates, was both impractical and unnecessary for Fanny and Clare, as they could take turns playing the role of model. The Boy Scout system appears to have had some drawbacks, as the SJAB rules cautioned that different boys were to be used for successive examinations, "as cases have not infrequently been noticed in which the models have given information (erroneous or otherwise) to candidates."[46] Having passed her exams to earn her certificates in first aid and home nursing, a woman was now eligible to enrol as a VAD nurse in an SJAB nursing division.

Despite her hours of training and study, Frances Cluett readily acknowledged that they did not entirely prepare her for VAD nursing in the overburdened military hospitals of England and France. After a full year of overseas nursing, she acknowledged to her mother, with characteristic self-deprecating humour, "It's very laughable sometimes for the [medical officer] orders things I never heard of before; so I wonder to myself how in the world am I going to write that down in the dispensary book; Ah mother, there is a funny side to it sometimes."[47]

When Canada's VAD scheme was finalized in the months prior to the war, women were not expected to take the leading role. That a vast network of military convalescent hospitals would be established across the country was not foreseen, as the war in Europe was projected to be both brief and victorious, involving minimal casualties. The eventual requests for Canadian VADs to reinforce the nursing reserves of the British military hospitals were also beyond expectations. The detailed guidelines for conducting training programs for VAD nurses were seen as a precaution against possible invasion. Should this occur, the women's detachments might take temporary charge of sick or wounded men at evacuation stations or emergency hospitals, before their transfer to regular military hospital facilities. As members of a precautionary organization, the VADs were envisioned as doing little beyond the basic nursing tasks that Hazel Todd was rehearsing with her Ottawa Division in the autumn of 1915. Lacking real nursing work, Todd kept them busy setting up railway rest stations and preparing food and refreshments for troops en route to military camps.[48]

Far more elaborate and public preparations had been ongoing in Britain since 1909, long before St. John began organizing VADs in Canada and Newfoundland for war service. The threat of war, even invasion, was far sharper in Britain, with the enemy on the doorstep, and it was essential to keep the

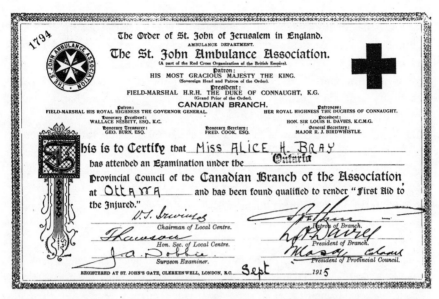

St. John Ambulance Association first aid certificate issued to Alice Bray, Ottawa, September 1915. *Courtesy of City of Ottawa Archives, MG042/A2004–0161*

St. John Ambulance Association home nursing certificate issued to Alice Bray, Ottawa, April 1916. *Courtesy of City of Ottawa Archives, MG042/A2004–0161*

VAD nursing members active and engaged in readiness for hostilities. VAD training camps were established on a regular basis, allowing VADs to practise how to "pitch and strike tents, dig trenches for camp fires, load wagons, make beds and straw mats" for the wounded, with the redoubtable Boy Scouts serving as surrogate soldiers fresh from imaginary scenes of battle. Anne Summers believes that these activities also made an exciting contrast to the usual VAD chores of "elementary nursing skills and housewifery."[49] By contrast, the Canadian VAD wartime nursing program was not seriously pursued until August 1914. With this, however, came the tantalizing possibility of an overseas assignment. Even as late as October 1918, when Bessie Hall began her VAD training at a Halifax hospital, the remote prospect of an overseas post was still a powerful motivator in her decision to enter the program:

> As my services are perfectly voluntary I have the privilege of leaving when I like. But really this is a dandy experience for now, and will make things ever so much easier for me if I ever do get over. It will be great knowing something of hospital life, and I shall come home quite content to rest on my oars until my call comes.[50]

The military-styled framework of the St. John Ambulance Voluntary Aid Detachments was in keeping with the organization's historical and imperial ties. As with the examination guidelines, however, there is evidence that it too was flexible. So few of the ambulance division members were still available following the call to arms that maintaining the required quota of fifty-five men per detachment was probably impossible. Finding sufficient numbers for the women's detachments posed no problem, but the actual organizational structure outlined in the government's "Organization of Voluntary Medical Aid in Canada" appears to have been adapted as the situation required. The expectation of establishing emergency field hospitals faded quickly in 1915, as nursing members in various regions began to enter regular VAD service at military convalescent hospitals. The government proposed the following structure:

MEN'S DETACHMENT

1 commandant, not necessarily a medical man
1 quartermaster
1 dispenser
4 section leaders
48 men (divisible in four sections of 12 men each)

Note - The object of having four sections is to enable small places in rural districts to organize single sections, four of which will be combined to form a complete detachment.

This is merely a suggestion, no doubt the St. John Ambulance Brigade will wish to utilise its Companies for this purpose, in whatever manner it thinks best.

WOMEN'S DETACHMENT

- 1 commandant (man or woman, not necessarily a medical man)
- 1 quartermaster (man or woman)
- 1 trained nurse, as lady superintendent
- 20 women, of whom four should be qualified as cooks.[51]

Photographs taken both before and after the war show VAD nurses lined up for a formal military review, often by distinguished visitors such as the Prince of Wales on a postwar visit to Canada, illustrating St. John's deep roots in a military tradition. In Britain, with its history of jurisdictional friction between the BRCS and the Order of St. John, such exercises sometimes prompted derision. Archie Loyd, a founder of the BRCS, criticized the order for demonstrating an upper-class tone and pretensions, with its ornate uniforms and military-styled hierarchy.[52] On one occasion, Loyd referred to the order disparagingly as "the claptrap and mutual decoration crowd." Some of this sarcasm stemmed from the fractious division of responsibilities between the BRCS and St. John in regard to VAD organization and Loyd's perception of War Office favouritism toward the order.[53] Fortunately, the simplified VAD structure in both Canada and Newfoundland negated any similar jurisdictional spats, despite the smaller dominion's closer affiliation with the British VAD system.

Training for VADs averaged five to six weeks per course, or about ten to twelve hours of lecture and demonstration per course, often conducted consecutively over a three-month period. As the case of Fanny Cluett and Clare Janes demonstrated, however, exceptions could be made depending on the requirements of time and place. Overall, the time devoted to VAD training was similar to that allocated to transforming a raw recruit into an infantryman with the Canadian Expeditionary Force (CEF).[54] Just as the CEF did not presume to convert a delivery boy or labourer into a professional career soldier, neither did St. John promote its newly minted VADs as the equivalent of fully trained graduate nurses. The goal was to create a force of capable auxiliary nursing assistants who had enough skill and knowledge to be useful in a medical

emergency and if necessary to assist in military hospitals at home and overseas. The basic training that VADs received in Canada and in Newfoundland,
whether with St. John or the British Red Cross, used the same manual and
syllabus. From 1914 through late 1918, when the Canadian VAD program was
revised as the Women's Aid Department (WAD), the training evolved as far
as possible to keep pace with the changing needs of wartime hospital care.[55] In
some locations, retired nurses took on the role of "lady superintendent," with
the responsibility for training and organizing the nursing divisions. Their duties
were also adaptable, and the position was not restricted to trained nurses,
permitting experienced SJAB members, such as the Ottawa Division's Hazel
Todd, to assume the role. Working as a secretary for the federal government,
Todd recruited qualified instructors from the Ottawa medical and nursing
community to train the VADs. She followed up by rigorously drilling them in
the practice of their new skills.[56]

Training the VADs

By 1916, Canada's VADs were actively involved in war service at home and
abroad, with the St. John nursing lectures continuing to be offered across the
country. In November 1916, Dr. Margaret Patterson initiated a VAD nursing
program at the University of Toronto, offering weekly campus training sessions
that were specially adapted to attract the ideal candidate, both intellectually
and socially. The sessions were held late in the day, after regular university
classes, to ensure that undergraduates could attend. The rapid growth in the
number of military convalescent facilities brought a greater sense of urgency
to expedite the VAD training and accommodate more recruits, as reflected in
the university's recruitment notice:

> To become a VAD worker it is necessary to take a course in First Aid and an-
> other in Home Nursing. The usual number of lectures in each course is six, but
> the work may be compressed into five. Every applicant for examination is re-
> quired to have attended at least four lectures. The length of a lecture is an hour
> and a half, part of which time is spent in practical work, such as bandaging and
> taking temperatures, etc. A class should have at least twenty members, prefer-
> ably from thirty to forty.[57]

During the extended wartime university vacation period, many Toronto
undergraduates entered VAD work in one of the city's military convalescent

hospitals. Shirley Gordon enrolled in the special campus VAD program as her personal patriotic contribution. With the academic year ending early, she took up VAD work in the summer of 1918, assigned to the new veterans' orthopaedic hospital in North Toronto: "I was a St. Johns [sic] Ambulance VAD. And the courses were given in Home Nursing and First Aid, and you took them say during the winter. And you were trained in that and then you volunteered, or signed up for voluntary service in the hospitals."[58]

Gordon did not elaborate on her St. John training program, but she probably learned emergency bandaging techniques, which were emphasized throughout the war. Just how useful this was for regular ward duties is hard to assess, but none of the Canadian or Newfoundland VADs offered any criticism in their personal accounts. The VADs in training had no knowledge of where or how these skills might be used. They regarded the medical and nursing professionals who taught their classes as the experts and did not seem to question their authority. For their part, the instructors appear to have conformed to the syllabus, at least in spirit, but how individual teachers interpreted the material is impossible to know. As trainees, Frances Cluett and Clare Janes were certainly motivated to practise their bandaging skills. Later, on the wards, Fanny was more concerned with mastering the skill of applying clean dressings to wounds. Just remembering the many types of dressings was a challenge, as she confided to her mother: "There are so many with different dressings, that I assure you, you must not be asleep on the wards; there are thousands of things to remember."[59]

Some VADs did indicate indirectly that their knowledge of bandaging proved useful in their work. Annie Wynne-Roberts had taken leave from a Toronto bank to serve as a VAD at the Royal Army Medical Corps 1st Southern General Hospital in Birmingham, England. She knew that her brief training had not equipped her with the skill of a qualified nurse, but her assistance at the bedside, applying clean dressings, helped the nurses treat their charges more efficiently and contributed to healing:

> By virtue of my lengthy stay I am now senior V.A.D. in the block and have a good deal more interesting work to do. Instead of the eternal cleaning or supervising of cleaning I now spend my mornings and evenings doing surgical dressings with a sister or an assistant nurse, going the rounds with scissors, forceps and probe, applying fomentations, putting packages of gauze into big holes in the flesh and winding yards and yards of bandage round arms and legs and heads. Rather a change from banking anyway.[60]

Annie Wynne-Roberts,
Toronto VAD and Bank of
Commerce employee, c. 1917.
Courtesy CIBC Archives

Wynne-Roberts wrote detailed letters to her former colleagues at the bank, aware that they would be shared publicly. She usually adopted a lighthearted tone, perhaps to mask her true feelings about the war situation and its consequences for her patients. And perhaps her commentary, with its reassuring message that despite their wounds, the men were doing well and were being cared for by nurses and VADs, allowed her letters to pass the censor.

The core of the St. John VAD training program was the home nursing course. Although the students were also required to complete the first aid course, VADs in the home-front convalescent hospitals rarely handled sprains, burns, fractures, or similar emergency conditions.[61] Overseas, however, they were frequently assigned to surgical wards where hemorrhage was a constant concern. In triage situations, with a rush of new cases following a military offensive, VADs sometimes dealt with emergencies when no qualified nurse was available. As described by Canadian VAD Marjorie Starr, at the Scottish Women's Hospital near Amiens, the ability to recognize the signs of hemorrhage was critical:

The one poor soul with his arm shattered and both legs badly wounded was in great pain and I was trying to comfort him. When I looked at his dressings and saw the bright red blood on the bed, I just flew for sister. She, of course, rather lost her head. She is an awful fool and knows nothing of surgical work, so then I flew to wake the Doctor. Got her down, and a jolly good thing too as he would have bled to death – it was the Brachial artery that had been pierced by a bit of shattered bone that worked its way in.[62]

In this instance, Starr reacted promptly, having been taught to recognize the warning signs, but fixing the problem was not her responsibility. New-foundlander Sybil Johnson was equally attuned to the quick detection of a hemorrhage, demonstrating that her VAD training complemented her hospital work: "I was rather nervous watching two cases for possible haemorrhage too. A man can bleed to death so quickly and doesn't always feel it himself, just gets weaker and weaker."[63]

The stipulation that the VADs qualify in both the first aid and home nursing courses points to the gendered expectations that allocated the tasks of a Voluntary Aid Detachment. Unlike the female students who went on to assist the qualified nurses, the working men who handled the heavy labour of the ambulance service needed only first-aid instruction, which was taught mainly by demonstration and required a practical test only. As a St. John executive explained after the war,

> While women have the natural and divine instinct of nursing, yet a certain education in that subject adds greatly to that natural instinct and gift that they have. We have noticed continually that a result of the efforts of the Association in home nursing was increased efficiency, in this most splendid work.[64]

The home nursing course blended traditional nursing practices with modern scientific concepts in a concise program to familiarize the VADs with basic nursing. St. John made no claim to teach a standard nursing program. The VAD nursing course outlined essential procedures, such as bed making and sponge bathing. Lectures provided a brief scientific overview of anatomy and physiology, and addressed standard routines for pulse and temperature monitoring, diet preparation, feeding techniques, and other basic nursing skills.[65] Students also briefly covered the fundamentals of personal and family hygiene in the final lecture, but they were not required to take the separate home hygiene course offered by St. John.[66]

The second lecture in the home nursing syllabus (see Appendix 2) covered infection and disinfection, providing instruction on how to quarantine a patient and the types and application of disinfectants. Preventing and controlling infection had become standard nursing practice by the early twentieth century, illustrating Kathryn McPherson's "fundamental transformation" of nursing work, which was now firmly grounded in the concepts and practical application of the germ theory of disease.[67] Infection control was to prove critical in the military hospitals of Europe. The ravages of gas gangrene, and the bacteria that oozed from the heavily fertilized and gas-infused soils of Belgium and France, often proved more devastating to a patient's body than the original wounds.

In designing the home nursing program, Dr. James Cantlie perceived the VAD nurse as occupying a middle ground between the qualified nurse and the amateur practitioner. She was to act as a buffer against uninformed but well-meaning amateurs, many of whom had overwhelmed the British military medical services during the South African War.[68] The new twentieth-century VAD was certified as a capable assistant to the qualified military nurse, alert for signs that more expert attention was needed. She was not expected to take the initiative without instruction or guidance from a qualified nurse or physician; her role was to efficiently assist rather than lead.[69]

Not surprisingly, the nursing establishment in Canada was not pleased by the emergence of the VAD. The concept of professional versus amateur lay at the crux of its arguments against having VADs as nursing assistants in the CAMC hospitals overseas. No matter how vehemently St. John asserted that VAD certification was not intended to equate to graduate nursing qualifications in any context, the nursing community was not convinced. Late in the war, Jean Gunn, president of the Canadian National Association of Trained Nurses (CNATN), made the case that veteran soldiers would receive better care from third-year student nurses than from VADs, "who had six hours of classes."[70] Gunn recognized no middle ground between amateurs and professionals. Nevertheless, she did concede that experienced VADs could make ideal student nursing candidates.[71] She recognized that nurses' training required more than a few hours of classroom time. The greater portion of a student nurse's preparation took place in the hospital wards, where she had immediate contact with patients under the supervision of her instructors and experienced senior students. A critical problem for VAD trainees, particularly for service abroad, was the fact that experience in a hospital was not guaranteed. Much of this was due to local circumstances.

Sybil Johnson was recruited as a VAD through the BRCS in St. John's and had only minimal preparation before she was sent overseas. Although brimming with enthusiasm, she was uneasy about the gaps in her training and had many misgivings as she embarked for England:

I suppose we *are* VAD. I'm not quite sure if we are or not. I believe girls who
don't go in for Home Nursing or anything and who just offer their services for
any work are VADs but there isn't much difference. Mrs. B. [Adeline Browning]
said we counted as six month probationers, but I suppose that is still VAD.[72]

Sybil was billeted at the St. Mary's Hostel for Nurses in London while she
completed her VAD training in the Queen Mary's Convalescent Auxiliary Hospital.[73] There she was designated as a "VAD Special Service Probationer," a
category for uncertified VAD nurses who were willing to learn on the job.[74]
Although she had the benefit of this experience before being posted to the
1st Western General Hospital in Liverpool, she felt like an untried amateur
during her first few weeks on the wards. Fanny Cluett also started her hospital
training in London at the Queen Mary's Hospital prior to being transferred to
the 4th Northern General Hospital in Lincoln.[75] Both Fanny and Sybil Johnson
began their overseas VAD service in late 1916. Writing to her mother while
she was still training in St. John's, Fanny referred to Sybil and her sister Jill,
noting that "Judge Johnson's two daughters are studying Red Cross too."
There is no indication that they knew each other personally, and Sybil did not
mention Fanny in her letters or diary.[76] Some six months later, in mid-1917,
Jeanette Coultas described a very different introduction to VAD work that
began at the Newfoundland General Hospital in St. John's:

> Before they took me, however, I had to take a course of training at the General
> Hospital. I arranged with Mr. Knowling to go to work in the afternoons only,
> as I had to go to classes at the hospital from early morning until 1 p.m. At the
> hospital I learned to bathe the feet of men patients and you never saw such funny
> knobby looking things as men's feet! Anyway, I kept my repugnance to myself,
> for I was determined to let nothing stop me from getting overseas.[77]

Although the hands-on experience that Coultas received in Newfoundland was far removed from the realities of overseas wartime nursing, it did
give her some knowledge of hospital culture. Even the qualified military nurses
in CAMC hospitals often had little more experience with wartime nursing
abroad than the VADs. They did have the advantage of their rigorous hospital
training, which initiated them in the rituals of discipline and the strict regimen
of routines and procedures that supported the demands of their work. The lack
of such training was the greatest deficit in the VADs' preparation. Officially,
the colonial VADs were required to have some hospital experience before

Sybil Johnson, c. 1916.
Courtesy of the Centre for
Newfoundland Studies,
Memorial University Libraries

taking up a post overseas, but the reality often deviated from the ideal. The
man in charge of the SJAB VAD program in Canada, Dr. Charles Copp, acknowledged the issue in his 1918 address to the CNATN. Although he admitted
that "in some parts of Canada young women have been taken who have not
had any hospital experience whatever," he asserted that they still achieved
"remarkable records."[78]

The problem for St. John was primarily one of trainee access to hospitals.
Nursing directors in civilian hospitals did not want amateurs upsetting the
routines of their regular probationers. In this era, nursing students were still
the primary workforce of the public hospitals. Under the direction of a limited
number of full-time qualified nursing supervisors, they handled all the basic
nursing tasks, working their way up the hierarchy, from lowly probationers
to third-year seniors, and from basic cleaning tasks to those with greater responsibility, such as providing medications and other more detailed treatments. In
the opinion of nursing supervisors, disrupting this process with a continual
influx of untried amateurs could potentially undermine the efficient operation
of civilian hospitals.

Initially, the introduction of VADs into military convalescent hospitals was
opposed on the same grounds. The point was also made that the public might
deem VADs to be inappropriate caregivers for war veterans, who deserved
only the best nursing. A few prominent civilian physicians also weighed in.

The director of the Canadian National Committee for Mental Hygiene, Dr. C.K. Clarke, bluntly dismissed staffing convalescent hospitals with VADs on the basis that "the unqualified woman is a nuisance."[79] Jean Gunn's worries were more specific. The VADs' certification, combined with their hospital experience, could be converted into civilian nursing jobs in the event of postwar nursing shortages and could ultimately create "a loophole" for the lowering of nursing standards.[80] Nursing activists like Gunn were particularly alarmed by the eagerness with which the Canadian government appeared to embrace the concept of VAD wartime nursing. She and other nursing educators had worked hard to overcome the lingering perception of nursing as unskilled "women's work." They hoped soon to see it recognized as a respected occupation for educated women. The war offered the CAMC hospitals a prominent stage on which to display the skills and knowledge of trained military nurses, and it was hoped that their example would promote nursing's goal of professional recognition.[81]

From its inception, nursing activists in Britain had been no less wary of the regressive possibilities of the VAD scheme. Mary Burr, director of the National Council of Trained Nurses in England, vigorously argued that the VAD training program was full of "glaring faults," including minimal instruction time and an "over-emphasis" on the roller bandage. In her view, the casually trained VAD was less valuable than a nursing probationer, whose six-month trial period demanded specific standards of achievement. Burr was adamant that no probationer could master in six months what a VAD was expected to internalize in just ten or twelve hours of instruction. Although she did not advocate cancelling the program, she suggested that it would be of practical value only if it were directed by qualified nurses.[82]

Regardless of the scathing reviews, wartime hospital staffing needs expanded rapidly through 1915. As a consequence, the VADs increasingly assumed a far more prominent role in the British military hospital organization than originally envisioned. At the same time, with volunteer nursing unexpectedly gaining in popular approval, the British nursing critics became concerned that their objections to the VADs might be seen as unpatriotic. Tempering their criticism, British nurses heeded Burr's advice to become more involved in VAD training. Being seen as fostering the abilities of the nursing volunteers in the best interests of the state was better than being perceived as self-interested and unpatriotic.[83]

Much of nursing's criticism for the British VAD scheme must be viewed against the backdrop of its ongoing struggle for registration. Pre-war nursing shortages contributed to this issue, as qualified nurses found opportunities for military and territorial nursing in the colonies.[84] New openings for women's employment early in the century had also dipped into the reserves of prospective nursing students. This in turn gave rise to concerns that the standards of British nursing were being diluted by lower-qualified women who were being brought in to fill the gaps.[85] The war simply exacerbated the situation. Staffing needs in the civilian hospitals did not diminish, as military hospitals, at home and overseas, increasingly demanded that vacancies be filled with the most qualified nurses. VAD nursing assistants were educated, did not require payment, and were readily adaptable to both local and military needs.[86] Their abundance and popularity were problematic for the British nursing community. On the one hand, their help was sorely needed, but on the other, they demonstrated that well-bred, intelligent, motivated women, equipped with basic training and an intense practical experience, could be competent probationers and highly capable assistants.[87]

In September 1914, the limited reserves of experienced VADs were of minimal concern to Canada's nursing community. But its anxiety began to mount as the war intensified and growing numbers of volunteer nurses now assisted in the home-front military convalescent hospitals. Instead of applying tourniquets and temporary shin splints in emergency field hospitals, as originally expected, the VADs were working regular shifts in the convalescent hospitals. They did more than make the beds and scrub the floor: they helped to feed and bathe patients, dress wounds, and change bandages, and they generally undertook a far greater role than either the St. John Ambulance or the civilian nursing community had anticipated. Whether they were suitable as nursing assistants was an ongoing source of tension and debate throughout the war. St. John continued to defend its training procedures, which were primarily directed toward emergency nursing situations. The VADs continued to learn how to set up emergency hospitals and railway rest stations long after the first of them had embarked for military hospital work in England and France.

Hospital training was the most valuable experience a VAD could receive in preparation for service abroad, but for most, whether in Canada or Newfoundland, it was generally brief or non-existent. Training lay at the core of the arguments that kept Canada's VADs out of the CAMC hospitals overseas. Uncontrolled by rank or salary, the CAMC argued, they could easily disrupt the discipline and efficiency of the military hospitals. Matron-in-Chief Margaret Macdonald also feared that they might undermine the status of the qualified military nurses. Civilian nursing activists in Canada also wanted to ensure that the VADs did not endanger nursing's long-term professional aspirations by damaging the positive image that CAMC nurses created during the war. Despite the distrust of the nursing communities, and the restrictions imposed by the military nursing service, Canadian VADs soon emerged as popular representatives of women's contribution to the war effort. Their steady progress from a collection of enthusiastic onlookers to an army of nursing volunteers in home-front and Royal Army Medical Corps hospitals went far beyond all expectations.

Chapter Two

ENTHUSIASTIC AND ANXIOUS
Mobilizing the Voluntary Nursing Service

ALTHOUGH NOT ALL VAD nurses were eager for overseas service, many found the prospect tantalizing. Their zeal was fuelled by the adventure of travel abroad but also by a romantic idealism, which was reinforced by the VAD uniform. The uniform closely resembled that of military nurses, with its flattering white linen scarf evoking piety and femininity.[1] The imagery was underscored by the delicate styling of official VAD photographs.

In addition, young Canadian and Newfoundland middle-class women of British heritage shared a patriotic sensibility. Their social milieu had instilled a sense of service, responsibility, and allegiance to the Crown. This imperial consciousness was common among young men who rushed to enlist and the young women who immersed themselves in war service.[2] Many VADs were the daughters of British émigrés and often members of the first generation born and raised in the optimism of a new century "that belongs to Canada."[3] Their mothers and grandmothers were familiar with the women's organizations of the late nineteenth century, among them the Imperial Order Daughters of the Empire (IODE) and National Council of Women of Canada, active political groups that advocated a strong sense of social responsibility.

Having lost her brother in France, VAD Jean Sears understood her family's ambivalence when she was selected for service abroad:

My parents refused to let me go because they thought they had given enough to the war. I could work at home for the cause. And I was young and had never

Official VAD photograph
of Gwen Powys, SJAB
Fort Rouge No. 6 Nursing
Division, Winnipeg,
c. 1918. *Courtesy of
Debra B. North*

been away from home. However, one day my mother called me and said "if I
had the chance to serve my country like you and my mother kept me from it I
would feel very badly. So I won't keep you my dear. You can go if your father
will let you."[4]

Volunteer nursing enabled young women to wear a uniform like the enlisted
men but to serve in a manner that was deemed appropriate for their gender and
class. In the early months of the war, their unexpected enthusiasm for VAD
work was both gratifying and problematic for the program's organizers. The
St. John Ambulance wanted to encourage them but needed to maintain their
interest and commitment once they were certified as VADs. In early 1915, with
no men to nurse at home and no immediate prospect of work overseas, commandants in many divisions endeavoured to diminish the restlessness of the
VADs by substituting "military drill and discipline" for nursing. But the
VADs needed more to occupy their energies as they watched the casualty lists
grow through 1915 and saw increasing numbers of men being invalided back
to Canada.[5]

Sick and wounded soldiers sent back to Canada were initially the responsibility of the newly established civilian Military Hospitals Commission (MHC),
mandated in mid-1915 to provide "hospital accommodation and convalescent
homes for the officers and men of the Canadian Expeditionary Force" who
were returning from France.[6] The urgency to provide convalescent accommodation mounted steadily with the intensity of the fighting. This need was
met by private initiative as early as February 1915, through the donation of
independent hospital facilities, sponsored by individual citizens and groups.
The first of these hospitals was established by the IODE in a vacant Winnipeg
building that was loaned by the Hudson's Bay Company and converted to
care for the injured of the 2nd Contingent. Montreal's Khaki League followed
suit in April and August of 1915, opening its first two homes, with room for
just over a hundred patients. In Sydney, Nova Scotia, a private home for thirty-
three soldiers was established by an independent donor in June 1915; across
the country, many more such homes would be set up.

The rapid increase in convalescent hospital facilities led Prime Minister
Robert Borden's government to elevate the status and responsibility of the
MHC. In mid-October 1915, the MHC was given oversight of all military convalescent facilities, including the eleven that were already caring for some six
hundred men.[7] With the unceasing repatriation of thousands of invalided soldiers, the commission's mandate was extended in 1916 to include the rehabilitation of sick and wounded veterans to a "semblance of economic self-sufficiency."
With this amplified responsibility, relations between the Canadian Army
Medical Corps (CAMC) administration and the civilian-led MHC became
progressively more strained. Arguments centred on which of the two should
be responsible for the care and recovery of the men invalided home for further
treatment, including their rehabilitation back into civilian life, and on who
should provide bedside care.[8]

As the MHC hospitals scrambled to meet the demand for adequate and
cost-effective nursing personnel, they became the first proving ground for the
St. John Ambulance VADs.[9] Across the country, MHC authorities gradually
accepted the assistance of VADs to supplement the overburdened military
nursing personnel. Despite the apparent economic benefits of this, initial attempts to introduce VADs into MHC hospitals frequently encountered strong
resistance.[10] The problem was not one of gender or class, since the VADs, as
respectable, educated women, were well suited to auxiliary nursing. Instead,
their rapid transition from emergency nursing reserves to regular hospital assistants tested the boundaries of nursing professionalism and questioned the
popular perception of who were appropriate caregivers for wounded heroes.

Framing the Dimensions of VAD Service

The growing need for convalescent hospital space was the catalyst that transformed the Canadian VAD movement from a "standing army" on the sidelines into an active participant in the war effort. As private and public buildings were converted for convalescent use, requiring an ever-increasing supply of scarce nursing resources, resistance to VAD assistance gradually abated. The temporary hospitals, already staffed with physicians, surgeons, and qualified military nurses, began to take on VADs to help with routine housekeeping and nursing tasks.[11] As veteran Toronto VAD Shirley Gordon observed, "I think it is pretty true that the volunteers were a necessity, there were not enough nurses and enough trained people to do the job, so they taught what we needed to know, to volunteers, and we did the work in the hospitals."[12]

When the MHC converted the former Ottawa residence of Sir Sandford Fleming into a convalescent hospital in December 1915, VAD members were credited with helping to complete the renovation within a few short weeks. Soon, "this ardent band of ladies" was on duty, providing regular nursing assistance.[13] When the VAD program was first introduced into the home-front hospitals, there was often not enough work for everyone. Like many other smaller facilities, the Fleming hospital initially operated on a rotation of four VADs per week, while the fifty-six other members of the Ottawa Division waited patiently for their turn. Larger cities such as Toronto ran a sizable number of convalescent hospitals, many specializing in particular treatments, all readily welcoming VAD nurses. The St. John Ambulance College Nursing Division, under Lady Superintendent Dr. Margaret Patterson, was centrally located in downtown Toronto, and it recruited a large cohort of VADs from the undergraduates at the University of Toronto. These young women, including Shirley Gordon, served in convalescent hospitals during the university's extended wartime summer break.[14] Others often balanced VAD work with full-time employment in schools or offices, opting for weekend or part-time hospital duty as an alternative to regular VAD service.

The VADs became hands-on nursing assistants, functioning as "probationers under graduate nurses in convalescent homes" in the expanding network of veterans' hospitals.[15] With their formal recognition as regular nursing assistants, directly exposed to sick and wounded men, they had moved beyond expectations. The ongoing repatriation of invalided soldiers brought the war directly into the community, and the steady march of young female volunteers into convalescent hospitals further altered normal life in Canada.

St. John carefully monitored the VADs to guard against any negative assumptions about their character and fitness for the work. Like the St. John membership itself, which was drawn from professional and business sectors, with a sizable representation of clergy, physicians, and former military officers, VADs were generally white, Anglo-Protestant, and middle class. Many boasted strong family ties to Britain. Entering the VAD program was not contingent on a connection to a St. John member, but many VADs were the daughters or sisters of members. Apart from social profile, age and marital status were also key determinants of eligibility. The age generally ranged from the early to mid-twenties through the mid-thirties, and except for a few childless widows or wives of servicemen, VADs were unmarried.[16]

Some resistance to having VAD nurses assist in home-front convalescent hospitals emerged when the hospitals were still a new phenomenon, as was the case in Montreal, with the opening of the first Khaki Convalescent Home in April 1915.[17] This early wartime call to service for the VADs was largely influenced by Mrs. Viola Henderson, the lady superintendent of the Montreal St. John Ambulance Brigade. A retired nurse, she was a formidable force in the Montreal VAD program. Well aware that the civilian nursing community disapproved of the VAD scheme, she championed the work of her VADs through the pages of *Canadian Nurse*, the journal of the CNATN, emphasizing that "the VAD is warned not to trespass on the authority of the professional nurse."[18] Near the end of the war, she described the early resistance as "a passing evil" that had to be endured:

> Foes within and without in the form of sceptical minds tried to show many and varied reasons as to why it was unnecessary for such an organization to exist in Canada ... Having had experience with many kinds of probationer, we still felt that a good probationer is a most valuable asset to any ward and the work continued to grow.[19]

The Montreal VADs were primarily anglophones, reflecting St. John's connections to elite English-speaking business leaders in the city. Ascertaining how many Montreal VADs were francophones is not possible. Many came from prominent Westmount families in the Golden Square Mile, whether French or English.[20] They were well educated and frequently bilingual, like Marjorie Starr, who was often called upon to translate for the unilingual medical staff of the Scottish Women's Hospital in the Abbaye de Royaumont, north of Paris: "We had a soldier from Champagne in the outpatients today, who had burned his foot ... and came to us to get his foot dressed. I was called out of the Ward to attend to him, while the Doctor looked at it, and translate for her, and then dress it."[21] Although the bilingual capabilities of the Canadian VADs are unknown, bilingualism was not unusual in Montreal and Ottawa – and in the corridor between the two cities. Despite its strong British connections, the St. John Ambulance Quebec Provincial Council began to promote a greater francophone involvement as early as 1911 by making training materials available in French. In 1916, in an effort to encourage Quebec men to join the ambulance division, Dr. James Cantlie's manual *First Aid to the Injured* was translated as *Premiers soins aux blesses* and sold for thirty-five cents a copy. In 1918, Cantlie's *British Red Cross Society Nursing Manual, No. 2* was also made available in French.[22]

Viola Henderson readily acknowledged that not all recruits were suited to VAD nursing, despite their apparent qualifications. Many of the young women who came to her St. John Ambulance nursing classes displayed "a feverish unrest characteristic of the time" rather than a true interest in VAD work. As early as 1914, when she initiated the Montreal VAD program, Henderson believed she could spot the truly committed, those "clever, keen-eyed, earnest young women, with good social standing as an extra asset."[23] Their timely start meant that the Montreal VADs were trained and ready for service when the first Khaki Home opened in April 1915. In 1916, when the call came from London to send Canadian VADs overseas, ten of the Montreal women were immediately sent to hospitals in France.[24]

This apparent preference for the Montrealers generated some resentment among VADs who had trained elsewhere and who went only as far as the military hospitals in England for their first posting. Alice Bray expressed her disappointment in a letter to her mother in Ottawa. For Bray and her colleagues, the battlefields of France were the epicentre of the war. Being sent to the 1st Southern General Hospital in Birmingham, not even in London, was contrary to their idealized view of VAD nursing. As she wrote, "Gladys and I go to Birmingham. I suppose it is as good a place as any. Not so very far from London – but of course we are disappointed we aren't in London or Folkestone, or some place where we might run into some Canadians."[25]

Bray's perception of favouritism was unfounded, since the Ottawa VADs lacked the long hospital apprenticeship that their Montreal counterparts had enjoyed in the Khaki Homes. As a small city, Ottawa offered far less opportunity for nursing experience in a convalescent hospital, and Bray could claim no hospital experience whatever, not even part-time in Ottawa's Fleming Hospital. Despite this deficit, she felt fully confident of her capabilities after only a few weeks in Birmingham. She proudly informed her mother that "the nurse in charge wouldn't believe I had had no hospital experience, they were short handed so I had to go right into the gruesome part right away – ah my love it is gruesome – oh just fearful."[26]

It is not known why, with her lack of hospital training, Bray was selected for overseas work. Her friend and travelling companion, Gladys Humphrys, had at least two weeks of service in Ottawa, and three of the four other Ottawa women who sailed with Alice and Gladys had already done some hospital work. Edna Johnson and Alice Houston had completed a month of hospital training, and Betty Masson had almost two months of experience in the Fleming hospital and another outside Ottawa. Like Bray, Marion McLean seems to have had no hospital training. Of the six, only Houston and Johnson were eventually transferred to France, despite Alice Bray's high hopes at the outset.[27]

Ontario and Quebec produced the largest proportion of VAD personnel overall. Both provinces had a large urban population and well-established St. John Ambulance programs by 1914. The Montreal VADs may also have benefitted from their early access to regular work in local convalescent facilities, as well as Viola Henderson's professional nursing experience and her determination to override the skeptics. As the war ground on, they were eventually welcomed into the large Sainte-Anne-de-Bellevue military hospital complex near Montreal. By the end of the war, some 130 VADs from Montreal area St. John nursing divisions had worked in military hospitals at home and overseas.[28]

Viola Henderson's "sceptical minds" were not confined to Montreal. Military convalescent hospitals elsewhere in Canada also resisted attempts to introduce VAD workers. The VADs of the Halifax Nursing Division were little more than glorified cheerleaders when the war began, sending off the troops at dockside with candy and cigarettes. Their slow transition to more useful work began in the military convalescent hospitals. As the numbers of returning wounded continued to rise, VADs were assigned to assist on the incoming hospital ships, helping prepare the patients for transfer to hospital or onto trains bound for home. As a key point of departure for the troops, and subsequently for the return of the wounded, Halifax was one of the original six military detachment locations. Early in 1916, despite the demands on its nursing reserves, military medical authorities initially rejected the St. John offer of its "probationary nurses" to assist in the military hospital. Halifax activist and reformer Edith Archibald recounted the resistance in a chronicle of local women's war work:

This offer, after some delay, was accepted, and not long afterwards the first three V.A.D.s, Miss Edith Pyke, Miss Marion Doull, Miss Madelaine Scott, were appointed to the Pine Hill Military Convalescent Hospital, not without a good deal of opposition on the part of some authorities. These young ladies made good "in the face of many difficulties," and thus opened the way for the constantly increasing number of V.A.D. nurses, who did such splendid work throughout the rest of the period of the war, both in Canada and overseas.[29]

The VADs had yet to demonstrate that they were more than eager amateurs. The extra work and disruption involved in their training was also an added burden for the qualified nursing staff. Once the VADs crossed the threshold, the next step was to secure a broad public acceptance that they were competent and appropriate caregivers for sick and wounded soldiers. To this end, the St. John Ambulance authorities in Halifax employed subtle propaganda, with a photographic portrait of Edith Pyke, Marion Doull, and Madelaine Scott, the first VADs who were assigned to the Pine Hill Military Convalescent Hospital. Characterized as its "Three Shining Lights," the women are posed in a tableau reminiscent of "the three little maids from school" in the popular Gilbert and Sullivan operetta *The Mikado* that features the precocious trio.

This type of propaganda helped to distract from the VADs' lack of accredited nursing qualifications. It affirmed the wisdom of admitting them to the hospital wards by visually underscoring their femininity, virtuous innocence, and good breeding. Of the three, Marion Doull went on to serve as a VAD in England with the Royal Army Medical Corps (RAMC).[30] Following the initial period of uncertainty, the VADs were well represented in the many

The Three Shining Lights of the Pine Hill Military Convalescent Hospital. Courtesy Nova Scotia Archives

TABLE 2.1 Canadian and Newfoundland VADs who served overseas during the First World War

Province	Overseas VADs	% of total known VADs overseas	% of population of Canada by province (*1911*)
British Columbia	34	7	5
Alberta	25	5	5
Saskatchewan	35	7	7
Manitoba	34	7	6
Ontario	213	44	34
Quebec	51	11	27
New Brunswick	18	4	5
Nova Scotia	5	1	7
Prince Edward Island	4	1	1
Newfoundland and Labrador	36	8	3
Unrecorded	24	5	

Sources: Numbers are drawn from multiple sources, primarily British Red Cross Society Museum and Archives, Personnel Record Indexes; and Canadian city directories, 1914–30.

military convalescent hospitals in the Maritimes. Despite the enthusiasm, however, Maritime VADs who served abroad were outnumbered by those from Newfoundland and elsewhere in Canada (see Table 2.1). A combination of factors may have contributed to this imbalance. In New Brunswick, the VAD program did not get under way until mid-1917, and it was not organized in Prince Edward Island until mid-1918. In Nova Scotia, the aftermath of the December 1917 Halifax explosion engaged the energies of many VADs, both locally and beyond, well into 1918.

It was more than a lack of access that kept Bessie Hall from entering the Halifax VAD program until late in 1918. St. John had established a VAD nursing division in the city in 1916, the year Bessie graduated from Dalhousie University, but she needed to shore up her finances through teaching before enlisting for VAD work. Even with her late start, she hoped for an overseas posting until the armistice intervened. Learning there would be no further deployment abroad, she wrote home, describing a possible silver lining:

> First of all let me relieve your apprehensions by announcing something which will be a great relief to you and a terrible disappointment to me – there is no chance of going overseas now. Orders came last night to that effect. Heavens I'm sorry, but to "continue on" – there is to be a Hospital ship in on Friday also

a troopship and Mum! There is need of nurses and "V.A.D.s" to take charge of the train load for the west – right out to the coast! Mum just imagine! But *KEEP this dark* till you hear from me again. Remember it's not to be known.[31]

For women like Bessie, the hope for an overseas placement was fuelled by newspaper and magazine articles about the British VADs who worked in military hospitals in England and France. Yet when students enrolled in the VAD classes, St. John emphasized that being sent overseas was not guaranteed. Nor was their enthusiasm dampened by the many notices published in both the Red Cross and St. John literature cautioning against independent applications for VAD work abroad, one of which read,

Advice has been received through the office of the St. John Ambulance Brigade Overseas, within the Dominion of Canada, which office has been dealing with all applications from those desirous of serving in the capacity of probationers or nurses' assistants in the hospitals of Great Britain, that there are NO vacancies whatever for volunteer workers at the present, and that those who proceed to England with this end in view do so entirely at their own risk. A large waiting list exists at St. John's Gate, so that it will be some time before volunteers are called for.[32]

Nevertheless, as mandated by the government, St. John continued to build its reserve of VAD nursing assistants regardless of the limited expectations for deployment abroad before 1916. As the momentum grew, VAD organization charted a steady, if uneven, course across Canada, following the path of the St. John Ambulance pre-war regional development (see Table 2.2).

The first VAD nursing division in Manitoba was founded before the war, established in 1913 to assist the ambulance division in its emergency support for Winnipeg's extensive railway industry. The early start contributed to some thirty-seven Manitoba VADs being chosen for work in hospitals overseas.[33] Due to heavy snowstorms during the winter of 1911 and the challenges of geography, St. John did not include Alberta in its first western organizing campaign, and consequently the province's VAD program had a relatively late start.[34] It was established in September 1916, just as the first official group of sixty VADs from central and eastern Canada arrived in England. Because of the delay, only sixteen Alberta VADs were selected for service overseas.

The more limited opportunities for Alberta women did not dampen Violet Wilson's determination. After losing her brother and three cousins to the war during the summer of 1916, she enrolled in VAD training in Edmonton. Upon

TABLE 2.2 St. John Ambulance Brigade nursing divisions, Canada and Newfoundland, 1912–18

Province / Nursing division (officially established)	Province / Nursing division (officially established)
Alberta	*Ontario*
Calgary No. 39 (September 5, 1917)	Brockville No. 36 (June 3, 1917)
Celia Lucas No. 35 (Edmonton) (September 7, 1917)	College No. 15 (Toronto) (February 29, 1916)
Edmonton No. 20 (September 26, 1917)	Guelph Central No. 25 (April 3, 1917)
	Hamilton No. 16 (April 18, 1918)
British Columbia	Kingston Central No. 21 (November 1, 1916)
Vancouver No. 18 (August 7, 1916)	
Victoria No. 34 (May 11, 1917)	London No. 4 (April 12, 1914)
	Lord Kitchener No. 28 (London) (April 12, 1917)
Manitoba	
CPR No. 8 (Winnipeg) (March 1, 1915)	Ottawa No. 32 (March 19, 1917)
Fort Garry No. 2 (Winnipeg) (May 1, 1913)	St. Catharines No. 22 (December 8, 1916)
	St. Thomas No. 30 (February 20, 1917)
Fort Rouge No. 6 (Winnipeg) (November 19, 1914)	Toronto Central No. 1 (August 6, 1912)
	West Toronto No. 14 (March 17, 1916)
New Brunswick	Windsor No. 11 (April 6, 1915)
Fredericton No. 31 (May 1, 1917)	
Saint John No. 27 (May 11, 1917)	*Prince Edward Island*
	Charlottetown No. 41 (January 1, 1918)
Nova Scotia	
Amherst No. 50 (January 1, 1918) .	*Quebec*
Halifax No. 17 (June 1, 1916)	Montreal Central No. 19 (September 9, 1916)
	Montreal North No. 24 (December 19, 1917)
Saskatchewan	
Devonshire No. 40 (Regina) (July 16, 1917)	Montreal Western No. 38 (June 11, 1917)
	Mount Royal (Maple Leaf)
Edith Cavell No. 13 (Saskatoon) (November 29, 1915)	No. 43 (October 23, 1917)
	Quebec Central No. 29 (March 20, 1917)
Regina No. 10 (March 28, 1915)	Sherbrooke Central No. 12 (May 25, 1915)
Saskatoon No. 7 (January 12, 1915)	
	Newfoundland
	Avalon (St. John's) (April 21, 1913)
	Lady Davidson (St. John's) (September 17, 1914)

Sources: British Red Cross Society Museum and Archives, Personnel Record Indexes; Canadian city directories, 1914–30; Nova Scotia Archives, St. John Ambulance Brigade Overseas, *Report of the Chief Commissioner for Brigade Overseas, 1 October 1915 to 31 December 1917* (London: Chancery of the Order, 1918).

completing the program, she strategically relocated to join a Toronto nursing division, believing this would improve her chances for an overseas post. Her equally resolute brother Charlie had been among the first westerners to enlist in the Canadian Expeditionary Force (CEF), the day after war was declared. His eagerness was grounded in the heady sense of patriotism and adventure that many young Canadian men shared at the time.[35] Violet noted that the ties to Britain were particularly strong for young westerners:

> The first Western regiments were made up largely of Englishmen who flocked by the hundreds from all over the north to enlist in Edmonton ... The men of my brother's age were the first generation to be born in the West and were old enough to enlist when the war broke out, and there were not so many of them.[36]

Out on the east coast, tiny Prince Edward Island managed to send four VADs for work in RAMC military hospitals in England, despite a very late start in VAD organization (January 1918) and a small population (see Table 2.3).[37]

The four PEI VADs conform to the larger Canadian profile. Their ages range from twenty-five to twenty-nine, and all belonged to the comfortable, if not affluent, middle class. Notably also, all four were gainfully employed in white-collar female jobs, which they willingly put aside for VAD work abroad. Perhaps their ability to do so reveals that they did not depend solely upon their wages for financial support. Despite their late start, all four served at least one full VAD contract of five to six months overseas, and they continued to care for convalescent soldiers in England after the armistice.

The St. John VADs conformed closely to the expected requirements for regular nursing applicants. As Viola Henderson emphasized, the VADs in the Khaki Homes were regarded as the equivalent to regular nursing "probationers" in their experience and expertise.[38] As such, they were expected to mirror the probationers in every way, including their racial and ethnic identity. Also at this time, VAD membership was largely urban, since there were no northern or rural St. John branches in Canada. Some VADs did come from rural regions, particularly in western Canada, but had often moved to the city for better employment opportunities prior to volunteering for VAD service. The thirty-six St. John Ambulance nursing divisions established across Canada by the war's end were all situated in urban centres.

The eagerness of the new recruits to be engaged in VAD work sometimes outstripped the available opportunities before the home-front convalescent hospitals became widespread. In late 1915, in anticipation of caring for sick and wounded veterans, the St. John nursing division in Victoria acquired a large

TABLE 2.3 Prince Edward Island VADs overseas, Nursing Division No. 41

Name	Age in 1918	Occupation	UK post	Duration	Father's occupation
Florence Aitken	25	Librarian	1st Southern General Hospital, Birmingham	Oct. 1918 (1 month)	Not known
			1st War Military Hospital, Reading	Nov. 1918 to Jul. 1919 (8 months)	
Nellie Gillespie	28	Steno, PEI premier's office	1st Southern General Hospital annex, Stourbridge	Oct. 1918 to Jul. 1919 (10 months)	Not known
Belle Macmillan	25	Bookkeeper	1st Western General Hospital, Liverpool	Oct. 1918 to Feb. 1919 (5 months)	Customs clerk
Emma Nicholson	29	Steno	1st Western General Hospital, Liverpool	Oct. 1918 to Mar. 1919 (6 months)	Donald Nicholson, MP

Sources: British Red Cross Society Museum and Archives, Personnel Record Indexes; St. John House Archives and Library, Box Xa, "List of V.A.D. members who served in military and naval hospitals overseas"; *Charlottetown City Directories.*

unoccupied residence on its own initiative and set about converting it to a military convalescent home. But as the local newspaper reported, the government and the MHC had other plans: "It is not, however, anticipated that much nursing will be required, as sick men will be cared for at the naval hospital, which is being put in order."[39] Yet hopes were rekindled a few days later, with a subsequent announcement that certified VADs would "be placed in charge of all voluntary nursing at the convalescent home for returned soldiers," which would be renamed the Esquimalt Military Convalescent Hospital once the reconstruction of the former naval hospital was complete.

The newspaper characterized the commitment of the nursing volunteers as "prompted solely by a desire to apply in a practical and useful manner the knowledge they have acquired through hard study and work and to be of some assistance to the Empire in the present crisis."[40] Historian Robert Rutherdale argues that the stirring rhetoric in the press, which portrayed Canadian women as "standing by their fighting men," was part of a larger discourse of home-front propaganda.[41] The language of empire and patriotism bolstered the community's faith in the righteousness of the war, even as increasing numbers of severely damaged soldiers returned home.

The paper affirmed that Victoria's volunteer nurses had been granted access to hospital wards specifically because of their "exceptional qualifications" and were more than equal to "their sisters of the Red Cross Society in England" with regard to their nursing skills. The MHC authorities in charge of the Esquimalt Military Convalescent Hospital appear to have been more cautious about the neophyte volunteers. VADs were to go on duty at "about 10:30 am and will be free to leave at 5 pm. During that time their efforts will be controlled by the hospital's matron who is to be assisted by one or more trained nurses."[42]

In 1916, St. Chad's convalescent hospital in Regina was established in a vacant Anglican boys' college and staffed by VADs on a continuous rota; a year later, a VAD was appointed matron. There appears to have been no resistance to having VAD staff at St. Chad's, possibly because they had become a fixture in other Canadian hospitals. The overall enthusiasm for VAD service in Saskatchewan was particularly high. In 1916, 3 Regina women were among the first group of Canadian VADs to be sent to British military hospitals. They were chosen from a short-list of 41 candidates, only a small fraction of the 368 Saskatchewan VADs who volunteered for service abroad.[43]

Most Canadian VADs were based in Ontario, where thirteen St. John Ambulance nursing divisions had been established, all situated along the Ottawa-to-Windsor corridor. Toronto had three VAD nursing divisions (see

Table 2.2). The city's size and central location also led to the creation of several MHC convalescent facilities.[44] The smaller, private residences that had been used as convalescent homes were gradually replaced by larger, more practical installations. Vacant schools, church halls, and other suitable buildings were employed, their renovation necessitated by the increasing numbers of patients who required specialized long-term rehabilitation.[45] With the growing need for nursing support, Toronto-area VADs also met with less resistance, and hopeful overseas applicants found more opportunities for hospital training and preparation. The demand for their assistance grew as the war lengthened, and those who satisfied the basic criteria for the work were readily accepted. Among them was the future American aviation pioneer Amelia Earhart, who worked as a VAD in Toronto's Spadina Military Hospital for several months in 1918. As she recalled,

> Nurses' aides did everything from scrubbing floors to playing tennis with convalescing patients. The patients called us "sister" and we hot footed here and there to attend to their wants.
>
> "Please rub my back, sister. I'm so tired of lying in bed." Or, "Won't you bring me ice cream today instead of rice pudding?"
>
> We were on duty from seven in the morning until seven at night with two hours off in the afternoon. I spent a great deal of time in the diet kitchen and later in the dispensary, because I knew a little chemistry. Probably the fact that I could be trusted not to drink up the medical supply of whisky counted more than the chemistry.[46]

Earhart had come to Toronto in late 1917 to visit her sister, where she was confronted with the consequences of the war, seeing for the first time maimed and debilitated veterans, "without arms and legs ... paralyzed and ... blind. One day I saw four one-legged men at once, walking as best they could down the street together." She stayed on to train with a Toronto nursing division, hoping eventually to join the American Red Cross overseas; instead, she remained in Toronto through the influenza outbreak and the armistice.[47]

Earhart began her VAD service late in the war, when nursing help was much in demand. The Spadina hospital had a ten-hour work day for all nursing personnel, with VADs assuming many of the extra tasks, such as recreational activities with ambulatory patients and preparing the special diets and even basic medications that the regular nursing staff were too busy to manage. By the time Earhart arrived, VADs had become hospital fixtures, helping with the thousands of men now resident in MHC facilities across Canada.

Amelia Earhart in VAD
uniform in Toronto, 1918.
Courtesy Schlesinger Library,
Radcliffe Institute, Harvard
University

Earhart's work and that of most other VADs was legitimized by their reliability and aptitude rather than their nursing qualifications, or even citizenship. There is also little doubt that Earhart's status as a well-educated member of a prominent American family underscored her suitability as a VAD.[48] As Robert Rutherdale emphasizes, middle-class women's voluntary patriotic community work with uniformed men was shaped "by class boundaries and gendered significations." Earhart was more than qualified to play tennis with her patients, who were almost certainly officers. Like Earhart, many of the Toronto-area VADs were university students from middle-class homes, unlikely to have considered working for wages in an arms factory as their wartime occupation.[49] By 1916, several VADs were being recruited directly from the University of Toronto campus by the local health activist and VAD organizer Margaret Patterson.

When overseas placement finally became a reality in 1916, Toronto-area women appear to have had some advantages. Perhaps this was due to their larger enrollment or the strength of the VAD leadership in the province. Of the 150 VADs in Margaret Patterson's College Nursing Division in Toronto, 40 were selected for overseas service, equalling the number of all Saskatchewan VADs sent abroad. Regardless of their location, not all VADs were content to wait for the official call: impatience drove many to take the initiative, fund their own transport to England, and enlist directly with the British Red Cross at Devonshire House. Ontario's St. John Ambulance organization reported in September 1915 that several of its VAD "certificate holders have proceeded to England and are engaged in the various hospitals of the Red Cross as nurses' assistants."[50] The initial scarcity of overseas postings through official St. John channels did not diminish the enthusiasm of the applicants. Enrollment for training continued unabated, and by the end of 1915 some 4,100 students had completed the required courses; many went on to apply for full VAD certification.

St. John continued to seek out recruits in suitable venues, as evidenced by Margaret Patterson's special undergraduate VAD classes at the University of Toronto. Female enrollment had increased at universities, as capable and intelligent women filled the spaces left by the male students who were serving overseas. In Toronto, this development presented St. John with an ideal source for VAD candidates.[51] Patterson's classes were initiated just as the first official contingent of Canadian VADs reached England, showing that overseas service was now a real possibility. The Women's University Association was quick to assure the students and their families that opting for VAD training entailed "not the slightest obligation to join a division" – it was preparation only "for service if needed."[52] Furthermore, most female undergraduates were too young to undertake work abroad, as twenty-three was the minimum age for service overseas. Most students who completed their training and signed on as VADs worked in the Toronto military convalescent hospitals during the summer vacation, and others helped prepare dressings at the local base hospital.[53]

The pattern of development was much the same in the Dominion of Newfoundland, although there the VAD training and organization were shared between St. John and the Red Cross. During the war, at least forty Newfoundland VADs served overseas as nurses or ambulance drivers. When Devonshire House suddenly called for colonial VADs in 1916, some Newfoundland women undertook a rapid training program or completed their training overseas, spending seven months as "special service probationers" in an English hospital.[54] St. John in Newfoundland recorded that twenty-three "nursing sisters" travelled to England "to serve as VADs" in 1917 and noted other women who had "undertaken hospital and Red Cross work" under the guidance of trained nurses.[55] This ambiguous categorization blurred the professional identities of the 175 Newfoundland women who nursed in some capacity overseas during the war and would underscore nursing's concerns regarding the distinction between nurse and VAD.

Like their Canadian counterparts, many Newfoundland women had strong ties to Britain, which helped fuel their interest in VAD work. Their patriotic sensibilities were intensified in 1916 by the decimation of the Newfoundland Regiment during the Battle of the Somme.[56] Patriotism was critical to the growth and popularity of the St. John VAD program. Charles Copp, assistant commissioner of the St. John Ambulance in Ontario, who was responsible for the Canadian VAD program, was adamant that the VADs were motivated only by "pure patriotism." He countered the rumour that the VAD program was simply a marriage bureau, citing the "remarkably good" service record of Canadian VADs abroad.[57]

Maintaining the Boundaries between the CAMC and the VADs

Canada's VAD program was of little concern to the nursing community when the war began. In September 1914, nursing leaders were fully engaged in ensuring that only qualified nurses would be chosen for service overseas as CAMC nursing sisters. When Jean Gunn, president of the CNATN, learned that several partially trained and poorly recommended women had managed to evade the selection process by using their contacts at the Militia Department, she feared the potential consequences.[58] Thinking that the image and status of all trained and qualified Canadian nurses, civilian or military, might be debased, she warned that "Canadian nurses would be judged and compared to those who were sent on active service regardless of their merits."[59] As the underqualified women had had their appointments personally approved by the minister of militia and defence, Sam Hughes, Gunn forwarded an official complaint to Prime Minister Borden.

The intervention of CAMC matron-in-chief Margaret Macdonald ensured that the integrity of the nursing service was not compromised. However, as Macdonald's biographer Susan Mann makes clear, this required some "delicate manoeuvring" around the demands of the CNATN, the sensibilities of the underqualified nurses, and the poor judgment of Sam Hughes.[60] Macdonald needed both tact and diplomatic agility to avoid the political pitfalls.[61] She assured Gunn that the substandard nurses would function solely as support staff, would handle non-nursing tasks, and would not bear the commissioned rank of lieutenant, which was accorded to a regular CAMC nursing sister. No doubt dismayed that it had failed to gain control of the CAMC selection process, the

Louise de Salaberry, VAD,
c. 1917. *Rare Books and Special
Collections, McGill University
Library*

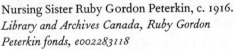

Nursing Sister Ruby Gordon Peterkin, c. 1916.
*Library and Archives Canada, Ruby Gordon
Peterkin fonds, e002283118*

CNATN chafed at the knowledge that unqualified women would wear the CAMC uniform and to all outward appearances carry the status of qualified nursing sisters. Its concerns regarding identity were reinforced by the grey and white uniform of the SJAB VADs, which was very similar to the blue and white uniform of the CAMC nurses. To the casual observer, both might appear to convey the same authority and expertise.

Macdonald shared these concerns: with the skills and professionalism of Canadian nursing in the public gaze, she was fully aware of the risks from inferior representation. In 1914, most Canadian nursing graduates were not yet designated as registered nurses under provincial legislation. In most provinces, no legal restriction prevented an underqualified woman from seeking employment as a "nurse."[62] The idea of professional status was bound up with the recognition of nursing as a scientific, knowledge-based skill that required a rigorous standard of qualification. Nightingale and other early nursing advocates had worked to standardize training procedures. Their efforts promoted a greater awareness of nursing competence and the association of nursing with middle-class respectability.[63] By the onset of the war, the vestiges of the Sarah Gamp stereotype had been erased, transforming nursing into a respectable occupation for educated women.[64] Canadian civilian and military nurses alike recognized that excluding underqualified women from the CAMC nursing service was essential to promoting the modern, professional image of Canadian nursing. Ensuring that the VADs did not enter CAMC hospitals became no less critical to the image of nursing overall. Status and professionalism were central to nursing's aspirations, and maintaining a visible distance between the volunteer and the trained nurse was vital to these goals. To this end, Matron-in-Chief Margaret Macdonald was committed to keeping VADs out of Canadian military hospital wards overseas.

The numbers of sick and wounded Canadian men increased dramatically in the wake of the gas attacks that killed seven thousand during the Second Battle of Ypres in April 1915. The unexpected intensity of loss and injury inflamed patriotic feeling at home, motivating more young women to seek a direct involvement with the war through VAD work. Doreen Gery recalled the onslaught of posters and images exhorting both men and women to do their patriotic duty and felt driven to train for VAD nursing when her younger brother and fifteen of his classmates left school to enlist. She eventually followed him overseas, having secured a posting in France.[65]

Throughout the war, Matron Macdonald received countless letters from Canadian VADs, begging for the chance to nurse overseas with the CAMC. With no shortage of qualified nurses and a firm resolve to deny casual appointments, she refused them.[66] Her consistent reply was that "Canadian hospitals do not employ V.A.D. nurses, but only trained nurses." The same message was conveyed to the many CAMC administrators who dutifully forwarded importuning letters from friends or family requesting VAD work in the military hospitals.[67]

Macdonald's position was bolstered in 1916 by a controversial review of the CAMC's overseas organization, compiled by Colonel Herbert Bruce, inspector general of the CAMC.[68] During the first years of hostilities, convalescent hospitals staffed with VAD nurses had rapidly become integral to the RAMC in Britain, with the constant stream of recovering men being discharged from primary care into the massive military hospital complex. As the much larger counterpart of Canada's National Relief Committee, the Joint War Committee

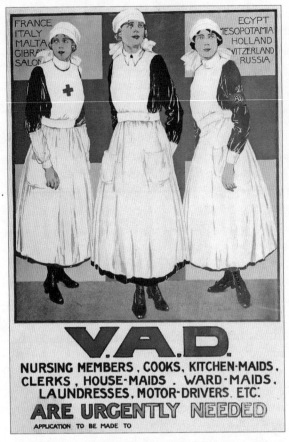

British Red Cross VAD recruitment poster, by Joyce
Dennys. *Courtesy British Red Cross Society Museum and
Archives, acc. 2355/1*

in Britain managed more than three thousand auxiliary home hospitals staffed
by the RAMC.[69] As in Canada, these facilities were generally adapted from
large private homes and other serviceable buildings offered by their owners
for the duration of the war. Before the CAMC and Canadian Red Cross hospitals were established in Britain, the auxiliary hospitals frequently housed
convalescent Canadian soldiers. Midway through the war, this arrangement
provided considerable ammunition for political manoeuvring in Canadian
military medical circles, and it fuelled the Bruce inquiry's criticism of the
CAMC organization under Director General of Medical Services, General Guy
Carleton-Jones.[70]

Published in September 1916, the Bruce Report pilloried the CAMC operations under Carleton-Jones's direction, employing the emotive imagery of Canadian soldiers lingering in British convalescent hospitals, "asking and begging to be taken to Canadian hospitals."[71] The report was particularly scathing in its criticism of the British VAD auxiliary hospitals, characterizing the VADs as eager and patriotic but with little or no training.[72] As Bruce stated,

> Most of the Voluntary Aid Detachment Hospitals are merely dwelling houses, roughly adapted to serve as hospitals, with a medical staff from the neighbouring civilian practitioners.
>
> As a rule there are one or more supervising graduate nurses, but most of the nursing is done by young ladies who, previous to the war, had no hospital training.[73]

His words confirmed Margaret Macdonald's arguments for keeping Canadian VADs well away from CAMC hospitals. In the wake of the report, Bruce took over control of the CAMC from Carleton-Jones. Ironically, he was soon replaced due to his own apparent incompetence.[74]

In an autobiographical postwar review of his experience with the politics of war, Bruce revised his earlier criticisms of the British VADs. Had he been allowed to continue with his reorganization of the CAMC, he stated, he would have introduced Canadian VADs into the CAMC hospitals, regardless of Macdonald, "who I found very much opposed to the idea."[75] He noted that Canada was one of the very few Allied nations that did not use its own VADs in its military hospitals overseas, and he acknowledged the enormous economic value of VAD nursing assistance. He likened the role of the VADs to that of probationers, who performed the bulk of the menial tasks "at little or no expense" in contemporary civilian hospitals. He concluded that after a VAD had served for eighteen to twenty-four months in a military hospital, her work had become "indistinguishable" from that of a fully trained nurse. Had these opinions been published in 1916, Macdonald's response can only be imagined. As it was, she viewed the Bruce Report as a grave injustice to General Carleton-Jones, even though it endorsed her own views on VADs.[76]

With Bruce removed from authority, Macdonald's policy of refusing VAD assistance prevailed, although the Canadian VADs who hoped for a CAMC placement remained largely unaware of the political roadblocks. The St. John Ambulance continued to recruit and train them, also apparently oblivious to the political turmoil within the CAMC. With the introduction of regular VAD service into home-front convalescent hospitals by mid-1915, women's eagerness to nurse "the boys" overseas continued to grow. Ironically, on the heels of the Bruce Report, the first official contingent of sixty St. John VADs was preparing to embark for service overseas with the RAMC, at the request of the British Joint War Committee. Canadian VADs were elated to finally have an opportunity to serve overseas, if only in the British hospitals.[77]

Enlisting for VAD Service Abroad

Early in the war, Britain's military hospitals rapidly came to depend on their seemingly infinite supply of VADs. In February 1915, Devonshire House had begun screening its reserve of volunteer nurses for regular service in the home-front military hospitals and on the Continent. The escalating conflict soon demanded a continuing expansion of military hospital beds and a ready supply of nurses to manage them. Acknowledging that unpaid VAD service was not without personal expense, the War Office was soon working to encourage the enrollment of even more women, with a suggested stipend of twenty pounds a year. This amounted to only half the wage of a trained and certified staff nurse of the era, but VADs were also guaranteed accommodation, an allowance for board and washing, and one pound per quarter for the upkeep of the uniform. Although they would no longer be cost-free volunteers, the stipend was little more than a living allowance, a bid to attract less affluent women by defraying some of their expenses. By mid-1916, the RAMC began to look to its colonial allies to help replenish the VAD reserves, as sick and wounded men continued to arrive in an endless stream.[78]

By the conclusion of 1915, despite the cautionary messages from St. John and the Canadian Red Cross, a number of determined and resourceful Canadian and Newfoundland women had already gone overseas, preceding the first official contingent. Influenced by the propagandized reports of British VAD work in the popular press, they travelled independently or with friends and family in search of VAD work.[79] Some trained with the British Red Cross once they arrived; others hoped that their Canadian St. John qualification would enable them to enlist as British VADs. Many financed their own passage to London and then secured a hospital post by applying in person to Devonshire House.

Money was a critical factor in determining whether a woman could take this path. The VADs who were sent under the auspices of St. John had their travel costs covered by the organization (see Appendix 3). Once abroad, they also received a basic living allowance from the RAMC, a payment that was increased as enthusiasm for VAD work began to lag with fatigue and war weariness.[80] A few Canadian women of limited means mistakenly assumed that if they financed their own trip to England, they would be taken on as a CAMC nurse or VAD and have their travel costs reimbursed by the government. One of these, Sophie Smethurst, left Saskatoon "with the intention of joining the Canadian forces," apparently unaware that the CAMC did not accept VADs. She was inevitably rejected by the Canadian military, but her VAD training secured her a placement in an RAMC hospital. A few months later, she confidently reapplied for VAD work with the CAMC, citing her British hospital experience: "I have been working with a fully trained sister and have had to take her place when away. I am now on night duty with [four] patients to look after alone. I have good experience in dressings."[81] She had acquired an endorsement from Colonel Munro, in charge of No. 8 Canadian Stationary Hospital, for the reassessment of her application. Nonetheless, as Cynthia Toman's study of the CAMC nursing service illustrates, Macdonald remained unimpressed with Sophie's credentials. Her response was unequivocal: "VAD nurses are not at present being employed in our hospitals."[82]

With so few opportunities, most Canadian VADs were content simply to be working overseas, regardless of which hospital they served in. As Alice Bray acknowledged to her mother after being assigned to the RAMC's 1st Southern General Hospital, in Birmingham, "Really, if you saw the awful need of nurses here you would be glad you had let me come – I wouldn't be happy not doing my part."[83] Her observation spoke to the RAMC's problem of qualified nursing reserves that were sorely depleted well before the war ended, unlike the CAMC, with its surfeit of nurses waiting for the call. The British military nurses had little option but to rely on their VADs and to accept and adapt to the Canadian and other colonial volunteers who worked with them at the bedside.

In September 1916, St. John finally received a request from Devonshire House to select sixty Canadian VADs to serve abroad in the RAMC hospitals. For this and the seven subsequent calls, a VAD's selection would depend on her record of hard work, plus a measure of determination and luck, with luck often the most critical element. From the outset, the selection process was erratic. Prior experience in a military hospital did not guarantee an overseas posting, as Bessie Hall discovered. The great majority of applicants could only wait and hope to be chosen, often frustrated by the uncertainty and irregular selection process. Ultimately, most would be disappointed, as Devonshire House issued only eight formal calls between 1916 and the end of the war (see Table 2.4), and Matron Macdonald's position regarding the employment of VADs did not change.

TABLE 2.4 St. John Ambulance Brigade, Canadian VAD
contingents selected for overseas service

Year	Month	Number	Total by year
1916	September	60	60
1917	July	35	
	December	27	62
1918	February	25	
	March	54	
	June	41	
	July	54	
	September	49	223
Total			345

Following the September 1916 call, the College Nursing Division in Toronto
reported that, of the more than eighty women who had been on regular duty
in local military convalescent hospitals, "twenty volunteered, seven were selected and twelve went overseas by their own expense."[84] Toronto's Central
Nursing Division sent seven members overseas with the first group in 1916
and another eight in the summer of 1917. Across Canada, the selection process
was equally uncertain. Three of the eleven Saskatoon VADs who had volunteered only "provisionally" were chosen by late 1917. Four of the eight Regina
volunteers were accepted by their St. John nursing division but were still waiting to be called overseas at the end of the year. Fredericton had no St. John
nursing division prior to mid-1917, but two of its VADs were selected for
service abroad within the first six months of its operation. Halifax, with more
than a hundred women engaged in regular VAD service throughout the war,
sent only six.[85]

The unpredictable selection pattern shared some similarities with that of
the CAMC nursing service, where the candidates for overseas placement far
outnumbered the available opportunities. In Edmonton, VAD Violet Wilson
calculated that she would have a much better chance of being chosen if she
moved to Toronto and joined a nursing division there. Her move embodied
the mix of determination and good luck that seems to have been a key requirement for selection. As the daughter of a prominent Edmonton physician and
politician, Violet was well connected through family and friends in both cities.
Educated at Toronto's Bishop Strachan School for girls, she maintained a

forthright independence and thirst for adventure throughout her life. Yet unlike her brother, who had enlisted the day after hostilities began, she did not immediately rush to aid the war effort. It was the sudden loss of her brother, followed by the loss of three cousins "during that awful summer of 1916," that fixed her resolve to do so:

> I went to Toronto, and taking various nursing courses, and worked in a military hospital. And then I took a motor mechanics course. This was considered quite something, as there were not many cars around in those days and very few women drivers. After completing the course, in order to get more practical experience, I worked in a garage for six weeks doing the ordinary repair work as it came in. One day I heard an Aunt say to a friend disappointedly: "Hardly feminine work!!" But I loved it![86]

Although Violet was selected to go overseas in 1917, her departure date was repeatedly changed. She finally resorted to family connections and secured an interview with Assistant Commissioner for the St. John Ambulance Brigade in Canada Sir Henry Pellatt. He was an old family friend, "in his youth an admirer of my mother's." The meeting, however, was not quite as expected:

> Shown into his luxurious office, I asked whether he could hurry my departure. I was terrified when this great fat man, who seemed as old as the hills to me, pulled me down on his knee and began kissing me! As I was struggling to get away his secretary came in and showed no surprise whatever at the scene. Apparently there was nothing unusual in this situation! But this was my first experience with a licentious old man, I was overwhelmed! However, he did promise me that: Not another girl will leave Canada before you! And they didn't.[87]

Wilson went on to serve as a VAD in England and France.

The records indicate that among the initial overseas contingent, VADs from Montreal divisions had a greater chance of selection for France, though the reason for this is not clear. However, as mentioned above, many had volunteered in the Khaki Homes and, by April 1916, were also working in the Grey Nuns' Convalescent Home. The eleven Montrealers who travelled with Alice Bray in the first contingent were experienced hospital workers. Of this group, ten went directly to France, and one was sent to Egypt. Viola Henderson described their work in Montreal:

During the year 1915 to July 1916, the workers performed all the duties in what finally was not one but three homes, serving three months at a time, day and night duty, the day duty being divided into two periods, night duty regular hospital hours. In 1916 the call came for Overseas and found the V.A.D.s ready to answer "Send Me."[88]

Alice Bray resented the apparent preference shown to the Montreal VADs who went directly to France. She felt that they received special treatment from Devonshire House due to their association with Henderson. Bray and her Ontario colleagues were given less glamorous first assignments in England, with some hope for a transfer to France: "Betty Masson and Mary McLean and that bunch go to Lyster [Leicester]. Miss Johnson and Miss Houston went to Lincoln, and of course the dear Montrealers went straight to France, imagine, but we all will get the chance to go to France they say, if we make good, so here is hoping."[89]

Having overcome the obstacles to overseas selection, VADs still faced an arduous and sometimes dangerous ocean voyage before reaching their final destination. Violet Wilson finally set sail in mid-1918 with a western contingent of forty VADs and found the experience "a ghastly voyage in every way. The food was as bad as the accommodation, the weather was foul, and worst of all we had to wear life-belts all day." The women were "billeted six in a cabin designed for two," and after three weeks of zigzagging across the Atlantic to avoid submarines, it was "not surprising that none of us were on speaking terms." The physical discomfort was matched by the drama of potential danger. One day, the VADs were summoned to their boat stations and left "standing on deck for four hours nervously watching one of our convoy as she was attacked by a submarine." Violet's unexpected compensation for this ordeal was a chance encounter with George Bennett, an old friend from Edmonton, the brother of future prime minister R.B. Bennett, who invited her to his cabin "for a forbidden but welcome drink" when it was over.[90]

Always ready for a challenge, as her narrative reveals, Violet breached VAD protocols even before the ship left port. Although she was pleased to be under way, she was far less happy with her "unbelievably ugly" VAD uniform and was determined to remedy its most offensive feature:

Worst of all was the hat. At the time small hats were the fashion, with large crowns, and any woman will appreciate the depressing effect of having to wear a wide, low-crowned hat. I rushed mine to a milliner, and with the crown raised it didn't look quite so bad. When nothing was said about the change I thought

I had got away with it. Unfortunately it was decided that before we left Canada one of those awful group photographs should be taken, and as I was tall, I was put in the back row, and so silhouetted against the background. I was given a good "ticking off," as I paraded before the Commandant, and told to obey the rules in future and not destroy government property: "Did I realize that taxpayers had paid for my hat?" I was ordered to get a new one at my own expense. This I did, but I carefully kept my improved version, and as soon as I was safely at sea, I threw the regulation one overboard.[91]

Decades later, two other VADs recalled this memorable voyage. Agnes Wilson, also from Edmonton but unrelated to Violet, mentioned the discomfort: "But you know we had an awful crossing. We had to go with a convoy, and the rate of the convoy was just as slow as could be. I think we were twenty-two days crossing ... and everyone was desperately sea sick."[92] Regina VAD Daisy Johnson recalled being delayed for more than a week in Halifax after leaving

Western contingent of VADs in Toronto en route for embarkation for England, July 1918. Violet Wilson is second from the left, back row. *Glenbow Archives, NA-2267–6*

Montreal and then setting off with a convoy of eleven ships, including one loaded with TNT, a sobering thought after the disastrous December 1917 explosion in Halifax. Daisy remembered that "sports were organized; also a concert and we were kept on lifeboat stations for an hour when someone thought they saw a submarine. The destroyers appeared on the 26th and from then on we had to sleep partly dressed and with our boots and lifebelts on – very uncomfortable."[93]

Three Newfoundland VADs who made the crossing much earlier, in 1916, recorded a quite different experience in their letters and diaries. There were two voyages, only a few weeks apart, but both were far less eventful and much more comfortable than that of the Canadians. The Newfoundlanders sailed on civilian ocean liners, reaching England only a week to ten days after leaving New York. For sisters Sybil and Jill Johnson, members of the St. John's elite, ocean travel was a familiar experience. Despite the "good orchestra" onboard, Sybil found the journey particularly "boring," with nothing out of the ordinary to dispel the monotony.[94] But this was Fanny Cluett's first ocean voyage, and she thoroughly enjoyed every minute of it, particularly the food: "Breakfast is served in the dining room from 8 a.m. until 10 a.m. Chicken broth is served at 11 a.m. on the deck. Luncheon at 1 o'clock. Tea and cakes and biscuits at 4 o'clock. Dinner at 7 o'clock. In fact breakfast and luncheon are dinners too, as there are so many, many, many courses."[95]

The Newfoundland VADs were not escorted by a naval convoy. They travelled instead in the company of wealthy and influential British and American civilian passengers. The Johnsons were completely at ease in this environment, but Fanny Cluett was overwhelmed by the liner's lavish decor, the unexpected benefits of free writing paper, and a live orchestra during meals. The glamour of the passengers amazed her:

> I wish you could see some of the tables, ladies drinking coffee, playing che-
> quers, smoking cigarettes and talking, dressed in silks and laces. At night dia-
> monds are worn. I looked at the Countess' rings last night. Dear me I never saw
> such a display of jewellery in all my life as I have seen this week. I never thought
> I would see life as it is.[96]

But the war soon dramatically altered the travel experience of Newfound-land VADs. Just six months after Fanny and the Johnsons made their cross-ings, Jeanette Coultas of St. John's embarked from Halifax instead of New York, now that the Americans had entered the war.[97] Her memory of the trip was far more in line with what the Canadian VADs recounted in 1917:

We landed at Halifax and there we had to wait for 23 days. Then one night we were alerted and led to the docks. We didn't know what ship was taking us nor were we encouraged to ask. One person, however, did vouchsafe the information that the ship was a tub. On board we found the ship was no floating palace – but we didn't care. We were on our way at last!

Our ship was one of a convoy and we learned later was called the City of Marseilles. We had a few scares during the crossing. One of the ships in our convoy, the Kenilworth Castle, was torpedoed. We didn't feel very brave, but it would never do to show any nervousness – All of the officers and crew looked so brave.[98]

Once in London, all VADs, colonial or British, had to confront the female bureaucracy at Devonshire House, headquarters of the Joint Women's VAD Committee, before beginning work in the RAMC hospitals. At Devonshire House, Canadian and Newfoundland VADs rapidly discovered that they were all on an equal footing as "colonials," regardless of class or national origin. This was of no concern to Fanny Cluett, as she marvelled at the grandeur of the Devonshire House reception hall, with its "sixteen great pillars, eight on either side, running the length of the room, and a famous oil-painting over the mantlepiece." Once again, she was moved to declare, "I never thought I would ever see the like."[99] In contrast, Sybil Johnson was oblivious to the surroundings and clearly unimpressed with her welcome at VAD headquarters:

Went to H.Q. this morning as instructed, dutifully arriving a bit before 12, the appointed hour, to be told that the lady who had summoned us had "gone out a few minutes ago but would be back." So we waited for more than an hour, when she appeared and sailed past us, flat heels, high collar, glasses and all. After a while we sent a message to say we'd been there since 12 and were duly received (with a freezing glance). She didn't even say "sorry." If I hadn't been keen on my job I should have said, "Where were you dragged up?" – Still she was more human than before, so by the time we've spent a few mornings in attendance she'll be shaking hands, and asking us to sit down. I felt as I evidently [was] intended to feel. Like a servant asking her to take us into service.[100]

As a member of a leading St. John's family, Sybil was unaccustomed to being ignored or kept waiting, but she knew little of large, anonymous bureaucracies. At Devonshire House, she was just one of thousands of VAD applicants, many boasting a far more influential pedigree than hers. She did not know that the Devonshire House organization relied on limited human resources – the many unpaid volunteers from the middle and upper classes, one of whom was the young Princess Mary.[101] Alice Bray's first impression of Devonshire House in September 1916 was more positive. It was still adjusting to the new category of "colonial" VAD, which included women from other nations and dominions, such as Australia and New Zealand. Alice's sole memory of her visit was of being "paraded up" for a group inspection by a commandant and being pronounced "quite smart." Far more notable was their reception at "Lady Winston Churchill's," followed by an outing to "Mme Tussaud's Waxworks," probably arranged by the St. John Ambulance in England.[102] After being scrutinized by a lady official at Devonshire House, the VADs were assigned to one of the many hospital facilities that came under the auspices of the Joint War Committee.[103]

By 1918, Devonshire House had processed well over twenty-two thousand VAD applicants. The Joint Women's VAD Committee was recruiting for all British military hospitals, which included large RAMC complexes and dozens of small VAD auxiliary hospitals, convalescent homes, camps, and hostels. All were designed to meet the varying needs of sick or wounded men at many stages of recovery. It was the lack of medical expertise and suitable equipment in these facilities that had originally prompted Colonel Herbert Bruce's criticism in the Bruce Report rather than the VAD nurses themselves. He sympathized with one Red Cross VAD commandant, who readily acknowledged the problems but was powerless to improve conditions.[104] Not surprisingly, Britain's director of Army Medical Services, Sir Alfred Keogh, staunchly defended this system of small hospitals, which numbered more than three thousand by the war's end, as providing excellent personal care.[105] In Britain, as in Canada, these hospitals ranged from town halls, schools, and commercial buildings to sometimes opulent stately homes, and in France and Belgium even converted abbeys and chateaux were not uncommon. Temporary additions, such as huts or tents, were often made to these structures, as in the case of the Wandsworth Hospital in London, which occupied the former classrooms of the Royal Patriotic School. It cared for many colonial casualties, including men from the Newfoundland Regiment and the Anzacs of Australia and New Zealand. It had expanded from an initial 520 beds "cooped together in those first days in every available room and corner," more than tripling in size to accommodate 1,800 beds by the end of 1916. The result was a maze of huts linked by endless corridors and subdivided into wards, much like a small town.

The Wandsworth Hospital was not unique, as is revealed in a letter written by Annie Wynne-Roberts in late 1916, describing the 1st Southern General Hospital, Birmingham:

Balloon view of the 3rd London General Hospital, Wandsworth. Drawn by A. Henry Fullwood in 1915, this view shows the original Royal Patriotic School building encompassed by a growing number of temporary pavilion wards. *Australian War Memorial, ART19782*

We arrived on Saturday night. On Sunday morning we were told in what wards to work, and now we feel as if we had been here for months ... I have not found out the exact number of patients yet, but I am told that it is well over 2,000. The main corridors are each over a quarter of a mile in length. Imagine walking that distance every time one needs something from the nurses' home![106]

Whatever preconceptions the Canadian and Newfoundland VADs may have entertained before experiencing the reality of overseas hospitals, they quickly learned to expect the unexpected.[107]

Non-nursing VADs

In their postwar retrospective, Wealtha Wilson and Ethel Raymond claim that "theoretically women are unfitted for war; in actual practice they are the real supporters and approvers of war. It could never be waged were it not mothered by women."[108] A successful conclusion, they argue, was unattainable without the efforts of women, whether they were at home knitting comforts to support the efforts of the boys in the trenches or nursing in military hospitals to restore the sick and wounded to fighting form. Wilson and Raymond regard the VAD nurse as a vital part of this mothering army, but not all women who opted for VAD work chose nursing as their preferred assignment.[109]

They were encouraged by a CAMC policy change of mid-1917, which permitted non-nursing VADs to serve as social convenors in the Canadian Red Cross recreation huts attached to the hospitals in England and France, a new approach that was notable enough to be cited by the principal matron for the British Expeditionary Force in France, E.M. McCarthy.[110] The huts offered a respite to convalescing patients who needed a change from the monotony of the wards. However, the new policy was not generated by a sudden recognition of the value of VAD assistance. It was an expedient response to increasing demands for more fighting men, which resulted in able-bodied male orderlies being released for active service. The Canadian Red Cross was careful to avoid the political pitfalls of placing female volunteers in CAMC hospitals against the wishes of its matron-in-chief. It emphasized their non-nursing status when the assistant commissioner overseas announced the change in June 1917: "We are making a change in our Recreation Huts and have been getting out young Canadian ladies as V.A.D. members to replace the orderlies in these huts; the change so far has been very satisfactory indeed."[111]

As the need for available and cost-effective auxiliary personnel continued to grow, journalists and propagandists were tasked with putting a positive spin on women's war service overseas, particularly those jobs that were not normally associated with nursing. Experienced newspaper publicists such as Mary MacLeod Moore skilfully improvised, producing heartening vignettes of young Canadian VADs working abroad in the Canadian Red Cross recreation huts. Early in 1918, following a visit to a CAMC hospital, Moore penned a reassuring piece on the care of recovering Canadian wounded. The men who could leave their beds for some recreation in the huts were being capably assisted by sensitive and respectable Canadian VADs:

> It was a charming sight to come in from visiting wards full of sick and wounded men and find a young girl in the indoor uniform of the VAD with its white veil in charge of a hut full of men wearing the badges of famous regiments ...
>
> Some of the men were writing letters, others reading, others playing cards and billiards, and some merely talking and laughing together in the best of spirits. The girls in charge, who appear to be the embodiment of tact, as well as of kindness and energy, understand when to leave the men alone, and when to talk and make suggestions.[112]

The "badges of famous regiments" attest to the well-bred, chivalrous character of the men, and the "white veil" demonstrates the purity of the VAD assistant in the informal environment of the hut. The uniform framed her work, even in a recreational capacity, providing her with the socially approved identity of "nurse." Working in a hut also facilitated close contact with the wounded warriors, but not necessarily at the bedside. Surprisingly, a few of these volunteers had briefly served as nursing assistants in No. 3 Canadian General Hospital in France, where "the Recreation Hut has been turned into a ward during the recent rush and the V.A.D.s there have been assisting the nursing sisters."[113]

A report by Matron E.M. McCarthy on the CAMC nursing service in France noted that fifteen non-nursing Canadian VAD volunteers had been assigned to the huts and other clerical duties, most having reached England well before the first official contingent of September 1916. Some had been certified as British Red Cross VADs after their arrival; consequently, their identity as Canadian VADs was largely invisible, as they blended in with the more than twenty thousand British volunteers who wore the Red Cross VAD uniform.[114]

Men who convalesced in England often returned to combat less swiftly than those who remained in a military hospital in France and also had a greater chance of being reassigned to a non-combat role. The huts were intended to promote their recovery and to return them to active service as quickly as possible. In France, ensuring that a man's recovery was reasonably congenial also benefitted the war effort. In her postwar retrospective on Canadian Red Cross work, Mary MacLeod Moore championed the installation of both the huts and the VADs, continuing the theme of the "motherly" influence:

> The Huts were a stroke of genius. Men who were not ill enough or sufficiently badly wounded to be sent to England were often in hospital for some time, and after passing through a "Con. Camp" [convalescent camp] returned to duty. The Red Cross Huts were their happiest reminders of home and of a woman's care, for the Huts were in charge of Canadian girls, members of the V.A.D., who acted as hostesses and organizers, arranged entertainments, decorated their Huts for special occasions, and were often confidantes of the boys and men, far from their own relatives, who shyly displayed family photographs and letters to these sympathetic friends.[115]

Although the CAMC's official policy change in regard to non-nursing VAD assistance dated from 1917, some VADs had not waited for this development. As early as 1916, a few Canadian VAD workers were providing clerical support in some Canadian hospitals. Matron Cameron-Smith of the CAMC nursing service discovered the "special work of the lady VAD helpers" while touring the Canadian treatment centres on the south coast of England. The twenty-eight CAMC nurses who cared for three hundred patients at the Westcliffe Eye and Ear Hospital were assisted by two VADs and a home sister who managed the nurses' quarters. Cameron-Smith remarked,

> This was of interest, as very few of the CAMC hospitals as yet, have employed VAD assistants. One lady, Mrs. Aver of Hamilton, Ontario has been connected with this institution from its commencement almost, and takes charge of the main telephone – Another, Miss Baldwin, is the link between Westcliffe Hospital and the Canadian Red Cross Branch in Shorncliffe, looking after the comforts, which that generous lady supplies ... This is one person's work and the fact that Miss Baldwin does it so capably, allows a Nursing Sister to be free for the more technical duties that are here, as everywhere, in abundance.[116]

In a revelation that countered the CAMC nursing community's opinion regarding VADs as society women who would disrupt both hospitals and the authority of qualified nurses, Cameron-Smith found "no evidence of friction between sisters and VAD workers, or the latter and the servants." This positive comment was bolstered by her description of the "eighteen VAD helpers, enthusiastic, capable, gentle and strong," that she had also observed at the Queen's Canadian Military Hospital in rural Kent. Cameron-Smith's remarks appear to suggest that she may have been open to seeing more VAD assistance in the CAMC hospitals had she been consulted.[117]

Beyond the CAMC hospitals, the nursing sisters came into contact with Canadian VADs in a variety of settings, one of which was the Hôtel du Nord in Boulogne. Formerly a summer retreat, the hotel opened as a CRCS Red Cross Nurses' Rest House in April 1918, and thirteen Canadian VADs were assigned to it. Established as a hostel by the Canadian Red Cross for Allied nurses and VADs travelling to and from France, as well as a respite for those on leave, it accommodated more than 6,800 guests in less than a year. Nurses arrived at all hours, day or night, to be picked up from the harbour or the train station. Characteristic of his time and class, Colonel H.W. Blaylock, CRCS chief commissioner overseas, reported that the home had been founded to alleviate the problems faced by travelling nurses, who were forced "to go to dirty French hotels where they were crowded and overcharged."[118] Mary MacLeod Moore praised the hotel's transformation, under the direction of Mrs. Ethel Gordon-Brown and her VAD assistants, who "turned a hotel into a real home, with the prettiest chintzes and freshest curtains, good china and restful furniture, and the willing service of a staff of charming Canadian girls."[119] The furnishings for the earlier Canadian nurses' Rest House in London had been a point of contention between Matron Macdonald and Colonel Charles A. Hodgetts, the Red Cross commissioner overseas during the war. As Susan Mann notes, Macdonald had wanted a truly welcoming atmosphere for tired nurses, one whose fine china and linens evoked the comforts of home, but Hodgetts had argued for basic army blankets and had used quilts to save money for the Red Cross hospitals.[120] Not surprisingly, Macdonald appears to have won the match, but even with the more luxurious trappings, coziness was not always achieved.

Despite the chintzes and linens, the Boulogne establishment had its problems. One Canadian VAD who was posted there mentioned several discomforts associated with a converted summer hotel, which lacked both a heating system and a fireplace – "We nearly died of cold!" Eva Morgan also recalled that during the heavy bombing raids along the coast of France in late 1918, the VADs and guests were often forced to retreat to the cellar, along "with the mice and the rats and all the rest of it!"[121] Canadian engineers had reinforced the cellar as an air raid shelter, and it could be entered from within the building or from an exterior courtyard. Journalist Moore reported that when the warning sounded, guests and staff together, "sometimes to the number of 100, descended to the cellar by the light of electric torches," where they waited out the bombardment. Her account, written for readers in Canada, including the families of the young VADs and CRCS subscribers, carefully avoided any mention of rats and mice. Instead, it emphasized the amenities of the home, including Canadian touches such as the corn grown by the VADs in the courtyard garden.[122]

Another, much smaller group of Canadian VAD assistants was unexpectedly granted an unofficial place in the CAMC nursing service much earlier in the war, when Matron Macdonald created a special class of worker to help with the operation of the nurses' residences. As mentioned above, she discovered in late 1914 that the minister of militia and defence, General Sam Hughes, had appointed some twenty underqualified women to the CAMC nursing service overseas, which prompted CNATN president Jean Gunn to complain to Prime Minister Borden. Macdonald cleverly mollified the sensibilities of everyone involved by devising a new category of nursing assistant and specifying that "the only possible way in which their services could be utilized was as housekeeper in the Sisters' quarters."[123] Although functioning as non-nursing VADs, the women were identified as home sisters and remained within the purview of the CAMC, receiving the pay and allowances of military nurses but not the rank. Already accustomed to managing household staff, they were suited to organizing the domestic arrangements of the nurses. The CAMC ensured that Hughes made no further ill-advised nursing appointments, and any subsequent housekeeping positions appear to have been filled by VADs.[124]

For most Canadians, women in a VAD uniform nursed, but the cheery news items in the society pages did not convey the true nature of their work. Although the distinction between nurse and VAD was often blurred, it was sufficient for the public to acknowledge that women in nursing uniform, regardless of their affiliation, were handling the feminine task of caregiving. Nursing was an accepted patriotic task for middle-class women, though war work that did not fit this category was another matter.

Whereas the idea of the war nurse was generally popular, the nursing and medical communities were far less enthusiastic about the VAD. The MHC gradually accepted the entry of VADs, who proved both cost-efficient and useful in convalescent care, but the CAMC proved far more resistant. For their part, the VADs who were sent to British hospitals were happy to join the war effort. Even those who did not work at the bedside were glad to assist with the recovery of "the boys," if only in an adjunct capacity. Those who looked on from the outside perceived little difference between nurse and VAD, British or colonial, and saw only women doing the necessary work of caring for the sick and wounded.

Chapter Three

EVERY WOMAN IS A NURSE
Framing the Image of the VAD

IN THE 1933 MEMOIR OF her experience as a British VAD, Vera Brittain recalled that she had first viewed the war "not as a superlative tragedy, but an interruption of the most exasperating kind to my personal plans." She concluded that her initial response sprang from the selfish perspective of her privileged upbringing.[1] Brittain's eloquent narrative of love and loss, set against sadness and suffering in the war hospitals, firmly established the romantic mythology of VAD service. Much as Nightingale became the "lady with the lamp" in the Crimea, Brittain's young, delicate, well-bred VAD identity created an enduring image that came to represent the thousands of Imperial VADs.[2] Her memoir established British VAD service as the domain of the fragile daughters of the upper classes, women otherwise lacking in practical experience of the working world. This mythology has obscured the larger and more varied role of countless other British and colonial VADs, including the Canadians and Newfoundlanders.[3]

The depiction of VAD service as an extension of the mission work of elite Victorian-era women has rarely been challenged. Anne Summers's intensive history of British military nursing identifies the pre-war VADs primarily as privileged women like Vera Brittain. Most VADs of this early organizational phase had limited formal education and practical skills, and were largely "outside the labour market altogether."[4] This image is supported by Lyn Macdonald's history of wartime nursing, emphasizing the strength and stamina of the VADs given their upbringing as "gently nurtured girls ... straight out of Edwardian drawing rooms." More recently, Janet Watson characterizes the

British VADs as having been "more comfortable," in a socio-economic sense, than the qualified nurses whom they worked under or alongside.[5] Many VADs did fit this profile, but there is also evidence enough to challenge it. In 1916, the Joint Women's VAD Committee conducted a survey, taking a random sample of two hundred VAD nurses in regard to their previous employment. Predominantly middle to upper class, the subjects were representative VADs, but some sixty-eight had held pre-war employment, most in a skilled-women's occupation such teaching, practical nursing, or clerical work. More significantly, however, a few had performed domestic and industrial labour or other jobs typical of working-class women.[6] Although far from conclusive or scientific, the survey does suggest that VAD nursing was not the exclusive preserve of elite women, a conclusion that is bolstered by the record of the Canadian and Newfoundland VADs.[7]

Overshadowed by the more dominant model of the British volunteer, Canadian and Newfoundland VADs have been regarded as the "wives and daughters of the wealthy," an image that was reinforced in the contemporary print and visual media.[8] As the public face of the VAD, the "Red Cross nurse" as she was frequently identified, was assumed to represent all Imperial female volunteers.[9] Official propaganda, much of which came from Britain, routinely championed the self-sacrifice of the genteel woman who rolled up her sleeves for unaccustomed hard work: "Women in the highest ranks of society are content to scrub and clean; many a highly intellectual woman is working in the kitchen or the pantry or the linen-room of hospitals in France with the dogged determination to overcome the awful fatigue entailed by these physical labours."[10]

As Anne Summers shows, this imagery did apply in the pre-war period, when most British women who enlisted for VAD training were unencumbered by the need to earn a living. However, many of the colonial and British women who undertook VAD service during the war gave up paid employment to do so, a fact that the contemporary propaganda obscured. The Canadian and Newfoundland VADs represent a much more complex and nuanced model of the wartime nursing volunteer than the young and inexperienced British women who came from "the highest ranks of society." Closely aligned to the emerging "new woman" of the early twentieth century, they were far more practical and adventurous than the ethereal women of the propaganda. Although they lacked the professional training of Canada's military nurses, they and the nurses were alike in age, education, social background, and the gendered expectations of their middle-class values.

Women from the Best Homes

Despite their absence from the historical record, the work of the VADs was widely publicized and promoted during the war. The women's pages of newspapers and women's journals and magazines regularly featured articles about volunteers heading overseas or VADs at work in hospitals at home or abroad. With shameless excess, society journalists championed women's volunteer work for the many war relief agencies. The discourse served to reassure a largely middle-class readership that women's public patriotism was a natural extension of their feminine sensibilities, now redirected from community work to the care of sick and wounded soldiers.[11] Popular society journalists were effusive propagandists of women's war work. For example, Mary MacLeod Moore boldly declared that "if the Great War had nothing else to its credit it should be thanked for the development of the maternal instinct."[12] In pre-war Canada, similarly exaggerated prose helped to mitigate discomfort with the increasing numbers of well-bred young women who were seeking employment or had espoused feminist causes such as female suffrage. During the hostilities, the idealized notion of energized motherhood legitimated women's national war service. Romanticized depictions of well-bred young women soothing the fevered brows of wounded soldiers confirmed that they were merely fulfilling their natural maternal instincts.

In reality, the journalists had limited access to the military hospitals and were privy only to the peripheral aspects of medical and nursing work. For the most part, they met solely with select representatives of the Canadian VADs, mainly the social convenors in the Red Cross recreation huts or ambulance drivers in France. The VADs who worked in the Allied hospitals were instructed not to speak to the press, or to anyone outside the hospital, about their work. As a result, society-page columns were filled with positive, but well-embellished accounts of VAD life overseas. A Moore article titled "Canadian Women in the War Zone" characterized the non-nursing VADs who worked in the recreation huts as talented hostesses, welcoming visitors like Moore herself with "their social gifts which in happier times would be used in entertaining in their own homes." This portrayal promoted the femininity and good breeding of the VADs while masking both the seriousness of their commitment and the realities of the wartime hospital.[13]

That only women from the right class were chosen to undertake VAD work was also reinforced by authoritative professionals such as Dr. Maude Abbott. Attempting to validate the VADs' function as nursing assistants, she told an audience of qualified Montreal nurses that they were "drawn chiefly from the highest and best educated class of society."[14] This comment was meant to convey that the VADs would not discredit the honourable reputation of nursing. Abbott also intimated that under different circumstances, the VADs, with their middle-class background and good education, would make ideal candidates for formal nurses' training. Such messages were also designed to reassure Canadians that VADs were both respectable and capable of assisting with the care of soldiers, which included their sons, husbands, and brothers.

During the war, status and privilege were manipulated to either promote or discount the value and legitimacy of VAD work. In England, the St. John Ambulance charged a fee for VAD training to ensure that it attracted the right candidates, a practice that was followed in Canada. Conversely, the British Red Cross (BRCS) offered VAD training at no cost. In the atmosphere of prickly rivalry between the two British organizations, the BRCS accused St. John of elitist recruiting practices. The accusations stemmed in part from St. John's practice of charging a fee for training materials; in addition, some divisions' VAD uniforms were not necessarily supplied free of cost. This was true of St. John, both in Canada and Britain. In response, a St. John (SJAA) spokesman stated that "authorities connected with the Red Cross Society appear to consider it more desirable to have quantity than quality."[15] Clearly, in Britain at least, St. John did not regard elitism as a negative aspect of VAD membership.[16] The Canadian branch of SJAA also saw "quality" as an asset in rendering the VAD more acceptable to the nursing community. Addressing an audience of nurses in 1918, Dr. Charles Copp informed them that VAD applications had been received "in endless numbers from young women from the best homes," countering rumours that VADs might be anything less than respectable.[17]

Whatever "best homes" might imply, the Canadian and Newfoundland VADs were predominantly young, unmarried, and still living at home, with a professional father who was active in local politics or community work. Unlike their British sisters, few could claim aristocratic or titled connections, although wealth and power certainly existed in their resource-rich and rapidly industrializing young nation. Copp may have based his notion of the "best homes" on the sizable representation of merchant bankers, stockbrokers, and industrialists, some with honorary titles, whose daughters had enlisted as VADs. More probably, however, he was thinking of the middle-class business and professional families whose daughters constituted the greater number of VADs in Canada and Newfoundland (see Table 3.1).

Despite Copp's claims, a few VADs were the daughters of artisans or tradesmen, including a carpenter, a stone mason, a tailor, several railway workers, an asylum employee, and a herdsman.[18] Thus, despite Copp's assertions, not

TABLE 3.1 Fathers of Canadian and Newfoundland VADs, by occupation

Occupation	Newfoundland	Maritimes	Quebec	Ontario	West
Financiers and business leaders			5	2	1
Small-business owners	3	4	12	23	5
Politicians	2	1	2	4	1
Professionals, law, medicine, and clergy	3	1	15	19	5
Academics, engineers, civil servants, and managers	2	6	17	30	15
Skilled or unskilled labourers		1		16	3

Sources: City directories; newspapers; *Canadian Who's Who;* and contemporary reports.

all Canadian VADs came from the higher socio-economic strata; applications were accepted, provided the VAD candidate could pay the fee for instruction and materials. We can only speculate that the inflated patriotic sentiment of the war prompted a working-class family to support a daughter's ambition to take up VAD work, much as it may have supported a son's decision to enlist.[19] Most fathers of VADs were business or professional men, including several physicians who served with the Canadian Army Medical Corps (CAMC) during the war. Unsurprisingly, many belonged to local and national service organizations such as the St. John Ambulance and the Red Cross, and their wives were equally active in church, community, and women's groups.[20] Their numbers also included a sitting federal cabinet minister, a prominent banker and shipping magnate, some city mayors, and clergy of varied ranks. Clergymen were rarely wealthy, but their daughters were seen as ideal VAD candidates because of their impeccably respectable background and long experience of community service.[21] Overall, the Newfoundland VADs were equally varied in social class. Sybil and Jill Johnson were the daughters of a Supreme Court judge, and several others were the daughters of prosperous St. John's merchants. By contrast, Fanny Cluett was a schoolteacher from Belleoram, some 265 miles west of St. John's by sea, who came from several generations of shipbuilders and merchant fishers.[22]

    Although the socio-economic base of both the Canadian and Newfoundland VADs was evidently far more varied than both historians and contemporaries have suggested, the Anglo-Protestant influences were clear. In 1914, the St. John Ambulance in Canada regarded the British diaspora as the core of its membership. Many VADs were first- or second-generation British immigrants with a strong sense of loyalty to the mother country. Toronto VAD Jean Sears identified her family as "British-Canadians" and cited patriotism as her reason for volunteering, admitting that she had very little understanding of why Britain was at war. As she put it, "England was in danger, Canadian men were going over, and if Canadian women got a chance to go, they should go and help."[23]

St. John was closely aligned with the Anglican Church in Canada, and its membership and executive included many church officials, several of whom could boast VAD daughters. Despite its link with the Protestant churches, and the often bitter debates surrounding Quebec's support for the war, St. John did attempt to encourage francophone participation in the VAD nursing and ambulance programs by translating some of its training manuals. Regardless of church affiliation, however, a Christian association was generally assumed. The ideology and imagery of Christian doctrine, which were prominent in Allied propaganda, helped to shape the VAD program. Popular discourse often portrayed the war as "a crusade in defence of Christian principles," and the symbolism of resurrection carried over into postwar memorialization.[24] The propaganda that promoted recruitment, encouraged the purchase of victory bonds, and solicited donations to the Red Cross and other patriotic organizations was heavily infused with Christian imagery. Depictions of wounded or dying soldiers in the nurturing care of a nurse stylized as an "angel of mercy" were a powerful incentive in Red Cross fundraising campaigns.[25] A.E. Foringer's illustration *The Greatest Mother in the World*, created for the 1918 American Red Cross campaign, captured this perfectly with its potent evocation of *Michelangelo's Pietà*.[26] Draped in classical white robes, with a red cross emblazoned on her cap, the nurse clasps a miniaturized wounded soldier to her heart. The illustration evokes her healing ability, while representing the qualities of Christian motherhood as more essential than the acquired training and skills of nursing.

Beyond class and culture, the fundamental determinants of VAD membership were age and marital status. The list of regulations issued by the Joint Women's VAD Committee at Devonshire House stated that British women must be between twenty-one and forty-eight to qualify for VAD service at home. The same rule applied to VADs in Canada. Foreign service outside of Britain was limited to twenty-three- to forty-two-year-olds, to ensure both maturity and vitality. The category of "foreign service" carried a different interpretation for Canadian and Newfoundland women. Prior to 1916, the few Canadian VADs who went overseas before they were twenty-three were assigned to military hospitals in England. As of September 1917, the age threshold

The Greatest Mother in the World, by Alonzo Earl Foringer,
1917. *Library and Archives Canada, e010696790*

was reduced to twenty-one, reflecting both the increased demand for nursing
assistance and the dwindling pool of British VAD and qualified nursing
reserves.[27]

The long-established myth, in which legions of post-adolescent girls
stream into the horrors of the war hospitals, as perpetuated by Vera Brittain's
memoir, is not sustained by the Canadian or Newfoundland experience. Hoping
to circumvent the age restriction, Brittain had claimed to be twenty-three
when she started work as a VAD in London's Camberwell Hospital. In fact,
she was twenty, although as she describes, she looked more like "an unsophis-
ticated seventeen." According to Devonshire House records, very few of the
Canadian or Newfoundland VADs were taken on before they reached the
required age.[28] With a few exceptions, most VADs who nursed overseas ranged

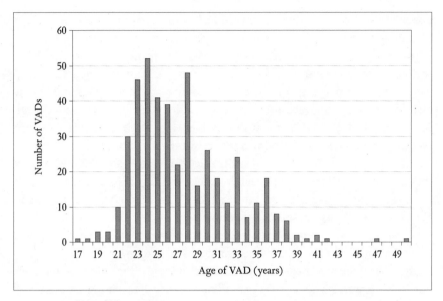

Age distribution of Canadian VADs.

in age from the mid-twenties to the early thirties. Fanny Cluett was thirty-three when she embarked for England, older than many VADs but still within the designated age range, and Lillian Brown was thirty-eight when she left Halifax for a post in a Cambridge military hospital. Although Shirley Gordon was just twenty when she began VAD work in a Toronto military hospital in 1918, she was still living at home under the watchful eyes of family.[29]

The future novelist Agatha Christie began her VAD work early in the war, at one of England's smaller auxiliary VAD hospitals. Initially, the older, middle-aged women had assumed the nursing work at her hospital, leaving the basic cleaning chores to the younger VADs like Christie. When they discovered that their duties involved far more than "a good deal of pillow smoothing and gently murmuring soothing words over our brave men," they quickly relinquished the nursing tasks to the "hardy young girls."[30] The age restrictions seem to have been discretionary, depending upon the place, the time, and the availability of nursing reserves, particularly in the British hospitals. Vera Brittain's application was accepted despite her obvious youth, as was probably the case with many others at either end of the age scale.

Beyond the age restrictions, the conventions governing married women's participation in the workplace applied equally to VAD service, despite its voluntary status. Asked why she had become a VAD, Shirley Gordon was unequivocal: "You married or you worked ... In other words it was a job."[31] The Joint Women's VAD Committee kept a record of VAD marriages until the program was disbanded in 1920. There is no indication that a serving VAD was immediately required to retire upon marriage, but most appear either to have postponed marriage or retired soon afterward. It was the same for the qualified nurses, who were also expected to retire when they married, though some applicants for CAMC nursing seem not to have understood this. Matron-in-Chief Macdonald had to inform several women that married nurses were "not being recommended for appointment."[32] Despite the social upheavals, the crisis of war did not disrupt gender norms with regard to married women's responsibilities for home and family. Most Canadian and Newfoundland VADs were also English speaking and well past adolescence when they began VAD work; very few could claim either elite or aristocratic status. Indeed, a small, but significant number were respectable working-class women. Over-all, the VADs did represent the "best homes" in an ideological sense, but their homes were more often on quiet, suburban avenues than among the mansions on the hill.

Workers, Students, and Volunteers

The Canadian and Newfoundland VADs of the First World War cannot be described as feminist in the political sense. If they were interested in the women's issues of the time, their writing or narratives did not show it. Never-theless, many did exhibit some characteristics of the independent new woman, through their higher education and gainful employment or their active, un-paid role outside the family home.[33] Several acquired a good education and marketable skills, and many were earning a salary in a female occupation be-fore they began VAD work, giving up their jobs for the duration of the war. Like the men in uniform, they temporarily discarded their civilian identities in the classroom, office, bank, or department store to pursue an uncharted course as nursing auxiliaries (see Table 3.2).[34] Unlike the men, however, they were not remunerated, which restricted full-time VAD service to those who did not rely on a weekly salary to support themselves or assist their families.

Most VADs possessed a high school education. Several had aspired to a university degree, and some undergraduates performed VAD work during the long summer break (see Table 3.3). Not all relied on family to support their higher education; a few worked to finance their studies, often as teachers. The vestiges of Edwardian upper-middle-class ideology still prevented some of the more elite VADs from attending university.[35] Their ambitions were frustrated

TABLE 3.2 Occupations for 185 of the 900 identified Canadian and Newfoundland VADs

Occupation	Newfoundland	Maritimes	Quebec	Ontario	West	% of total
Arts	2			2	2	3
Bank		3		5	5	7
Clerical		5	1	22	26	29
Factory or domestic		1		5	1	4
Government				17	20	20
Librarian	2				2	2
Professional	1			3	1	3
Sales and service			1	3	7	6
Teacher	2	1	1	10	26	22
Telephone operator				3	3	3
Unpaid Service		2				1

Sources: City directories and contemporary reports.

by families who saw women's higher education as an impediment to marriage and motherhood. Prior to her VAD training, Alice Lighthall, the daughter of writer and scholar William Doux Lighthall, had enrolled as a "partial student" in the women's program at McGill University. Her mother feared that if Alice obtained a degree, thus risking "the opprobrium of being considered an intellectual," her chances of making a good marriage could be jeopardized.[36] Alice left her studies in September 1916, as one of eleven Montreal VADs who were chosen for the first overseas contingent of sixty. She was also among the ten whom Viola Henderson selected to continue directly to the Royal Army Medical Corps (RAMC) No. 5 General Hospital at Rouen. In 1916, Alice was a well-educated, intelligent, and mature woman of twenty-nine. These qualities, as well as her family connections, probably secured her posting to France.

The daughter of McGill pathologist Sir Andrew Macphail, Dorothy Macphail was younger than Alice Lighthall, but she came from the same Montreal Westmount social environment and encountered similar academic restrictions. At twenty-one, she was enrolled as a "casual" student at McGill, in an effort to "exercise my brain a little" but was too young for overseas service in 1918, when she qualified as a VAD. Despite her father's misgivings, she was determined to assist in a local emergency hospital during the influenza crisis later that year.[37] From a different social background, but no less tenacious in mindset, Elizabeth (Bessie) Hall had earned an undergraduate degree from

TABLE 3.3   VADs identified as university graduates

VAD	Academic institution
Flora Edna Abernethy	Queen's
Laura Katherine Aitken	BA, Toronto, 1913
Mabel Atwill	Methodist College, St. John's
Janet Miller	Bishop Spencer, Law School, St. John's
Betty Maude Beatty	BA, McGill, 1913
Lucy Frances Dorothea Bidwell	BA, Toronto, 1916
Isabelle Marjorie Bleasdell	Toronto
Grace Errol Bolton	McGill, 1913
Mary Gladys Burns	BA, Toronto, 1919
Norine Butler	BA, Toronto, 1909
Lilian Mary Campbell	BA, McGill, 1912
Margaret Mackay Carlyle	BA, Toronto, 1914
Dorothy Leslie Code	BA, Toronto, 1914
Felicia Hannah (Nan) Cook	BA, Toronto, 1914, MA, 1915
Eva Coon	BA, Queen's, 1915
Louise Ashmore Creelman	Macdonald Institute, Guelph, 1916
Ethel G. Dickinson	Business School Chicago, Macdonald College, Guelph [Macdonald Institute, University of Guelph]
Shirley Gordon	Toronto, 1920
Dorothy E. Greensmith	Law, Saskatchewan, 1925
Emily Jane Guest	BA, Toronto, 1899, MA 1901
Bessie Hall	Boston, 1911, BA, Dalhousie, 1916, MA, Toronto, 1921, PhD, Bryn Mawr, 1929
Jean Harstone	BA, Toronto, 1913, MA 1914
Helen Christine Hope	Victoria College, Manchester, UK
Margaret Helen Kilmer	Toronto, 1908
Elizabeth Margaret (Bessie) Ritchie Kilpatrick	BA, Toronto, 1908
Marion St. Clair Leitch	BA, Toronto, 1919
Anna Mary MacKeen	McGill, 1908
Ruth Isobel Moffat	BA, Toronto, 1915
Christobel Robinson	Toronto, 1904
Geraldine Wickstead Sewell	BA, Toronto, 1911
V. Sparling	Toronto, 1917
Margaret Taylor	McGill, 1910
Mary Maud Isobel Thomas	BA, Toronto, 1912, MD 1926
Frances Marion Walwyn	Toronto, 1913
Agnes Kathleen Wilson	BA, Alberta, 1912
Annie Wynne-Roberts	BComm, Battersea Polytechnic, n/d

Dalhousie University, financed with her teacher's earnings. When the war was over, she returned to teaching to fund graduate studies that led eventually to a doctorate in social work. Her letters hint that her family initially had some doubts about her academic ambitions. After being awarded the Governor General's Medal for her bachelor's degree, she wrote to her mother: "Ask papa what he thinks of me now!"[38]

The women who were attracted to VAD work, at home or overseas, were in no sense rebels. Despite their intellectual attainments, they gave little indication of strong feminist or suffragist inclinations. Nor were they a privileged, homogeneous group, wholly unprepared for wartime service. They did share a determination to achieve their goals, an essential characteristic for wartime hospital work, and an independent spirit, often enhanced by a strong academic and employment record. Grace MacPherson's business school training and experience as a stenographer in Vancouver enabled her to support herself in London while she waited for a coveted post as an ambulance driver. As one of the first seven women to graduate from the University of Alberta in 1912, Agnes Wilson opted for a teaching career. She soon realized that it was not for her, but there were few alternatives until the VAD program enabled her to abandon the classroom for volunteer nursing overseas in 1918, as one of forty VADs selected from western Canada.[39]

Unlike most women who performed voluntary war work, VADs who went overseas relinquished their paid employment, suspending careers and a secure wage for a token stipend.[40] Agnes Wilson, Grace MacPherson, and others were willing to take this chance. For many, the expectation of reclaiming their jobs probably influenced the decision to volunteer for service abroad. All veterans who had held government jobs were entitled to return to them, including women, unless or until they married. For example, after a year of working as a VAD in a London hospital, Daisy Johnson returned to Regina in mid-1919 and resumed her work as a secretary with the Saskatchewan government, in the office of a deputy minister.[41] The provincial and federal governments appear to have respected the war service of unmarried female employees, just as readily as for veteran soldiers. Many VADs who were attached to the St. John Ambulance Ottawa Nursing Division were federal employees. Most of the fifteen VADs who were sent abroad resumed their government work within six to twelve months, the length of one or two standard six-month VAD contracts.

Following the armistice, many former VADs were hired as new federal employees, most often in the recently established departments that handled veterans' resettlement. Among the largest, the Department of Soldiers' Civil

Re-establishment (DSCR) also assumed responsibility for the Military Hospitals Commission. The DSCR established branches across the country to administer veterans' medical facilities, rehabilitation, and retraining, as well as employment and financial services.[42] Whether the VADs were hired as "veterans," with priority over other female applicants, is not clear. Perhaps VAD nursing abroad was seen as valuable experience for dealing with the needs of returning veterans and their families. Whatever the reasons, Violet Wilson was both surprised and pleased when her application for veteran status with the federal government succeeded. She was hired as an immigration officer with the Department of Immigration and Colonization. Her job was to interview war brides and other prospective female immigrants from Scotland, work that was not deemed suitable for a man, even if he were a veteran.[43] It also required that Violet work in Scotland, which she was happy to do:

> After the war there were many English and Scotch women coming into Canada to join their husbands, and they were a problem in that these men had neither jobs nor homes for them. So that was why the women officers were appointed, to check on this, to see what the conditions were at home. The women were required to prove that jobs or homes awaited them, and then they were issued a permit.[44]

Despite the Borden administration's apparent support for female veterans, the federal Civil Service Association (CSA) complained that it was negligent in celebrating the wartime service of its employees, whether male or female. Throughout the war, the CSA attempted to compensate, using its bi-monthly journal, the *Civilian,* to applaud and encourage the efforts of all federal employees serving abroad. The journal published an ongoing "Roll of Honour," including reports on the wounded and obituaries for the dead. It also provided biographical profiles and photographs of the twenty qualified nurses and VADs who were on leave from the government and serving overseas.

The government could not be perceived to be stopping its male employees or nurses from undertaking active service, but it preferred that its female staff remain in place, filling the gaps in the bureaucracy that opened as the men departed. Although this represented an improvement in status for the women, who had hitherto been viewed as marginally important, a *Civilian* editorial criticized the government's treatment of them. As it noted, a mere 20 were on active service abroad, out of a pool of some 4,817 potential female candidates. The editorial also alleged that "two or three times as many of our girls would have been in the hospitals overseas had not the departments placed every

Alice Houston, VAD,
c. 1916. *Rare Books and
Special Collections, McGill
University Library*

obstacle in the way of their joining the military service." Given the uneven
selection of VADs for work abroad, this accusation is debatable, but it is interesting to consider the possibilities had the CAMC hospitals been open to
the VADs.[45]

Fifteen federal employees are known to have served overseas as VADs, but
not all at the same time. Of these, nine resumed their original jobs during the
war, one took a new government position, and the remaining five married and
did not return to their jobs. Georgette Dufour was overseas from September
1916 to early 1920, longer than most VADs, completing all her war service in
England. Due to complications from influenza, she missed a chance to transfer
to Salonika. Georgette came home to Ottawa, where she continued to work
for the post office for at least a decade after the war. Alice Houston was another
longer-serving VAD, embarking with Georgette in that first September 1916
group from central Canada. She too returned to the post office after nineteen
months overseas. At forty-three, she had been one of the oldest Canadian
and Newfoundland VADs sent abroad. In 1918, she became the first Canadian
VAD to be "Mentioned-in-Dispatches," a singular military honour, awarded
for her ability to "carry on" when her hospital in St. Omer came under fire and
had to be evacuated. Military honours were a rare distinction for a woman in
this era, particularly one who lacked the official rank of a CAMC nurse, and
Houston was duly praised in the *Civilian*.

The journal had encouraged the nurses and VADs to send letters detailing their experiences overseas, as much as they were allowed. Muriel Wainwright, who left her post in the Marine Department to work as a VAD with the RAMC in Italy, corresponded regularly with the Women's Branch of the Civil Service. Knowing that the *Civilian* would publish her letters, she complained bitterly that she could give very few specifics about her work because "the censor won't allow us to mention such mundane matters."[46] Instead, Muriel provided a travelogue of Italy, along with gratitude for gift boxes filled with scarce luxuries such as tea, chocolate, and sugar. When the war ended, she returned to Ottawa, where she resumed her work in the Marine Department. Unlike other VADs, Edmontonian Adine Geach found that her job with the Department of the Interior had disappeared during her absence. Although an interim place was found for her with the Alberta Legislature, the *Civilian* protested vehemently that she had been neglected. Within the year, when a branch of the DSCR opened in Edmonton, Geach was reinstated as a federal employee; possibly this was due to CSA protests, or perhaps it reflected a new department's need for experienced staff.[47]

Unmarried VAD veterans had a good chance of being re-employed by the government, but a study of the Department of Agriculture suggests that this may have arisen more from expediency than from a recognition of their patriotic service.[48] Laura Mulvaugh's job as a seed analyst was designated specifically for women: as "fine, close work, very trying to the patience," it was considered unsuitable for a man.[49] The sex-stereotyping of job categories also permitted some women to circumvent the marriage bar. For Mulvaugh, it guaranteed reinstatement and that she would keep her job even if she married. In December 1918, the secretary of state announced that all female government employees who were adequately supported by a spouse were to be "released from duty unless the circumstances of her employment made her indispensable."[50] In 1920, Ottawa established a formal marriage bar to facilitate the re-employment of male veterans in government positions, but six VADs who had returned to the public service had already left their jobs for marriage, conforming to the social conventions of their time.[51]

Many VADs also came from offices in the private sector, and assessing how easily they returned to their jobs can be problematic. Some employers, such as the Canadian Bank of Commerce, were publicly supportive of the war work of their female staff. Among the eleven VADs who are known to have been employed at a bank, six were with the Bank of Commerce. During the war, the bank's monthly newsletter published "Letters from the Front," excerpts of correspondence from employees on active service, both male and female. After the war, a two-volume "roll of service" was compiled, with profiles, photographs, and the published letters of all staff who went overseas, including the two nurses and six VAD employees. Annie Wynne-Roberts, who boasted a commerce degree, had been with the bank for six months before she was sent to England as a VAD in September 1916. During her three years overseas, Annie became adept at circumventing the censor's pen. She regularly sent newsy anecdotes about her life and work in the hospitals of England and France, but she also included surprisingly explicit details: "Some of the wounds are so horrible, so bad that one wonders if it would not be more merciful to let the men die." After the war, Wynne-Roberts reclaimed her job, as did four of the five other female veterans who had worked at the bank, perhaps because the banking sector needed trained female workers during a period of rapid growth. Their ready reinstatement, like that of public service employees, may have owed as much to the demand for their skills as the acknowledgment of their war work.[52]

Apart from those employed in clerical work, the largest identifiable single cohort of trained and educated Canadian and Newfoundland VADs were the teachers. Of the approximately two hundred VADs whose pre-war employment is known, at least forty taught in elementary or secondary schools. Their average length of service abroad was twelve months before they returned to the classroom. Many other teachers remained at home but did part-time VAD work in a military hospital. One notable exception was Anne Bredin, who gave up teaching to become a full-time VAD at St. Chad's convalescent hospital in Regina.[53]

Schoolboards also seem to have tolerated the temporary absence of a female teacher on active service, just as for their male staff. The predominance of female teachers at the elementary level helped facilitate this situation: with a continuous supply of new female teachers and the ongoing retirement of women leaving the profession to marry, there was a regular turnover of female staff in positions not readily filled by men. Female teachers had a history of frequent mobility, often using their earnings to finance higher education or a new career path, as demonstrated by Bessie Hall.[54] Just how many Canadian teachers trained as VADs in the hope of overseas service is not known, but their strong representation among those who were selected suggests that St. John officials saw teachers as ideal candidates for the position. As hard-working, educated women, they had a proven ability to learn new skills, organize a complex environment (the classroom), and supervise a population of unpredictable individuals (the students). Experienced in negotiating the tightly structured hierarchies of the school administration, and with a documented employment record, they were perfect for St. John VAD service overseas.

The question remains as to why so many teachers readily exchanged wage and job security for the minimal VAD stipend to work in the unfamiliar and highly specialized world of hospital nursing. Some may originally have been dissuaded from a nursing career by family who considered it unsuitable, or perhaps too strenuous, for respectable women. No doubt, job dissatisfaction as expressed by teacher Agnes Wilson in Edmonton, propaganda campaigns, and the prospect of overseas service were also incentives. Arguably, as volunteer nurses, the teachers exchanged their maternal role as "nurturer" in the classroom for that of "caregiver" on the wards.[55] As a patriotic undertaking for teachers, VAD nursing was to some extent reinforced by wartime discourse that characterized soldiers, whatever their ages, as "our boys." In their personal accounts, VADs commonly equate hospital ward camaraderie with the antics of lively children. Annie Wynne-Roberts's letters contain several cheerful references to her patients: "The boys are dears ... And the pranks they are up to! The place is in an uproar half the time"; or "The boys are so plucky, always ready with a smile and a joke."[56] The move from nurturer to nurse can be seen as an acceptable gendered response for all VADs, not only the teachers.

Volunteer nurses occupied the lowest rank in the strict matriarchy of British hospital nursing. Here too, familiarity with the structured hierarchy of the school administration may have helped teachers adapt to hospital discipline and the pseudo-military role of VAD. They appear to have been well received by the nursing personnel, and they recorded few problems with their supervisors. VADs who had not worked in a hierarchical setting more often expressed difficulty with the discipline.[57] Teaching and nursing also enjoyed a comparative social value as women's occupations. As trained educators with defined careers, teachers posed little threat to the future job security of the nurses. On the other hand, their competence and independence helped compensate for their lack of formal nurses' training. The easy transition from teacher to nurse potentially posed a greater challenge to the professional goals of the nursing leaders.

Among the VADs were some two dozen members of the respectable working class who were employed as factory and service workers. Following more than two years of VAD service in England and France, Ellen Scobie returned to her job as a "press feeder" for the British American Bank Note Company, producing the bank notes for the Canadian Mint. Like Alice Houston, her colleague in the Ottawa Nursing Division, Scobie had been Mentioned-in-Dispatches "for heroism under fire," two of eight Canadian VADs to be so honoured. On her return, she was quickly promoted from the factory floor to "nurse" in charge of the first aid room.[58] The military award had elevated her status, but her promotion can also be seen as neutralizing her somewhat ambivalent situation as a decorated veteran female "soldier." It acknowledged her achievements, leaving a vacancy that could safely be reassigned to a deserving male veteran.

The only women who were officially denied admission to the VAD ranks were the qualified nurses themselves, whose skills were reserved for the real work of civilian or military nursing. Only retired nurses, such as Viola Henderson, were recruited by St. John as instructors and supervisors for the VAD program, and realistically, it is unlikely that a fully qualified nurse would have settled for the lower status and small honorarium of a VAD. However, seven women identified as trained nurses were listed among the active VADs at home and overseas. They included a masseuse at Montreal's Sainte-Anne-de-Bellevue military hospital and a nurse who worked for two years as a VAD in England, but they may not have met the CAMC criteria for fully trained nurses. In an era of unregistered practitioners, the designation of nurse was often loosely defined.[59]

VADs Behind the Wheel

Although the nurse may have been the most recognized of overseas VADs, arguably the most glamorous VAD role was behind the wheel of a Red Cross ambulance. However, they were not the first to challenge the male monopoly of the motor vehicle. In this respect, the First Aid Nursing Yeomanry (FANY) led the way; founded in early 1908 in anticipation of war, this independent women's volunteer organization initiated its ambulance service in 1915.[60] Citing the FANY and the non-traditional work that women performed during the war, Janet Lee argues that the conflict "encouraged social and personal autonomy for women at the very same time that it relied on traditional tropes of gender to stabilize the war effort and contain women's independence."[61] Thus, characterizing ambulance driving as appropriate for women was problematic for publicists and propagandists.

Smart and gender-neutral, the serviceable navy-blue uniforms worn by the Red Cross drivers lacked the femininity of the VAD nursing dress. Driving an ambulance was more masculine than nursing and thus more difficult to champion to a Canadian readership weary of war and its social upheavals. Rarely at a loss for words, Mary MacLeod Moore described her first impression of the drivers: "We got out of the car into the very midst of an exciting hockey match and ducked in and out among the healthy, cheerful girls who were enjoying a little recreation in their off time."[62] If the drivers could not be portrayed as feminine and spiritual, their schoolgirl exuberance on the playing field projected an appropriate image of youthful innocence and high spirits.

Although mastering a man's machine seemed daring and adventurous, driving an ambulance filled with gravely ill soldiers over rutted French roads was far from romantic. The BRCS VAD drivers spent long days and nights slogging over rough and muddy terrain in all weather, often without a windshield to ward off the elements. Initially, there were no mechanics, so they handled their own vehicle maintenance wherever and whenever it was needed. Often this required changing tires, refilling the oil and water, and cleaning and washing the cars inside and out after every run. It was understood that all vehicles must be returned to base, regardless of breakdowns, even if the driver had already completed three round trips of forty miles in a day.

Like the nursing and hospital support workers, the drivers were extremely circumspect about their experiences, and their personal documents reveal little about their work. Concealing the less palatable details preserved the aura of glamour and excitement, and few at home had any true understanding of the drivers' responsibilities. It is only in a postwar novel, written by Evadne Price and published under her pseudonym of Helen Zenna Smith, that a more accurate image emerges. Based on the diaries of an actual driver, possibly a VAD, *Not So Quiet ... Stepdaughters of War* is a gruelling account of ambulance work in France. The book quickly shatters any illusions that the drivers led carefree lives. As the narrator explains,

> Cleaning an ambulance is the foulest and most disgusting job it is possible to imagine ... We do not mind cleaning the engines, doing repairs and keeping the outsides presentable – it is dealing with the insides we hate.
> The stench that comes as we open the doors each morning nearly knocks us down. Pools of vomit from the poor wretches we have carried the night before, corners the sitters have turned into temporary lavatories for all purposes, blood and mud and vermin and the stale stench of stinking trench feet and gangrenous wounds. Poor souls, they cannot help it. No one blames them.[63]

If Mary MacLeod Moore knew of the true experiences of the "healthy, cheerful girls" whom she wrote about, she probably would not have revealed them. As Moore and her publishers understood, families wanted to be reassured that their daughters were safe and secure in every respect. The unconventional nature of the work was worrying enough, and the revelation that it was also dirty and difficult may have prompted many families to demand their return. The BRCS ambulance convoys were responsible for transporting the sick and wounded between the ambulance trains and hospital ships, and the military hospitals. Female drivers and nurses were not permitted near the battlefields, portrayals in film and fiction notwithstanding. As Marjorie Starr, with the Scottish Women's Hospital at Royaumont, north of Paris, noted in her diary in late 1915,

> I went out in one of the ambulances to fetch in wounded (it sounds very warlike, but really it isn't). Nurses don't go to the battlefields these days for their wounded, but our ambulances go to Creil, which is the clearing station, and quite in the war zone, and at the railway station they meet the trains from the firing line.[64]

An independent hospital, Royaumont ran its own ambulance service with female drivers from the outset. The first of the women's BRCS convoys replaced a male ambulance unit in April 1916 at Étretat, on the Normandy coast. The unexpected success of its twelve female drivers led to the regularization of "motor ambulance work" as a division of the BRCS VAD program. Ambulance work steadily evolved into a sizable arm of Red Cross VAD service in Britain and France. Initially in 1916, two BRCS women's motor ambulance units were formed in separate districts in France, each responsible for several convoys.[65] Over time, new BRCS convoys were added along the French coast, and later one in Paris attached to the Canadian Red Cross. The BRCS women's ambulance service steadily expanded to an average of 110 drivers per unit, including some Canadians and Newfoundlanders (see Table 3.4).[66] During this period, a large contingent of VAD drivers also began to replace the men in the general service motor convoys. Although they drove large transport trucks, moving supplies between the Red Cross depots and the hospitals, they did not enjoy the prestige of the female ambulance drivers. As general service VADs, they were paid a salary and were of much less interest to the readers of the women's pages.

Qualification and selection for British Red Cross ambulance work outside of Britain were extremely uncertain, given both distance and the limited openings for drivers. Very few Canadian and Newfoundland women secured a place in the BRCS convoys, and several opted to join other volunteer ambulance divisions, including the FANY and the French Service Automobile

TABLE 3.4 Canadian and Newfoundland VAD ambulance drivers

Name	Age	Home	VAD division	Convoy	Duration
Martha Marguerite Allan	20	Montreal	BRCS	France	c. 1916–17
Phyllis Baker		Montreal	Canadian Imperials	Étaples	1917 or 1918
Norine Butler	28	London, Ontario	Lord Kitchener No. 28	Étaples	Oct. 1917–Oct. 1918
Elsie Chatwin	27	Regina	Regina No. 10	Étaples, Boulogne, Chatham, England	Sep. 1918–Feb. 1919, Feb.–Mar. 1919, Mar.–Dec. 1919
Kathleen Farrar		Toronto	BRCS		
Evelyn Gordon-Brown		Ottawa	Canadian Imperials	France, FANY	1918
Jean Harstone	28	Peterborough, Ontario	Canadian Imperials, BRCS	Étaples, Le Tréport	Mar. 1917–Jun. 1918, Dec. 1918–Mar. 1919
Charlotte Leitch	22	St. Thomas, Ontario	St. Thomas No. 30	Étaples	Mar. 1917–Oct. 1918
Grace MacPherson	21	Vancouver	Canadian Imperials, BRCS	Étaples, London, US. M.Hq.	Apr. 1917– Jul. 1918, Jul.–Aug. 1918, Aug. 1918– Feb. 1919
Annie Alexandrina McArthur		Montreal	Le Service Automobile Sanitaire	France	1917-18
Jessie McLaughlin	24	Ottawa	Canadian Imperials	Étaples, Paris	Mar.–Jul.1917, Dec. 1917– Jun. 1918
Mary Coonan		Newfoundland			
Elsie Crowdy	26	St. John's	BRCS	Étaples, Italy	Nov. 1917– Aug. 1918, Aug.–Oct. 1918

▶

Name	Age	Home	VAD division	Convoy	Duration
Harriet Armine (Annie) Gosling		St. John's	BRCS	Étaples	With MacPherson
Mary Rendell		St. John's		Calais, FANY	

Sources: British Red Cross Society Museum and Archives, Personnel Record Indexes; Mary MacLeod Moore, "Canadian Women in the War Zone," *Saturday Night*, March 16, 1918, 17; Margot I. Duley, *Where Once Our Mothers Stood We Stand: Women's Suffrage in Newfoundland, 1890–1925* (Charlottetown: Gynergy Books, 1993), 116–18; Canadian Newspaper Service, *National Reference Book on Canadian Personalities*, 9th ed. (N.p.: Canadian Newspaper Service, n.d.); Sarah Hampson, "The Tragic Tale of a Star-Crossed Canadian Family," *Toronto Globe and Mail*, November 10, 2015, 1, 11.

Sanitaire. In the early twentieth century, access to a car was largely determined by class, and relatively few women knew how to drive; of necessity, women who joined an ambulance unit already possessed the skill. Some knowledge of auto mechanics was also an asset, but the BRCS drivers needed only the St. John first aid certificate, since trained nurses or VADs cared for the patients in transit. A few drivers did have full VAD qualifications, including Elsie Chatwin, a twenty-seven-year-old Regina stenographer. She worked part-time as a VAD nurse at St. Chad's convalescent hospital in Regina before being selected for the Étaples motor convoy in September 1918. As she recalled,

> Five girls went as VADs and I as an ambulance driver, but I'd always driven! My father bought a big McLaughlin Buick car. He couldn't drive it, nobody in the family could drive. So I was the second youngest, and I got busy and I learned to drive quickly. And I drove for a long time, you know, in Regina, but then I could drive as well as any man! I mean that, I could![67]

By early 1916, twenty-one-year-old Grace MacPherson was also an experienced driver, with her own vehicle, courtesy of a doting mother. Having completed a course at a local business college, she was working as a secretary in Vancouver in September 1915, when news came that her older brother, Alex, had been killed at Gallipoli. With the subsequent loss of one of her boyfriends, the first to die in the war, Grace resolved early in 1916 to "do her bit" at the wheel of a BRCS ambulance.[68] The first hurdle was getting to England, but the only result from Grace's many applications to the War Office and Devonshire House were non-committal replies. Her application was acknowledged, but a personal appearance in London would be necessary before any decision was made. Unable to afford the voyage overseas, Grace relentlessly petitioned the clerk at the Canadian Pacific Steamship offices in Vancouver daily for two months, until the company finally granted her free passage to England. Arriving in early August 1916, completely alone without a friend or relation in the country, she presented herself at Devonshire House, only to be disappointed again.[69] She wrote in her dairy, "I went to the Women's Voluntary Aid at Devonshire House, and found I had by one day missed bear of a job in FRANCE, all expenses paid. B.R.X. uniform & £1 a week which would buy stamps & chewing gum! I was simply broken hearted about it."[70]

Next, she appealed in person to Minister of Militia and Defence Sam Hughes at Argyll House in London, hoping that his endorsement might win a place for her. Instead, as she put it, he declared that "France was no place for me!" but he condescended to recommend her for more suitable work with the Canadian Red Cross in London.[71] Forced to endure an ongoing ritual of applications, interviews, and waiting during the next eight months, Grace took a job as a clerk in the Canadian Pay and Records Office. The longed-for call to join a BRCS convoy in France finally arrived at the end of March 1917.[72]

Grace was one of the very few Canadian and Newfoundland women who were selected as ambulance drivers with either the BRCS or the FANY.[73] For those who qualified, the work offered a unique role. Part of the appeal was its challenge to gender norms. The drivers broke the barriers to women's active service and mastered a symbol of modern masculine power at the same time, even if the weapons of mechanized war remained beyond their reach.[74] In 1916, their distinctive working uniform also confronted popular notions of feminine war work. Its goggles and leather jacket signified action and adventure, unlike the chaste dresses and demure white head scarves of the nurses or VADs, which emphasized the maternal aspects of their role. The dress uniform was no less respectable than that of the nurses but was more military in style, with its navy-blue serge jacket and skirt, white blouse, black necktie, and blue gabardine cap.[75]

Whereas for Sam Hughes and his generation, accepting ambulance work as appropriate for women was often difficult, modern female observers, such as the journalist and novelist F. Tennyson Jesse, extolled the androgynous identity of the drivers, perhaps exacerbating the anxiety of readers who were uncertain about the gender upheavals of the war. Writing for a British women's magazine, she recounted her night with a VAD convoy in France, describing the female drivers in their "goggles and gauntlets and the dashing black leather trench coats and aviator helmets" – although after spending the night on the road, she recognized that these garments were in reality more practical than romantic:

> They pulled a leather cap with ear-pieces down on my head and stuffed me into woolly jackets, and wound my neck up in a comforter, and finished up with a huge leather coat and a pair of fur gloves like bear's paws, so that when all was done I couldn't bend and had to be hoisted quite stiff up to the front of the ambulance.[76]

Despite the heavy and confining garb, Jesse anticipated taking a joyride with these seemingly free-wheeling adventurers, who "went at a good pace" with an empty rig. On the return journey, however, she grasped that the trip was a serious undertaking as the drivers focused on the road, navigating slowly and carefully through the darkness, "for we carried that which must not be jarred one hair's breadth more than could be helped."[77]

The directors of the BRCS motor ambulance division knew that permitting women to take on the unconventional and flamboyant task of ambulance driving was a somewhat risky experiment. As with the VAD nurses, they were careful to portray the drivers as respectable and feminine. Soon after Grace MacPherson joined the convoy, her supervisor chastised her for being "rather too free to Stretcher Bearers in my talk and that it was probably the different way Canadians had but S.Bs. did not understand it. I told her I was sure I had not been so and that all the world over, Canadian or otherwise, propriety seemed to me to be the same."[78]

The accusation was an affront to Grace's character and her national identity, but her offence was merely one of many that surfaced during the acculturation process that she and her mainly upper-class British co-workers and supervisors experienced. She was not allowed to wear her lucky "Little Black Devils" badge, a gift from a beau in the Winnipeg Regiment, and was told that she *"MUST NOT"* continue to wear her favourite red sweater with her uniform.[79] The desire that these young, single women should not appear to challenge social convention was reinforced by a very real concern for their security in a potentially insecure environment. Although propaganda portrayals of the Imperial forces stressed their heroism and chivalry, the actuality could be otherwise. The huge Allied medical and military training installation at Étaples on the Normandy coast had a history of turmoil and discontent, which came to head in September 1917, when the arrest of a soldier by the local military police sparked several days of rioting.

Although the women of the BRCS ambulance division espoused the patriotic commitment of the VAD nurses, they often presented a more boisterous and independent character. Grace MacPherson radiated this exuberance, a trait she shared with another "colonial," Newfoundlander Harriet Armine (Annie) Gosling, and the two became close friends. Gosling was the daughter of a prominent and politically active upper-middle-class St. John's couple whom Terry Bishop-Stirling describes as a "liberal reforming father and a feminist mother."[80] Her background complemented MacPherson's own outgoing western Canadian temperament, and together they faced the conservative upper-class bias of their British sisters in the convoy. MacPherson recalled,

> My first two months there were utterly miserable, and had it not been for some of the Canadians, girls whom I met at the various hospitals, I am sure I could not possibly have remained. We Canadian drivers were only three in number then, and our popularity amongst the other girls was not particularly noticeable, unless by its absence, nor did we stand in high favour with the Commandant and four section leaders.[81]

The character and demeanour of the women who worked in the war zone were critically important to a government in need of support for its wartime policies and the medical care it provided for the wounded. The unique dimensions of ambulance service required that propagandists such as Mary MacLeod Moore, Beatrice Nasmyth, F. Tennyson Jesse, and others stress the respectability and femininity of the drivers.[82] Moore fell back on the "high-spirited schoolgirl" analogy, emphasizing youthful exuberance, though twenty-three was the minimum age. One driver was described as a "rosy young person" whose living quarters were decorated with "pretty hangings and cushions" like those in school dormitories. Beatrice Nasmyth admitted her disappointment in discovering that the drivers did not wear the "romantic frills" rumoured to be part of the uniform, but her faith was restored when they demonstrated "the same delightful ease" of entertaining that any well-bred young woman would exhibit in a Canadian drawing room.[83] Nasmyth also conceded that the drivers knew their jobs and should be commended for their expertise despite its unfeminine character: "Their hands were not lily white but they looked extremely efficient as they plunged in and out of pails of water or polished some shiny surface ... Their faces glowed ruddily in the frosty air. Their whole appearance suggested sturdiness and pluck."[84]

Harriet Armine (Annie) Gosling with a British Red Cross ambulance in France, c. 1918. *Courtesy of the Centre for Newfoundland Studies, Memorial University Libraries*

Grace MacPherson, VAD, ambulance driver, May 1917. *Library and Archives Canada, Department of National Defence, PA-001368*

Regardless of their own admitted misgivings about women's suitability for the work, the commanding officers of the ambulance units were pleased, and surprised, by their eagerness and professionalism. Even during the heavy bombardments along the French coast in the final months of the war, the drivers proved "very efficient, turning out quickly and smoothly in reply to calls and establishing a reputation for punctuality." They frequently functioned with very little sleep and had no time for rest during the day. As the commandant for the convoy at the Normandy coast town of Le Tréport reported,

> During August [1918] the Drivers had only eight nights in bed. This meant that they were out for two hours during some part of each night of the month except on the eight nights mentioned. Twice there were two trains in one night and once two trains and two evacuations between 7 p.m. and 7 a.m. On this occasion the drivers had three hours sleep during the whole night. There was practically no chance of a rest during the day for the cars had to be attended to and the funerals, station and other day calls had to be attended to.[85]

Reports from other convoys offer similar descriptions. In May 1918, drivers stationed at Étaples came under particularly heavy bombardment, as did the entire Allied hospital complex. No ambulances were hit, but three CAMC nurses were killed and a fourth was badly injured.[86] The officer commanding the ambulance convoys reported that "no grumbling or self-pity was ever heard" during these attacks; nor did anyone complain when the influenza epidemic depleted their numbers and increased the workload. Following the armistice, as the work of the convoys slowed, the strain on the "health and spirits" of drivers began to emerge, much to the surprise of the male officers in the camps, "who apparently deduced, from their [the drivers'] easy acceptance of hard physical work and mental strain during the severe fighting, the unwarranted conclusion that they were capable of working at that pitch and in that spirit for ever and at all times."[87]

A brief memoir composed by Jean Harstone, one of the Canadians at Étaples with MacPherson, provides a vivid picture of the often perilous night driving along the French coast during Harstone's two years with convoys at Étaples and Le Tréport:

> The moon had vanished behind the clouds, the wind was wailing in the pine trees and the spirits of the night lashed the rain into torrents and they vanished in long trailing moans. This time I had one case, he uttered no word nor did he

appear to suffer, he was about beyond that. A Sister sat beside him and watched him anxiously, talked to him quietly though he did not hear. I ground slowly into the darkness, eagerly listening for the merest sounds through the wailing of the wind and the slapping of the curtain. At the hospital I looked at the Sister and knew we were too late.[88]

St. John in Canada initiated its VAD program two years before the BRCS women's ambulance convoy was put in place in 1916. When driving an ambulance overseas became an option, many women saw it as far more appealing than volunteer nursing. Devonshire House required a first aid certificate, "six months' thorough experience in driving," and "a good knowledge of running repairs" to qualify as a driver. Candidates also attended the BRCS driver-testing school in London to determine their "capabilities and general suitability."[89] Satisfying this latter requirement was essential and put potential drivers under close scrutiny. As Violet Wilson discovered, being qualified did not guarantee selection. Having earned the Devonshire House stamp of approval, the few Canadian and Newfoundland women who made the cut as ambulance drivers still had to brave the censure and judgment of their British peers. Just how their unconventional role was perceived at home was a greater concern for government authorities, who were ardently promoting their participation to relieve the strain on military personnel and public coffers.

Propaganda and Perception

A photo portrait of the young Princess Mary, daughter of King George V, in her British Red Cross VAD uniform embodies the image of the ideal volunteer nurse. Her pose was echoed in countless official photographs of VADs throughout the empire in an effort to capture the same delicacy, innocence, and regal aura. Just seventeen when the war began, the princess was never expected to take her turn on the wards, but she was an active role model and participant in the work of the Joint Women's VAD Committee at Devonshire House. She supported many other wartime groups that involved young women, including the Women's Army Auxiliary Corps (WAAC), whose membership consisted primarily of young single women from the working classes. In public, however, the princess did not wear the WAAC uniform. As Janet Watson argues, "a Princess could be a VAD, but not a WAAC," since the perceptions of "class differences (or lack thereof) were used either to authorize or deny gender appropriate activity in wartime."[90]

Princess Mary, Countess
of Harewood, by Vandyk.
© *National Portrait
Gallery, London*

   With the development of the hospital nursing schools from the late nineteenth century, the uniform of the graduate nurse had steadily evolved as a
proud symbol of her association with a particular training school.[91] Trading
her civilian uniform for the distinctive blue dress of a CAMC nursing sister
signified her unique role as both a nurse and a commissioned female officer on
active service. Although the honour of commissioned officer was not shared
by other Allied military nursing orders, each had its own uniform. The nurses
of Britain's Queen Alexandra's Imperial Military Nursing Service (QAIMNS)
were easily identified by their red capes. The numerous other British military
nursing services sported various greys, blues, and reds on their capes or dresses.
The Red Cross and St. John Ambulance VAD nursing members also wore
different uniforms. The standard St. John service uniform was the traditional
grey, black, and white of the Order of St. John, with a crisp white apron and
an armband that displayed the insignia of the order. On the wards, the Red
Cross VADs wore a blue dress with a prominent red cross on the apron bib.
Both the military and VAD nurses had a separate uniform to be worn outside
the hospital and for formal occasions. That of the CAMC nurses was navy
blue, with a double-breasted jacket and a skirt, whereas the St. John version
was dark grey, single-breasted, and belted, with a stiff white collar and cuffs.
Both wore jaunty felt hats of the appropriate colour. By mid-1916, the British

Red Cross had introduced new divisions of non-nursing VADs as ambulance drivers and general service workers. They wore practical brown uniforms that were appropriate for their work, and the drivers did not need aprons. The various independent voluntary medical and nursing organizations had their own uniforms.[92]

The result was a profusion of women in uniforms, nursing or otherwise, often indistinguishable to the untrained eye. Like those of the military nurses, VAD uniforms, whether Red Cross or St. John, were designed to be both functional and austere, with wrist-length sleeves and a hemline that was a regulation seven to eight inches above the floor. The early VAD service uniforms had stiff white collars and cuffs that chafed mercilessly with starching, but over time, many VAD divisions adopted a softer, flatter Peter Pan collar and detachable over-sleeves. All were enhanced by some form of headwear, such as caps, bonnets, or the more practical white scarf favoured by the military nurses, which was also the preferred VAD model. The starched white apron remained a classic accessory, and the cross on the bib of the Red Cross VAD became the iconic symbol of the war nurse, regardless of qualifications or affiliation.[93]

A patient could be forgiven for addressing the nurse with the generic title of "Sister," not appreciating the difference between graduate and volunteer nurses, a confusion that merely exacerbated the tensions between nursing co-workers. Beyond the hospital walls, artists, illustrators, and propagandists appropriated the BRCS VAD red cross as a convenient symbol for the war nurse, a casual disregard for the tradition and expertise of the qualified nurses that sometimes prompted resentment and recriminations. Early in the war, an anonymous commentator in the British *Nursing Times* declared, "These ignorant amateurs ... these young women with their express training are assuming full nurse's uniforms with the addition of a large red cross and being called and treated as trained nurses."[94] Generally unaware of the rancour in the nursing communities, most Canadian and Newfoundland VADs took pride in their uniforms. Bessie Hall was ecstatic when presented with hers. Despite starting work in a Halifax hospital rather than an overseas post, she felt a tremendous sense of accomplishment simply for being accepted as a VAD: "I have a thick grey coat (a beauty) and two hats and a lot of nursing clothes, aprons, etc. You should see my Cap! Wow! ... We wear a grey dress, white apron with bib, stiff linen collar, stiff cuffs, white belt and the cap, Mecca of my existence!"[95]

Few VADs reacted with quite the same enthusiasm when issued with their uniform. Though less effusive, Sybil Johnson was particularly pleased with the head scarf, finding "the white kerchiefs rather pretty and most saintly and becoming."[96] Violet Wilson was far more critical, and though she did concede that the scarf was comely, she declared it "the only attractive thing about the outfit." Indeed, she condemned the ensemble as an "unbelievably ugly uniform" and described it with disgust: "The nursing uniform consisted of a dull grey cotton dress with long sleeves and high, stiff white collars and cuffs, black cotton stockings (there were no such thing as silk ones then) dark grey coat and a dark woolen dress ... These clothes were government issue for VADs who were going overseas, and were of the most frightful cut."[97]

Having tossed her regulation hat overboard while sailing for England, the fashion-conscious Wilson set about remedying the rest once she reached London. Locating a "good military tailor," she ordered a uniform that was more to her taste:

> He was aghast! Army regulations! He couldn't do this, you couldn't do that! Not an extra pleat, not even a button moved. No! After a long argument I decided not to order the outfit, and as I went out of the door he rushed after me and whispered that, if I would promise to tell no-one he could make the suit, that he would do it. But he could not, dared not, put his name in the coat. So much for army regulations![98]

Whether or not a VAD approved of its style, the dress uniform did confer some unexpected benefits. Bessie Hall was delighted to find that Halifax shops and restaurants gave her the same discounts that men in uniform received. In her autobiography, Katharine Furse, VAD commandant-in-chief at Devonshire House, pointed out the unexpected "triumphs" of the uniform. The VADs were granted free bus travel in London, enjoying the same public acknowledgment of their patriotic service as the enlisted men, which made them "feel most warrantably superior to mere civilians in plain clothes."[99] The military nurses fully appreciated the symbolic value of their civilian uniforms, which signalled both professional competence and moral character.[100] There was no less respect for CAMC nurses in their military uniforms, which were almost too respectable in the view of veteran Canadian nursing sister Maude Wilkinson. Her assessment of the uniform was not unlike Violet Wilson's:

> There were fittings for our long navy dress uniforms and for our blue cotton service uniforms. The service uniforms were worn with voluminous white aprons, muslin veils, ankle length navy cloth coats and unbecoming navy blue hats. Looking at the group photo taken before we left makes it clear, no anxious

father had to warn his daughter to beware of the men overseas. In those uniforms even the most adventurous male would hesitate before casting an amorous glance in our direction.[101]

Despite the asexual neutrality of the uniforms, military or volunteer, the official propaganda struggled to cast a positive glow on the uncommon public prominence of women in uniform. To encourage support for the war effort through recruitment or monetary contributions, it embraced the maternal and spiritual symbolism of wartime nursing, particularly the Christian iconography of the red cross and the white scarf covering the head. The idealization of nursing was intensified in 1915, when the German command executed British nurse Edith Cavell in Brussels for treason. Cavell was instrumental in conducting some two hundred Allied servicemen safely out of German-occupied Belgium, as well as nursing German soldiers. Allied and Western powers were outraged that a woman, and a nurse, should be brutally executed by firing squad. Her story rapidly evolved into an icon of the nurse as a model of heroic sacrifice in war.[102]

Countless illustrations and photographs promoting the war effort linked women's contributions to Western notions of class, patriotism, and maternal duty. They drew heavily on the Nightingale legacy of women's instinctive nursing abilities in the Victorian model of femininity and on Christian spirituality. Wartime propaganda represented the nurses and VADs as demure and chaste, regardless of their often intimate ministrations to their male patients. The rare official photographs taken in the military hospital wards were designed to show the public that recovering soldiers were receiving superior care. In his study of the British wartime hospital experience, Jeffrey Reznik compares the organizational framework of the hospitals to the systems of scientific management that were employed in the munitions factories. Since fighting men were equally valuable weapons, the public image of the hospitals was framed as "nothing less than havens for heroes who had bravely served King and Country." This vision, Reznik argues, may have applied to the experience of officers but was often at odds with the realities of hospital life for the lower ranks.[103]

The hospital photographs almost invariably display neat rows of seemingly well-disciplined, solemn patients resting in immaculate cots, attended by erect and aseptically proper nurses and VADs. For an uncertain public concerned about the welfare of its sons and the virtue of its daughters, such images reinforced Victorian notions of order, decorum, and propriety between patient and nurse in the modern, scientifically managed military hospital.[104] The reality

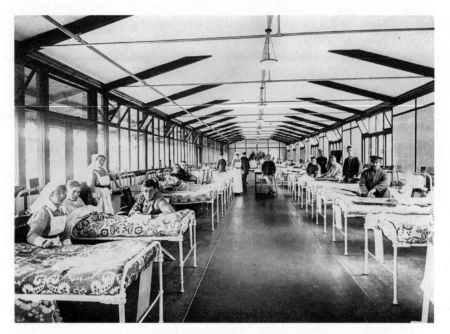

New Brunswick ward, Duchess of Connaught Canadian Red Cross Hospital,
Cliveden, c. 1916. © *Imperial War Museum*, Q 53611

of VAD and nursing work often differed markedly from these representations.
The work of BRCS VAD ambulance driver Grace MacPherson was more ac-
curately presented in photographs taken for the Canadian War Records Office
to record Canadian women's service abroad. The shots show MacPherson as
a healthy, hard-working, and energetic young woman, with a clear, open smile
and a handsome attractiveness. Dressed in a plain service overall, hair tousled
and hands covered in oil, she exudes rugged elegance and efficiency as she sits
at the wheel of her ambulance, changes a tire, cranks the engine, or fills the
radiator. But despite her apparent confidence and capability, MacPherson
confessed to her diary that her day with the photographers was "an awful
ordeal."[105]

Such photographs demonstrated that Canadian women, performing "masculine" work abroad, could remain wholesome and healthily feminine. In
recounting her night with a BRCS motor convoy in France, journalist F.
Tennyson Jesse characterized the drivers not as "pretty" in the conventional
sense but rather as "touched with something finer, some quality of radiance
only increased by their utter unconsciousness of it."[106] The hyperbole aside,

Grace MacPherson, Canadian VAD ambulance driver with
BRCS Étaples motor convoy, May 1917. *Library and Archives
Canada, Department of National Defence, PA-001305*

Jesse was struck by the drivers' lack of concern for the expectations of middle-
class femininity, but she found them no less "feminine" because of it.

Ample evidence shows that vigilance was essential to maintaining the un-
tarnished image of the VADs and military nurses. Numerous less edifying
representations appeared in the popular press and other print materials, prompting military and nursing officials to ensure that they had no basis in reality.[107]
Female war work was essential, and reassuring families at home, and society
overall, that it had no corrupting effect was critical to maintaining their continued support. The less savoury images of nurses and VADs that circulated
in the popular media fed on the deviance ascribed to women in uniform, using
base humour and innuendo to diminish their work as inept and morally suspect.
The publication *Our Girls in Wartime*, purporting to promote women's efforts,
includes an illustration in which "Nesta the VAD," dressed in a well-fitted
uniform, attends to a smirking patient as he intones in tortured doggerel,

> Nesta's nursing down our way
> V.A.D.
> I met Nesta yesterday
> And henceforward I shall pray
> That D.V. [God willing?]
> In her hospital I'll stay,

Nesta the VAD, 1917. *Thomas Fisher Rare Book Library, University of Toronto*

If some bits of bullet stray,
Into me .....
Nesta if you see this lay
R.S.V.P.[108]

Similarly juvenile humour appeared in the ubiquitous wartime postcards, illustrating the ambivalence of society regarding the female workers, particularly nurses and VADs, who had such close contact with sick and wounded men. In one popular series, "nurses" wearing a red cross on their apron bibs strike a range of poses from patriotic to provocative. One sits on a patient's lap while smoking and drinking, another suggestively offers an apple over the caption "Second Aid!" and a third leans over a smiling patient and touches his hand. The accompanying caption reads, "The Patient is not yet out of Danger."[109] With the stress of war disrupting gender and class roles, such depictions found a ready place alongside the equally prolific portrayals of nurses as angels of mercy. Patriotic propaganda also featured heroic soldiers

SECOND AID!

Second Aid!, by Arthur Butcher. *US National Library of Medicine, D05201*

framed by the Union Jack, as well as light-hearted sketches to bolster the morale of fellow comrades in arms and faraway family, in an effort "to trivialize the dangers of combat," as Jeffrey Keshen explains.[110] The salacious postcards of nurses and VADs were also designed to offset the realities of the wartime hospital.

The idea of nursing was complex in this unprecedented era of dependence on nursing care and the work of women. Sharon Ouditt suggests that the prominence of the military nursing uniform was a problematic aspect of nursing identity. At a time when the nurse had become a symbol of strength in relation to her debilitated male patients, it challenged the ideology of female vulnerability and need for protection. Its severe cut and lack of adornment, including jewellery, were an extension of civilian practice and were intended to render it asexual, as Christina Bates demonstrates. This dress code was strictly enforced in the military hospitals and for all VAD workers, to minimize any hint of sexuality.[111] On both sides of the Atlantic, nursing leaders, civilian and military, struggled to redress the balance between the popular commercial representations and the actualities of wartime nursing. Propaganda posters and illustrations presented nurses as chaste, maternal, and caring, whereas the postcards, which omitted and thus discredited their hard work, depicted them as sexual objects for male consumption or as preying on vulnerable wounded soldiers. And though the reality of nursing work was not revealed to the public, at least one VAD was grateful that "the people I knew would be ignorant for ever of certain duties which come into the nursing province," believing this knowledge to be far more embarrassing than any prurient suppositions.[112]

Despite the uncertainty and innuendo, popular opinion of nurses and VADs improved during the course of the war, as is confirmed by Ian Miller's examination of Empire Day parades in the city of Toronto. In 1916, the wives and mothers of soldiers preceded the nurses and Red Cross workers, but by 1918 they had changed places.[113] The maternal representation of VAD nursing competed with the identity of nurses as skilled practitioners, but it supported the temporary role of VADs. Despite their amateur status, prevailing notions of gender and class enabled the VADs to access the military hospitals as nursing assistants; their femininity, respectability, and inherent maternal nature were their keys to entry.

Chapter Four

NO TIME FOR SENTIMENT
Making a Useful Contribution

FEW VADS BELIEVED THAT their training was equivalent to the expertise and experience of the qualified military nurses who supervised their work. Their value as assistants was proven in their ability to fit quickly and quietly into the hospital routine, helping to lighten the burden on the nursing staff. Although they were idealized by the press and in propaganda, most of their work was neither romantic nor glamorous. Whatever previous hospital experience they may have had, the realities of the work shattered any preconceptions, particularly for those who served abroad. Whether it was situated in a converted abbey or a vast assemblage of huts and tents, the war hospital was dedicated to returning soldiers to the field, rehabilitating the disabled, and rendering the last hours of the dying as comfortable as possible. The health and well-being of the nurses and VADs who cared for them was secondary. Fanny Cluett's voluble letters from Rouen offer insights into hospital work, demonstrating that fatigue was not an option for a VAD:

> I go on duty at ten minutes to eight in the evening and come off at 8 am. Night duty is no laughing matter especially if the wards are heavy.
> I have the care of five wards at night; so you can imagine I am kept a bit busy. I sometimes feel very sleepy around the hours of one and two; but sleep must be sacrificed on all accounts, as one must keep a look out for all sorts of things, such as amputation bleedings, deaths, drinks, etc.[1]

Cluett wrote this letter after several months of experience; novice VADs were generally all-purpose assistants. Their tasks varied from scrubbing floors to assisting in the operating theatre, depending on the location and the needs of the nurses and medical staff. The Canadian and Newfoundland VADs were regularly sent overseas with just a few weeks of basic training and little or no hospital experience. Often, they were expected to assist immediately with the treatments and procedures for horrific wounds that tested the stamina even of the seasoned nursing personnel. They were much like untried probationers, experiencing their first encounters with the seriously ill or injured, though their patients were likely to be far more grievously wounded.[2] They met a mixed response from the military nurses. During her early weeks as a VAD, Sybil Johnson complained that the nurses were endeavouring to "impress on us that we needn't think we're anything wonderful, that they are trying to tolerate the blundering inefficients put under them but find it difficult."[3] Similarly, as a newly minted Red Cross ambulance driver, Grace MacPherson quickly learned that she was a far from perfect recruit: "I think my really and truly worst experiences were being 'on the carpet' for various misdeeds – but we never seemed capable of doing the correct thing in the eyes of the 'powers that Be.'"[4] Any sense of heroism on the part of the VAD was quickly dispelled, but VADs and their supervisors generally managed to work together effectively despite their often uneasy relationship.

VADs on the Home Front

After VADs were granted access to military convalescent hospitals early in 1915, most home service VADs were assigned to local facilities, and this work comprised the greater proportion of the Canadian VAD experience. Their written records and much later oral interviews show that it was constant and demanding, although far less stressful and physically exhausting than that in England or the Continental theatres of war. It typically concentrated on healing persistent wounds, rehabilitating patients, and providing post-operative care for men who needed follow-up treatment after returning from overseas. However, this routine was disrupted by two crises that occurred in 1917 and 1918. The first began on December 6, 1917, when the SS *Mont-Blanc* exploded in Halifax Harbour, devastating the city and its environs. A few months later, the second crisis – the influenza pandemic – demanded an unprecedented nursing and medical response. For a time, its impact on the civilian population seemed to overshadow the needs of veterans being invalided home to Canada and Newfoundland for continued hospital care. This excessive demand was

Elizabeth (Bessie) Hall,
c. 1916. *Courtesy Dalhousie
University Archives*

compounded by Halifax's situation as a terminal port for hospital ships carrying the wounded home from overseas.

The crisis was reaching a peak in October 1918, just as Bessie Hall was entering VAD service. A recent graduate of Dalhousie University, she was excited
by her new challenge as a VAD nurse. Her regular letters home to Bridgewater,
Nova Scotia, offer a vivid picture of her transition from student to VAD, with
her first assignment to the civilian Victoria General Hospital in Halifax.[5] Unlike
the first three Nova Scotia VADs, who prevailed against the resistance to civilian women volunteers and penetrated the inner sanctum of the Halifax Pine
Hill Military Convalescent Hospital in 1916, Bessie Hall encountered no objections from the nursing staff when she entered Victoria General in late 1918.[6]
She was brought in to help alleviate both the demands on the nursing reserves
in the aftermath of the explosion and the continuing need of nurses for the
military and naval hospitals. Like much VAD correspondence, her letters
typically focus more on her social life than on her work, beyond noting that
she put in eleven-hour shifts. She was assigned to the pediatric ward, many of
whose patients had been orphaned by the explosion and had no family to provide convalescent care at home.

Hoping that her young charges would not discover her inexperience,
Bessie described "taking temperatures and looking wise," characterizing her
duties as "steady" but not taxing.[7] Her supervisor was a "particularly nice"

ward nurse, and the nursing staff were friendly, lending her dresses for parties, inviting her to socialize with them in local restaurants, and exchanging invitations to visit after the war.[8] By late October, she realized that she had "no chance of going overseas now." Ever positive, she nurtured the hope of being selected for a hospital train convoy taking convalescent veterans home to the west coast over Christmas.[9] Instead, she and a qualified nurse were sent to the Nova Scotia town of Bedford to provide home care for flu victims. Although Hall's late entry into VAD work did not result in the travel and adventure she had hoped for, she persisted with it into early 1919, through the final wave of the epidemic. Assigned to the Camp Hill Military Convalescent Hospital, she was not tasked with regular ward duties; instead, she prepared special meals in the diet kitchen and served meals in the dining room to disabled veterans.[10] Unfortunately, Camp Hill proved less congenial than her previous assignments. The VADs were being used more as maids-of-all-work than as nurses:

> We had a "fight" about Camp Hill the other day, at least we V.A.D.'s got on our dignity about our position there, and walked out until they made it better for us ...
>
> Now about the Camp Hill matter. You see its this way. Mrs. Bligh thought we ought to be willing to do any old sort of work there. Well we didn't see it that way. We had not been doing any nursing at all, so we told them they'd better hire maids and *pay* them! Then we quit. Well now we hear rumours that we are to be requested to come back for the proper work. All right. We'll do it.[11]

After a few more weeks at Camp Hill, Bessie moved to the Infants' Home and finally to the Pine Hill Hospital, where she stayed until she left VAD service in early May. The nursing, and the friendship of fellow VADs, kept her involved in the work well into 1919, but it was winding down and she needed to earn the funds that would finance her next challenge as a graduate student.

Shirley Gordon was still an undergraduate at the University of Toronto when she trained as a VAD in Margaret Patterson's campus program during the winter of 1917–18. With the start of the long summer break, she embarked on regular VAD work, which stretched into the fall of 1918 after the epidemic closed the university. She began in Toronto's Davisville Military Orthopaedic Hospital, assisting with patients who had survived the first stages of critical care overseas and been invalided home for further surgery and rehabilitation. Although she was performing regular VAD duties, much like those of probationers in a hospital nursing school, they were far removed from the front-line triage undertaken by many VADs overseas. Gordon's work included "helping with dressings in the Dressing Room, and in that case you might put on top bandages." She also accompanied the doctor or nurses on the ward rounds to assist with "top" bandages and to "hand things and wring out compresses ... so that they could accomplish more than they could without that help." These tasks were always performed under supervision and only after a lengthy apprenticeship of far more menial chores.[12]

On the home front, new VADs had time to absorb hospital routines and procedures. Gordon started with the drudgery of cleaning the wards, moved on to preparing the patients' special diets, and finally graduated to the basic nursing tasks of applying top bandages to the dressings, which she implied was a step up from helping with regular dressings.[13] The length of a VAD's shift at Davisville denoted her level of experience and expertise. Beginners worked four-hour shifts, gradually moving up to a full eight-hour day. All VAD work was closely monitored by the nurses. Like Bessie Hall, Shirley Gordon enjoyed a congenial relationship with most of them, and though she did encounter a few who seemed "somewhat resentful," possibly worried that the VADs "were taking their jobs," they were the exceptions.[14]

Some fifty years later, Gordon assessed her Toronto VAD work as similar to "what ward aides and nursing assistants do now."[15] Her recollections offer a clear picture of how the VAD nursing assistant fit into the hierarchy of a military convalescent hospital in Toronto. The authority of the VAD program and that of the military hospital administration were well defined, which helped to offset any potential conflicts:

> We were under the direct jurisdiction of a VAD officer. She posted us to our posts and was responsible, for instance, carrying around a tape measure to see that our skirts weren't more than eight inches from the ground! ...
>
> Eight inches was the thing they had to be ... She did do the general administration and the regulating and the placing of the volunteers, but while you worked you were under the direct control of the Nurse in charge of your work. In the kitchens we worked more or less under the Orderly Sergeant.[16]

The dress code was universally enforced. To their consternation, VADs who were assigned to military hospitals in England had their skirt lengths measured with equal rigour by a matron rather than a VAD supervisor. The St. John Ambulance in Canada appears to have maintained a greater degree of control over its nursing members in the local hospitals than the VAD organizations did in the British war hospitals, where the matron reigned supreme.

In Canadian military hospitals, the VADs were expected to maintain a respectful separation from the nursing personnel. This included lunching in the ser-
geants' mess rather than with the commissioned nurses in the officers' mess.
Regardless, Shirley Gordon found the atmosphere to be more relaxed in practice
and largely dependent on the attitude of individual nurses. While she was assigned to assisting with the dressings, she lunched in the officers' mess with
her supervising nurse, "just because she was a nice person."[17] In home-front
hospitals, the routines and working relationships between VADs and military
nurses were well established before the second and most virulent wave of the
influenza epidemic arrived in the autumn of 1918. With this infection, the
hospitals were battling an invisible enemy as deadly as any tangible foe.[18] This
crisis, and the earlier Halifax explosion, dramatically reinforced the value of
the VAD scheme on the home front and bolstered growing arguments that
favoured a more permanent role for Canada's VADs as the war was drawing
to a close.

On the morning of December 6, 1917, a Belgian relief vessel and a French
cargo steamer loaded with munitions collided in the "Narrows" of Halifax
Harbour, resulting in a cataclysmic blast that levelled the north end of the
city and seriously damaged most of the nearby area. More than 1,600 people
were killed and countless others badly injured.[19] In the immediate aftermath,
thousands of the injured sought medical aid. The home of Dr. George A. and
Clara MacIntosh was badly damaged but still standing, and Clara, a trained
nurse and member of the Victorian Order of Nurses, set up a makeshift clinic
in her husband's absence. As lady superintendent of the Halifax VAD Nursing
Division, she quickly issued a call for all VADs to report for duty at the local
hospitals, only to discover later that "it was unnecessary, they were all there."[20]
Within twenty-four hours, she began supervising the VADs and co-ordinating
untrained volunteer men and women to assemble an ad hoc emergency relief
body. This was later formalized as the Medical Relief Committee, just as personnel and supplies began to pour in from American and Canadian sources.[21]

All but 18 of the 129 Halifax VADs had reported for duty, despite illness
and injury to themselves or family members, as well as damaged or destroyed
homes. As Clara MacIntosh later reported, all were ready to provide first aid
wherever it was needed, "in the streets, in the parks, on the Common and nearest hospitals." The most frequent injuries were caused by flying glass, when
windows imploded from the concussion. In MacIntosh's estimation, the value
of the VAD training program was fully realized in this crisis, as the women set
about "arresting haemorrhage, removing glass, plaster and splinters from
wounds, applying dressings and splints." Many injuries closely resembled battle

wounds, and she believed that the VAD training in asepsis helped prevent serious complications.[22] The scenes of carnage in the hospitals rivalled any in the war zone, and like their sisters overseas, many Halifax VADs found themselves substituting for qualified nurses in improvised operating theatres.[23]

During the first twenty-four hours, more than seventy VADs reported for duty at seven hospitals. Their numbers were augmented by ten VADs from Saint John, New Brunswick, and six others who were visiting from outside Halifax. Some thirty VADs continued to work in the community for the next several days, having improvised first aid kits to deal with minor injuries and burns. As word of their presence spread through a neighbourhood, they often set up impromptu clinics, and Clara MacIntosh arranged medical care for the more serious cases. By the third day, hospital matrons were calling for more VADs to relieve the exhausted nurses (a year later, VADs such as Bessie Hall could still be found on duty in some of the civilian chronic care wards). In the weeks following the disaster, several VADs also acted as public health nurses, assisting doctors on home visits and investigating home-bound cases. Others served as community workers, reuniting family members, locating missing children, helping to distribute food and clothing, and doing whatever else was needed.

The experiences of numerous VADs were later recorded, including that of Daisy Shrum, who was working in the offices of Maritime Telephone and Telegraph when the blast struck. Everyone onsite escaped injury, and once she knew that her family was safe, Daisy reported for duty at the Camp Hill Hospital. There, she assisted the nurses for the next five days, all the while feeling frustrated that it was "almost impossible to help everyone." In the heat of the moment, she had forgotten to notify her employer, and she learned later that he was anxiously trying to discover if she was injured or dead.[24] In the aftermath, Clara MacIntosh was full of praise for the many other VADs like Daisy, who had only minimal hospital experience prior to the disaster:

> I can never express the admiration I have for our girls, who unaccustomed to the horrors of this kind have shown the greatest endurance ... I know of cases where they have stayed on duty twenty hours at a stretch and rendered service which at any other time would have been considered impossible. One member assisted in any way possible at the Morgue where the scenes baffled description.[25]

By the end of December, an estimated one hundred VADs had contributed over a thousand days of service to the sixteen hospitals in the Halifax region, and another thirty had worked in the community for more than a week. Two weeks later, when an outside medical unit finally arrived to take over the district work, Clara MacIntosh somewhat smugly noted that they found "little or nothing to do." Not without some pride, the district superintendent for the St. John Ambulance Brigade in Nova Scotia, Reginald V. Harris, who was also Clara's brother, concluded that the VADs had "saved hundreds of lives" through their prompt, efficient, and effective work, and their "perfect organization."[26] Suddenly called upon to fill in for trained nurses during the crisis, the Halifax VADs had fulfilled their mandate as a domestic reserve of emergency auxiliary nursing assistants. One legacy of the episode was a new peacetime public health role for the Halifax Red Cross as well as a demand for more trained public health nurses, a role that had necessarily fallen to many VADs following the disaster.[27]

The Canadian National Association of Trained Nurses (CNATN) took note of these developments, calling for a National Nursing Service Corps modelled on the American Red Cross unit that came to Halifax immediately after the explosion. However, it emphasized that the division should consist of nurses, not VADs, who would be "ready at a moment's call for mobilization."[28] Ironically, the call for a standing nursing reserve echoed the rationale for in-itiating the VAD program at the start of the war. The national and provincial directors of the St. John Ambulance knew that the Halifax relief work had validated the VAD scheme. In his report to St. John, Superintendent Harris rather proudly acknowledged this: "It must be a great satisfaction to you, as well as to me, to realize that after several years of preparatory work the mem-bers of the Association and Brigade responded so magnificently to the call."[29] Local nurses also acknowledged their reliance on VAD assistance during the emergency. In a *Canadian Nurse* article, a nurse from the Halifax Naval Hospital described being alone and desperate for help, with fifty injured patients, includ-ing physicians and other members of the nursing staff. She recounted how she had "snagged a nurse and a VAD" from the Camp Hill Hospital. She praised the VAD, who "was a brick, and absolutely dependable," helping to cope with amputations, fractures, and even brain surgery in conditions that rivalled hospitals at the front.[30]

In the autumn of 1918, less than a year after the Halifax disaster, Canada's nursing reserves were again severely tested as the second wave of the influenza epidemic spread across the country. In Halifax, the VADs were again called on to work in hospitals and private homes, and when a third wave of the epidemic struck in early 1919, some, like Bessie Hall, stayed on well into the new year. One group volunteered in a Massachusetts hospital for three weeks, returning the favour of help given after the explosion. In New Brunswick, qualified nurses were scarce outside the urban areas, and VADs were enlisted to accompany them to isolated districts. In cities such as Saint John, they followed the example of their Halifax sisters after the explosion, assisting in special emergency hospitals, helping in the diet kitchens, and preparing and delivering meals to stricken families.[31]

With its larger population, Ontario initiated an Emergency Volunteer Health Auxiliary to help co-ordinate essential volunteer nursing relief. The program enlisted VADs as well as many other women who had taken the St. John home nursing course, assisting about a thousand families during the crisis. In Toronto, Margaret Patterson adapted her regular VAD classes to focus on diagnosing and treating influenza. She also established an emergency VAD network, the Sisters of Service, or SOS, to respond to the needs of Torontonians. Similar organizations were created in cities and towns across Canada, including Prince George, British Columbia, where VADs were sent to Indigenous communities devastated by the virus.[32]

Throughout Canada, VADs whose experience consisted largely of classroom instruction suddenly became full-time nurses, often without the oversight of a qualified nurse when demand overwhelmed resources. To assume her role as a VAD, Dorothy Macphail, the daughter of McGill pathologist Andrew Macphail, had to battle through her family's presumption that her health was as delicate as her late mother's. Her letters to her father demonstrate her determination to aid the war effort. When the epidemic took hold, she was twenty-one and had just completed VAD training in Montreal. Her correspondence with her father, who was overseas with the Canadian Army Medical Corps (CAMC), maps the progress of the virus. In her words, it was more "a plague than an epidemic," averaging a hundred deaths per day in Montreal by mid-October and not discriminating by class or age. In Montreal alone, it killed more than three thousand people during October 1918, some two hundred of them on the worst day, October 21, when the epidemic peaked. In the midst of the crisis, Dorothy dutifully requested her father's permission before undertaking VAD service in an emergency hospital. She bolstered her request by arguing that the city was "crying out for helpers and being young and strong I felt I ought to."

Dorothy revelled in the new challenge of assisting the nurses at the Grenadier Guards Emergency Hospital in the local armoury, oblivious to the risk of infection. She was extremely happy with her VAD role, and there was no friction or resentment from the qualified nurses. She wrote with much enthusiasm to her father, "I got to love my work more and more, I have never been so contented with my work before and all the nursing sisters are so good to me." As the disease quickly depleted the nursing reserves, their grateful acceptance of willing and efficient volunteer help is understandable. Like many front-line healthcare workers, Dorothy did not escape the virus but fortunately recovered quickly from a mild infection and was soon back at work, giving the lie to her family's protests of delicate health. Across the country, however, the strain on medical and nursing personnel was acute.[33]

Of the 125 certified VADs who were available to help in Ottawa, many were government employees, since only a few public service VADs had been released for work abroad. During the epidemic, they often did double duty, working at the office by day and helping in private homes or hospitals as VADs overnight. Some were seconded to municipal offices, presumably substituting for ailing staff in the organization of relief efforts.[34] The double day was common for unmarried women during the emergency. Lacking children to care for, they were expected to look after their relatives or others outside the home. Professional nursing may have been a specialized female occupation, but voluntary nursing was the unquestioned purview of all women in times of need or crisis.

Community leaders, including Ottawa mayor Harold Fisher, affirmed this fact, reminding women of their duty to volunteer. With qualified nurses becoming scarce in his city, Fisher declared that "knitting socks for the soldiers is very useful work but we are now asking the women of Ottawa to get into the trenches themselves." Far from reacting with outrage, the women of Ottawa, including the trained VADs, were already responding to this need, and the mayor was simply voicing the assumptions of society. Elsewhere, Beth Dearden travelled from Toronto to North Dakota to help with the office work at her uncle's grain elevator business, taking her VAD uniform in case it was needed. When the epidemic struck, she continued to work the day shift for her uncle but donned her uniform for night duty with a stricken family, stoking the wood stove and supplying her charges with tea and soup. The situation was not helped by the bitterly cold temperatures – Beth's uniform froze solid in the washtub on the porch – but her patients all survived, including infant twins.[35]

The rapid immersion of neophyte VADs into full-time nursing was common during the crisis. As public buildings were hastily transformed into emergency hospitals, VADs were often the only recourse as large numbers of qualified nurses contracted the virus, and no qualified personnel could be found. At times, completely inexperienced VADs such as Gertrude Murphy found themselves temporarily alone and in charge of numerous patients. A teacher, Murphy had reported for VAD work at the Calgary General Hospital when the epidemic closed her school. Instead, she was sent south by train to work in a makeshift emergency hospital in Drumheller, which was reportedly suffering the "worst type of Flu in Alberta." When her fellow passengers learned that she was a VAD en route to a quarantined community, they treated her with a combination of fear and curiosity, cautiously avoiding physical contact and even declining to pass by her seat to get to the washroom, as if she were a potential plague carrier.

Drumheller was a small mining town in 1918, and all of Murphy's initial twenty patients were young miners, most of whom were eastern or southern European immigrants. The only English speaker among them was a Welsh boy. Twenty-three men had already died in the emergency hospital set up in the local school house, but they had yet to be buried because the locals were either "too sick ... or too scared" to do it. The mine owner and his assistant were the only volunteers until Murphy arrived, and they immediately turned to the task of transporting convalescents back to town and the dead to the morgue. Although a trained nurse and a second VAD had been promised, they had not yet appeared, and Murphy was horrified to find herself alone with nearly two dozen critically ill men to care for. The mine owner dismissed her pleas that she was "only a VAD" and did not know what to do, stating that he himself had managed to cope without any training, implying that she at least had the natural benefit of her sex.

With no alternative, Murphy resolutely began to "pitch in," making beds, emptying bedpans, bathing hands and faces, and feeding anyone who could manage the soup provided by a local restaurant.[36] In any event, there was little more that could be done. Although physicians were in high demand during the crisis, medical historians generally concur that competent, or even available, amateur nursing was more valuable. As John Barry writes, "nursing could ease the strains on a patient, keep a patient hydrated, resting, calm, provide the best nutrition ... Nursing could save lives."[37] Two VADs and finally a qualified nurse reached Drumheller a few days later. As elsewhere, the nurse did not object to Murphy's lack of training and even praised her efforts as more than adequate to the task. She delegated Murphy to "special" the sixteen most critical cases, as the patient count rose steadily to more than eighty.[38] In this emergency, the need for competent assistance outweighed any tensions about professionalism that might have surfaced under less exceptional circumstances.

Arguably, the demand for nurses had never been greater than in the autumn of 1918, when the pandemic peaked in Canada, and neither local public health authorities nor military hospitals could afford to refuse willing and competent nursing assistance, whatever its source. Unfortunately, whereas Mayor Fisher of Ottawa was urging women to help save people from "dying in our midst," some public figures attempted to exploit the opportunity to politicize the nursing situation. Prior to the epidemic, an ongoing jurisdictional dispute had been simmering between the CAMC and the civilian Military Hospitals Commission (MHC) as to which of the two could better care for convalescent veterans invalided home to Canada. By February 1918, the CAMC had prevailed, separating the medical and vocational aspects of veteran rehabilitation. Most MHC hospitals now came under the authority of the military and the CAMC, although organizational skirmishes persisted.

The summer of 1918 saw the war turn in favour of the Allies, but at great human cost, resulting in the heaviest Canadian casualties of the conflict. The ripple effect put an enormous strain on the military hospitals at home and abroad. Just as the epidemic was entering its deadly fall peak, thousands of convalescing wounded began arriving home for further treatment. Many died of influenza in the veterans' hospitals at a time of heightened stress and war weariness. Public accusations of "military incompetence and neglect" emerged because few understood that the virus tended to prey on healthy young adults. In a Toronto military hospital that admitted 2,100 influenza cases, some 270 developed pneumonia, 90 of whom died. As Morton and Wright suggest, these statistics were not unreasonable in a pre-antibiotic era. Unfortunately, Toronto mayor Tommy Church, a "populist civic leader," used these figures to incite outrage. He maximized the publicity, bringing the matter to court, where a grand jury denounced the military for negligence and "bad nursing." The latter accusation referred to the VAD assistants in the convalescent hospitals, implying substandard nursing on the part of the CAMC. The court's conclusions fuelled the arguments of the CNATN, which was protesting against an emerging government proposal for continuing postwar VAD assistance in military hospitals to provide a cost-effective solution to the long-term care of convalescent veterans.[39]

Despite the accusations of inadequate nursing, first-hand accounts of VAD work during the influenza crisis attest to the value of their contribution. A young Amelia Earhart was one of many VADs who worked in the military convalescent hospitals and one of the few entrusted with night duty on a pneumonia ward, where she helped the sisters to "ladle out medicine from buckets in overcrowded wards." The voluntary services of Earhart and countless other VADs were welcomed by the beleaguered nursing staff and readily received in hospitals.[40] Like Dorothy Macphail, Earhart was a healthy young woman, and she too gave little thought to the risk she was taking. At the time, few statistics demonstrated the unusually high proportion of influenza deaths among

young adults between the ages of twenty and forty, although the general observations of medical and public health authorities may have raised some
alarm.[41] Inevitably, several VADs did succumb to the disease at home, as well
as overseas, where it was equally devastating. There are only seven confirmed
Canadian and Newfoundland VAD deaths, all seemingly the result of complications with influenza, but given their exposure and the statistics, more
seem likely. .

In this era of unprecedented societal dislocation, with the destruction of
war compounded by domestic disaster and disease, the sacrifice of civilian
women in the care of others seems not to have been regarded as unreasonable. The declaration that Ottawa women needed to get into the trenches
was received without rancour. It did not conflict with the popular belief that
women were natural caregivers and that young unmarried women should
volunteer as nurses when needed, without concern for their own well-being.
Gender dictated their duty in this time of crisis, and VADs saw their work as
a form of selfless "soldiering" – a necessary patriotic service to the state.

The Stress and Strain of VAD Service Abroad

Referring to the more difficult aspects of her VAD work overseas, Jean Sears
described having performed some unimaginable tasks that "you never thought
you were going to do ... terrible things to look at, see and do. And you had to
just grit your teeth and do it!" Sears started her VAD work in a Toronto hospital
before being sent to England. Despite the rigours of the work, she believed
that her experience in a British military hospital brought her much closer to
the realities of the war, and in retrospect she felt "thankful for the privilege"
of being part of "a great thing."[42] Nursing overseas allowed VADs to realize
their goal of patriotic service, a privilege that, for most, justified the hardships
and stress. VAD work commonly varied from the propaganda depictions in
magazines and newspapers, and the demands of wartime nursing were often
well beyond the scope of even the experienced military nurses. For untried
volunteers with scant medical knowledge, the sights, sounds, and particularly
the smells of hospital work fully realized the cliché of being thrown into "the
deep end." For example, VAD Doreen Gery recounted her experience for a
film crew, her soft, gentle voice difficult to reconcile with her horrific description of her first case in France. He was a soldier who had been "bayoneted
right down, in the abdomen ... and he was dying." His breathing was impeded
by his own intestines, which were rising out of his abdominal cavity. Gery was
assigned the task of pushing them down, holding two gauze pads "to use quietly

and get them back down into position again." This was far more harrowing than anything she had imagined. Completely unprepared, she protested, "I can't do it. I'd rather die than do it!" To which a weary and overburdened sister snapped, "Well, die then! You're of absolutely no use to me!" These harsh words were like a splash of cold water, steeling Gery's resolve to prove her worth. She was rewarded a few weeks later with an approving pat on the back from the same sister, silently acknowledging her useful assistance.[43]

To be useful was the goal of most VADs as they coped with the stress of the unfamiliar hospital environment, the endless physical and emotional demands, and the numbing fatigue of long shifts. The length of their shifts varied, depending on the individual hospital organization, its location in England or on the Continent, and the previous experience of the VADs themselves. Fanny Cluett began her VAD work in late 1916 at the 4th Northern General Hospital in Lincoln. Her detailed letters home describe average work days that stretched over eleven hours, beginning at seven in the morning but including a three-hour off-duty period; and "sometimes we have extra time."[44] Few VADs provide the same amount of detail. Fanny's initial schedule in England was far more routine, and much less stressful, than that of Doreen Gery and most other VADs who were posted to France. Fanny also possessed a calm and pragmatic temperament, more measured than that of many VADs, who were conscious of their lack of preparation. Like Doreen Gery, they often dreaded the scorn or impatience of harried nursing supervisors, who were more accustomed to subservient probationers than to raw volunteers who lacked the discipline of hospital training.[45] For some VADs, the first six months abroad were a trial by fire, and not all contracts were renewed. Few VADs remained overseas for more than a year. It can only be speculated whether this was due more to the nature of the work or to the need for funds or other personal reasons.

After completing her probation in England, a VAD could apply for deployment to France. Several Montreal VADs who travelled with the first Canadian contingent in 1916 managed to bypass this requirement, perhaps on the recommendation of Viola Henderson, whose standing as a retired nurse may have given her endorsement some weight.[46] Although she may have vetted them because she knew of their work in the Khaki Convalescent Homes, their posting to France may also point to the elite status of many Montreal VADs, with their prominent connections. Given the membership of the St. John Ambulance during this era, particularly in the Ottawa-Toronto-Montreal triangle, the VAD program was able to enlist the daughters of some influential families. There is no proof that they received preferential treatment, but the uneven selection process for overseas service did leave room for the possibility. Many were

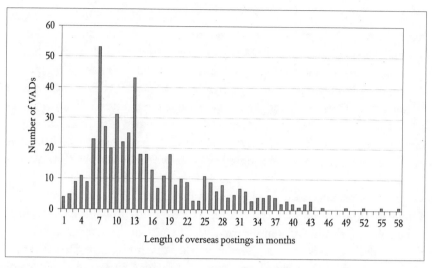

VAD overseas postings by month.

Note: The average total posting was 15.4 months.

Sources: British Red Cross Society Museum and Archives, Personnel Record Indexes: Military Hospital Files/Record Cards. Based on known length of overseas posting for 494 Canadian VADs.

connected through church and community women's groups and service organizations, such as the May Court Club in Ottawa, whose membership included women from prominent political and professional families, as did Montreal's elite Junior League. As Elise Chenier reveals, at least seven VADs who were sent to France belonged to the league, and some forty-two were involved in VAD nursing by 1918.[47] Middle- and upper-middle-class women were well represented among the Canadian VADs, and class was certainly a key aspect of membership, but it is difficult to estimate just how much privilege and family connection influenced selection for overseas postings.

Although St. John praised the training of its VADs, the question of how well prepared they were for work abroad remained problematic. While discussing the quality of the VAD program at the CNATN convention in 1918, Dr. Charles Copp carefully sidestepped the issue. He noted truthfully that it was neither "possible, nor ... feasible or desirable" for VADs to train alongside nursing probationers in Canadian civilian hospitals before they were sent overseas. His comment implied that there was neither enough time nor enough space to accommodate all the VADs who went abroad and cautiously evaded the fact that the civilian hospitals had wanted no part of amateur volunteers.[48]

Shortly after arriving at the 1st Southern General Hospital in Birmingham, Annie Wynne-Roberts wrote that she already felt as if she'd been there for months. One of five Canadian VADs deployed to the hospital in 1916, she had enjoyed a brief apprenticeship in Toronto's Davisville Military Orthopaedic Hospital while still employed by the Bank of Commerce. In Birmingham, she began her VAD work in a convalescent ward and confessed to feeling somewhat deflated because she was not immediately assigned to the surgical wards, unlike other VADs who had "started in" on dressings. Despite the delay, the rapid turnover of personnel soon advanced Wynne-Roberts to the status of "senior VAD" on her ward, where she assisted with dressings, and within the year she was transferred to a hospital in France.[49] During her Atlantic voyage, and again in the London hospital where she took her probationer's training, Sybil Johnson had heard rumours that VAD work was little more than glorified domestic service. She was relieved to learn that both she and her sister Jill would be posted to the same Liverpool hospital, where they would have "some real nursing to do, and hardly any cleaning up. No dishes or scrubbing, etc., glory be!" This news was especially welcome, as, like many Canadian VADs, the Johnson sisters came from a class that was "little used to" cleaning up.[50]

Possessed of a more adventurous spirit than Sybil, Violet Wilson hoped to become a VAD ambulance driver rather than a nurse, and she took a six-week motor mechanics course in Toronto to further her goal. She was understandingly dismayed when she was posted to Devonshire House and assigned to "cleaning and scraping the mud and dirt from military cars that had been returned from France." The longed-for ambulance duty never materialized, but within a few weeks she was mercifully reassigned to nursing amputees in London's Gifford House convalescent hospital.[51] Latecomers to overseas service, Canadian and Newfoundland VADs were a small cohort compared to their British counterparts, whose numbers exceeded twenty thousand. With so many suffering men, there was little time or patience for individual preferences.

Marjorie Starr had travelled from Montreal in September 1915 to become the only Canadian VAD in the Scottish Women's Hospital, which was situated in the Abbaye de Royaumont near Amiens. How she attained this position is unclear, as she was not part of an official St. John contingent, and the hospital operated independently of the Joint Women's VAD Committee. Her prior hospital experience is unknown, but in this all-female institution established in an ancient abbey, she was designated as an "orderly," its term for a VAD. Whatever the mechanism for her engagement, she was put to work as soon as she arrived: "I had 15 beds to make myself, and a perfect stream of bedpans, three horrid dressings to prepare and then bandage up, and clear away, and when the other sister came back, if she didn't set me to scrub lockers, and I jolly well had to smile and do it."[52]

English hospitals were generally less stressful assignments than those in France, which often admitted men directly from the casualty clearing stations. At Royaumont, they were frequently transported straight from the battle front. Physically, however, working in England could be just as demanding. Fanny Cluett's letters record the standard routine of her first month in the British 4th Northern General Hospital in Lincoln. She rose before 6:00 a.m., took a half-hour for breakfast at the hostel, and then walked a mile to the hospital to be on duty by 7:05 a.m. The work day began with scrubbing tables, sorting laundry, washing towels, sweeping, dusting, preparing for washing the patients by hand, and ensuring that the wards were spotless before the mid-morning milk break. Preparations for dressings followed, erecting screens around patients, readying the fomentations and sterilizing all the instruments, and then clearing everything away once the dressings were done to be ready for midday dinners and feeding the patients. Following her own dinner break, Fanny was back to washing patients, making beds, and serving tea, which she prepared herself, having declared the cookhouse version "unpalatable." There were yet more dressings and a "general clean up" before Cluett went off duty at 8:00 p.m. and walked the mile back to the hostel. As she put it in her own singular style, "we don't stop hardly to draw a breath," and the work was doubly demanding on the days when she lacked an assistant.[53]

Sybil Johnson followed a similar routine in the 1st Western General Hospital, Liverpool, although her morning shift began at the more congenial hour of 8:15 a.m. In most other respects, the cleaning, sweeping, dusting, and keeping patients washed and in clean linens was little different from Lincoln or the other hospitals in England. Sybil was also responsible for taking "temperatures and pulses," and helping to lift patients into the large outdoor Bath chairs for walks in the hospital gardens. This was hard work, a world away from her comfortable life in St. John's, but she seems to have revelled in it, "especially helping people round and making them clean and comfortable." Like Doreen Gery, she was pleased to be performing tasks that were both manageable and useful.[54] Whereas the recruitment posters elevated VAD service to a spiritual calling, new VADs were grateful simply to survive the fatigue and unfamiliar tasks of the early weeks. Unlike in the home-front hospitals, they had no time to adjust and were expected to adapt, follow directions to the letter, take responsibility for their work, and complete all tasks without question or complaint.

In the war zones of Belgium and France, the hospital workload was often unpredictable, and much was contingent on the pace of battle. A major offensive signalled an onslaught of casualties to the nearest hospitals, which then rippled out to other medical facilities offering differing levels of care, all the way back to "Blighty."[55] The hospitals nearest the battlefront dealt with the worst of the carnage and the greater proportion of deaths. The VADs stationed in more distant hospitals, often on the French coast and back in Britain, cared for the survivors, and though deaths certainly did occur, most of their patients were struggling to recover from major surgery and often to adjust to disfigurement or permanent disability. Conversely, some feared that their injuries would heal too quickly, forcing their return to the terrors of the trenches and potential death. Among the VADs, adjusting to so much pain and suffering varied from woman to woman. Fanny Cluett relied on humour as a buffer against tragedy, which probably contributed to the length of her overseas service. Marjorie Starr, who proved far less adaptable, endured great emotional torment and completed just one term as a VAD. Most appear to have found a middle ground, taking strength from the realization that their efforts were useful and sometimes valued by patients and nurses alike.

Perhaps Fanny Cluett's unflappable approach secured her rapid secondment to France, only three months after she applied for a transfer. Her prompt selection was unexpected, and it caused some embarrassment among her peers at Lincoln, most of whom waited a year or more. Cluett was devoid of pretense and well aware of her limitations as a VAD, readily conceding that she lacked the knowledge and experience of a trained nurse:

> I shall never forget one day; the M.O. [medical officer] asked what kind of dressing one of the patients had on his leg; for the life of me, I could not just remember then whether it was Hydrog Ammon Oil ointment or Red Lotion. I said at first it was one thing, then another; but at last I remembered rightly, and told him. I had not had time to dress him before the doctor came through; and there are so many with different dressings, that I assure you, you must not be asleep on the wards; there are thousands of things to remember.[56]

Even under pressure, Fanny rarely panicked, but the more sensitive Marjorie Starr lacked this sang-froid and regularly suffered bouts of insomnia due to the trauma of watching men suffer and die. Many of the patients at her Royaumont hospital came directly from the trenches, often in great numbers and in perilous condition, and she frequently felt overwhelmed by an inrush of new cases:

It was Starr here and Starr there till I didn't know if I was on my head or my heels, but I managed somehow, but it is rather awful to be told to get something in a hurry you never heard of ... Then had to fly for the priest, then the head surgeon, the man was dying, then off to the Office to have them send another urgent wire to his people, so altogether it was a nerve-racking day.[57]

However, depending on the situation, she could sometimes disassociate the practical and the personal aspects of the work, even when unorthodox methods were applied. She recounted having to assist "at the dressing of the two amputated arms; not nearly as bad as I thought it would be ... not like the man's leg when I had to positively sit on his chest to keep him down while the Doctor dressed it." She sympathized with "the poor VAD yesterday who got a leg to burn."[58] The eager young women who had enrolled for VAD training back in Toronto or Saskatoon could never have imagined such a task. Even the experienced nurses had rarely encountered this excess of injury and pain in their civilian work. Despite her acute distress on the wards, Starr could often detach the emotional aspects of the work from its clinical elements, particularly the marvels of modern surgery:

Really today each one seems worse than the last: one arm will simply have to be amputated, he had poison gas as well, and the smell was enough to knock one down, bits of bone sticking through and all gangrene. It will be marvellous if Miss Ivens saves it, but she is going to try it appears, as it is his right arm. He went to x-ray, then to Theatre, and I believe the operation was rather wonderful, but I had no time to stop and see, as I had to help carry stretchers.[59]

Starr proved reliable in the operating room and was thus frequently sought out to assist the theatre nurse:

Down came a Theatre Sister with a message from Dr. Ivens that I was to go up to an Operation. It wasn't from our Ward, but the V.A.D. from his ward couldn't stand the Theatre, so Dr. Ivens said I was to go: it doesn't worry me, but I must say it was a beastly affair, a bullet in a man's inside, and they couldn't get it. I was there a whole hour holding up a leg in that hot air.[60]

Had she been permanently assigned to the operating room, Starr might have extended her time at Royaumont. Unfortunately, the suffering patients, unpredictable routines, and insomnia gradually became too much, and she was reassigned to kitchen duties ahead of the rotation, which will be a great relief to the strain, as although it is hard work washing dishes and setting tables all day, it is monotonous and so a rest to the awful strain ... It will not be so interesting, of course, but I am not thinking of seeing things now, I just want to rest my mind and get away from the horrors for a little. Several of the girls have given up completely under the strain, but I hope this change will just pull me up in time, and I won't mind the hard work if I have no responsibility.[61]

At one point, Starr was given some relief from the wards through an unexpected opportunity to make some much-needed hospital garments:

I have heard a rumour which delights me, that I may be put to do some sewing for a week or so ... When the matron heard I could sew, she thinks she may give me a turn at it for a change, as we are all entitled to a little lighter work every little while. It will be fine to sit down for an hour or so, as my feet are what bother me, and certainly the dressings take it out of one if you are a bit sympathetic.[62]

Henriette Donner sees Starr's reallocation to non-nursing tasks as humiliating proof that she had failed as a nurse.[63] In this first instance, however, Starr regarded the change as a respite, welcoming it as a chance to regain her stability. Unfortunately for her, it did not solve her problems. Like Starr, many VADs had difficulty adjusting to night duty, which compounded the stress and fatigue of a heavy workload. Sleep deprivation was often accompanied by feelings of inadequacy in not being able to cope with the suffering. The relationship between emotional and physical illness was little understood at the time, as is tragically underscored by the treatment of shell shock patients.[64] Few Canadian or Newfoundland VADs continued their overseas service beyond eighteen months; Fanny Cluett's four years were very much the exception. After repeated bouts of illness and insomnia, Marjorie Starr regretfully conceded that she could not remain beyond her first six-month contract.

As mentioned above, Starr was the only Canadian VAD at Royaumont. Her isolation was unique, as the Devonshire House administration worked to ensure that new VADs had a support system of friends or relatives serving with them at their first hospital. Siblings Sybil and Jill Johnson were assigned together to the 1st Western General Hospital in Liverpool, and they also had family nearby.[65] Many Newfoundland VADs were posted to the Lady Roberts' Convalescent Hospital in Ascot or to the 4th Northern General Hospital in Lincoln, where Fanny Cluett and three other Newfoundland VADs were also assigned in late 1916.[66] Alice Bray and her close friend Gladys Humphrys were sent to the 1st Southern General Hospital in Birmingham on the advice of Viola Henderson. Gladys was originally to be paired with another Canadian, but as Alice wrote to her mother, "when Mrs. H. found G and I were such good friends she changed it – so I took quite a lot about her back" (in this remark, Alice conceded that her many complaints about Henderson's preference for her own Montreal VADs may have been unfair). Birmingham proved an unpleasant first assignment for Alice and Gladys, which was mitigated to some degree by their mutual support. They eventually moved on to a second contract at the much more agreeable Royal Herbert Hospital in London, where, as Alice wrote enthusiastically, "all the girls seem so happy and content and the whole atmosphere of the place is that you are expected to be a lady not a thieving servant girl." Though demonstrating the prejudice of her upbringing, Alice refrained from condemning all servant girls, declaring the staff at the London VAD hostel to be far more congenial than in Birmingham: "We don't have a thing to do about looking after our own rooms. The nicest little maid keeps everything spotless."[67]

Class perceptions clearly contributed to Alice Bray's somewhat uneven adjustment to VAD service. Regardless, the presence of a close friend undoubtedly helped her to remain at the Royal Herbert for eighteen months, well into the postwar period. Marjorie Starr did not have this kind of support, and though she was not excluded from the camaraderie of the primarily Scottish-born VADs and nurses at Royaumont, she felt a degree of detachment that arose from both cultural and class differences. She declined to join the hospital hockey team of VADs, characterizing the players as "a burly lot, a good many of them suffragettes," which was not surprising for workers at a feminist hospital, but she did concede that they were "a jolly lot just the same."[68] Jean Sears felt equally alone when she arrived at the 2nd London General in 1917 but was befriended by an older, more experienced VAD and "taken under her wing."[69]

Regardless of their heritage or status, all Canadian and Newfoundland VADs qualified as "colonials." As they quickly learned, their social position at home guaranteed neither privilege nor acceptance in the hospital culture of the Royal Army Medical Corps (RAMC) or in any other VAD work environment. Grace MacPherson discovered this when she started work as an ambulance driver with the British Red Cross in France. The daughter of a Vancouver civil engineer, she had trained as a stenographer and, with her mother's help, was one of the first women in Vancouver to drive her own car. Popular, pretty, with an effervescent personality, she arrived in France full of energy and enthusiasm, but her outsider status put her at a social disadvantage, and she suffered an unaccustomed crisis of confidence as a result. Feeling excluded from the clique of upper-class British drivers whom the supervisor apparently favoured, she bitterly complained to her diary that "in all the hundred odd girls here, about 25 can play the game ... and the others are not fit to wipe one's boots on!"[70] With time, camaraderie, and shared experience, she gradually became acculturated, and by the end of the war she acknowledged that "these same girls are my best friends."[71] During those first few months, however, without the support of a close friend, Grace often felt very much alone and discouraged.

Carroll Smith-Rosenberg discusses the supportive networks of nineteenth-century schoolgirls, in which senior students eased the transition of new arrivals, providing a comforting cushion of female friendships.[72] Some VADs may have encountered a similar dynamic in their communal experience as nursing volunteers or drivers. Indeed, the analogy of carefree schooldays was a favourite of female journalists who wrote about VADs in the war zone, and perhaps they did take comfort in the familiar homo-social patterns of their school years as a means of countering the tensions and uncertainties of their work. Identified only as K.M. Barrow, one British VAD used the image of the school in discussing her experience in France: "Life in a Military Hospital is a school within a school. Inside the big school of experience, there is a type of school-life which is not unlike that which we lived in our 'teens, with its friendships, its sops, its frenzied activities and its recreations."[73]

The nurses and VADs contributed immeasurably to the survival and recovery of countless sick or wounded men, particularly through the promotion of hygiene and the prevention of infection. Christine Hallett's study of trauma containment in war hospitals notes that the British military nurses and their VAD assistants placed a high priority on hygiene. She argues that this emphasis subtly influenced the health of patients by instilling order amid the chaos of war.[74] Marjorie Starr recounted Royaumont's rigorous hygiene regimen when wounded men arrived by ambulance:

> We lift the stretchers out and lay them on the floor: then they are portioned off to each Ward. If they are stretcher ones they go to an Out-patients' Room quite near, where we blanket bath them, and all their clothes go into a sack. The other ones that can walk go to the Cleansing Room: there is a bath there behind curtains. We take their belongings and put them into sacks and label them, and then they go behind the curtains, and one of the not badly wounded men that we have had for some time, bath them: then we finish them up and get them to bed.

I never saw such filth, or wounds as we have had today, straight from the trenches, and all gory and muddy.[75]

As vividly described by Desmond Morton, the bacteria-laden mud of France and Flanders, steeped in decades of animal fertilization and now contaminated by "rotting corpses, rats, feces," killed far more men than snipers' bullets or shells. Cleaning and draining open wounds, after the surgeon had cut away the infected tissue, was a complicated but essential process.[76] VADs frequently mention fomentations – moist compresses or poultices – as one of the most painstaking, but critical, weapons in the fight against infection. Developed under normal hospital conditions to cleanse an open wound, fomentations were extremely labour intensive and even more difficult to apply under wartime conditions. As Kathryn McPherson explains, they entailed

placing strips of cloth in a linen holder attached to wooden handles. Nurses lowered everything except the handles into a vat of boiling water and when the fabric was hot enough the nurse carried it to the patient's bedside, placed it on the infected site, and then covered it with more dry cloths. This might be performed up to three or four times an hour and each time the nurse had to be careful to avoid burning the patient.[77]

After being "taken to task" for coming late to breakfast following night duty, Sybil Johnson complained of the heavy workload to her diary and criticized the sister for not doing her share:

I have even to change the foments, (2 of which are four-hourly) and moisten two dressings and fill the tubes (5 of them) in the very tender knee. That means that each wound must be unbandaged and all carefully done up again. Then temps, drinks, medicines and cough mixtures, getting our own meal and clearing up, washing, dress a safe hip and change the man's drawsheet and make his bed alone! Endless jobs.[78]

Johnson did not question the need for these tasks, only the lack of time or assistance. Even with such exacting procedures and an adherence to precise "scientific" hygiene routines to minimize infection, the demands of the moment could override protocol, particularly in front-line hospitals. Marjorie Starr's account of conditions at Royaumont illustrates the endless challenges, when expediency could outweigh scientific practice:

There is no time to put on rubber gloves, so I just trust to chance and go in for all with bare hands: one has to touch septic things, as the bad wounds are drained by rubber tubes in them, and these are taken out and given to me in a bowl, and in two minutes I have to have them back to the Doctor washed and sterilized, so I just have to squeeze them with my fingers and a piece of cotton wool, a thing never dreamed of in a proper hospital, but everything here is primitive, naturally no time to think of nurses' fingers: we just have to have no cuts or long nails.[79]

Even as a volunteer, Starr was aware of the standards for preventing and controlling infection. Her actions were not the folly of an untrained amateur, but a response to the physician in charge, whose instructions she followed without question, as any qualified nurse would do. It is likely that her "trust to chance" was greater than she realized, as infection and injury plagued both nurses and patients. The RAMC compiled a lengthy list of the serious medical problems, including tuberculosis and blood poisoning, that had forced the retirement of dozens of VAD nurses, in some cases requiring the amputation of fingers or even a limb.[80] In Sybil and Jill Johnson's Liverpool hospital, the infection of VAD and nursing personnel was common. When Jill's thumbs became infected, Sybil casually observed, "septic fingers are so tricky. People lose fingers and even arms all the time." Having a septic thumb "cut" three times, poor Jill "suffered a lot"; on the third occasion, the doctor removed half the nail, all of which Jill endured after refusing the anesthetic. Further debilitated by loss of sleep due to the pain, she insisted on continuing to work until both thumbs were bandaged.[81]

Severe back injuries were also common among VADs, typically the result of lifting and carrying heavy stretcher patients. They were a particular problem at Royaumont, with its medieval stone staircases. As Starr recounted, "carrying men up those stairs is much too heavy work ... even four of us sometimes," but in a converted abbey staffed entirely by women, there were no brawny male orderlies to help with the lifting.[82] The problem was not unique to Royaumont. A VAD at Sybil Johnson's Liverpool hospital was bedridden for weeks due to an internal injury suffered when lifting a stretcher, despite having male orderlies on staff. Strenuous physical work was perhaps the most unexpected aspect of VAD duties overseas, but male orderlies came at a premium in the war zone because healthy men were needed at the front. Annie Wynne-Roberts described the wounded as having "poured" into her hospital during the 1916 Somme offensives. They all needed to be "bathed, clothed and surgically dressed" before being transferred to an auxiliary hospital, often

Marie Estelle (Jill) Johnson,
c. 1916. *Courtesy of the Centre
for Newfoundland Studies,
Memorial University Libraries*

within twenty-four hours of their arrival. This rapid turnover made room for the next wave of wounded, sometimes totalling up to three hundred a day. Annie wrote that the front-line hospitals in France were sometimes "crammed to the doors" with men who were too badly injured to be moved, often suffering from wounds that had not been dressed for several days.[83] In such circumstances, there was little time to consider the strain on VADs or other personnel.

Fanny Cluett seems to have adapted better than most, but she was not immune to the stress of standing by a bedside in a darkened ward, "watching for the last breath." She could dismiss the swish of the rats as they pushed under the beds but could not "forget some of the more piteous sights that could ever possibly be."[84] Annie Wynne-Roberts was much less complacent about the ubiquitous vermin that prowled the French hospitals. She made her rounds "lantern in hand, Florence Nightingale style," hoping to avoid tripping over tent ropes or encountering many rats: "Ugh! Their name is legion here and they are as tame as cats and about the same size."[85]

Rats were less a feature of night duty in England, and the pace was less fevered. At her Liverpool hospital, Sybil Johnson made her rounds every twenty minutes, with only a dim hall light as her guide; the nights on her ward were very still, beyond "a sigh or mutter." After 11:00 p.m., a male orderly came to assist in the event that a post-operative or dying man needed special care. But even in England, night duty could be demanding, and its quiet rhythm could suddenly be shattered by the arrival of a convoy invaliding patients back from France. This usually followed an offensive, and it signalled the start of a "fortnight of frenzy," with a continuous influx of new cases.[86] Late in the war, the attacks of enemy Zeppelins and bomber aircraft exposed hospitals in London and all along the south coast to new night terrors. Violet Wilson was stationed at Gifford House convalescent hospital for amputees in southwest London during the Zeppelin raids of 1918. When the attack began, the patients had to be moved outside, since the combination of shock and their recent amputations made them panic and cry out, pleading not to be left in their beds. Like shell shock, their reaction to the raids was little understood. Though the nurses and VADs found it "pretty hard to bear," they dutifully remained outdoors with the men, helping to calm them until the clamour of the raids subsided.[87]

Marjorie Starr never adjusted to night duty, especially in an old abbey made eerie by lantern light. She found nights on the wards to be "much more responsibility" than the daytime hours and could not relax enough to sleep when off duty. The private sleeping cubicles reserved for night duty nurses lacked window coverings, and noises penetrated from overhead and through the doors.[88] There were other unexpected discomforts. Barely ten days after her arrival at Royaumont, Starr found her first flea. It probably came from a new patient fresh from the trenches, since the endless scrubbing and cleaning of the hospital wards left no "corner for them [the fleas] to live in." To her dismay, Starr discovered that certain home comforts were also unavailable: "No bath now for two weeks, and none in view for another fortnight. If I had only known and brought a rubber one with me. Not nearly so tired today ... just dirty. It is wonderful what one can get used to."[89]

Food rationing was another hardship for some, as Muriel Wainwright acknowledged in a letter to the Women's Branch of the Civil Service, thanking it for a gift box of restricted provisions that included chocolate and sugar. While in Lincoln, Fanny Cluett lamented the rationing of bread and sugar but discouraged her mother from sending an emergency parcel of cake: "I should dearly love to have it – but I assure you mother the postage is not very small ... All we hear these days is 'Economy in wartimes.'"[90] She wrote of meatless days and fish on Fridays for the VADs and nurses, but there were no food restrictions for the patients, who thoughtfully shared their scones and bread with the nursing staff. Despite the privations, Cluett declared that her health was never better, apart from a lingering cough that disappeared once she reached Rouen.[91] Minor mishaps and illnesses, like Cluett's cough, were part of life overseas. Attributing her persistent sore throat to "climate and exhaustion,"

Jean Sears decided not to ask for a transfer to France, believing that the chronic condition would foil her chances.[92] Other VADs also found that poor nutrition, sleep deprivation, fatigue, and the strenuous workload left them vulnerable to illness and injury. Many nurses and VADs required a convalescence period in one of the Canadian Red Cross rest homes established for Imperial nurses in England and France.[93]

When the influenza epidemic struck, nurses and VADs overseas put their own health at risk in the care of servicemen, as was expected of them. An RAMC report underscored this assumption, citing the "good fortune in the fact that nursing of the sick and wounded is a natural act," despite the "hazardous nature of the calling" and, at times, the danger to "life and health." The report did concede that many nurses had died as a result of enemy action, but others had "suffered life-long damage to health" due to work-related illness and injury.[94]

The damp and cold, inadequate heating, uncomfortable sleeping arrangements, constant fatigue, exposure to illness and infection, and endless lifting of heavy men all took a tremendous physical toll on the VADs, no matter how healthy and robust they were when they arrived in England or France. The emotional stress of watching men suffer and die, often helpless to ease their pain, proved a greater test for the more sensitive women. In a situation where "one's little ills are nothing at all in comparison to the ills around us," Marjorie Starr was often frustrated by her inability to rise above her personal problems. The VADs had merely to look at their patients to feel shame for any self-indulgent complaints. Their reward for discomfort was the constant gratitude of the patients for their efforts. Often, they found that humour was the best defence against the rigours of the work. In a letter to her fiancé, written after nearly six months of VAD service in England, Sybil Johnson declared that she was now "not only muscular and managing but also enveloped in an air of conscious virtue and piety and sisterly love, and unpleasant, nay infuriating smugness!"[95]

Nurses and VADs Negotiating the Bedside

Once they began active service, VADs had to make a quick adjustment to hospital routines and procedures, as well as the strenuous physical and emotional demands of their work. They also had to adapt themselves to assisting the qualified military nurses, all of whom, regardless of age or seniority, were their superiors in the hospital hierarchy. The enormity of this adjustment is evidenced in the list of proscriptions, titled "Don'ts for V.A.Ds," that they received upon registering at Devonshire House for their first assignment. It was just one of many lists and regulations, including a personal message from Dame Katherine Furse, that they were expected to internalize (see Appendix 4):

DON'TS FOR V.A.Ds.

DON'T talk about anything you hear in Hospital.

DON'T criticize anybody, but do all you can to see that your own bit of work needs no criticism.

DON'T forget you are under Military discipline – therefore under absolute obedience to all seniors.

DON'T forget to stand up when seniors come into ward or room.

DON'T forget that when in uniform all members should be immaculately clean, trim and tidy.

DON'T forget that the outside public often judge the Association by the individual members.

DON'T forget that duty comes before pleasure.

DON'T expect your own particular feelings or likes to be considered. You are but one of many.

DON'T think you can pick and choose your own work at *first*. Do all that comes your way with your whole heart, and others will soon see what you are best fitted for.

DON'T forget to "Bring your will to your work, and suit your mind to your circumstances – for that which is not for the interest of the whole swarm is not for the interest of the single bee!" *(Marcus Aurelius)*[96]

VADs on active service were not permitted to discuss their work or experience beyond the hospital walls, and the censor's hand can often be detected in their letters home. Graduate nurses absorbed this maxim of discretion during their student years and knew just how readily they could be brought to book for any lapse. When budding author and VAD Enid Bagnold published her first book, an idealized impression of her time at London's Royal Herbert Hospital, she was summarily dismissed from her post "for breach of military discipline."[97] To a lesser degree, the point was made clear to novice BRCS VAD Diana Manners, when she was summoned to the matron's office to explain an incautious remark made at the family dining table: "Did I not realize what a sacred thing a hospital was? How vowed we should all be to discretion and respect? In our hands were the sick and dying. The responsibility of their death was often with us. Outside its walls it should not be talked about and certainly not ridiculed."[98]

Anxious to craft heroic tales of suffering and service, journalists were often frustrated by the dearth of information on the inner workings of the hospitals. In 1920, well into the postwar period, an editorial in the *Hospital* lamented that the "veil of secrecy which hid the operations of the nursing sisters during the war has not yet been lifted," thus limiting public appreciation of their efforts.[99] Equally dissatisfied, Canadian Red Cross publicist Mary MacLeod Moore complained that though Canadian nurses and VADs had contributed much to the war effort, "thanks to censorship especially, comparatively little is known of their work."[100] Often this void was filled with portraits of young ingenues casting off the remnants of adolescence as they assisted at the bedside of sick and wounded men. Just as sporting analogies shrouded the true nature of trench warfare, so youthful schoolgirl imagery created messages of a patriotic feminine "esprit de corps."[101] The VADs were playing for "their side," enjoying the "exhilarating" experience of being part of "a great and complicated organization."[102] Conversely, they were often likened to a cloistered community, and late Victorian "high diction" and the poetic imagery of Rudyard Kipling, which would have been familiar to Canadians of British heritage, were employed to elevate their work to a divine undertaking.[103]

Despite the rhetoric, VADs had few illusions about their work as assistants to the military nursing staff. Their letters and diaries contain no cloying assertions of devotion and fortitude. Indeed, Annie Wynne-Roberts frankly acknowledged that in the early weeks of her VAD service, "the smell of antiseptics and lotions made my head ache and the sight of poor battered bodies made me dizzy."[104] Fanny Cluett's letters are equally devoid of spiritual or idealized pretensions. She admitted to having "fainted dead away" on her fifth day of service while helping the sister to change dressings and equally unromantically recorded that "when I came to myself I was stretched out on the floor."[105]

Handicapped from the start by inexperience, limited training, and unfamiliarity with hospital culture, some Canadian and Newfoundland VADs also encountered unexpected isolation and distrust due to their colonial status. Others brought their own biased assumptions about the British nursing class, which coloured their initial impressions. Whether volunteer or professional, all nursing personnel were coping with the demands of wartime hospital conditions while learning to work together in exceptional circumstances. The Johnson sisters arrived with minimal VAD training, and Sybil feared that her probationary period in a London hospital might be supervised by "a certain kind of

Englishwoman who is infuriating, self-satisfied and perfectly inhuman." Her time as a schoolgirl in England may have prompted this unease. The words of a more experienced VAD simply inflamed her anxiety: she dismissed the British nurses as "infuriatingly superior ... positively rude and overbearing," although she did concede that "most of them are not that bad." Having worked herself into a state of nervous anticipation, Sybil nonetheless allowed that it was "quite useless to be against those in authority, though ... it doesn't do to be too docile and weak." Ultimately, she rationalized that it was "rather hard to strike a happy medium." During her nineteen months overseas, she never fully overcame her ambivalence. She admired the dedication and hard work of the nurses but often criticized their seemingly gruff and impatient treatment of both VADs and patients. A month into her service, she wrote to her father, cheerfully declaring that on some wards "the sisters are pigs and the nurses are horrors. But mine are all nice and quite jolly."[106]

Overall, the VADs on the home front described much less tension in their interaction with the nurses. Shirley Gordon enjoyed a comfortable relationship with her nursing supervisor at the Davisville Military Orthopaedic Hospital in Toronto. Jean Sears, who began her VAD work at Davisville, moved to a hospital in Chelsea, where she found much greater friction between the British nurses and the VADs. The military hospitals in Britain were more rigidly organized than those in Toronto; as Sears put it, in Toronto there was "not the discipline there was in England, not quite."[107] The colonial VADs often found English hospital life difficult to comprehend and accept. Soon after arriving at the 1st Southern General Hospital, Birmingham, Alice Bray observed that "everything is done absolutely according to military rule you get up by the Bugle (Réveille) and you go to bed by 'Lights Out.'"[108] Jean Sears was amazed by the imperious authority of the matron at her Chelsea hospital. In the dining hall, the matron, senior sisters, and hospital administrators sat at an elevated table, and the matron's entrance was purposely delayed for dramatic effect. When she arrived, the VAD nearest the entrance scurried from her seat to hold the door, and as matron swept in, the VADs and nurses rose together and proffered "a little bow." Sears and the other VADs accepted this ritual without complaint, as "the hierarchy didn't affect us," but Sears also found that some of the ward sisters could be very imperious. There were a few whom she simply "couldn't bear," which inevitably led to a confrontation:

> One of them was so rude to me one day that I just turned round and sauced her back. I said, "I haven't come 3000 miles to work voluntarily to be spoken

to like that by anybody." Of course she reported me to the matron and I was up on the carpet, so that I was changed from that ward.[109]

As VADs could not be disciplined by a loss of salary or rank, penalizing their lapses could be a challenge. A few were dismissed outright, as Alice Bray nervously observed: "One of our girls is being sent away on Saturday absolutely no reason given, only that she is to go – if it did happen I feel I wouldn't feel disgraced or anything for I know I have done my very best."[110] It was not unusual for VADs who came up against the hierarchy to find that their contracts were discontinued at the end of their six-month probationary term. Given that reliable nursing aid was at such a premium, the extreme sanction of outright dismissal probably indicated that the Birmingham VAD was guilty of more than poor work habits. Alice Bray's contract at Birmingham was not extended, apparently because she was a colonial. The matron made it clear that she disliked this "class," and of the six Canadians posted with Bray, only Welsh-born Annie Wynne-Roberts had her contract renewed, because she at least was "British."[111] Whether the bias was related to class or cultural differences, or simply to a general resentment of VAD intrusion, is not clear, but several VADs noted the stigma of colonialism.

Violet Wilson was posted to the Gifford House convalescent hospital in London, thankful to be relieved of her car-cleaning duties at Devonshire House. A high-spirited woman, she radiated independence and self-confidence, qualities that probably did not impress the hospital matriarchy, accustomed as it was to deference. A clash was predictable. Violet saw the English nursing sisters as antagonistic to all VADs and as going out of their way to be unpleasant, most particularly to the colonials:

> We had to take a good deal from them, but when it was announced that we were to get up half an hour earlier in the morning in order to take hot water to them in their bedrooms I rebelled. I said I'd come to help wait on the men, not the Nurses, and I said it very loudly!
>
> Told by Matron that COLONIALS, amongst our other awful characteristics, "had no sense of discipline," I was put on night duty as a punishment.[112]

The VAD nurses in the war zone experienced much less friction or cultural discrimination from their military nursing supervisors. Distanced from the oversight of the more senior generation of British nursing administrators, the military nurses who were sent to the Continent were probably younger, more adventurous, and less conservative or constrained by the hierarchical traditions of hospital organization. They were also functioning in far more stressful conditions that frequently demanded flexibility.[113] Moreover, the VADs who worked under their watch generally had some level of experience and had come with a reference from a previous posting. In France, as elsewhere, hospitals were often an amalgam of canvas tents and wooden huts, a maze of rooms connected by wooden boardwalks. There, out of necessity, the nursing framework lost some of its formality. Weeks of comfortable routine could suddenly erupt into days and nights of caring for streams of patients, many caked in mud from the trenches. Under such circumstances, co-operation was essential. During calmer intervals, VADs and nurses often strolled through the countryside or had tea together in a local cafe. In Rouen, Fanny Cluett shared her free afternoons with both VADs and nurses, touring the public gardens, investigating quaint little shops, and sipping café-au-lait at the nearby hotel.[114]

By 1918, British nurses were in diminishing supply, and capable VADs were often given more responsibilities and autonomy than would be permitted in England. To encourage superior VADs by acknowledging their competence and long-term service, and to promote morale, the Joint Women's VAD Committee eventually devised a visible ranking system – service bars or stripes that were worn on the sleeve of the uniform dress and coat, much like the stripes denoting military rank. Initially, they identified a "senior" VAD of at least thirteen months. Gradually, red and blue stripes were added to indicate rank, seniority, and the type of hospital service. These extended categorizations enabled VADs with a good report from matron to take an exam and be elevated to the rank of "Assistant Nurse."[115] The system was flexible, facilitating Ottawa VAD Muriel Wainwright's rapid promotion to join the staff of a new military hospital on the Italian Mediterranean. Her honour was duly noted in the pages of the *Civilian:* "Within the year she was made a senior VAD. When it was decided to send a party of 40 nurses to Italy, Miss Wainwright was asked to go as an assistant nurse – a promotion that usually takes two years to achieve. Before leaving she was given scarlet stripes for excellent service and shoulder straps with A.N. (assistant nurse)."[116]

Following her transfer to France, Annie Wynne-Roberts was also elevated to the status of night duty nurse "in sole charge" of her hospital under canvas.[117] Some qualified nurses were uncomfortable with the promotion of volunteers, and when Royaumont's chief medical officer, Dr. Frances Ivens, proposed raising the status of the VADs and partially trained nurses on staff, they registered their concerns. As Ivens explained, some VADs

Muriel Wainwright,
c. 1917. *Courtesy Rare
Books and Special
Collections, McGill
University Library*

have had a considerable amount of experience, and could be trusted to act as
seconds in the wards ... They should be promoted to Auxiliary Nurses, be given
a salary of £20 and wear Army Sisters' caps with ordinary uniform which would
make a distinction. I am sure that some feel that they do not get promotion here,
and really they do more work, and with more intelligence, than an inferior type
of fully-trained nurse.[118]

To avoid dissention, Ivens eventually settled on the designation of "staff
nurse" rather than "auxiliary." This helped ease the affronted sensibilities of
the partially trained (two years) nurses, whom Ivens then designated as "assistant nurses," raising the nurses' status with suitable adjustments to salary. On
the whole, the issue revolved around class rather than training. Although Ivens
ardently promoted the rights of women in the medical profession, she also
recognized that in background and education, the majority of the VADs were
more closely aligned to her own class than partially trained nurses. Some
Royaumont VADs were "very wealthy society girls" and thus were not atypical

of the British VAD movement, in which class affiliation was seen as more important than training.[119] Despite the disagreements between the nursing staff and administration, Marjorie Starr mentioned little discord between the nurses and VADs at Royaumont. She considered herself to be a good friend of the second matron and recorded one experience when they visited an American military hospital together. To Starr's delight, both women were introduced as Scottish nurses, "because they were unaware that I was a humble VAD swanking around with the Matron."[120] Although Lyn Macdonald's claim regarding the "happy-go-lucky" atmosphere of the French hospitals seems somewhat overstated, Canadian and Newfoundland VADs do give the impression that the relationship between themselves and the nursing personnel was more comfortable outside of England.[121]

In England or elsewhere, the VADs were always cognizant of their minimal training and subordinate position in the hospital hierarchy. Intelligent, hard working, and committed to patriotic service, Sybil Johnson was content to work with any of the nurses in her Liverpool military hospital, as long as her efforts were appreciated: "My sisters are very nice, though the one in charge rather oppressively acts up to *her* idea of a super-woman among imbeciles."[122] Less assertive and more sensitive, Sybil's younger sister Jill was acutely conscious of her amateur status. On one occasion, she was moved to tears by a patient's pain. As Sybil wrote in her diary,

> Poor old J. has a dreadful case in her ward. Her Sister got an orderly to help her, but he very soon staggered into the ward and fainted. Then she got another new RAMC man who just looked and went out and nearly crumpled up. So she tried J., the Baby, who did see it through and held him. He told her he saw tears running over her cheeks (she didn't know she cried) and said it made him feel better, although his "fuss" hadn't been about nothing. He said "I didn't know nurses wept" to which Jill responded "I'm *not* a nurse, only a sham one."[123]

For Sybil, the hallmarks of a good supervising nurse were intelligence and industry. Initially assigned to a "happy ward" under a supervising sister who was "very nice and capable," she was moved to a new ward within a month and soon became angry and frustrated: "When my own (night) sister told me to clear the trolley, of course I did so and was violently attacked for it in the middle of the ward by the charge sister. I said *my* sister had told me to do it. But most of these people have the manners of pigs. They make me furious."[124]

By early 1918, problems had become widespread in the Liverpool hospital, prompting its VADs to resign "in droves." Sybil noted that more than 160 of them left the service in the six months following the appointment of a new matron. In her opinion, the matron was insensitive to the needs of the VADs, refusing reasonable requests for time off when brothers or fiancés came back on leave – "so they simply go." The matron also seemed unable to manage her nursing staff, who in turn began to harass the VADs, prompting Sybil to comment, "No decent maid would put up with it – such abuse and impudence." Perhaps her rancor stemmed from general weariness with the war and the difficulty in finding fresh nursing reserves to lighten the burden. Except for this particular matron, Sybil felt that her nursing supervisors were reasonable and capable people.[125] During her much shorter VAD career, Marjorie Starr was ambivalent about her supervisors, some of whom became friends, though others were a trial:

> I have had the most trying sister in the Hospital to train me, and now I have another, and what a difference: the other used to lose her head in a rush, and really I never knew if I was standing on my head or my heels, and I never seemed to get through, as she never let me finish anything in peace, always fly away to get this and that, then why wasn't this done?[126]

The more complacent Fanny Cluett had few complaints about her supervisors. In Rouen, Sister Horrocks put great trust in her judgment and abilities, often leaving her to oversee half the wards alone. Fanny's common sense and ability to laugh at her own shortcomings were assets at her often chaotic front-line hospital. Frequently left in sole charge when a sister had a half-day leave, she was rarely flustered or distressed and freely admitted her mistakes. Once, when she had forgotten to report a patient with gas blisters to the medical officer, she calmly acknowledged that the sister would not be pleased – "However there it is." Reserving her energy and emotion for the patients, she refrained from impassioned recriminations against the nursing staff and developed strategies for managing the hierarchy, smoothly navigating the rules and procedures. Her letters were composed with the immediacy of personal conversation. Late one night, she confided to her mother that she was using a forbidden candle and would need to extinguish it if "Matron or Super Night Sister is prowling about. Then relight it again."[127] Fanny's equable demeanour helped her surmount the stress of her exceptional situation, unlike the more emotional and judgmental Sybil Johnson, who worried constantly about the friction between

VADs and nurses. Sometimes unfairly, she tended to blame the nurses for any difficulties, and though willing to concede that her own efforts were not always perfect, she needed constant appreciation of her work from women whose background and education did not match her own. From her point of view, the nurses would have been more productive had they accepted that they too were ordinary women, "not a separate, superior and privileged race."[128]

VADs and Their Soldier Patients

Annie Wynne-Roberts wrote of how her perspective altered during her transition from civilian onlooker in Toronto to VAD nurse in a British hospital. In a rare uncensored letter, she recalled her feelings as she watched Canadian soldiers proudly marching off to join the conflict: "So spick and span in their new uniforms, so splendidly virile, [they] used to give a queer sensation of tightness in the throat." But now, she added, "the coming of these boys straight from the fight, war-scarred and weary, brings tears perilously near. However, there is no time for sentiment in war."[129]

It was the sick and wounded men who gave meaning to the work of the VADs, not the nursing per se. Unable to take up arms, they fought the war as gender dictated, by assuming the identity of nurse. This, as Janet Watson argues, "was their symbolic battlefront, and the hospital served as their trench."[130] They were well aware of the differences between themselves and the military nurses, who had extended the scope of their civilian training and experience into the military hospitals. Canadian and Newfoundland VADs overwhelmingly showed little interest in pursuing nursing as a career. As Charles Copp struggled to convey to a skeptical CNATN in 1918, they "had no previous desire to enter the nursing profession, and have no more now – it is pure patriotism on their part." In mid-1918, the Militia Department proposed paying a salary to VADs in the military convalescent hospitals, "as the girls are under definite orders instead of voluntary service." The St. John Ambulance College Nursing Division in Toronto threatened to disband in protest, arguing that accepting payment would signify renouncing VAD work as a purely patriotic gesture on behalf of "the boys."[131]

The majority of civilian women were involved in a range of patriotic services, paid and unpaid, far removed from the trenches and the fighting men. The VADs and nurses enjoyed a unique connection to the realities of mechanized warfare and its human cost, both at home and overseas. On the wards, VADs could take a stand against the enemy, particularly those who went overseas. The VAD nurses and ambulance drivers were later recognized for their "active service in the field" by the British War Office, with the same General Service and Victory Medals that were issued to Allied soldiers at the war's end.[132]

Most families could countenance an unmarried daughter taking up volunteer nursing in a local military hospital, but few imagined that she would perform such work in the war zone. More than the horror of the *Lusitania* or the fate of Edith Cavell, parents feared for the moral and social reputation of their daughters, living far from home while ministering to the needs of unknown men. The issue of class appears to have been more difficult for the parents of elite British VADs. Stella Bingham cites the example of one well-bred young Englishwoman who informed her family that she was about to start VAD work: "The fact that I was going to nurse other ranks and not convalescent officers was spoken of in hushed whispers and with much head shaking."[133] Bingham attributed their reaction to protectiveness rather than snobbery, but both were probably involved.

Canadian and Newfoundland VADs were not immune to the social dimensions of the work, but their personal accounts speak more to their admiration of the men, regardless of their rank, for their courage and cheerfulness despite pain and debilitation. This may not always have outweighed class considerations, as some expressed surprise that courage was not confined to the officer class. Jean Sears acknowledged that "a great many of the patients were lower class British. Wonderful, wonderful people! The backbone of the British Army ... the Tommies!" Sybil Johnson was more consciously condescending, describing her patients as "honest and cheery and clean looking and some of course, the very roughest ... as far as social class goes." Violet Wilson had nothing but praise for her patients – "The cheery courage of those men, with no arms or legs, sometimes neither, was unbelievable" – and made no qualification in assessing them.[134] At Royaumont, most of Marjorie Starr's patients were *poilus*, the lowest-ranked French troops, and only a few officers were brought in while she was there. The hospital was near the front and the men usually arrived fresh from the trenches, smelling of filth and putrid wounds. The experience was well outside Starr's social conditioning amid the Montreal Westmount elite, and it took some adjustment. Initially, she felt most positively disposed toward a group of patients of a "much nicer class and very intelligent and well educated." They spoke a French that she easily understood and offered much-wanted news about the progress of the war.

This class perspective gradually faded from Starr's writing as she became accustomed to her situation. By the end of her time at Royaumont, she was far more attuned to the suffering of the patients than to their social origins, preferring to nurse the wounded rather than those who were only sick, and "so uninteresting."[135] Sybil Johnson expressed a similar view, remarking that wounded men were "so terribly appealing ... so helpless." This reaction reinforces Janet Watson's argument that VAD identity was more grounded in an involvement with the war effort than in the role of nurse. Watson contends that whereas qualified nurses preferred to look after sick soldiers, regarding this as *real* nursing work, the VADs focused on caring for the wounded, seeing it as validation of their patriotic service.[136] In helping to nurse the true casualties of the conflict, they were making their most useful contribution.

The military hospital system itself promoted class distinctions in providing differing forms of care for officers and other ranks. Violet Wilson discovered the advantages of being an officer when she transferred from Gifford House in London to a special convalescent home for Canadian officers in Deauville, on the coast of France. Established in a luxurious summer villa belonging to the Rothschilds, the hospital ensured that its patients were well supplied with the ample food and rest deemed necessary for their recovery and return to the field. In a later interview, Wilson stated,

> I've never really forgiven myself, or forgotten the shame I felt while enjoying the luxury of this, and all the other Canadian establishments in France and England. When the English hospitals, and the French ones ... were starved of necessities and were so terribly short of food, we were living in luxury. Coming from Gifford House where our amputee cases received bread and dripping only for their evening meal, and where nine times out of ten the milk puddings provided were made from musty rice or tapioca, it made a deep impression on me.[137]

Wilson was ashamed to be little more than a glorified servant amid such largesse, instead of performing useful nursing. The lower-ranked but far more critically injured patients at Gifford House got by on much more limited resources. She did acknowledge that her own brother would probably have benefitted from the privileges of rank had he survived, as would the brothers and fiancés of most VADs. The perks of separate wards, greater privacy, and individual care were much disparaged by the military nurses, but according to Watson, the special treatment was not entirely grounded in class. In France at least, it served a practical purpose. Sending officers home to convalesce in England often enabled them to circumvent returning to the theatres of war on the Continent. Keeping them in France, and well supplied with comforts and favours, made them less eager to return to Blighty and more accessible to be called back to active service once they recovered.[138]

Families on either side of the Atlantic adjusted to the idea of their daughters ministering to wounded men, regardless of rank. Nursing German prisoners of war (POWs) was beyond the imagining of most parents. Within four months of Fanny Cluett's arrival at the 4th Northern General Hospital in Lincoln, her request for a transfer to France was approved. She was baffled by the speed of her reassignment to Rouen and even more surprised when she learned that she was to nurse POWs. Knowing that her family back in Belleoram would be less than comfortable with her new situation, she abandoned her usual newsy style of letter writing for several months. To conceal the details of her work in Rouen, she adopted a mysterious cover story worthy of a spy novel, insisting, "I cannot tell you anything about the hospital here, as we must keep absolutely quiet on these matters in France." When her assignment ended, Fanny could no longer contain herself and confessed the truth to her family:

I don't think I ever told you I did night duty in the German compound for Prisoners of War. I had five German wards to look after, and one of the wards was an acute surgical, where amputated legs and arms had to be watched for hemorrhages.

I think had you known that was where I was doing night duty you would have felt a bit uneasy. Of course, there was an English night orderly also. It was funny, I did not feel at all scared, but perhaps I did feel a bit nervous some-times. I knew they could not harm me there, or at least I suppose they couldn't: I have passed through their wards with them lying on either side; sometimes I used to think, if they would only jump up; but then on the whole I had nothing whatever to complain about, they were always very respectful to me.[139]

The likelihood of being assaulted by patients in any surgical ward was limited. More worrying for nursing supervisors were romantic attachments between the patients and nursing personnel. The opportunity for such rela-tionships was severely circumscribed by the rules and by the acknowledged social divide between VADs and most patients, but they did occur. Jill Johnson was engaged to a former patient before the war's end, having apparently already "broken the heart" of another, both probably officers.[140] She was not alone in forming a close bond with a patient, but there is little to indicate any intimate contact, even with a fiancé. The watchfulness of nursing supervisors reflected their concern for the difficulties that could arise from contact between nurses or VADs and their patients. In her published "diary," British VAD Enid Bagnold recounted having crossed a line simply by intimating a too familiar relationship with a patient, letting him "stand near me and talk." On Bagnold's next shift, the patient had vanished, transferred to another hospital before she even knew his name. Whether this episode was a novelist's fabrication or a true account is unknown. True or not, it demonstrated the vigilance exercised by supervisors to prevent any hint of impropriety between nurse and patient.[141] The status and image of nursing had to be preserved, and as nursing personnel, the VADs were expected to follow the rules for conduct.

Of course, this does not mean that the rules were never broken. In more than one instance, Violet Wilson tested the limits and survived unscathed. She was a natural risk-taker, rarely letting the rules get in her way. During her time at Gifford House, she spent her free days touring around London with a variety of escorts. On one outing, she and her male companion missed the last bus to Putney and were obliged to walk the twelve miles to the hospital. Arriving after the 10:00 p.m. curfew, they found that the gates were locked. Undaunted, Violet had her friend boost her on his shoulders to scale the high stone wall that surrounded Gifford House. Since the wall was topped by broken glass, Violet was forced to balance equally on her handbag and the shards of glass before leaping to the ground, tearing her clothes and "bleeding freely." She managed to elude the guard, but she moved painfully around the wards for the next few days, her "behind plastered with bandages."[142]

Although Violet Wilson was in no danger from her companion of the evening, the vulnerability of nurses and VADs was not overlooked by the military authorities, particularly in the war zone. In France, VAD ambulance driver Elsie Chatwin recounted one occasion when she was ordered to drive two ambulatory Portuguese patients the twenty-five miles from the military hospital to their base at Boulogne. As she set out alone, the two men became increasingly "obstreperous," so she stopped at convoy headquarters to ask for a second driver who would ride along with her, "because I didn't think it was very safe with these soldiers." Instead of a second driver, the commandant ordered a soldier to accompany her as an escort. Although she now had three men in her vehicle, Elsie felt completely secure with a British soldier.[143] The rapid response to her request for aid confirms that the military authorities were alert to the security issues for women in a combat zone.

Perhaps the ethnicity of Elsie's passengers fuelled her apprehension, or that of her commandant. Like class, ethnicity influenced the relationship between VADs and their patients. As mentioned above, even the usually calm Fanny Cluett admitted to some disquiet when she began night duty with the

POWs. The isolation of the night shift, in conjunction with the pervasive anti-German propaganda, doubtless contributed to her unease. By contrast, Jean Sears had only positive memories of the Romanian soldiers whom she nursed. One had even declared his love for her, and she had briefly and innocently reciprocated, admitting that "he was very attractive!" Such flirtations, however innocent, were worrying for nursing supervisors, who were conditioned to forestall any potential liaisons. Sears acknowledged that VADs were expected to behave themselves but admitted the difficulties: "We had ideals in those days ... To be thrown in with men ... from all over the world, it took some doing to keep level ... not to have your head turned. But you had your heart hurt very often!"[144]

For some VADs, flirtation developed into a lasting bond. Daisy Johnson helped nurse Harry Cook at the King George Hospital in London after his release from a POW camp, and she married him in Regina in 1919. Other similar marriages probably occurred as well. Some VADs married their fiancés from home while both were serving overseas. Tragically, both Janet Miller from St. John's and Ruby Pinfold from St. Thomas, Ontario, were widowed before the war ended.[145] From the perspective of family, marriage was not really a problem if the couple were a suitable match; more concerning was the temptation for casual liaisons. In this regard, VADs were more at risk from the young medical officers than from the weak and incapacitated patients in their care. Healthy, handsome, and eager for distraction from the horrors of war and its toll on their patients, the medical officers were far from home – and perhaps from wives and sweethearts. They were particularly appealing to VADs as well-educated young men from the same social circles as their own brothers and boyfriends.

Eva Morgan, a Canadian Imperial VAD from Montreal, met perhaps the most eligible bachelor of her day when she was assigned to the Red Cross nurses' Rest House at Boulogne. The nurses and VADs regularly hosted dances in the converted hotel and invited any Allied officers who were stationed in the area. One of these, attached to a local Canadian division at the time, was Edward, Prince of Wales, a dashing and romantic figure. Though a frequent guest at the dances, he had never learned how to dance, being forbidden by his disapproving mother, Queen Mary. Released from her gaze and far from home, "he was dying to learn how," particularly now that the waltzes and polkas of an earlier era had given way to "the Bunny Hug and Fox Trot ... and we taught him how to dance!" Like the prince, Eva Morgan was testing parental boundaries. She was fully aware that if "father and mother had known what we were doing they'd have had me back ... in a minute, but they didn't

... You can be sure I didn't tell them!"[146] Although Morgan's clandestine dancing now seems far from compromising, some VADs did form more questionable attachments. At the end of the war, while she was working as the recreation director of a demobilization camp in Wimereux, Violet Wilson formed a relationship with a British officer. As she recalled, "I would sometimes dine with him in Boulogne. We sat cowering in the darkest corner in the restaurant because ... regulations forbade English officers in France to be seen eating in public with women, and this was months after the Armistice!"[147]

Vera Brittain's memoir of her war years has garnered considerable analysis and speculation for its revelation that her VAD experience awakened her sexuality. Hardly salacious, Brittain describes the natural response of a sheltered twenty-one-year-old suddenly exposed to a much wider world. She admitted to feeling no shyness or embarrassment in confronting the naked bodies of her patients, only "gratitude for their simple acceptance of my ministrations." She also believed that this asexual intimacy allowed her an "early release from sex inhibitions," which seemed to haunt many of her female contemporaries.[148] Referencing Brittain's awakening sexuality and newfound freedom, literary analyst Sandra Gilbert sees the war as a liberating force for nurses and VADs. She suggests that with the hospitalized men rendered "invalid and maybe invalid," the healthy young VADs were the "triumphant survivors."[149] This notion is refuted by Brittain's biographer, Deborah Gorham, who argues that she was required to subvert her sexuality as a VAD, to conform to the acceptable response of "traditional female nurturance."[150] The theme of sexual neutrality in the hospital milieu is reinforced by Fanny Cluett's discussion of the strict code of detachment that governed interactions between VADs and patients. She wryly commented that the VADs at Lincoln were "allowed to speak but little to the patients, and to tell the truth we scarcely have time to speak to ourselves sometimes."[151]

In their personal accounts, Canadian and Newfoundland VADs frequently employ maternal images to describe their relationship with their patients. Sybil Johnson even admitted to a sense of guilt for usurping the maternal role of one visiting mother: "I thought how mean it must seem to her when she couldn't stay and nurse him. It seemed so odd to think of me wandering in a perfect stranger and washing his face and generally waiting on him and keeping her waiting outside while I did it!"[152]

Johnson appears to have relished the role of surrogate mother, identifying herself as the "nanny" in a nursery of small boys, helping to "give them their meals nicely and keep their hot bottles hot and get them drinks, make their beds and wash them and get them clean clothes." In one passage, she described spoon feeding a patient "like an old mother bird." This reversion to the mother-child relationship seemed to help the men cope with their weakness and disability, and with the intimate but necessary treatments that emphasized their temporary loss of masculinity. As they regained strength and mobility, the "up-patients" often performed some of the lighter VAD chores, much like young children hoping to please mother, a face-saving fiction that concealed any diminishment of masculine identity.[153]

Fanny Cluett took on a maternal identity in helping an eighteen-year-old soldier who required an extended hospital stay while he recovered from a painful spinal injury. Under her doting attention, he became "a very mischievous boy," demanding increasing amounts of her time to alleviate the boredom of hospital life. Much like an indulgent parent, she empathized with his pain and encouraged his antics, even playing tricks on him on April Fool's Day.[154] The age difference between them – more than fifteen years – helped to legitimize their unusually close relationship. Older patients also welcomed the retreat into childhood, as a respite from the trauma of war and their painful wounds. One patient wrote in the autograph album of Canadian nursing sister Beatrice Mack, "She tucks me in like mother did/in the dark days long ago/she treats me like a little kid/it'll make me better I know."[155]

The VADs may have had some justification for viewing their patients as children. Many were little more than boys, having concealed their age in their eagerness to enlist. However, Nancy Nygaard's study of VAD writings offers an alternative interpretation. She argues that infantilizing patients maintained the illusion that VADs were caring for innocent boys, not "men who killed others," often young German soldiers like themselves, and who could kill again if they returned to the front.[156] Marjorie Starr's reference to her poilus patients seems to support this idea: "Really they seem like a lot of children here, and one really can't realize that they can kill people."[157] Yet the perception of maturity could also be based more on physical appearance than on a psychological impression: referring to the death of "the old tubercular chap," Starr wrote, "he was quite childish (one speaks of him as old he looked so aged, but he was only thirty-two)."[158] Fanny Cluett was fully aware of her own young patient's age and consequently treated him like the "boy" he was.

Even without a nurse's training and experience, the intense world of the war hospitals soon taught VADs that a patient's emotional well-being needed support. The up-patients, who were able to move around the wards but not yet ready to resume active service, often took on the role of orderly. Sybil Johnson referred to one such man after he was discharged: "My friend Jack went out today. I called him 'Priceless,' because he was so good. Did everything possible with such a quiet willing energy, and between whiles kept us amused with really witty banter in broad Scotch!"[159]

Johnson encouraged their laughter as an antidote for pain and boredom, recounting one occasion when an up-patient dressed as a VAD and was led around the ward by another patient, posing as the medical officer. It became all the more uproarious when the "nurse" unexpectedly encountered the vice-matron, "a severe and dignified (tho' an awfully nice) woman. I believe she was amused, but pretended she didn't notice."[160] The VADs and sisters collaborated to make special days such as Christmas as enjoyable as possible for their patients. In Rouen, Cluett and her ward sister purchased cakes and other delights from the Expeditionary Force canteen "for the boys' tea on Xmas day!" and an up-patient helped her trim the ward with paper decorations and tissue, hung "in festoons from the ceiling of the tents." Sybil Johnson's patients also received Christmas stockings stuffed with combs, razors, and other useful items, as well as cigarettes, candy, and noisemakers, all "going like pandemonium" as soon as they were found.[161] For these grown men, the maternal nurturing of the VAD was part of the healing process, a refuge from the awkward, unpleasant, and intimate aspects of hospital care that usurped their dignity and independence. Creating a comfortable and relaxed atmosphere also helped the VADs to bridge the divide between civilian life and the exceptional demands of their volunteer service. The maternal dimensions of their work accentuated its usefulness for the cheerful and courageous men under their care, and balanced out the harder days.

Chapter Five

SAYING GOODBYE

Forgetting, Remembering, and Moving On

WHEN ASKED ABOUT HER year overseas as a VAD in London some fifty years earlier, Agnes Wilson responded, "Oh it was a marvellous experience! Really, I wouldn't have missed that for anything!"[1] As recent studies reveal, other veteran VADs shared her enthusiasm, despite what we know about the war.[2] The Canadian and Newfoundland VADs had participated in a collective movement that was far removed from any previous experience. Consequently, when celebration and dancing in the streets heralded the armistice, many felt some ambivalence regarding the long-awaited peace. The news arrived in Drumheller, Alberta, just as Gertrude Murphy and the local doctor were heading out of town to care for a stricken family:

> Suddenly the stillness was shattered by a shrieking blast from the locomotive at the station, followed by another and another ... Church bells began to ring wildly and clamorously. Then the fire bell clanged and car horns blared ... People were running out of the houses, down the streets, waving flags, shouting, dancing, singing in a frenzy of excitement. A car filled with screaming people waving Union Jacks and Stars and Stripes, horn blaring, slowed down as they passed us. "What's the matter with you?" they screamed, "Don't you know the war is over?" We had forgotten the war.[3]

Worldwide, the influenza epidemic was still exacting its toll, killing some fifty-five thousand in Canada alone. More than sixty thousand Canadian service personnel had died as a result of the war, and an estimated seventy thousand were coming home permanently disabled. Canada was not alone in its losses, and the grim statistics had an understandably dampening effect on wearied spirits worldwide.[4] In France, the VADs and nurses in Doreen Gery's hospital wept behind doors for brothers and lovers lost to the war: "We were just so tired that I don't think we could have kept going for much longer."[5] Alice Bray watched the first joyous crowds surge into the streets of London upon hearing the news: "It was perfectly marvelous – everyone just flew outside – a sound like the surge of the sea over the whole country." Later in the day she sensed a change, as the crowds merged into a "sort of disquieting throng," possibly a harbinger of the restlessness and uncertainty that came with the realization of what peace had cost and the changes it would bring.[6] For the women and men on active service, peace meant adapting to a world no longer framed by the war that had shaped their lives for four long years. There would be no return to a misty "golden age." The VADs, like the soldiers they had cared for, would soon discard their well-worn uniforms and resume their civilian lives.

The structure of Canadian society changed rapidly as war industries promptly shut down, leaving thousands of female workers without the exceptional wages of their wartime jobs. War and epidemic also left countless women without their anticipated marriage prospects, as well as unprecedented numbers of young widows, all needing to support themselves. For those who had the means and ability, higher education might substitute for marriage. Some might find a place in the white-collar workforce alongside the many veteran VADs who returned to their careers. For others, the future was less defined.[7]

Most of the 150 Canadian and Newfoundland VADs who are known to have been employed during the 1920s entered white-collar occupations, in keeping with their class and education. In the early postwar years, some 85 of them took up clerical work, whether in the public service, private financial and professional offices, or in other private businesses. Not unexpectedly, another 30 taught school, many in their former classrooms. More notable were the 20 who continued in some form of salaried nursing work, as ward aides, first aid assistants, and one dental nursing assistant. The definition of "nurse" in this era was still casually applied to a range of women's caregiving roles, although 4 veteran VADs did earn graduate nursing qualifications after the war. The remaining 15 whose employment could be traced worked in several female occupations: a dietician, a chiropodist, 2 librarians, and 11 in various sales and service jobs. All these work roles met traditional gendered expectations. Canadian women may have gained the vote, but they were still governed by the conservative dictates of the pre-war world. Newfoundland women were still waiting for the franchise.[8] For many VADs who had enjoyed the freedom and sense of purpose and responsibility of the war years, peace was a welcome but uncertain prospect.

It meant a loss of the autonomy, prestige, and collectivity that had defined the VAD movement. The constant hum of activity had faded, and Violet Wilson found her homecoming "too quiet and too sudden a change from all the wartime hustle and bustle." Like many returning soldiers, she felt "restless and dissatisfied."[9] Sandra Gilbert describes the similar, if more extreme, response of veteran British war workers who felt trapped by "embittered unemployment or guilt-stricken domesticity."[10] Rather than sinking into despair, Violet Wilson was galvanized into action by her discontent. Rejecting an offer of marriage as too restricting, she decided to seek out new experiences for work and travel. Not all veteran VADs shared her adventurous spirit, and many suffered due to their loss of freedom and status. Nevertheless, women's increasing visibility in the workplace was challenging convention, even within traditional gendered boundaries. Many VADs adapted the skills and experience they had acquired in wartime to develop a new peacetime occupation.

Whatever their prospects, few seemed inclined to pursue nursing as a career. In the final months of the war, Canada's nursing activists were challenged by the potential intrusion of VADs into veterans' hospitals, as a cost-effective government remedy to projected nursing shortages. When the VADs proved uninterested, the debate ended. For the overwhelming majority, their volunteer work had been an expression of patriotism but only for the duration of the war; they were not transformed into peacetime nurses. As the soldiers abandoned the trenches and laid down their arms, most Canadian and New-foundland VADs also saw the armistice as the end of their own service. For Doreen Gery, Gertrude Murphy, Alice Bray, and their peers, the advent of peace was more a time for reflection than for raucous fanfare. Nevertheless, their work did not come to a sudden halt with the armistice. At home and over-seas, there were many months of labour ahead, assisting in winding down the veterans' hospitals and helping to care for the men who were too debilitated to make the journey home. Gertrude Murphy had been too busy with the in-fluenza crisis in Drumheller even to contemplate the cessation of hostilities, although many had already left VAD work much earlier. This effectively ended their letters and diary entries, such as those of Marjorie Starr, whose experience had differed so markedly from what she had expected or could endure. Even the determined Grace MacPherson gave up her ambulance work in the months before the armistice, finding the stress was taking a toll and much in need of replenishing her finances. Whatever their experience, the VADs' personal documents convey a certain satisfaction with their wartime experience. Sybil Johnson returned home in the summer of 1918, following eighteen months as a VAD in a Liverpool hospital. On her final day, she wrote in her diary, "So here's an end to my little trip as a VAD and I'm most glad I came."[11]

A Community of Canadians

Although the St. John Ambulance enjoyed sole responsibility for the training and certification of Canadian Voluntary Aid Detachments, it was not ultimately responsible for all of Canada's VADs overseas. Some VADs had not waited to be selected and found their own transport to Britain, eventually applying directly to Devonshire House. Others bypassed St. John altogether, funding their voyage overseas and taking up service as Canadian or British Red Cross workers. Some also trained as British Red Cross VADs overseas, hoping this would guarantee them a place in a military hospital. Whatever their route, a varied group of Canadian women were volunteering overseas as nurses, ambulance drivers, and non-nursing hospital workers by the war's end.

Those who arrived under the aegis of St. John constituted an identifiable cohort. Those who did not inhabited a limbo identity, being neither British in origin nor Canadian in their VAD affiliation. In 1918, this disparate community was unexpectedly drawn together under the umbrella of an independent VAD organization called the Canadian Imperial VADs, or "Imperials." Offering the unattached VADs both leadership and an identity, the Imperials filled a gap.

They evolved in response to an urgent request from the Joint Women's VAD Committee in April 1917, asking for increased colonial VAD support. Hoping to appeal to a wider pool of applicants, the Joint Women's VAD Committee at Devonshire House authorized the creation of "reserve detachments" from Britain's colonies and dominions. The goal was to augment the dwindling supply of British VAD nurses and non-nursing general service workers as the war took an ever-increasing toll on both its manpower and its woman power. The new Imperial detachments would operate in parallel with the Devonshire House VAD program and would not be directly affiliated with either the British Red Cross or St. John, although their nurses and female ambulance drivers were still required to obtain official certification through one organization or the other. This "separate but equal" structure was rationalized as a means of preventing existing detachments from being overwhelmed with new members. Each Imperial detachment was to have its own independent "recruiting commandant," who was not subject to Joint War Committee oversight.

Lady Milly Perley, Canadian
Imperial VAD commandant,
by Fayer. *Library and Archives
Canada, PA-034148*

In recruiting for the Imperials, socially influential women in the colonies
and dominions appealed to the elite, who might otherwise not have responded
to the more middle-class VAD leadership. Thus, Imperial VADs tended to be
of a higher class status than those who had entered the original program organized under the Joint Women's VAD Committee. For example, Princess Mary
became commandant of a British Imperial VAD unit, despite her youth.[12] All
but one of the Imperial detachments in Australia, New Zealand, South Africa,
and Canada were led by a titled commandant. At the time of the armistice in
November 1918, the detachments boasted some eight hundred colonial members. The ongoing recruiting and deployment of the St. John Ambulance VADs
in Canada was unaffected. The new Imperial program circumvented the various
national and colonial VAD organizations and appealed directly to the govern-
ors general of the dominions, encouraging the creation of the independent
Imperial VAD units. The commandant of the Canadian Imperial VADs was
Lady Milly Perley, who, as the wife of Canada's acting high commissioner in
London, put her own interpretation on the request for a new VAD unit. Rather
than recruiting a detachment of entirely untried neophytes, she focused instead
on the many Canadian volunteers who were already engaged in Red Cross
VAD work in England or France.[13]

Officially launched in February 1918, the Canadian Imperial Voluntary Aid Detachment had some 187 members by the end of the war. As most were drawn from the upper echelons of Canadian society, their backgrounds were less varied than those of the St. John VADs. Many were older and married, and had travelled to England early in the war to work with the Canadian Red Cross in London. Others were serving as British Red Cross VADs, but not all of the 115 Canadian Imperials who held VAD nursing credentials were active in nursing roles.[14] There were some new recruits, but most Imperials were already working overseas, "having practically no status or official recognition of their services," as journalist Anne Merrill reported. She argued that joining the Imperials appealed because it linked the women together and identified them with a Canadian unit.[15] During their early months in London, the Perleys had been chastised by the Canadian press for leading a seemingly lavish lifestyle amid the privations of war. Since that time, Lady Perley had become active in the Canadian Red Cross and many other patriotic endeavours, but none afforded the leadership role of the Imperials. Personable and energetic, she took it on with enthusiasm. She created a distinctive commandant's uniform for herself, but to avoid confusion, and expense, the Imperial VADs were permitted to wear their own regular St. John Ambulance or British Red Cross uniforms, with the addition of a small crescent-shaped "Canada-R" badge on the shoulder.[16]

The Imperial umbrella took in a broad cross-section of volunteers who could now be identified as Canadian. They included those driving British Red Cross ambulances in France and any Canadian VADs enrolled in British Red Cross nursing detachments.[17] The unit also enjoyed the advantages of Milly Perley's position as wife of the acting high commissioner. Her diplomatic status gave her access to some of the Canadian Army Medical Corps (CAMC) facilities in the war zone, which permitted her to propose one of her Imperials should an appropriate opportunity arise. As a result, at least twenty Imperials worked in CAMC hospitals in a non-nursing capacity. Others were posted variously to St. Dunstan's Home for Blind Soldiers, the Canadian Red Cross nursing hostels in England and France, and the Canadian Red Cross head-quarters in London. When one of the Imperial assistant commandants, Mrs. Ethel Gordon-Brown of Ottawa, was put in charge of a new Canadian Red Cross Nurses' Rest House in Boulogne in 1918, she selected thirteen Canadian Imperials to assist her.[18]

Regardless of their advantages, the Canadian Imperials were no less com-mitted to VAD work than their sisters in the St. John divisions. Most remained in their assigned posts but with the added benefit of joining a Canadian volunteer

Ethel Gordon-Brown *(back row, centre)* and Canadian VAD staff of the Canadian Red Cross Nurses' Rest House, Boulogne, July 29, 1918. © *Imperial War Museum, detail Q 9140*

community abroad. They cut across middle- and upper-class lines to forge a strong bond. Although the scheme offered Lady Perley a prominent public service role, she can be credited for recognizing their need to be identified as part of a national community. After retiring from ambulance driving, Grace MacPherson worked briefly as Perley's secretary in London and later warmly described her as "the most delightful and charming person I have met in my travels ... a mother to all Canadian girls overseas."[19]

Nurses or Volunteers?

The wartime emergence of the VADs had presented unexpected challenges for Canada's nurses. From early in the century, nursing schools had sought to standardize training, reinforce the rituals of nursing practice, and demonstrate immutable models of femininity and decorum, ultimately aspiring to professional recognition.[20] Not until early 1915, when the VADs first entered the home-front military convalescent hospitals, did the Canadian National

Association of Trained Nurses (CNATN) become concerned about their potential admission to the CAMC hospitals overseas. As the pool of experienced VADs gradually widened, anxiety increased about postwar competition that might undermine the status and job security of qualified nurses. Matron Margaret Macdonald successfully blocked VAD access to most CAMC hospital wards during the war, but neither she nor her civilian counterparts had anticipated the minefield of veterans' convalescent care. By the spring of 1915, with optimism for an early victory fading and casualty lists lengthening, the Allied forces overseas had begun to recognize a growing urgency to rehabilitate and restore the wounded and maimed. Among the more significant developments of wartime military medical care was an effective physiotherapy service.

The evolution of therapeutic physiotherapy as a healthcare occupation for women was an unanticipated offshoot of the war. Remedial massage and various other physical therapies steadily became essential elements of convalescent rehabilitation treatment. The training of female physical therapists that developed in conjunction with the treatment was a key component in restoring men to fighting strength, or at least to a level of self-sufficiency as civilians.[21] Wherever possible, the CAMC endeavoured to return men to the field following their release from convalescent care in England and France. Trained physiotherapists were increasingly needed to provide their rehabilitation, which in turn gave rise to debates over who was best qualified to handle this task. Early in 1915, certified masseuses began applying for work with the CAMC, but Matron Macdonald refused them, accepting only nurses who were qualified in massage, despite the rapidly growing need for massage therapists. She believed that nurses' training was a prerequisite for massage therapy. Rather than importing civilian personnel from Canada, she referred CAMC nursing sisters to the massage course at the Granville Special Hospital for orthopaedic care in the south of England.[22]

The Militia Department had its own concerns about the mounting costs of rehabilitation. When full control of VAD organization in Canada was transferred to the St. John Ambulance Brigade (Overseas) in 1917, plans were developed to train VADs for massage work in the CAMC hospitals, irrespective of Macdonald's policies.[23] The Military School of Orthopaedic Surgery and Physiotherapy was established at Hart House, on the University of Toronto campus, during the same year. Here, some 250 women were subsequently qualified in specialized physical and occupational rehabilitation programs between 1917 and 1919.[24] In 1918, the St. John Ambulance reorganized the VAD program to include a new category of masseuse, responding to the Militia Department's recognition that diversifying the VAD organization to address the complex needs of veteran rehabilitation would be of economic benefit. Although the VAD program was to be renamed the Women's Aid Department (WAD) to reflect its true gendered identity, the administrative structure would not change.

Organization and training still rested with the St. John Ambulance Brigade (SJAB) under the auspices of the Department of Militia and Defence, but the VADs were to be designated either as nursing members or as function trainers (FTs) who specialized in physiotherapy.[25] The first aid and home nursing courses continued as before for nursing members, but FTs required additional courses in physiotherapy. These were taught at Hart House to prepare them for work as physical therapists in the convalescent hospitals. The proposed WAD was much broader in scope than the original VAD program, incorporating two salaried special service divisions in addition to the non-salaried volunteers. One division would provide basic housekeeping and cleaning services, similar to the British Red Cross general service VADs, and the other would supply more highly skilled function trainers and massage specialists who took a mandatory six-month course at Hart House.[26] From the government's perspective, this scheme would address both the projected nursing shortages in veterans' hospitals and the mounting costs of veteran rehabilitation. A 1918 directive from Sir Edward Kemp, the minister of Overseas Military Forces of Canada (OMFC), listed the benefits:

In regard to electrical remedial work ... would it not be better to employ VADs and train them, rather than take Nursing Sisters who have had upwards of three years' course in Canadian Hospitals to qualify for their particular branch of work.

In connection with massage, VADs are trained to this work who are not regular Nursing Sisters ... In other words owing to the possibility of Nursing Sisters becoming scarce it is desirable to conserve the personnel of this Branch of the Service as much as possible. From an economic standpoint there would be an advantage as young ladies trained for this work would not be Lieutenants.[27]

Kemp had obviously realized the economic value of the VADs as unremunerated volunteers. Harnessing women's unpaid labour for rehabilitation work was regarded as a greater benefit than paying additional qualified military nursing sisters for the same work. The potential for nursing shortages after the war was a real concern, and having a pool of minimally trained unpaid women available for basic therapeutic work could help offset the exorbitant costs of rehabilitation. This was worrying news for civilian nursing leaders such as Jean Gunn, who had long feared that the VADs might undermine the value and security of nursing work when the war ended. Gunn and her peers understood that this would simply open the door to a further exploitation of nurses' skilled labour. At the CNATN convention in the summer of 1918, Gunn stressed the need to be wary of lowering nursing standards: "We cannot afford to allow the crisis through which we are now passing to furnish a loop-hole for us to lower our standards, for while it is very easy to lower them, it is very difficult to bring the standards back where they were before."[28]

Gunn was well aware that allowing unpaid and unskilled women to assume the role of qualified nurses in any capacity not only devalued nurses' work, but women's labour overall. The CAMC administration was equally opposed to incorporating VAD therapists into the military hospitals. The director of medical services, General Gilbert L. Foster, diplomatically observed that though the VAD masseuse might "serve admirably," she had come too late.[29] He argued that the CAMC already had well-established training programs in massage and other therapies for nursing sisters, and was also employing "low category" men who were no longer fit for combat to provide remedial physiotherapy under supervision. Even unpaid VADs, in Foster's opinion, represented an additional cost to the military for transport, food, and lodging. He concluded that "unless it becomes the policy of the Department [of Militia and Defence] to bring over a number of young women from Canada, I would not recommend encouraging any of the girls from Canada ... to come here and take up this work."[30] Matron Macdonald was confident that military nurses who were trained in massage at the Granville Hospital were far more suitable than VAD masseuses who were the product of Canadian classrooms. She also felt that a rotation in massage work gave the CAMC nurses a break from their regular duties. Employing VADs as masseuses was "a doubtful economy" in her view, since the nurses were "naturally much more efficient and in a much better position to maintain proper discipline."[31]

Some prominent civilian medical voices echoed Macdonald's sentiments. Dr. C.K. Clarke of the Toronto General Hospital was an influential, if at times controversial, leader in the development of psychiatric treatment. He stated that volunteer women were "not amenable to discipline themselves, nor can they enforce discipline." Thus, they had no place in military hospitals, where they could undermine efficiency.[32] To reinforce the government's position, a delegation of Canadian senators was sent to tour the CAMC hospitals in mid-1918. The senators concluded that the military nurses were not qualified in massage and were therefore being inefficiently employed when not performing their regular duties. Their opinion was largely dependent upon the advice of the RAMC's inspector of massage services, Dr. Barrie Lambert, a massage pioneer who saw massage therapy and nursing as distinct fields. In the end, the nurses won by default. Not long after the senators' visit, VAD transport overseas was cancelled in anticipation of the armistice, and the debate was left unresolved. Margaret Macdonald had the satisfaction of maintaining the integrity of the CAMC nursing service, but the threat had been real, and another year of war might have seen economy triumph over principle.[33]

While the CAMC was successfully battling the potential intrusion of the VAD overseas, the CNATN was mounting a parallel defence against the permanent use of VAD nurses and masseuses in the veterans' hospitals at home. The challenge was threefold, turning on the impending return of thousands of convalescent veterans, the anticipated nursing shortage, and the large reserve of experienced VADs. The nursing shortage was caused by a combination of factors, including marriage, military service, and the incentive of higher-paying war work, which absorbed both prospective students and recent graduates, despite a significant increase in nursing graduates since the pre-war era. The situation was compounded by an unprecedented demand for convalescent nursing because of the war.[34] Aware that the government intended to staff veterans' hospitals with VADs, the CNATN developed a counter proposal, which was designed to transform them into qualified nurses. As graduate nursing candidates, they would complete part of their practical student training in the military hospitals, providing a cost-free benefit to the government. Converting VADs into a reserve of qualified nurses would alleviate the projected shortage, while diminishing competition from veteran VADs. As a bonus, the CNATN would gain control over the selection of VAD probationers, and the nursing schools would enjoy government funding for the necessary new residences and any other contingent costs of expanded enrollment. From the CNATN's point of view, this scheme was better than recruiting unqualified VADs directly into the veterans' hospitals, a course that, among other defects, offered no solutions for future nursing shortages.[35]

The CNATN was surprised and dismayed to discover that plans for the new Women's Aid Department were well under way before its own proposal had even been considered. The reorganization would produce seven hundred WAD volunteers for immediate work in military hospitals at home and overseas, at a tremendous cost saving for the government. Undaunted, Jean Gunn requested a meeting with Dr. Charles Copp, director of the VAD program, during which she suggested amending the original CNATN plan. St. John would have full jurisdiction over the non-nursing general service workers, but the selection and training of the VAD student nurses would still be left to the discretion of the hospital schools. The students would wear their VAD uniforms instead of standard civilian nursing costumes, signifying their St. John Ambulance affiliation. To the bewilderment of the CNATN executive, St. John rejected the proposal to accept VADs as student nurses, on the grounds that it closed "the opportunity for the enthusiastic young women to nurse the soldiers as a V.A.D."[36] Jean Gunn and her CNATN colleagues were incapable of seeing nursing solely as a patriotic gesture and had simply assumed that the VADs would welcome the opportunity to become fully qualified. They remained convinced that VAD work was an expedient means of launching a nursing career without undertaking the rigorous training.[37]

As the VAD program director, Copp was equally unable to appreciate the CNATN's deep concerns that VADs might endanger the employment prospects, or professional aspirations, of qualified nurses. He was adamant that the VADs were merely a voluntary supplement to the military nursing services, and he vigorously refuted suggestions that they intended to compete for nursing jobs after the war. Copp assured the CNATN that it was "absolutely against the rules" for VADs to "seek recognition" from the nursing community at the war's end. However, he did concede that once a VAD retired from the St. John Ambulance Brigade, "there was no regulation governing her actions, nor could they interfere if she adopted nursing."[38] For its part, the CNATN leadership had naively failed to recognize that the government interest in extending VAD service was purely a short-term, cost-effective solution to immediate military nursing shortages. There was no thought for the long-term needs of civilian nursing. Yet perhaps the most surprising aspect of the debate was the lack of understanding on the part of the CNATN, the military, and the St. John Ambulance that the war alone had been the catalyst for VAD service. Becoming a VAD had been an expression of patriotism; there was no significant interest in pursuing volunteer nursing, civilian or military, once the war ended.[39]

Despite the uncertainties surrounding the future of nursing, Jean Gunn and her CNATN colleagues did concede that the VADs had made a useful contribution to the war effort. They recognized that nurses and VADs were alike in class and education, and that with the proper qualifications, many VADs were well suited to nursing. As an incentive, the Canadian Association of Nurse Education suggested that the nursing schools might offer individual veteran VADs some credit for their overseas service, to a limit of six months.[40] In response, the Brandon nursing association in Manitoba agreed to a concession of one month of training for each year spent overseas, and the more generous Saskatchewan nurses offered two months of training credit per year of service.[41] Healthcare activist Dr. Helen MacMurchy urged the nursing community to show more flexibility, noting that some British VADs had been offered a full year's credit against the three years of training because their war service "had been so good and so helpful."[42] MacMurchy had also mistakenly interpreted the reluctance of some VADs to relinquish their work immediately following the armistice as proof of their interest in a professional nursing career, rather than a desire to prolong the independence, responsibility, and shared duties of their wartime experience.[43]

Predicted nursing shortages, government interest in ongoing VAD services, and the emerging peacetime public health initiatives of both St. John and the Canadian Red Cross reinforced the CNATN's desire to solidify the professional identity of graduate nurses.[44] These issues framed the CNATN convention in the summer of 1918, just as the proposal to insert VADs into hospital training schools as probationers was rejected. In addition to meeting the immediate needs of the veterans' hospitals and guaranteeing a reserve of trained graduates for the future, the plan averted the VADs' backdoor entry into a nursing career. Ultimately, Gunn rationalized that VAD work in the veterans' hospitals would not continue indefinitely. With this battle lost, she turned to the longer-term needs of nursing graduates, particularly to the three thousand military nurses whose CAMC contracts would soon end.[45]

A year later, in the summer of 1919, with the war and the influenza epidemic behind them, Gunn argued that the public had come to realize "the value of nursing and the need of nursing." She emphasized the urgency of capitalizing on the CAMC nursing service's legacy to promote future professional recognition and employment security for all nurses.[46] With a postwar push to complete nurses' registration, all nine provinces enacted "some form of nursing legislation" by 1922, although Kathryn McPherson suggests that it was disjointed and of variable quality. She argues that the provincial nursing associations did not gain the essential right to define who should practise, but only to keep unqualified women from promoting themselves as "trained" graduates.[47] Nonetheless, the completion of national registration can be viewed as a moderate achievement, influenced in part by the projected continuation of VAD nursing in military hospitals. Although registration put some restrictions on the ability of veteran VADs to enter directly into paid nursing, there were no guarantees. The plan to continue with peacetime VAD nursing had demonstrated that, immediately after the war at least, VADs still garnered sufficient public confidence to challenge the authority of qualified nurses.

Having lost the battle for VAD hospital training, Gunn and the CNATN regrouped for a campaign in the developing field of public health nursing as a potential new career path for CAMC veterans, consequently enhancing the future status and scope of nursing. The path was already crowded, with the St. John Ambulance and the Canadian Red Cross exploring possible outreach nursing programs in the Canadian northwest.[48] Here too, the CNATN remained anxious about the VADs, worrying that their availability might advance their chances for recruitment and "launch on the public a group of partly trained women to assume the responsibility of human life unlicensed and uncontrolled by legislation."[49] Indeed, the CNATN fear of the VADs enlarged their influence on developments in professional healthcare well beyond their wartime achievements. Ironically, the CNATN had simply failed to perceive that few VADs had any intention of continuing with nursing. Gunn and her colleagues reasoned that the limited continuation of VAD assistance in veterans' hospitals would be less damaging to nursing aspirations than their infiltration into the embryonic public health programs. In her address to the August 1919 CNATN convention, Gunn emphasized that whatever public health schemes were adopted, "we as a nursing organization have to supply the nursing personnel."[50] This goal was to be achieved by establishing the standards of qualified nursing through registration and working to elevate the professional authority of nursing through university accreditation.

Demobilization

In July 1918, as she prepared to depart for home, Sybil Johnson reflected on her experience with patients, nurses, and fellow VADs, "who were very mixed ... but one met them all on 'equal terms' and was quite at liberty to squash anyone who made herself disagreeable, which seldom happened." The patients had satisfied Sybil's standards: "So dear and good. About two men were indifferent out of all I have personally had to do with." The nursing staff received a less glowing review, revealing Sybil's ambivalence about her own performance as a VAD, her lack of conditioning as a probationer, and her privileged background:

> It is hard to understand how the nursing profession can be so variously filled. Some of the trained nurses were charming and refined, some rough but kindly and others who could not speak the King's English and who also had not the vaguest idea of what is commonly known as "manners," let alone consideration! I met specimens of all sorts, but was rather fortunate in those whom I came most in contact ... A sister could be most overbearing and positively insulting, especially in the ward before the patients, without actually giving one reason to report her to matron.[51]

The war was still raging, but Sybil knew it was time to go back to St. John's and her long-delayed marriage, and had been counting the weeks until she was to leave. She had few regrets, although other VADs had more difficulty detaching themselves emotionally from the war and their part in it. Like many VADs, Daisy Johnson delayed her departure until well after the conflict ended. She stayed on to nurse repatriated POWs in King George Hospital in London until July 1919, when the remaining two thousand men were finally transferred to more comfortable, purpose-built convalescent facilities. The hospital had been converted from His Majesty's Stationery Office, a government building with ceilings so low that patients whose beds were against the inside walls never saw the sky.[52] Daisy subsequently married a repatriated Canadian POW whom she nursed there, which accounts for the long delay in her departure.

This reluctance to leave helped fuel the notion that the VADs held a strong interest in pursuing nursing as a future career. Almost half of the Canadian and Newfoundland VADs posted abroad were still in service as late as May 1919, although many were simply working out the terms of the contracts they had signed with the Joint Women's VAD Committee. They were often redeployed to aid the slow process of demobilization and were reassigned to a variety of support roles, particularly in France where the military hospitals were rapidly dismantled following November 11, 1918. Patients who were not well enough to make the long journey home, to Canada or elsewhere, were sent to convalesce in England.

The Allied forces soon took charge of the vacated Red Cross installations and recreation huts in the former war zone. Convalescent camps were promptly converted into temporary staging centres for healthy men awaiting the discharge papers that would send them home. Red Cross support services for nursing personnel and visiting families were also rapidly evacuated. The many residences, hotels, and other buildings that had served as clubs, hostels, and convalescent homes were restored to their owners. The ambulance convoys and railway rest stations were put in the care of paid general service VADs until the final demobilization of the VAD program in the autumn of 1920.[53] No longer needed in the luxurious Deauville Officers' Home, Violet Wilson and two of her colleagues had a three-week leave before they were to report to VAD headquarters in Boulogne:

The job was done, and given three weeks leave I left with the two girls for a holiday in the south of France. They had passes to visit the trenches, and probably the first issued to any woman, it was still only December 1918. I was determined to go with them though I had no pass, and I went. Making our way to

Ypres and walking around the old trenches now deep in snow, the plain everyday misery of the war was brought back to us, and I remember my brother's description of how the rats ran around in those now deserted trenches.[54]

Following this sad pilgrimage, the rest of the trip was an adventure like no other. Unencumbered by chaperones, the three young women progressed across France, confidently dismissing the gendered constraints of the pre-war world. They spent a night in an empty POW camp, sleeping in a "deserted hut without water, toilet or heat," after accepting transport and a meal from the two officers in charge. For the next two nights, they revelled in the luxury of a chateau, headquarters of a British general who had offered them a ride in his staff car. As Violet enigmatically recounted, "wild would perhaps be a better word to describe those nights." The subsequent night found them back in a village, sleeping on camp cots in a tiny room "with a huge hole in the roof," freezing without the benefit of blankets. On the final leg of their journey, they travelled across Vimy Ridge into Amiens, where they boarded a Paris-bound train that lacked both windows and food. They were unexpectedly rescued from hunger by two former patients, who supplied them with chocolate, sardines, and gum. After a last stop in Cannes, they arrived late to Boulogne, where Violet was surprised by her warm welcome, though in the midst of the epidemic all help was needed:

> The men were coming back from the various fronts and the Flu epidemic went on, so I was welcome and no questions asked. It was a ghastly sight to see the trains come in from Germany filled with unhappy men who thought that at long last they were going home, only to be struck down at the last minute by that horrible disease. Put into a hospital at Boulogne, half of them were fated to die there, and not only the men. One worked beside a girl one day to hear the next that she was dead. The sound of the Last Post still rings in my ears, all day long and late into the night bugles could be heard.[55]

While the epidemic held sway in the Boulogne area, Violet's nursing services were much in demand in its many hospitals. As the emergency gradually subsided, the hospitals began to close, and Violet moved on to a demobilization camp in Wimereux. No longer needed for nursing, she and a general service VAD were the only women stationed at the camp amidst two thousand "tired, disillusioned, restless men." Their task was to keep the men occupied and out of trouble with recreation activities and entertainment, while they waited for the documents that would send them home. The two women shared a tiny hut with the camp sergeant-major, "supposedly as protection for us." Unfortunately, he was also the bandmaster, and the hut served as the only rehearsal space. Nearly driven mad with the noise of constant band practice, the ever resourceful Violet shrewdly invited the commanding officer to tea during a practice session, and a new rehearsal space was organized shortly thereafter. When the camp inevitably shut down, she returned to Boulogne, this time as housekeeper for the Canadian Red Cross headquarters in the Hôtel Christol. Her daily trips to the fish market for supplies would have unexpected consequences. As she recalled, "My French vocabulary increased rapidly, and quite innocently I absorbed some expressions rather in the order of the 'four-letter words.' That absolutely horrified my family when I innocently used them later in Paris." Although reluctant to abandon this carefree life, Violet dutifully returned to Canada upon learning that her mother had become ill.[56]

Although Fanny Cluett did not share Violet's free-spirited independence, she remained overseas until late October 1920, when the VAD program was finally disbanded. Her hospital in Rouen was closed in mid-1919, but she signed on again as a salaried general service VAD and was sent to the RAMC base in Constantinople, where she worked as the storekeeper. During her time as a VAD nurse, Fanny had been adamant that "nothing would induce me to give it up," and she held to this resolve until the program was terminated.[57] Others, such as Sybil Johnson, had been ready to retire before the war ended, though not all wanted to immediately abandon the heady atmosphere of wartime Europe.

In late summer 1918, Grace MacPherson worked briefly as secretary to Milly Perley at the Canadian Red Cross headquarters in London. She soon found a much better salary as the head driver for the American Military Hospital in London and managed to delay returning to Vancouver until the spring of 1919. She needed this time for "decompression," as she termed it, finding it difficult to suddenly separate herself from life abroad.[58] Jean Sears identified a similar sense of "dislocation" as the war came to an end. Like Grace, she had wanted to spend time in Europe after the armistice but was soon summoned home to help console her sister, who "was not a bit well," dealing with the loss of their brother and her own fiancé during the war. Jean did not argue; she understood where her duty lay, but "of course I wanted to stay. Peace had come and I just wanted to look around a bit, draw my breath. But I came home before Christmas."[59]

Some volunteers who had remained on the home front felt a similar reluctance to leave their VAD experience. Bessie Hall had accepted that she would not be sent overseas but hoped that she might be chosen to help escort a group of convalescent soldiers by train from Halifax to the west coast over Christmas. The rumour came to nothing, though Bessie continued her VAD work until the late spring of 1919, when the influenza crisis finally abated, loath to relinquish her cherished uniform and fade into civilian life.[60]

Retirement from VAD work brought anonymity and a loss of the unique identity as women in uniform engaged in patriotic service. Despite her concerns for the future of nursing, Jean Gunn conceded that the VADs deserved some recognition for their work. She was indignant that "no provision for a pension or any acknowledgement of the service of the volunteers has been made by the Dominion Government."[61] The Canadian Red Cross (CRCS) had been responsible for funding the VAD program during the war but was reluctant to continue in this role once hostilities ceased, as VAD Geraldine

TABLE 5.1   VAD deaths on service, at home and overseas

Name and nursing district	Date of death	Cause	Where
Bertha Bartlett, Newfoundland No. 2, St. John's	November 3, 1918	Influenza suspected	Buried Wandsworth Cemetery, London, England
Ruth Birch (Mrs. Wm. Gilbert), London, No. 4	November 1, 1918	Influenza	London, Ontario (hospital unknown)
Grace Errol Bolton, Montreal, Central No. 19	February 16, 1919	Influenza suspected	2nd Northern General Hospital, Leeds
Ethel G. Dickinson, Newfoundland, St. John's	October 26, 1918	Influenza	Grenfell Hall Emergency Hospital, St. John's
Isabel Henshaw, Beds 4, UK	June 14, 1919	Influenza suspected	Winnipeg General Hospital
Nora Young McCord (Mrs. Morgan) Toronto Central No. 1	November 28, 1918	Influenza suspected	No details
Dorothy Pearson Twist, Victoria No. 34	September 26 1918	Pneumonia/ influenza	Frensham Hill Military Hospital. Buried with full military honours, Aldershot, England

Sources: Imperial War Museum, Women at Work Collection, BRCS 25.3/10; Joseph R. Smallwood and Robert D.W. Pitt, eds., *Encyclopaedia of Newfoundland and Labrador* (St. John's: Newfoundland Book Publishers, 1981), 1:621; Obituary, "VAD Nurse Falls Victim," *St. Thomas Times-Journal*, November 4, 1918, 13.

Sewell discovered in 1924. During that year, her father petitioned the CRCS "to bear the expense of her operations and hospital treatment," attributing her health problems to her VAD work. Sewell had remained on active service abroad until June 1919, but the CRCS "would not admit any obligation," even though the St. John Ambulance had granted her three hundred dollars "on compassionate grounds."[62] The petition was rejected. For its part, the RAMC acknowledged that VAD nursing could give rise to serious health problems, a fact that is underscored by the deaths of at least seven Canadian and Newfoundland VADs from diseases that they contracted during their service (see Table 5.1).

Because the VADs were volunteers, they had no official standing with the CAMC, and it was unclear which body should compensate those who became ill or were injured during their time overseas. Their services abroad had been governed by the Joint Women's VAD Committee, as a branch of the British War Office. The War Service Badges later presented to Canadian VADs by the Order of St. John, as well as all other medals and distinctions, were awarded through the War Office. It was the same for Canadian soldiers who were presented with medals for service in the field. There were also eight Canadian VADs who had been Mentioned-in-Dispatches (see Table 5.2). This distinction was given for a specific act of valour, at the discretion of the commanding general of Allied forces. Holding particular significance for the military, it validated the work of all Canadian VADs who served overseas.

Unlike British VADs, Canadian VADs were not offered a postwar scholarship fund to train for a career in a health-related occupation. Acknowledging that many British women had sacrificed career or education to work as VADs, the Order of St. John also provided supports for those who were now unemployed or had suffered other deprivations due to the war.[63] As a public recognition, a special memorial service was held at St. Paul's Cathedral in April 1918, dedicated to the imperial nurses and VADs. The names of 340 British VADs who died on active service are also among those 1,400 women commemorated on oak screens in York Minister.[64] The name of VAD Dorothy Twist, of Shawnigan Lake, British Columbia, was also mistakenly included among those of the CAMC nursing sisters who died on active service. There was no official memorialization of VAD work in either Canada or Newfoundland, but two communities on opposite coasts chose to honour local VADs. In August 1918, after three years of VAD nursing in England, Ethel Dickinson had returned home to St. John's in poor health. She resumed her work as a teacher but was soon back in uniform when the schools were closed due to the epidemic, reopening in early October as emergency hospitals. Within a short time, she had

TABLE 5.2 Canadian VADs Mentioned-in-Dispatches

Name	Comments	Nursing district
Amy Augusta Bruce	No date	London 40 (UK) (Toronto)
Mary W.M. Gordon	January 14, 1918 (Egypt, two years), General Sir A. Murray, "for valuable service to the sick and wounded"	Fort Rouge No. 6
Alice Sophia Houston	December 21, 1917, General Sir Douglas Haig, "for gallantry in air raid in France" (59th General Hospital bombed while on duty)	Ottawa No. 32
Amy Eliza Haydon Luck	No date	No. 2/196 (UK) (Harrison Mills, BC)
Christobel Robinson	No date	Toronto (affiliation unknown)
Ellen Beatrice Scobie	December 30, 1918, General Sir Douglas Haig	Ottawa No. 32
Phyllis Madeline Taylor	Recreation huts, CAMC hospitals, France (non-nursing)	Canadian Imperials (Kingston)
Mary Maud Isobel Thomas	December 30, 1918, General Sir Douglas Haig, "valuable services in the field"	Toronto Central No. 1

Sources: St. John House Archives and Library (SJH), World War I – World War II Records: VAD Training, box X(a), "VAD Nursing Members Who Served in Military and Naval Hospitals Overseas"; SJH, SJAA, "Eleventh Annual Report, 1920," 21–22; SJH, SJAA, First Aid and the St. John Ambulance Gazette (UK) 28, no. 325 (July 1921): 12.

contracted the virus and died on October 26. Dickinson was well respected in St. John's as a teacher and for her VAD work. The community organized funds to erect a tall Celtic cross in the city's Cavendish Square, which was raised in her memory but also to honour the war service of all Newfoundland military nurses and VADs.[65] On the west coast, the small Vancouver Island community of Cobble Hill included VAD Dorothy Twist's name on the cenotaph dedicated to local fallen soldiers. Twist had succumbed to complications of influenza, contracted while she was nursing at the Frensham Hill Military Hospital in England, the first Canadian VAD who is known to have died on active service. She was accorded full military honours, as were all Allied soldiers who died

Ethel Gertrude Dickinson, c. 1914.
Courtesy of Archives and Special
Collections, Queen Elizabeth II
Library, Memorial University,
MF-329

Dorothy Twist. *Courtesy Cowichan Valley*
Museum and Archives, 2014.7.5.1

on active service, and was buried in the Aldershot Military Cemetery.[66] The
War Office medals for VADs did not arrive in Canada until November 1923,
by which time most had quietly slipped back into civilian life.[67]

Transitions

Like many soldiers, VADs often felt a restless discontent with the return to
normal conditions at the end of the war. Several initially hoped to continue
their VAD work in the Canadian convalescent hospitals. In early 1919, the
Sainte-Anne-de-Bellevue military hospital near Montreal engaged some fifty
VADs, both veterans and new recruits. Under the new WAD structure, they
were nursing assistants, masseuses, and function trainers, as well as waged
general service staff.[68] Barely twenty-one, Eugenie Marjorie Ross had been
part of the first overseas VAD contingent in 1916. After returning to Montreal
in 1917, she trained as a masseuse in one of the new programs being offered at
McGill University and the Military School of Orthopaedic Surgery and
Physiotherapy at the University of Toronto. Now Mrs. Finley, she worked as

Headstone of Dorothy
Pearson Twist, Aldershot
Military Cemetery, grave
AG 374. The insignia on
the stone is "British Red
Cross – Order of St. John."

a VAD masseuse at Sainte Anne's, transforming her wartime training into a
career in physiotherapy. She returned to Sainte Anne's during the 1940s to
establish a physiotherapy unit for a new generation of wounded Second World
War veterans.[69]

Several VADs managed to adapt their wartime experience into a range of
health-related careers. Dorothy Chown returned to Kingston, Ontario, following VAD work in the diet kitchen of an English military hospital, later
becoming a dietician in the Kingston General Hospital. Food preparation skills
had been much in demand in the overseas military hospitals during the war.
Many VADs first gained experience in the diet kitchens of the home-front
convalescent hospitals as part of their probationary training before assisting
with the patients on the wards.[70] For some, health-related careers evolved
unexpectedly out of their wartime experience. Blanche Thistle worked briefly

as a private duty nurse in St. John's until a former employer hired her as his dental nurse, initiating a new woman's healthcare occupation in Newfoundland.[71] Before leaving for overseas VAD service, Ellen Scobie worked as a press feeder for the British American Bank Note Company in Ottawa. On her return, she was promoted to the newly created position of first aid room nurse, apparently in recognition for being among the eight Canadian VADs who were Mentioned-in-Dispatches.

Although Hazel Todd did not serve abroad, as commandant of Ottawa's St. John Ambulance Nursing Division, she was responsible for the recruitment, training, and selection of all local VADs through the war years. She continued to work for the federal government during the conflict and then became the secretary of Ottawa's Social Hygiene Council.[72] Her long experience with St. John and her association with the VAD program probably helped her to secure the job. Even so, the considerable pressure on women who worked for the federal government to make room for returning veterans cannot be discounted. During the early postwar years, the VAD experience also helped shape the career path of several veterans within the St. John Ambulance (SJAA) organization itself. Marion Magee's appointment as travelling secretary to the Provincial Council of the New Brunswick Branch of SJAA rested on her "technical knowledge" of the association, resulting from her overseas VAD work. St. John records mention a further benefit of Marion's status as a VAD: the "wearing of the St. John Ambulance uniform on official occasions in this case has been found to add distinction and impressiveness to the office."[73]

The postwar career path of Mary Maude Isobel Thomas was particularly exceptional. Upon finishing her undergraduate studies in 1912, she had intended to become a teacher, but the war intervened. Serving as a VAD in both England and France, she was Mentioned-in-Dispatches and was later awarded the Royal Red Cross Medal, nursing's highest distinction. Her VAD work provided a catalyst for a medical career: returning to Canada, she entered the University of Toronto's Medical School and graduated second in her class in 1926.[74]

Her career as a medical doctor is unique among veteran Canadian VADs. Except for the handful who were later listed as "nurse" in various city directories, most left healthcare work when the war ended. Outside of marriage and motherhood, teaching and clerical occupations remained the most common postwar employment for VADs. For these young women, and thousands of others in Canada and Newfoundland, the war or the influenza epidemic had dashed their expectations of a traditional domestic future. There are many sad stories, such as that of Ruby Pinfold, who reluctantly returned to teaching as

a young widow in southwestern Ontario. She had married her Canadian soldier fiancé in England just as the war was ending. Two weeks later, and only
eleven days before the armistice, he died of influenza.[75]

A few fortunate VADs, such as Violet Wilson, used their war experience as
a springboard into new opportunities that were not related to healthcare. Violet
had no real interest in nursing, but she was eager to return to Europe, so she
applied for a Canadian government position that would send her to Scotland,
where she would work as an immigration officer. Although her VAD service
had been non-commissioned and voluntary, she trusted that the government
would accord her the same preference that male veterans received. As she
explained during a later interview, she passed the necessary public service exam
but had to wait for a ruling on her "veteran" status:

> At the time, preference in government appointments, all things being equal,
> were given to persons who served in the War, returned soldiers. The question
> now arose, did persons such as VADs, while serving with and under the Army,
> qualify? Were we literally returned soldiers? After three months pondering
> this question, the government decided we were and then I received the appoint-
> ment and went to Glasgow![76]

Violet's job was to process the transfer of war brides to Canada, and she
found the work fascinating, but after two years in Glasgow she was restless
and looking for a new challenge. She considered a marriage proposal from an
old beau – "he who had pushed me over the wall" at Gifford House – which
required becoming a poultry farmer on Vancouver Island. After one brief visit,
she knew she "didn't want to spend my life looking at the chamber-like faces
of chickens" and opted to accompany an aunt on another trip through France.
On her return, Violet began a long and varied career as a radio broadcaster,
concert promoter, public relations director at Chateau Lake Louise in Alberta,
and recreation director with an oil drilling camp in northern Alberta, a variant
on her brief time in the Wimereux demobilization camp. She finally settled
into a fifteen-year career as a European tour guide before retiring to Victoria,
British Columbia.[77]

Few women of this era, VADs or otherwise, enjoyed such an interesting
and unconventional career path. Agnes Wilson had happily exchanged teaching
for VAD service. A chance meeting on her return to Edmonton led to a new
role as secretary to the dean of arts and sciences at the University of Alberta,
despite a complete lack of clerical skills. For the first few months, Agnes spent
part of each day attending typing and shorthand classes, and remained in her

job until she married the university registrar in 1922.[78] As a rule, VADs relinquished their jobs when they married, becoming far less visible in the public record after they took on their new role as wives and mothers. There were a few exceptions: Eugenie Marjorie Ross Finley continued to work as a physiotherapist after her wedding, and Gertrude Murphy Charters, who returned to teaching after the war and subsequently married, embarked on a varied career, much like Violet Wilson. She was a prominent community activist, then the first female councillor in Grande Prairie, Alberta, and later the editor of the local newspaper.[79]

Many married VADs remained active in volunteer community work, and in the St. John Ambulance, into the next war and beyond. Daisy Johnson Cook worked as a VAD in Regina's Grey Nuns' Hospital during the Second World War. Ruby Pinfold Lawrence remarried but continued to teach in Port Stanley, Ontario, and was serving as secretary for the St. John Ambulance Nursing District in St. Thomas in 1938. Jean Sears was the social convenor for her Toronto Nursing Division in the 1930s.[80] Grace MacPherson's VAD status had qualified her for a job with the new federal Department of Soldiers' Civil Reestablishment in Vancouver, but she soon married and moved to northern British Columbia, never losing her characteristic drive and vivacity. She continued with community work in the local veterans' hospitals and according to Sandra Gwyn, marched proudly alongside the veterans in the Armistice Day parades. Like Daisy Cook, Grace was a St. John Ambulance volunteer in the next war, helping to train a new generation of VADs.[81]

Newfoundland VADs followed similar paths in the postwar era. Some were equally reluctant to give up their uniforms, whereas others returned home to work or marriage, often maintaining a public service role with the Red Cross or other community organizations. Fanny Cluett's overseas adventures began and ended with her four years as a VAD. She was one of the longest-serving VADs, remaining abroad until the program was disbanded in October 1920, finally returning home to Belleoram to resume teaching in the four-room school. She did not share Violet Wilson's restlessness, and she never married, but she was always busy. She helped to raise her orphaned nephew, continued to teach, operated a small general store, and functioned as the community's unofficial nurse.[82] By contrast, Sybil Johnson came home to marry her fiancé and take up her place as a prominent member of St. John's society, contributing her talents as violinist to many fundraising causes.[83] These women belonged to the first generation of well-educated Newfoundland women, and like all Newfoundlanders they were deeply affected by the tragedy of the Newfoundland Regiment at Beaumont Hamel, which took many of their husbands, brothers,

and fiancés. They returned from their war experience as mature, sophisticated women, and as one VAD daughter argued, they needed an outlet for
their physical and intellectual energies.[84]

Like Ruby Pinfold, Janet Miller was married and widowed in rapid suc-
cession while still overseas. In early 1915, she left St. John's, accompanied by
friends and family, to follow her brother and her fiancé, Eric Ayre, to England.
She and Eric were married in June 1915, but she was soon widowed, losing
both Eric and her brother at Beaumont Hamel on July 1, 1916. During her year
in England, she had qualified as a British Red Cross VAD nurse and trained
as a "motor driver" at the BRCS driver-testing school, hoping to join a Red
Cross ambulance convoy in France, but she chose to remain in England with
her grieving family.[85] At the end of the war, she felt "too old and out of touch"
to resume her law studies.[86] Eventually, she remarried but in the interim years
gave her energy and intellect to women's issues, working for local social and
health concerns, and for Newfoundland's burgeoning suffrage movement.[87]

Unlike Janet Miller and others who had gone overseas, home-based Newfoundland VADs had not been exposed to British feminism, but they were no
less motivated to lobby for the vote. May Kennedy was instrumental in organizing the Newfoundland suffrage movement. In the wake of the war, many
female Newfoundlanders, including former VADs, redirected their patriotic
energies toward "a reluctant Newfoundland legislature," which finally enacted
the suffrage bill in 1925.[88]

In Canada, the battle for the franchise had been fought and won well before
the last VADs returned home. Despite the long struggle to gain the vote, and
their involvement in the war, Canadian VADs had demonstrated little interest
in the suffrage movement. Jean Sears thought that the vote "was a wonderful
thing" but admitted to knowing "just a little" about the suffrage campaign.
Marjorie Starr had worked within the close confines of the ardently feminist
Scottish Women's Hospital but viewed the suffragists at Royaumont as an
ideological group quite separate from herself.[89]

Some VADs continued their St. John Ambulance connections long after the
armistice, but the postwar era saw a notable lapse of interest in volunteer nursing.[90] Although women's membership in St. John initially continued to outpace
that of the men, the numbers of nursing divisions steadily declined after 1925,
whereas the men's ambulance divisions doubled. Industrial accidents provided
an ongoing reason for maintaining an ambulance brigade, but there was little
need for a large reserve of VAD nurses in the postwar. Patriotism had motivated their VAD service, and one St. John Ambulance historian concedes that
in peacetime there was "no effective counterpart capable of calling volunteers

to humanitarian service."[91] The wartime volunteers had been united by a kinship of service, as Jay Winter argues. They shared the privilege of "standing vigil at the bedside," acting as surrogates for absent family, conscious of the responsibility this role entailed.[92] By the time the program was demobilized in late 1920, most Canadian and Newfoundland VADs had long since worked out their contracts, settling back into their former jobs, moving on to new challenges, or trading careers for domestic life.

Soon after the armistice, both St. John and the Canadian Red Cross redirected their focus toward the civilian population and new initiatives in public health and social services. The poor physical condition of the military recruits, the return of thousands of debilitated men, the recent influenza epidemic, and alarming new statistics on infant and maternal health all signalled a critical need for an effective public health infrastructure, both urban and rural. Particular attention was given to the health of children, who would become the mothers, workers, and soldiers of the future.[93] It was the qualified nurses, not VADs, who would fight these new battles. The VAD returned to the pre-war model of a St. John Ambulance Brigade nursing member, once again standing ready to assist the ambulance division at community events and tend to minor casualties or illness.[94] In the aftermath of the epidemic, community advocates had called for a register of VADs and other suitable volunteers, but women who hoped to take a leadership role in community health services now needed to look beyond the St. John Ambulance. The dominance of women in the brigade ended with the war, much as they were ushered out of the workplace to make room for returning veterans. The predominance of female membership in the brigade was a temporary phenomenon that existed solely during the war years. Afterward, women were quietly redirected to their supporting role as caregivers, with no discernible alteration in the traditional leadership role of men.[95] New female membership in the St. John Ambulance lapsed notably, as women eager for an active role in patriotic work looked to the IODE, which offered the benefit of female leadership. General interest in the St. John home nursing programs also declined, as the Canadian Red Cross, with its new peacetime mandate, took a strong organizational role in the voluntary public health sector.

Within a decade of the war, the St. John Ambulance had resumed its primary function of providing emergency ambulance and first aid services for labour and industry. Nursing activities found limited column space in its literature. In 1929, a St. John publication titled *Canadian First Aid* ran a brief article about "Miss Ellen Scobie, nurse at the Canadian Bank Note Company," who had been praised by an Ottawa medical specialist for her recent treatment of an eye injury. Although the article mentioned that Scobie had been a VAD and underscored her appointment as "head of first aid services for the company" as being more than honorary, it supplied no details regarding her war work.[96] Over time, veteran VADs who had maintained their connection with St. John were increasingly relegated to the footnotes, if they were mentioned at all.

This pattern also occurred in Britain. Anne Summers argues that VADs and other British women who had enjoyed an unaccustomed independence and freedom of choice during the war had largely been manipulated into serving the state. Once their service was no longer needed, they were shunted back into the private domain, where they presented no threat to traditional masculine dominance in the public sphere.[97] As the 1920s progressed, the qualified "expert" was increasingly called on for advice or assistance in matters of health. The Canadian Red Cross nursing stations and outpost hospitals in rural and western Canada would be staffed only by qualified public health nursing personnel. The VADs gradually faded into the shadows, to be recalled in their full regalia only for official functions or veterans' parades, as a backdrop to the larger story of the St. John Ambulance.[98] Their aid was much appreciated, their excellent work had won these "Very Able Darlings" accolades from the organizations that harnessed their energy, and they had helped returning veterans transition from war hospitals into rehabilitative care.[99] For a time, their names were inscribed on volunteer registries for future emergencies, but the war work was done and they were expected to return to the status quo.

Contrary to the predictions of the CNATN, the VADs did not pose a threat to the jobs of qualified nurses. In the immediate postwar years, nursing registration was completed across Canada, and the CNATN worked diligently to elevate the training standards to the university level, particularly in the developing field of public health. The nurses embraced the new public health opportunities, but retired VADs were excluded. The era of the well-meaning amateur volunteer was ending – qualified experts would dominate the new women's healthcare professions.

The end of the war also ended the sense of common purpose shared by all, at home and overseas. After the first heady hours of celebration, it was time to adapt to the new realities of peace. The VADs, particularly those who had served overseas, had a unique experience of the war, but now they were expected to put it behind them and return to diffidence and domesticity.

For many, this was neither desirable nor possible. Violet Wilson and her peers had enjoyed their independence and were still eager for new challenges. They often found that the social conservatism of the postwar era limited their life choices to teaching, nursing, or social work. Many returned to civilian life to become the working girls of the 1920s, the activist western farm wives of the 1930s, and the mothers of the peace movement as the next war loomed. It is hardly by chance that theirs was the first generation of Canadian women to take a seat in Parliament or fight for a place in the Senate as fully recognized "persons."

As the war began, the VADs had donned their crisp new uniforms with enthusiasm and pride, buoyed by a sense of adventure and a determination to prove their usefulness as bedside warriors. In the aftermath of war, many found the return to peace an uncertain and difficult process. They might have agreed with Alice Bray, as she prepared to leave her VAD life behind: "There seems to be a sadness in saying Good-bye to it all ... It is like saying Good-bye to a chapter in your life forever really."[100]

APPENDICES

APPENDIX I

British Red Cross Nursing Manual, No. 2

CONTENTS

CHAPTER   PAGE

1. THE NURSE 1

2. CHOICE OF THE SICK-ROOM—VENTILATION,
   ETC. 5

3. PREPARATION OF ROOM FOR RECEPTION OF
   PATIENTS 11

4. BEDS AND BEDDING 16

5. DETAILS OF NURSING 23

6. FEEDING THE PATIENT 33

7. INVALID DIET 40

8. MEDICINES AND THEIR ADMINISTRATION . 46

9. THE TEMPERATURE OF THE BODY—FEVER 53

10. THE PULSE 62

11. RESPIRATION 66

12. BATHS AND BATHING 75

13. INFLAMMATION 85

14. INFECTION AND INFECTIOUS DISEASES . 104

15. DISINFECTANTS AND DISINFECTION . . 124

CONTENTS

CHAPTER   PAGE

16. SURGICAL INSTRUMENTS AND APPLIANCES . 132

17. SUBSTANCES USED IN DRESSING WOUNDS . 141

18. THE NURSE'S DUTIES BEFORE, DURING, AND
    AFTER OPERATION 144

19. ROLLER BANDAGES 150

20. MOVING WOUNDED OR INJURED PATIENTS
    INDOORS—LAYING OUT THE DEAD . 182

APPENDIX 187

INDEX 213

Source: James Cantlie, *British Red Cross Society Nursing Manual, No. 2* (London: Cassell, 1914). Copy belonging to Eugenie Marjorie Ross, Woodlands, Quebec, May 1915, by kind permission of her late son E.G. Finley, Ottawa.

APPENDIX 2

St. John Ambulance Brigade Syllabus of Instruction

ADULT COURSE.

SYLLABUS OF INSTRUCTION—FIRST AID TO THE INJURED.

FIRST LECTURE.

A. Principles of First Aid.
B. A brief Description of the Human Skeleton and of the Muscles.
C. Fractures—Causes, varieties, signs, and symptoms.
D. Treatment of Fractures—General Rules.
E. The Triangular Bandage and its application.

SECOND LECTURE.

A. Treatment of Fractures (continued)—Details of treatment.
B. Dislocations, Sprains—Signs, symptoms and treatment.
C. The Heart and Blood Vessels. The Circulation of the Blood.
D. Hemorrhage and wounds—General rules for treatment.
E. The Triangular Bandage and its application.

THIRD LECTURE.

A. Hemorrhage and wounds (continued)—Details of treatment.
B. Internal Hemorrhage—Signs, symptoms and arrest.
C. Hemorrhage from Special Regions—Signs, symptoms and arrest.
D. Bruises, Burns and Scalds, Bites and Stings, Frost-bite.
E. Foreign bodies in the Eye, Nose and Ear.
F. The Triangular Bandage and its application.

FOURTH LECTURE.

A. The Nervous System.
B. The Organs and Mechanism of Respiration—Artificial Respiration.
C. Insensibility.
D. Poisoning.

FIFTH LECTURE (FOR MALES ONLY).

A. Improvised methods of lifting and carrying the sick or injured.
B. Methods of lifting and carrying the injured on stretchers.
C. The conveyance of such by rail or in country carts.

FIFTH LECTURE (FOR FEMALES ONLY).

A. Preparation for reception of accident cases.
B. Means of lifting and carrying.
C. Preparation of bed.
D. Removing the clothes.
E. Preparation for surgeon.

ST. JOHN HOME NURSING COURSE. SYLLABUS OF LECTURES.

LECTURE I. THE SICK ROOM.

Introductory Remarks, Selection, preparation and cleaning of room, Bed and bedding. Furnishing, Warming and Ventilation.
The roller bandage, and its application.

LECTURE II. INFECTION AND DISINFECTION.

Infectious and non-infectious cases, Quarantine of patient, History of a fever case, Disinfecting and Disinfectants.
The roller bandage, and its application.

LECTURE III. DETAILS OF NURSING.

The nurse, Regulation of visitors, Management of nurse's own health, Washing and dressing patients, Bed making, Changing sheets, Lifting helpless patients, Sick diet, Administration of food, medicines and stimulants.
The roller bandage, and its application.

LECTURE IV. DETAILS OF NURSING (continued).

Observation of the Sick, Rigors, Sleep, Pain, Posture, Skin, Appetite, Vomiting, Cough, Expectoration, Effects of remedies, etc., Temperature taking, Baths, Bed-sores, Delirium, Nursing sick children, What to prepare for the Physician's and Surgeon's visits.
The roller bandage, and its application.

LECTURE V. APPLICATION OF LOCAL REMEDIES.

Poultices, Fomentations, Blisters, Ointment, Leeches, Padding splints, Bandaging, Personal and family hygiene, Management of convalescents.

Source: Archives of Ontario, MU 6858, "Annual Report for 1913 of the St. John Ambulance Brigade Overseas within the Dominion of Canada," 23.

APPENDIX 3

The Grand Priory of
The Order of the Hospital of St. John of Jerusalem in England.

AMBULANCE DEPARTMENT.

The St. John Ambulance Brigade Overseas

WITHIN THE DOMINION OF CANADA

DEPUTY COMMISSIONER:
IRIG.-GENERAL SIR HENRY M. PELLATT, C.V.O., D.C.L.

ASSISTANT COMMISSIONER, ONTARIO DISTRICT:
CHARLES J. COPP, M.D., M.R.C.S.

554½ YONGE STREET

Toronto, Canada, Jan. 25th, 1918

Miss Gwendolyn Powys,

    Fort Rouge Nursing Division, No. 6.,

Madam:-

        On the occasion of your departure on Special Overseas
Service as probationer in the Naval and Military Hospitals in England,
for the duration of the War, the Deputy Commissioner for the Brigade
Overseas, within the Dominion of Canada, and your Officers, wish you
every success as you go forward to assist in the great cause which
our Empire has so deeply at heart.

        That you will discharge your duty to your King and Country,
to the Brigade Overseas, and to yourself, is expected; and that you
will uphold the traditions and glory of Canada's womanhood, whom you
represent, is known. It is the sincere desire of those who send you
forward that you will discharge whatever duty and responsibility is
reposed in you with the determined purpose to at all times give your
best. We trust you, and shall await in no uncertain confidence the
report of your service.

        You are on Military Service and will owe obedience to the
Officers under whom you serve. You will wear the uniform provided
from the time of mobilization until discharged unless otherwise
ordered.

        You will sail from   Halifax   under Dr. M.
Ellen Douglass,   Officer-in-Charge, Canadian Volunteer Probationer
Nurses. You will owe obedience to her until such time as she shall
have transferred you to the Commandant-in-Chief, Joint Women's V.A.D.s.
-Mrs. Lady. Ampthill---- Devonshire House, Piccadilly, London, W., under
whose command you will then serve.

        When the time comes for you to return to Canada, you should
apply to the Chief Commissioner, Brigade Overseas, St. John's Gate,
Clerkenwell, who will make arrangements for your return. When you return
to Canada, report of your return must be made to this office.

        I have the honour to be,

        Madam,

        Your obedient servant,

CJC/EMS.

        Assistant Commissioner, Dis't. of Ont.
        For the Deputy Commissioner.

In this letter to VAD Gwen Powys, Dr. Charles Copp outlined the expectations of her overseas service. *Used with permission of Gwen Powys's daughters Frances Powys MacNeil and Marjorie A. Cunliffe North and granddaughter-in-law Debra B. North*

APPENDIX 4

407/4

No...**1614**

*This paper is to be considered by each V.A.D. member as
confidential and to be kept in her Pocket Book.*

You are being sent to work for the Red Cross. You have to
perform a task which will need your courage, your energy, your
patience, your humility, your determination to overcome all
difficulties.

Remember that the honour of the V.A.D. organisation depends on
your individual conduct.

It will be your duty not only to set an example of discipline and
perfect steadiness of character, but also to maintain the most
courteous relations with those whom you are helping in this great
struggle.

Be invariably courteous, considerate, unselfish and kind.

Remember that whatever duty you undertake, you must carry it
out faithfully, loyally, and to the best of your ability.

Rules and regulations are necessary in whatever formation you
join. Comply with them without grumble or criticism and try to
believe that there is reason at the back of them though at the time
you may not understand the necessity.

Sacrifices may be asked of you.

Give generously and whole-heartedly, grudging nothing, but
remembering that you are giving because your Country needs your
help.

If you see others in better circumstances than yourself, be patient
and think of the men who are fighting amid discomfort and who
are often in great pain.

Those of you who are paid can give to the Red Cross Society
which is your Mother and which needs more and more money to
carry on its great work.

Those of you who are not paid are giving their best to their
Mother Society and thus to the Sick and Wounded.

Let our mottoes be—"Willing to do anything" and "The People
gave gladly."

If we live up to these, the V.A.D. members will come out of this
world-war triumphant.

Do your duty loyally.
Fear God.
Honour the King.

KATHARINE FURSE,
Commandant-in-Chief. B.R.C.S. Women's V.A.D.'s.

Document given to every VAD on active service by Dame Katharine Furse. *Courtesy
British Red Cross Society Museum and Archives, acc.1407/4*

NOTES

INTRODUCTION

1 The identification by name of Canadian and Newfoundland VADs now exceeds nine hundred. In her "Lectures on the History of Nursing," *Canadian Nurse* 19, no. 3 (March 1923): 149, Maude E. Seymour Abbott, M.D., states that 2,500 Canadian VADs served on the home front. No official lists or statistics were compiled by the St. John Ambulance Brigade (SJAB), the Canadian Red Cross Society, or the British Red Cross Society (BRCS) to confirm the exact number of Canadian and Newfoundland VADs at home or overseas. Current estimates for the total number of VADs are based on a combination of the BRCS Personnel Record Indexes, unofficial lists for overseas VADs compiled by SJAB in Ottawa, and other contemporary sources, including city directories. Recent additions have been located via genealogical researchers and family members. Although VADs tended to be nursing assistants, many were hospital clerical workers, ambulance and motor drivers, hospital social convenors, canteen workers, and massage therapists. Original records of Allied women's volunteer work in the war are rare, with the exception of the Imperial War Museum's invaluable Women at Work Collection.

2 Only the British Red Cross VADs wore a red cross on their aprons, but they far outnumbered the St. John Ambulance VADs in Britain, and this distinctive symbol dominated the popular perception of the VAD. A few St. John VAD official nursing division photographs show red crosses on the apron bibs, but close inspection reveals that these are irregular and were sewn on by the women themselves, not printed into the cloth.

3 Vera Brittain, *Testament of Youth: An Autobiographical Study of the Years 1900-1925* (1933, repr., London: Fontana, 1979); Alan Bishop, ed., *Chronicle of Youth: Vera Brittain's War Diary, 1913-1917* (London: Victor Gollancz, 1981).

4 Deborah Gorham, *Vera Brittain: A Feminist Life* (Toronto: University of Toronto Press, 2000); Alan Bishop and Mark Bostridge, eds., *Letters from a Lost Generation: First World War Letters of Vera Brittain and Four Friends* (London: Abacus/Little Brown, 1999); Enid

Bagnold, *A Diary without Dates: Thoughts and Impressions of a VAD* (London: Heinemann, 1918); Olive Dent, *A VAD in France* (London: Grant Richards, 1917); Henriette Donner, "Under the Cross: Why VADs Performed the Filthiest Tasks in the Dirtiest War: Red Cross Women Volunteers, 1914-1918," *Journal of Social History* 30, no. 3 (Spring 1997): 687–704. For recent analysis of British VADs and nurses, see Janet S.K. Watson, *Fighting Different Wars: Experience, Memory, and the First World War in Britain* (Cambridge: Cambridge University Press, 2004); Christine E. Hallett, *Containing Trauma: Nursing Work in the First World War* (Manchester: Manchester University Press, 2009); Sharon Ouditt, *Fighting Forces, Writing Women: Identity and Ideology in the First World War* (New York: Routledge, 1994), Chapter 1; and Sandra M. Gilbert, "Soldier's Heart: Literary Men, Literary Women, and the Great War," in *Behind the Lines: Gender and the Two World Wars*, ed. Margaret R. Higonnet et al. (New Haven: Yale University Press, 1987), 197–226.

5 For Canadian and Newfoundland VADs, see "Bessie Hall, 1890-1969," in *No Place Like Home: Diaries and Letters of Nova Scotia Women, 1771-1938*, ed. Margaret Conrad, Toni Laidlaw, and Donna Smyth (Halifax: Formac, 1988), 242–60; Sandra Gwyn, "The Education of Grace MacPherson," in Sandra Gwyn, *Tapestry of War: A Private View of Canadians in the Great War* (Toronto: Harper Collins, 1992), 435–60; Bill Rompkey and Bert Riggs, eds., *Your Daughter Fanny: The War Letters of Frances Cluett, VAD* (St. John's: Flanker Press, 2006); and Sarah Glassford and Amy Shaw, eds., *A Sisterhood of Suffering and Service: Women and Girls of Canada and Newfoundland during the First World War* (Vancouver: UBC Press, 2012). On home-front experience, see Ian Hugh Maclean Miller, *Our Glory and Our Grief: Torontonians and the Great War* (Toronto: University of Toronto Press, 2002); Desmond Morton, *Fight or Pay: Soldiers' Families in the Great War* (Vancouver: UBC Press, 2004); Robert Allen Rutherdale, *Hometown Horizons: Local Responses to Canada's Great War* (Vancouver: UBC Press, 2004); James M. Pitsula, *For All We Have and Are: Regina and the Experience of the Great War* (Winnipeg: University of Manitoba Press, 2008); and Jim Blanchard, *Winnipeg's Great War: A City Comes of Age* (Winnipeg: University of Manitoba Press, 2010). Susan R. Fisher, *Boys and Girls in No Man's Land: English Canadian Children and the First World War* (Toronto: University of Toronto Press, 2011).

6 For the CAMC nursing sisters, see Susan Mann, ed., *The War Diary of Clare Gass, 1915-1918* (Montreal and Kingston: McGill-Queen's University Press, 2000); Susan Mann, *Margaret Macdonald: Imperial Daughter* (Montreal and Kingston: McGill-Queen's University Press, 2005); Andrea McKenzie, ed., *War-Torn Exchanges: The Lives and Letters of Nursing Sisters Laura Holland and Mildred Forbes* (Vancouver: UBC Press, 2016); Cynthia Toman, *Sister Soldiers of the Great War: The Nurses of the Canadian Army Medical Corps* (Vancouver: UBC Press, 2016); and Cynthia Toman, "A Loyal Body of Empire Citizens: Military Nurses and Identity at Lemnos and Salonika, 1915–1917," in *Place and Practice in Canadian Nursing History*, ed. Jayne Elliott, Meryn Stuart, and Cynthia Toman (Vancouver: UBC Press, 2008), 8–24.

7 For other war workers, see Patricia A. Staton, *It Was Their War Too: Canadian Women and World War I* (Toronto: Green Dragon Press, 2006); Joan Sangster, "Mobilizing Women for War," in *Canada and the First World War: Essays in Honour of Robert Craig Brown*, ed. David MacKenzie (Toronto: University of Toronto Press, 2005), 157–93; Linda J. Quiney, "'Bravely and Loyally They Answered the Call': St. John Ambulance, the Red Cross, and the Patriotic Service of Canadian Women during the Great War," *History of Intellectual Culture* 5, no. 1 (2005), http://www.ucalgary.ca/hic/; Debbie Marshall, *Give Your Other*

Vote to the Sister: A Woman's Journey into the Great War (Calgary: University of Calgary Press, 2007); and Sarah Carlene Glassford, "'The Greatest Mother in the World': Carework and the Discourse of Mothering in the Canadian Red Cross Society during the First World War," *Journal of the Association for Research on Mothering* 10, no. 1 (2008): 219–32.

8 Sarah Glassford and Amy Shaw, "Introduction: Transformation in a Time of War?" in Glassford and Shaw, *A Sisterhood of Suffering*, 7–8.

9 John F. Hutchinson, *Champions of Charity: War and the Rise of the Red Cross* (Boulder: Westview, 1996), 350–51, 354.

10 Charles Dickens, *Martin Chuzzlewit, 1843*. A slovenly and drunken character, Sarah Gamp became a stereotype of the untrained, non-professional nurse.

11 Lynn McDonald, "Florence Nightingale a Hundred Years On: Who She Was and What She Was Not," *Women's History Review* 19, no. 5 (November 2010): 721–40; Mark Bostridge, *Florence Nightingale: The Making of an Icon* (New York: Farrar, Strauss and Giroux, 2008); Sioban Nelson and Anne Marie Rafferty, eds., *Notes on Nightingale: The Influence and Legacy of a Nursing Icon* (Ithaca, NY: ILR Press, 2010); Louise Penner, *Victorian Medicine and Social Reform: Florence Nightingale among the Novelists* (New York: Palgrave Macmillan, 2010).

12 Gail Braybon and Penny Summerfield, *Out of the Cage: Women's Experiences in Two World Wars* (London: Pandora, 1987); Nicole Ann Drombrowski, ed., *Women and War in the Twentieth Century: Enlisted with or without Consent* (New York: Garland Press, 1999); Susan R. Grayzel, *Women's Identities at War: Gender, Motherhood and Politics in Britain and France during the First World War* (Chapel Hill: University of North Carolina Press, 1999); Angela K. Smith, *The Second Battlefield: Women, Modernism and the First World War* (Manchester: Manchester University Press, 2000); Cynthia Enloe, *Does Khaki Become You? The Militarization of Women's Lives* (London: Southland Press, 1983); Cynthia Enloe, *Maneuvers: The International Politics of Militarizing Women's Lives* (Berkeley: University of California Press, 2000); Margaret Vining and Barton C. Hacker, "From Camp Follower to Lady in Uniform: Women, Social Class and Military Institutions before 1920," *Contemporary European History* 10, no. 3 (2001): 353–73.

13 G.W.L. Nicholson, *Canada's Nursing Sisters* (Toronto: Samuel Stevens Hakkert and Company, 1975); Anne Summers, *Angels and Citizens: British Women as Military Nurses, 1854-1914* (Newbury: Threshold Press, 2000); Jan Bassett, *Guns and Brooches: Australian Army Nursing from the Boer War to the Gulf War* (New York: Oxford University Press, 1992); Patricia Donahue, "Reflections on the Changing Image of Nurses in Wartime," *Caduceus: A Humanities Journal for Medicine and the Health Sciences* 11, no. 1 (1995): 53–58; Mary T. Sarnecky, *A History of the U.S. Army Nurse Corps* (Philadelphia: University of Pennsylvania Press, 1999); Anna Rogers, *While You Are Away: New Zealand Nurses at War, 1899-1948* (Auckland, NZ: Auckland University Press, 2003); Mercedes Graf, *On the Field of Mercy: Women Medical Volunteers from the Civil War to the First World War* (Amherst, NY: Humanity Books, 2010).

14 Nicholson, *Canada's Nursing Sisters*, 4, 33–37; E.A. Landells, ed., *The Military Nurses of Canada: Recollections of Canadian Military Nurses* (White Rock, BC: Co-publishing, 1995), 1:2–5; Mary W. Rode, "The Nursing Pin: Symbol of 1,000 Years of Service," *Nursing Forum* 24, no. 1 (January 1989): 15–17.

15 Summers, *Angels and Citizens*, 24.

16 Kathryn McPherson, *Bedside Matters: The Transformation of Canadian Nursing, 1900-1990* (Toronto: University of Toronto Press, 2003).

17 Ibid., 6; Natalie Riegler, *Jean I. Gunn: Nursing Leader* (Toronto: A.M.S. and Fitzhenry and Whiteside, ed., 1997); Judi Coburn, "'I See and I Am Silent': A Short History of Nursing in Ontario," in *Women at Work: Ontario, 1850-1930,* ed. Janice Acton, Penny Goldsmith, and Bonnie Shepard (Toronto: Canadian Women's Educational Press, 1974), 127–63; David Coburn, "The Development of Canadian Nursing: Professionalization and Proletarianization," *International Journal of Health Services* 18, no. 3 (1988): 437–56.

18 Barbara Melosh, *"The Physician's Hand": Work Culture and Conflict in American Nursing* (Philadelphia: Temple University Press, 1982); JoAnn Whittaker, "The Search for Legitimacy: Nurses' Registration in British Columbia, 1913-1935," in *Not Just Pin Money: Selected Essays on the History of Women's Work in British Columbia,* ed. B.K. Latham and R. Pazdro (Victoria: Camosun College, 1984), 315–26; Susan M. Reverby, *Ordered to Care: The Dilemma of American Nursing, 1850-1945* (Cambridge: Cambridge University Press, 1987); Celia Davies, *Rewriting Nursing History* (London: Croom Helm, 1989); Pauline Jardine, "An Urban Middle-Class Calling: Women and the Emergence of Modern Nursing Education at the Toronto General Hospital, 1881-1914," *Urban History Review* 17, no. 3 (February 1989): 179–90.

19 McPherson notes that the Canadian census listed 227 men as nurses between 1921 and 1941. McPherson, *Bedside Matters,* 116.

20 Margaret Darrow, *French Women and the First World War: War Stories of the Home Front* (Oxford: Berg, 2000); Margaret Darrow, "French Volunteer Nursing and the Myth of War Experience in World War I," *American Historical Review* 101, no. 1 (February 1996): 80–106; Janet S.K. Watson, "Khaki Girls, VADs and Tommy's Sisters: Gender and Class in First World War Britain," *International History Review* 19, no. 1 (February 1997): 32–50; and Janet S.K. Watson, "Wars in the Wards: The Social Construction of Medical Work in First World War Britain," *Journal of British Studies* 41, no. 4 (October 2002): 484–510.

21 Classic studies of Victorian-era women's service ethic include Nancy Cott, *The Bonds of Womanhood: "Woman's Sphere" in New England, 1780-1835* (New Haven: Yale University Press, 1977); Jane Lewis, *Women and Social Action in Victorian and Edwardian England* (Aldershot, UK: Edward Elgar, 1991); and Mariana Valverde, *The Age of Light, Soap, and Water: Moral Reform in English Canada, 1885-1925* (Toronto: McClelland and Stewart, 1991). For gender and work, see Louise A. Tilly and Joan W. Scott, *Women, Work and Family* (New York: Routledge, 1987); and Joan Wallach Scott, *Gender and the Politics of History* (New York: Columbia University Press, 1999).

22 Gwen Szychter, "The War Work of Women in Rural British Columbia, 1914-1919," *British Columbia Historical News* 27, no. 4 (Fall 1994): 8–9; Ceta Ramkhalawansingh, "Women during the Great War," in *Women at Work: Ontario, 1850-1930,* ed. Janice Acton, Barbara Shepard, and Penny Goldsmith (Toronto: Canadian Women's Educational Press, 1974), 261–307; Daphne Read, ed., *The Great War and Canadian Society: An Oral History* (Toronto: New Hogtown Press, 1978); Sangster, "Mobilizing Women for War," 157–93.

23 Barbara M. Wilson, ed., *Ontario and the First World War: A Collection of Documents* (Toronto: University of Toronto Press, 1977), lxxxvi; Gale Denise Warren, "The Patriotic Association of the Women of Newfoundland, 1914-1918," *Aspects* 33, no. 2 (Summer 1998): 23–32; Margot I. Duley, "The Unquiet Knitters of Newfoundland: From Mothers of the Regiment to Mothers of the Nation," in Glassford and Shaw, *A Sisterhood of Suffering,* 5–74; Terry Wilde, "Freshettes, Farmerettes, and Feminine Fortitude at the University of Toronto during the First World War," in Glassford and Shaw, *A Sisterhood of Suffering,* 75–97; Linda

J. Quiney, "'We Must Not Neglect Our Duty': Enlisting Women Undergraduates for the Red Cross during the Great War," in *Cultures, Communities and Conflict: Histories of Canadian Universities and War*, ed. Paul Stortz and E. Lisa Panayotidis (Toronto: University of Toronto Press, 2012), 71–94.

24 This attitude is epitomized in the official history of the wartime work of the Canadian Red Cross. Chapter 5 is titled "A Mothering Bureau" in reference to the work of both the VADs and the Canadian Red Cross Information Bureau in London under the direction of Lady Julia Drummond. See Mary MacLeod Moore, *The Maple Leaf's Red Cross: The War Story of the Canadian Red Cross Overseas* (London: Skeffington and Son, 1920), 67–85.

25 Watson, *Fighting Different Wars*, 6.

26 Alan R. Young, "'We Throw the Torch': Canadian Memorials of the Great War and the Mythology of Heroic Sacrifice," *Journal of Canadian Studies* 24, no. 4 (Winter 1989–90): 5–28. Only mothers of fallen sons made the "supreme sacrifice" and were rewarded with "undying glory" like their sons. See Wealtha A. Wilson and Ethel T. Raymond, "Canadian Women in the Great War," in *Canada in the Great War*, vol. 6, *Special Services, Heroic Deeds, Etc.* (Toronto: United Publishers of Canada, 1921), 177. The language of war as applied to women is discussed in Olive Dent, "How Women Rallied to the Call," in *The War Illustrated: A Pictorial Record of the Conflict of the Nations*, ed. J.A. Hammerton (London: Amalgamated Press, 1918), 9: 111.

27 Watson, *Fighting Different Wars*, 61.

28 As of April 1918, 350 VADs were listed on the official Roll of Honour for the Allied Services. See Imperial War Museum (IWM), Women at Work Collection, BRCS 25.5.4/26, "Memorial Service for Nurses Who Have Fallen in the War," April 10, 1918.

29 Olive Dent, "On Home Service," in Hammerton, *The War Illustrated*, 9:175.

30 The concept of a "warrior on the wards" is from Watson, "Wars in the Wards", 495; and Watson, *Fighting Different Wars*, 94.

31 McPherson, *Bedside Matters*, 17, 210–11.

32 IWM, Women at Work Collection, BRCS 2/18, "Terms of Service." The age restriction for home service (including in Britain) was twenty-one to forty-eight years, whereas it was twenty-three to forty-two years for foreign service.

33 McPherson, *Bedside Matters*, 17.

34 Summers, *Angels and Citizens*, 175, 212–32; Mann, *Margaret Macdonald*, 37–51; Sheila Gray, *The South African War, 1899–1902: Service Records of British and Colonial Women* (Auckland, NZ: self-published, 1993).

35 Maureen Judge, dir., *And We Knew How to Dance: Women in World War I* (Montreal: National Film Board of Canada, 1994).

36 British Red Cross Society (BRCS) Museum and Archives, Personnel Record Indexes, http://www.redcross.org.uk/about-us/who-we-are/museum-and-archives/resources-for-researchers/volunteers-and-personnel-records.

37 These include the letters of Elizabeth (Bessie) Hall from Halifax, Nova Scotia, to family in Bridgewater, Nova Scotia, and the letters of Dorothy Macphail to her father, Sir Andrew Macphail, overseas with the Canadian Army Medical Corps (CAMC). See Nova Scotia Archives (NSA), McGregor-Miller Collection, MG1, vol. 661; and Library and Archives Canada (LAC), Sir Andrew Macphail fonds, MG 30, D 150, Dorothy Macphail Letters, 1915–18.

38 The British Red Cross does not claim that the index is a complete record of VAD service. My identification of Newfoundland and Canadian VADs has been supplemented with information and documents acquired through personal contact with family members and other interested researchers.

39 This term "new woman" was used to describe the emerging late-nineteenth-century model of young, educated middle-class women, often employed and some demonstrating feminist interests. See Gail Cuthbert Brandt, Naomi Black, Paula Bourne, and Magda Fahrni, *Canadian Women: A History*, 3rd ed. (Toronto: Nelson Education, 2010), Chapter 7.

40 "Small army" is borrowed from a 1922 letter to the *Ottawa Journal*, which reads as follows: "Several hundred of our graduates in Home Nursing and First Aid rendered splendid voluntary assistance during the Great War in British Hospitals, where they served with thousands of their British confreres as VADs; indeed, the British hospitals could not have carried on without the aid given by this small army of 'volunteer nurses.'" Director General, St. John Ambulance Association, Letter to the editor, *Ottawa Journal*, c. January 1922, reprinted in St. John House Archives and Library, St. John Ambulance Association, *First Aid Bulletin* 3, no. 2 (February 1922): 3.

CHAPTER 1: THIS ARDENT BAND OF LADIES

1 G.W.L. Nicholson, *The White Cross in Canada: A History of St. John Ambulance* (Montreal: Harvest House, 1967), 33–34; John F. Hutchinson, *Champions of Charity: War and the Rise of the Red Cross* (Boulder: Westview, 1996).

2 The Dominion Council of the St. John Ambulance Association was established in 1897, with Surgeon-Lieutenant-Colonel George Sterling Ryerson as general secretary. See Strome Galloway, *The White Cross in Canada, 1883–1983: A History of St. John Ambulance, Centennial Edition* (Ottawa: St. John Priory, 1983), 28–29.

3 Christopher McCreery, *The Maple Leaf and the White Cross* (Toronto: Dundurn Press, 2008), 35–36. In 1892, the surgeon-captain of the military hospital in Halifax promoted the founding of a local St. John Ambulance, hoping to augment the limited resources of the Military Ambulance Corps with a paramilitary ambulance service. St. John House Archives and Library (SJH), Constitution and General Regulations of the St. John Ambulance Association Canadian Branch, 1910, 1–3; Deanna Toxopeus, "Women in the St. John Ambulance Brigade, 1916-1990: A Study of Change in a Conservative Organisation" (unpublished paper, Carleton University, Ottawa, 1994).

4 McCreery, *The Maple Leaf and the White Cross*, 45–65; Anne Summers, *Angels and Citizens: British Women as Military Nurses, 1854-1914* (Newbury: Threshold Press, 2000), 212.

5 Agatha Christie, *Agatha Christie: An Autobiography* (New York: Dodd, Mead, 1977), 209.

6 Elise Chenier, "Class, Gender, and the Social Standard: The Montreal Junior League, 1912-1939," *Canadian Historical Review* 90, no. 4 (December 2009): 687–89.

7 Library and Archives Canada (LAC), Voice of the Pioneer, 9861, acc. 1981–0111, Violet Wilson Interview, c. 1970. Wilson was the daughter of Dr. Herbert C. Wilson, a prominent Edmonton physician and politician (d. 1909). Aged twenty-four in 1914, she had recently returned from a year of travel overseas.

8 Canadian Red Cross Society, *What the Canadian Red Cross Society Is Doing in the Great War: Being an Outline of the Organization and Work of the Canadian Red Cross Society* (Toronto: Canadian Red Cross Society, 1918), 5, 8.
9 Sarah Carlene Glassford, "'The Greatest Mother in the World': Carework and the Discourse of Mothering in the Canadian Red Cross Society during the First World War," *Journal of the Association for Research on Mothering* 10, no. 1 (2008): 221–22; Gwen Szychter, "The War Work of Women in Rural British Columbia, 1914-1919," *British Columbia Historical News* 27, no. 4 (Fall 1994): 8; Natalie Riegler, "Sphagnum Moss in World War I: The Making of Surgical Dressings by Volunteers in Toronto, Canada, 1917-1918," *Canadian Bulletin of Medical History* 6, no. 1 (1989): 27–43; Canadian Red Cross National Archive (CRCNA), Canadian Red Cross Society, *Bulletin* (vol. 1, April 1915–vol. 41, January 1919); Mary MacLeod Moore, *The Maple Leaf's Red Cross: The War Story of the Canadian Red Cross Overseas* (London: Skeffington and Son, 1920), 37–47; Veronica J. Strong-Boag, *The Parliament of Women: The National Council of Women of Canada, 1893-1929* (Ottawa: National Museums of Canada, 1976), 240–42.
10 Summers, *Angels and Citizens*, 170; Mariana Valverde, *The Age of Light, Soap, and Water: Moral Reform in English Canada, 1885-1925* (Toronto: McClelland and Stewart, 1991).
11 Archives of Ontario (AO), MU 6858, "Annual Report for 1913 of the St. John Ambulance Brigade Overseas within the Dominion of Canada," St. John Ambulance Association, file, Amelia K. Prentice, 21.
12 Ibid., 14.
13 Brian D. Tennyson, *Canada's Great War, 1914-1918: How Canada Helped Save the British Empire and Became a North American Nation* (Lanham, MD: Rowman and Littlefield, 2015) 28. The army's senior command structure was reorganized in 1904 to create a Militia Council modelled on the British Army Council. The council had seven members that included the minister of militia and defence and six senior members of the department. See also "Canadian Military History Gateway," www.cmhg-phmc.gc.ca.
14 *The Organization of Voluntary Medical Aid in Canada* (Ottawa: Government Printing Bureau, 1914). See also Imperial War Museum (IWM), Women at Work Collection, BRCS 1/5, "St. John Ambulance Association Report of the Ambulance Committee, 1916," 32.
15 The three nursing divisions were in Toronto, Owen Sound, and Winnipeg.
16 Gale Wills, *A Marriage of Convenience: Business and Social Work in Toronto, 1918-1957* (Toronto: University of Toronto Press, 1995), 14.
17 *Scheme for the Organization of Voluntary Aid in England and Wales* (London: H.M.S.O., 1909). The scheme was revised and finalized in 1910 under the same title.
18 McCreery, *The Maple Leaf and the White Cross*, 64–65, 85–88; Cassie Brown, *Death on the Ice: The Great Newfoundland Sealing Disaster of 1914* (Toronto: Doubleday, 1972), 208.
19 The Rooms Provincial Archives Newfoundland and Labrador, Patriotic Association of Newfoundland Records, MG632, f.a.100, file 31, Adeline E. Browning to unknown recipient, November 3, 1915.
20 *St. John's Daily News*, November 5–6, 1915; Nicholson, *The White Cross in Canada*, 61.
21 Richard J. Kahn, "Women and Men at Sea: Gender Debate aboard the Hospital Ship Maine during the Boer War, 1899-1900," *Journal of the History of Medicine and Allied Sciences* 56, no. 2 (April 2001): 113.

22 Summers notes that 1,110 of the final total of 1,318 detachments were established by the Red Cross by February 1912. The remaining 208 were SJAB detachments. See Summers, *Angels and Citizens,* 218.

23 IWM, Women at Work Collection, BRCS 10.5/4, "St. John Ambulance Association, Executive Report, 1915," 9-10; Summers, *Angels and Citizens,* 265; Hutchinson, *Champions of Charity,* 253. Hutchinson notes that Queen Alexandra "muddied the waters" as both president of the British Red Cross and president of the Committee of Ladies of Grace of the Order of St. John.

24 Nicholson, *The White Cross in Canada,* 57. The St. John Ambulance requests for funds were promptly addressed. In January 1915, the commissioner for the St. John Ambulance in Canada, Sir Henry Pellatt, asked for and received $25,000 to send a division of male orderlies and trained nurses overseas. In July 1916, the Canadian Red Cross promptly authorized $15,000 to finance the travel costs for the first overseas contingent of Canadian VAD nurses. Canadian Red Cross National Archive, Canadian Red Cross Society, Executive Committee Minute Book 1, January 29, 1915, 156; Canadian Red Cross Society, Executive Committee Minute Book 3, July 25, 1916, 52–53; James Cantlie, *British Red Cross Society Nursing Manual, No. 2* (London: Cassell, 1914).

25 Centre for Newfoundland Studies, Memorial University Libraries (CNS), Frances Cluett Papers, Collection-174, file 2.02.001, Frances Cluett to Mother, mid-October 1916, written at the Seaman's Institute. Adeline Browning, president of the British Red Cross in St. John's, approved Cluett's VAD application. During her training, she lived in the women's section of the Seaman's Institute. Dr. William Reeves, a member of SJAA, trained the ambulance brigade in first aid. Clare Janes and Cluett became close friends following their VAD training, sailing to England and serving together. Bill Rompkey and Bert Riggs, eds., *Your Daughter Fanny: The War Letters of Frances Cluett, VAD* (St. John's: Flanker Press, 2006), 20–24.

26 Summers, *Angels and Citizens,* 217–24.

27 *St. John's Daily News,* November 5–6, 1915. The initial five Newfoundland VADs sent overseas were Madeline Donnelly, Jean Emerson, Isobel Le Messurier, Cecile Windeler, and Annie Worsley. Donnelly and Emerson served in both England and France. See British Red Cross Society Museum and Archives (BRCS MA), Personnel Record Indexes; and Nicholson, *The White Cross in Canada,* 61.

28 "Annual Report for 1913 of the St. John Ambulance Brigade Overseas," 12–13; *The Organization of Voluntary Medical Aid in Canada* (1914), 3.

29 Trained brigade members were quickly recruited into the CAMC, and some fifty were deployed to the Royal Army Medical Corps. Charles Copp, "St. John's Ambulance Brigade," *Canadian Nurse* 14, no. 7 (July 1918): 1165.

30 City of Ottawa Archives (COA), St. John Ambulance Association Records (SJAA fonds), Ottawa Nursing Division No. 32, 1910–27, MG26 D83, "Secretary's Report, 1915," 2.

31 Summers, *Angels and Citizens,* 253.

32 IWM, Women at Work Collection, BRCS 1/8 – Part II, "St. John Ambulance Association, Report of the Ambulance Department, 1919," 29. The report broke down the numbers by year: 10,443 in 1914; 14,742 in 1915; 10,024 in 1916; 13,076 in 1917; and 13,327 in 1918.

33 Ibid. The six detachments were created under the terms of *The Organization of Voluntary Medical Aid in Canada,* of 1914.

34 *Ottawa City Directories*, 1916-19; COA, SJAA fonds, Ottawa Nursing Division No. 32, 1910–27, MG26 D83, "Report of the Commandant," Ottawa Women's Voluntary Aid Detachment, November 8, 1915, 1. In late 1914, Hazel Todd was elevated from assistant general secretary for St. John in Ottawa to commandant of Nursing Division No. 32. The unmarried daughter of a senior parliamentary public servant, she had a brother on active service.

35 COA, "Report of the Commandant," 1.

36 Ibid., 2.

37 COA, "Report of the Commandant," 3.

38 Captain R.J. Birdwhistle, general secretary for St. John in Canada, "Address to the Organizing Session of the Saskatchewan Branch of the St. John Ambulance Association in Regina," as reported in the *Regina Leader*, January 28, 1911, 10; "Annual Report for 1913 of the St. John Ambulance Brigade Overseas," 21.

39 Birdwhistle, "Address to the Organizing Session," in the *Regina Leader*, 10.

40 Cantlie, *British Red Cross Society Nursing Manual, No. 2*.

41 "Annual Report for 1913 of the St. John Ambulance Brigade Overseas," 23.

42 Nova Scotia Archives (NSA), Red Cross Collection, MG 20 vol. 321, St. John Ambulance Brigade, "Report of the Chief Commissioner for Brigade Overseas, 1 October 1915 to 31 December 1917" (London: Chancery of the Order, 1918), 47–51. In Winnipeg, Dr. L. McPhee-Green was divisional surgeon, and Dr. M.E. Crawford was lady superintendent for the nursing division. Other female physicians associated with the VAD program included Dr. Ellen Douglass, the Fort Garry Division in Winnipeg, Dr. A. Ross of Guelph Central Division, and Dr. B.L. Collver of Simcoe Central Nursing Division. Also see *Winnipeg Tribune*, January 19, 1918.

43 *The Organization of Voluntary Medical Aid in Canada* (1914), Regulation no. 12, 6, and Regulation no. 14.

44 Constitution and General Regulations of the St. John Ambulance Association Canadian Branch (1919), 25, 31.

45 CNS, Frances Cluett, Collection-174, file 2.02.001, Frances Cluett to Mother, October 29, 1916.

46 Constitution and General Regulations of the St. John Ambulance Association Canadian Branch (1919), 31.

47 CNS, Frances Cluett, Collection-174, file 2.02.003, Frances Cluett to Mother, February 4, 1918, Rouen.

48 *The Organization of Voluntary Medical Aid in Canada* (1914), Regulation no. 12, 6, and Regulation no. 14.

49 Summers, *Angels and Citizens*, 220.

50 NSA, McGregor-Miller Collection, MG1, vol. 661, no. 8, Bessie Hall to Mother, October 2, 1918.

51 Proposed organizational structure of the Canadian SJAB men's and women's detachments under the original March 1914 *Organization of Voluntary Medical Aid in Canada*, 5.

52 Hutchinson, *Champions of Charity*, 253.

53 Archibald Loyd, quoted in Hutchinson, *Champions of Charity*, 254.

54 Tim Cook, *At the Sharp End: Canadians Fighting the Great War, 1914-1916* (Toronto: Penguin Canada, 2009), 1:50–54.

55 *Women's Aid Department (W.A.D.) – St. John Ambulance Brigade (Overseas) within the Dominion of Canada – Regulations* (Ottawa: King's Printer, 1918); Nicholson, *The White Cross in Canada*, 59.
56 *Women's Aid Department (W.A.D.) ... Regulations*, 1; Galloway, *The White Cross in Canada*, 92. Todd continued as lady district superintendent for the Ottawa division through the Second World War.
57 University of Toronto, *Varsity*, November 1, 1916, 1.
58 LAC, Great War and Canadian Society Project, Shirley Gordon Interview, A1 9903–0015, July 18, 1974. Casually referred to by the VADs as the Davisville Hospital for its Toronto location on the corner of Davisville Avenue and Yonge Street. The hospital was converted during the war from the National Cash Register Company factory as a special military hospital for orthopaedic cases. In 1919, it was renamed the Toronto Military Orthopaedic Hospital, but the name and function continued to evolve into the postwar era. See Nathan Smith, "Comrades and Citizens: Great War Veterans in Toronto, 1915-1919" (PhD diss., University of Toronto, 2012), 1, and Canadian War Museum (CWM), Beaverbrook Collection of War Art, Object number 19710261-0766, painted by Stanley Francis Turner, c. 1918. The painting depicts veterans at Davisville Avenue and Yonge Street in Toronto, outside the Military Orthopaedic Hospital.
59 Rompkey and Riggs, *Your Daughter Fanny*, 129.
60 "Annie Wynne-Roberts Letters," in *Letters from the Front: Being a Record of the Part Played by Officers of the Bank in the Great War, 1914-1919*, ed. Charles Lyons Foster (Toronto: Southam Press, 1920), 1:184. Annie Wynne-Roberts was a VAD at the Birmingham hospital from late September 1916 to late April 1917. She later served in three hospitals in France, until August 1919. See also BRCS MA, Personnel Record Indexes.
61 Constitution and General Regulations of the St. John Ambulance Association Canadian Branch (1919), 25.
62 IWM, Department of Documents (DD), Marjorie Starr Diary, 4572, October 8, 1915.
63 CNS, Sybil Johnson, Collection-201, file 2.03.002, Sybil Johnson Diary, August 19, 1917.
64 Sir Percy Sherwood, president's address in "16th Annual Report of the Canadian Branch of the St. John Ambulance Association," 1925, 9.
65 Constitution and General Regulations of the St. John Ambulance Association Canadian Branch (1919), 15.
66 AO, MU 6858, "Home Hygiene: Syllabus for Elementary Certificate," in "Annual Report for 1913 of the St. John Ambulance Brigade Overseas," 24.
67 Kathryn McPherson, *Bedside Matters: The Transformation of Canadian Nursing, 1900-1990* (Toronto: University of Toronto Press, 2003), 85–86.
68 Kate Adie, *Corsets to Camouflage: Women and War* (London: Hodder and Stoughton, 2003), 12–13. Both the "lady nurses" and the "social butterflies" of Cape Town, who disrupted the routines of the military hospitals, fit this description.
69 Jean Cantlie Stewart, *The Quality of Mercy: The Lives of Sir James and Lady Cantlie* (London: George Allen and Unwin, 1983), 209.
70 Natalie Riegler, *Jean I. Gunn: Nursing Leader* (Toronto: A.M.S. and Fitzhenry and Whiteside, 1997), 83.
71 Jean Gunn, "Nursing: Address Given before National Council of Women," *Woman's Century* 6, 5 (August 1918): 11.

72 CNS, Sybil Johnson, Collection-201, file 2.01.013, Sybil Johnson to Daddy and Mummy, December 16, 1916 (emphasis in original). Adeline Browning, head of the local "Virgonia" Red Cross Branch, also brought Fanny Cluett to St. John's for VAD training. Sybil did have some class time before embarking overseas but appears to have had less prior instruction than Fanny.

73 The Queen Mary's Convalescent Auxiliary Hospital in London seems to have been a common centre for Newfoundland VADs to complete their hands-on hospital training.

74 IWM, Women at Work Collection, BRCS 2/18, *Joint Women's VAD Department: Terms of Service* (15 March 1917) 2–3; BRCS MA, Personnel Record Indexes.

75 Cluett was posted to a Territorial Force hospital, the 4th Northern General in Lincoln. Established in 1908, the Territorial Forces were the reserve force of the British Army. During the war, they also established their own hospitals to supplement the RAMC hospitals and a Territorial Force Nursing Service. See Summers, *Angels and Citizens*, 207–9.

76 CNS, Frances Cluett Papers, Collection-174, file 2.02.001, Frances Cluett to Mother, mid-October 1916, Seaman's Institute.

77 Jeanette Coultas Wells, as told to Iris Power, "I Was a V.A.D.," *Atlantic Guardian* 11, no. 5 (July 1954): 26–27.

78 Copp, "St. John's Ambulance Brigade," 1166.

79 LAC, Sir Edward Kemp fonds, MG 27, II, D9, file 19, Dr. Clarke to Professor Mavor, February 16, 1917; LAC, Department of Militia and Defence, RG 9, III, B1, vol. 3419, file N-5-47, Colonel Rennie, A.D.M.S. Canadians, to Mrs. Lois Pringle Nickalls, August 21, 1917.

80 Jean Gunn, "Canadian National Association of Trained Nurses' Convention, 1918," *Canadian Nurse* 14, no. 8 (August 1918): 1211.

81 Pauline Jardine, "An Urban Middle-Class Calling: Women and the Emergence of Modern Nursing Education at the Toronto General Hospital, 1881-1914," *Urban History Review* 17, no. 3 (February 1989): 186–87; Riegler, *Jean I. Gunn*, 78–95, 217.

82 Hugh E. MacDermot, *History of the School for Nurses of the Montreal General Hospital* (Montreal: Alumnae Association, 1940), 53–54; Mary Burr, "The English Voluntary Aid Detachments," *American Journal of Nursing* 15, no. 6 (March 1915): 461–67. Burr's role as the director of the National Council of Trained Nurses of Great Britain and Ireland was equivalent to that of Jean Gunn, and like Gunn she was committed to the professionalization of nursing.

83 Summers, *Angels and Citizens*, 226–27.

84 Ibid., 151.

85 Ibid., 225.

86 Julia Roberts, "British Nurses at War, 1914-1918: Ancillary Personnel and the Battle for Registration," *Nursing Research* 45, no. 3 (May-June 1996): 167.

87 Summers, *Angels and Citizens*, 226.

CHAPTER 2: ENTHUSIASTIC AND ANXIOUS

1 Diana Condell and Jean Liddiard, *Working for Victory? Images of Women in the First World War, 1914-1918* (London: Routledge and Kegan Paul, 1987), 20.

2 Janet S.K. Watson, "Active Service: Gender, Class and British Representations of the Great War" (PhD diss., Stanford University, 1996), 23.

3 Sir Wilfrid Laurier, prime minister of Canada from 1896 to 1911, coined the phrase "The nineteenth century was the century of the United States. So I think we can claim that Canada will fill the twentieth century." It was quickly simplified to "the twentieth century belongs to Canada." See *Canada's Prime Ministers, 1867–1994: Biographies and Anecdotes* (Ottawa: Naional Archives of Canada, 1994).

4 Library and Archives Canada (LAC), Great War and Canadian Society Project, Jean Marita Sears Interview, A1 9903–0008, "Interview Notes," page 3, July 23, 1974. Sears was one of thirty-five Toronto VADs selected for service overseas in mid-1917.

5 "Decide to Nurse Invalided Soldiers," *Victoria Daily Colonist*, November 20, 1915, 11.

6 Desmond Morton and Glenn Wright, *Winning the Second Battle: Canadian Veterans and the Return to Civilian Life, 1915-1930* (Toronto: University of Toronto Press, 1987), 7, 8. The MHC was created by Order-in-Council on June 30, 1915.

7 Ibid., 19–20; Annmarie Adams, "Borrowed Buildings: Canada's Temporary Hospitals during World War I," *Canadian Bulletin of Medical History* 16, no. 1 (1999): 29–31.

8 Adams, "Borrowed Buildings," 29.

9 Morton and Wright, *Winning the Second Battle*, 84.

10 City of Ottawa Archives, St. John Ambulance Association Records, Ottawa Nursing Division No. 32, 1910–27, MG26 D83, "Secretary's Reports, November 11, 1915."

11 Charles Copp, "St. John's Ambulance Brigade," *Canadian Nurse* 14, no. 7 (July 1918): 1163; Adams, "Borrowed Buildings," 25–48.

12 LAC, Great War and Canadian Society Project, Shirley Gordon Interview, A1 9903–0015, July 18, 1974. Gordon worked as a VAD in 1918 while still an undergraduate at the University of Toronto.

13 Ibid., 3; Morton and Wright, *Winning the Second Battle*, 17–20. At least twenty facilities were in operation by the close of 1915.

14 G.W.L. Nicholson, *The White Cross in Canada: A History of St. John Ambulance* (Montreal: Harvest House, 1967), 58–59. With sixty members in total, Ottawa Division VADs had little more than a brief introduction to hospital work.

15 Archives of Ontario (AO), St. John Ambulance Association (SJAA): Administration Records, 1909–77, MU 6814, file Annual Reports, 1912–19, "Report of Ontario Provincial, Canadian Branch, St. John Ambulance Association," September 30, 1915, 16 (AO, "Report of the Ontario Provincial")

16 Nova Scotia Archives (NSA), St. John Ambulance Brigade Overseas, *Report of the Chief Commissioner for Brigade Overseas, 1 October 1915 to 31 December 1917* (London: Chancery of the Order, 1918), 17–19 (NSA, *Report of the Chief Commissioner*).

17 Viola Henderson, "V.A.D. Work in Montreal," *Canadian Nurse* 14, no. 8 (August 1918): 1245–46.

18 Ibid., 1247.

19 Ibid., 1246–47.

20 See François Rémillard and Brian Merrett, *Mansions of the Golden Square Mile, Montreal, 1850–1930*, translated by Joshua Wolfe (Montreal: Meridian Press, 1987). The Golden Square Mile was the euphemism coined for Montreal's most elite residential district in the Westmount neighbourhood. It was developed between 1850 and 1930 at the base of Mont Royal in the city's west-central downtown area.

21 Imperial War Museum (IWM), Department of Documents (DD), Marjorie Starr Diary, 4572, December 16, 1915.
22 James Cantlie, *First Aid to the Injured* (London: St. John Ambulance Association, 1914); James Cantlie, *British Red Cross Society Nursing Manual, No. 2* (London: Cassell, 1914). See also Christopher McCreery, *The Maple Leaf and the White Cross* (Toronto: Dundurn Press, 2008), 55, 83.
23 Henderson, "V.A.D. Work in Montreal," 1244.
24 Ibid., 1245, 1247; Maude E. Seymour Abbott, "Lectures on the History of Nursing," *Canadian Nurse* 19, no. 4 (April 1923): 208.
25 LAC, Alice Bray fonds, MG 30, E572, vol. 1, Alice Bray to Mother, September 29, 1916.
26 Ibid., October 1916.
27 All material pertaining to the VADs' service record overseas is drawn from the Personnel Record Indexes at the British Red Cross Society Museum and Archives. Alice Bray worked as a VAD in England for almost three years, first in Birmingham and later in a London hospital.
28 Henderson, "V.A.D. Work in Montreal," 1245–46; St. John House Archives and Library (SJH), World War I – World War II Records: VAD Training (Records: Training), box X(b), Register and Record Sheets: Ste Anne de Bellevue, No. 4 Military Hospital (1918-1919); SJH, Records: Training, box X(a), "VAD Nursing Members Who Served in Military and Naval Hospitals Overseas."
29 Edith J. (Mrs. Charles) Archibald, *Nova Scotia Red Cross during the Great War: Nineteen Fourteen-Eighteen* (Halifax: Nova Scotia Provincial Branch, Canadian Red Cross Society, c. 1920), 57.
30 Marion Doull served in the King George Hospital, London, from August 1918 to June 1919 and in Royal Victoria Hospital, Netley, Hampshire, from June 1919 to August 1919. The King George Hospital was established in 1912, became an emergency military hospital in 1915, and was converted back to a civilian facility in March 1919. The hospital was named for George V and referred to by VADs as King George, King George V, or King George Military hospital. There is no available information for Scott or Pyke.
31 NSA, McGregor-Miller Collection, Bessie Hall Letters, MG1, vol. 661, file 8, Bessie Hall to Mother, Wednesday evening, 1918 (emphasis in original).
32 Canadian Branch of the St John Ambulance Association, *First Aid Bulletin* 1, no. 1 (1916), 7. How many VADs applied for an overseas post and were subsequently selected is not known. Some did not pursue VAD work abroad, constrained by their employment or by family.
33 Winnipeg's Tuxedo Military Hospital housed 1,200 beds by 1918. The hospital employed VADs, two of whom worked at the summer home of Sir Augustus and Lady Nanton on Lake of the Woods, which was affiliated with the hospital. See Canadian Red Cross National Archive (CRCNA), Canadian Red Cross Society (CRCS), *Bulletin* 37 (June-July 1918): 5; Archives of Manitoba, Augustus Nanton Papers, MG14, C85, "Sir Augustus Nanton and the Town of Nanton, Alberta," 4.
34 *Calgary Albertan,* November 16, 1916. Snow and cold weather forced the cancellation of planned organizing meetings for the St. John Ambulance in Edmonton and Calgary.
35 Robert Allen Rutherdale, *Hometown Horizons: Local Responses to Canada's Great War* (Vancouver: UBC Press, 2004), 46–47.

36 LAC, Voice of the Pioneer, 9861, acc. 1981–0111, Violet Wilson Interview, c. 1970. At twenty-eight, Charlie Wilson was a lawyer and one of the original Edmonton Eskimos. "Obituary, 'Lieut Wilson,'" *Edmonton Bulletin,* June 8, 1916; Mike Jeffreys, "She Returns to Find Her City's Grown Up," *Edmonton Journal,* June 27, 1974, 19.

37 The Canadian census for 1911 puts the PEI population at 93,728, dropping to 88,615 by 1921. The population of Canada in 1911 was 7,206,643.

38 Henderson, "V.A.D. Work in Montreal," 1246.

39 "A Convalescent Home," *Victoria Daily Colonist,* November 14, 1915, 8.

40 "Decide to Nurse Invalided Soldiers," *Victoria Daily Colonist,* November 20, 1915, 11.

41 Rutherdale, *Hometown Horizons,* 201.

42 "Decide to Nurse Invalided Soldiers," *Victoria Daily Colonist,* November 20, 1915, 11.

43 K.J. Quarry, ed., *A Review of the History of St. John Ambulance in Saskatchewan, 1911–1983* (Regina: St. John Ambulance, 1983), 31–32. VAD Anne Sheppard was appointed matron of St. Chad's in 1917, with no record of any formal nurse's training. The 1911 census indicates that 6.8 percent of Canadians resided in Saskatchewan, compared to 35.1 percent in Ontario and 27.8 percent in Quebec. See also Saskatchewan Archives Board (SAB), Qu'Appelle Association Occasional Papers, R0705, autumn-winter 1915; SAB, Cullum Family Papers; and NSA, *Report of the Chief Commissioner,* 18–19.

44 AO, "Report of the Ontario Provincial," 16. There were thirty-nine SJAA branches in Ontario by 1918, offering classes for both men and women, but nursing divisions were founded only in larger centres. ; Adams, "Borrowed Buildings," 30.

45 Adams, "Borrowed Buildings," 29–30; Morton and Wright, *Winning the Second Battle,* 19–24.

46 Amelia Earhart, *The Fun of It: Random Records of My Own Flying and of Women in Aviation* (New York: Harcourt, Brace, 1975), 19–20.

47 Ibid., 9.

48 Earhart was the maternal granddaughter of a former federal judge and bank president, Alfred G. Otis, and daughter of lawyer Edwin Earhart of Kansas.

49 Rutherdale, *Hometown Horizons,* 202.

50 AO, *"Report of the Ontario Provincial,"* 1.

51 Judith Fingard, "College, Career and Community: Dalhousie Co-eds, 1881-1921," in *Youth, University and Canadian Society: Essays in the Social History of Higher Education,* ed. Paul Axelrod and John G. Reid (Montreal and Kingston: McGill-Queen's University Press, 1989), 41. The author notes that female enrollment at Dalhousie almost doubled during the war years, from twenty-three at the start to nearly forty by 1918.

52 University of Toronto, *Varsity,* October 20, 1916, 2.

53 University of Toronto, "Important News for Women Undergrads," *Varsity,* November 1, 1916, 1; AO, Report of Ontario Provincial, 2; Strome Galloway, *The White Cross, 1883-1983: A History of St. John Ambulance, Centennial Edition* (Ottawa: St. John Priory, 1983), 52–53; NSA, *Report of the Chief Commissioner,* 18. The VADs were assigned to Euclid Hall and Spadina Convalescent Homes; twelve went daily to the base hospital, established during the war by the Military Hospitals Commission (MHC) as a rehabilitation and training centre for physiotherapy in Hart House on the University of Toronto campus.

54 Centre for Newfoundland Studies, Memorial University Libraries (CNS), Frances Cluett Fonds, Collection-174, file 2.02.001, Frances Cluett to Mother, October 12, 1916; CNS,

Sybil Johnson, Collection-201, file 2.01.013, Sybil Johnson to Daddy and Mummy, December 16, 1916; Joint War Committee of the British Red Cross Society and the Order of St. John of Jerusalem in England, *Reports by the Joint War Committee* ... (London: H.M.S.O., 1921), 197.

55 Nicholson, *The White Cross in Canada*, 35–36. The St. John's branch of the SJAA in Newfoundland was established in April 1910. Cassie Brown, *Death on the Ice: The Great Newfoundland Sealing Disaster of 1914* (Toronto: Doubleday, 1972); NSA, *Report of the Chief Commissioner*, 26; Bill Rompkey and Bert Riggs, eds., *Your Daughter Fanny: The War Letters of Frances Cluett, VAD* (St. John's: Flanker Press, 2006), xxiii.

56 Gale Denise Warren, "The Patriotic Association of the Women of Newfoundland, 1914-1918," *Aspects* 33, no. 2 (Summer 1998): 23–25, 28–29. On July 1, 1916, during the Battle of the Somme at Beaumont Hamel in northern France, 780 members of the Newfoundland Regiment advanced into battle. Within minutes, 310 were killed, including all 22 officers. Another 360 men were wounded, effectively wiping out the regiment. The exact number of dead and wounded varies by source, but both Warren and Morton cite the same number. See Desmond Morton, *A Military History of Canada: From Champlain to the Gulf War* (Toronto: McClelland and Stewart, 1992), 143.

57 Copp, "St. John's Ambulance Brigade," 1166. Copp became assistant commissioner for Ontario in 1911. Christopher McCreery, *The Maple Leaf and the White Cross* (Toronto: Dundurn Press, 2008), 52.

58 Natalie Riegler, *Jean I. Gunn: Nursing Leader* (Toronto: A.M.S. and Fitzhenry and Whiteside, 1997), 78–81.

59 Ibid., 80.

60 Susan Mann, *Margaret Macdonald: Imperial Daughter* (Montreal and Kingston: McGill-Queen's University Press, 2005), 74–75, 87–89; Natalie Riegler, "The Work and Networks of Jean I. Gunn, Superintendent of Nurses, Toronto General Hospital, 1913-1941: A Presentation of Some Issues in Nursing during Her Lifetime, 1882-1941" (PhD diss., University of Toronto, 1992), 150–51; G.W.L. Nicholson, *Canada's Nursing Sisters* (Toronto: Samuel Stevens Hakkert and Company, 1975), 58.

61 Riegler, *Jean I. Gunn*, 79–80.

62 Nursing registration was initiated in Nova Scotia in 1910 but was not completed nationally until Ontario introduced it in 1922. Janet Ross Kerr, "Professionalization in Canadian Nursing," in *Canadian Nursing: Issues and Perspectives*, ed. Janet Ross Kerr and Jannetta MacPhail (St. Louis: Mosby, 1991), 27. The majority of training school graduates did not qualify under legal registered status until the mid-twentieth century, according to Kathryn McPherson, *Bedside Matters: The Transformation of Canadian Nursing, 1900-1990* (Toronto: University of Toronto Press, 2003), 20.

63 Sioban Nelson, *Say Little, Do Much: Nurses, Nuns, and Hospitals in the Nineteenth Century* (Philadelphia: University of Pennsylvania Press, 2001).

64 Charles Dickens, *Martin Chuzzlewit* (1843); Pauline Jardine, "An Urban Middle-Class Calling: Women and the Emergence of Modern Nursing Education at the Toronto General Hospital, 1881-1914," *Urban History Review* 17, no. 3 (February 1989): 186–87; and Riegler, *Jean I. Gunn*, 217.

65 Tim Cook, *No Place to Run: The Canadian Corps and Gas Warfare in the First World War* (Vancouver: UBC Press, 1999), 144–57; Morton, *A Military History of Canada*, 38–40. Of the sixteen boys who left school to enlist, fourteen did not return, including Gery's brother.

Maureen Judge, dir., *And We Knew How to Dance: Women in World War I* (Montreal: National Film Board of Canada, 1994).

66 How many CAMC nurses served overseas is difficult to ascertain, as Macdonald's biographer, Susan Mann, demonstrates. She hedges at "close to 3,000" and cites a variety of sources, each with a different breakdown, but the most accurate estimate is 3,141. See Mann, *Margaret Macdonald*, 74, 224n1.

67 LAC, Department of Militia and Defence, RG 9, III, B1, vol. 3419, file N-5-47, ADMS Canadians to Mrs. L. Pringle Nichalls, August 21, 1917, citing Matron Macdonald. Two VADs were assigned as support services at Westcliffe Eye and Ear Hospital in Folkestone, England, but it is not clear whether they were Canadian or British.

68 The advent of early nursing education in Canada dates from the 1880s, as nursing gradually evolved from a working-class to a middle-class identity. See Jardine, "An Urban Middle-Class Calling"; and Herbert A. Bruce, *Report on the Canadian Army Medical Service* (London, 1916).

69 Nicholson, *Canada's Nursing Sisters*, 59. The Joint War Committee included the Joint Women's VAD Committee, which oversaw the VADs from the St. John Ambulance and the British Red Cross. IWM, Women at Work Collection, BRCS 1/4, "SJAA Central Executive Report," 9; IWM, Women at Work Collection, BRCS 1/5, "SJAA Report of the Ambulance Committee, 1916," 7; Joint War Committee, *Reports by the Joint War Committee*, 230.

70 Desmond Morton, *A Peculiar Kind of Politics: Canada's Overseas Ministry in the First World War* (Toronto: University of Toronto Press, 1982), 86–87, 94–95.

71 Bruce, *Report on the Canadian Army Medical Service*, 7, 127–33.

72 Ibid., 24.

73 Ibid., 22.

74 Mann, *Margaret Macdonald*, 84–85; Morton, *A Peculiar Kind of Politics*, 86.

75 Herbert A. Bruce, *Politics and the Canadian Army Medical Corps* (Toronto: William Briggs, 1919), 55.

76 Ibid., 54. Bruce married a former British VAD after the war. Mann's biography mentions the depth of Macdonald's feelings regarding the injustice, to the extent that she was prepared to transfer to a nursing post in the field. See Mann, *Margaret Macdonald*, 85.

77 Abbott, "Lectures on the History of Nursing" (April 1923), 208–10. Fourteen members of the contingent, ten of whom went on to RAMC hospitals in France, were from Montreal. The remaining forty-six came from other towns and cities across Canada.

78 Anne Summers, *Angels and Citizens: British Women as Military Nurses, 1854–1914* (Newbury: Threshold Press, 2000), 270. Summers estimates that some twenty-three thousand British women served as VAD nurses during the war.

79 *The Times History of the War* (London: The Times, 1915), 4:247–50.

80 Copp, "St. John's Ambulance Brigade," 1165. Copp notes that in 1918 the British government paid VADs twenty pounds per annum for the initial six-month probationary contract, which then rose to thirty pounds a year, plus an annual four pounds for the uniform. This was in addition to landing and transportation costs paid by the Order of St. John and the Red Cross. These sums were intended to cover basic living expenses for laundry and other necessities, and were not seen as salary. Room and board was provided by the individual hospitals or other medical facilities.

81 LAC, Canadian Army Medical Corps (CAMC), RG 9, III, B 1, vol. 3419, N-5-47, Sophie Smethurst to Col. Munro, August 13, 1916; LAC, Canadian Army Medical Corps (CAMC),

RG 9, III, B 1, vol. 3419, N-5-47, Matron-in-Chief Macdonald to Col. Munro, August 21, 1916.

82 Cynthia Toman, *Sister Soldiers of the Great War: The Nurses of the Canadian Army Medical Corps* (Vancouver: UBC Press, 2016), 42–43; LAC, Canadian Army Medical Corps (CAMC), RG 9, III, B 1, vol. 3419, N-5-47, Matron-in-Chief Macdonald, to Col. Munro, August 21, 1916.

83 LAC, Alice Bray fonds, MG 30, E572, vol. 1, Alice Bray to Mother, October 13, 1916.

84 NSA, *Report of the Chief Commissioner*, 18–19.

85 Ibid. By 1917, CAMC personnel had grown to trust the capabilities of VADs working in local convalescent facilities. When the military hospital, which was devoted to orthopaedics, opened in the Davisville area of Toronto, its new matron brought her experienced VADs along with her.

86 LAC, Voice of the Pioneer, 9861, acc. 1981–0111, Violet Wilson Interview, c. 1970. Violet's brother, Charles Wilson Jr., was killed in action at the end of the Battle of Sanctuary Wood in 1916.

87 Ibid.

88 Henderson, "V.A.D. Work in Montreal," 1246.

89 LAC, Alice H. Bray fonds, MG 30, E572, vol. 1, Alice Bray to Mother, October 1916. "Lyster" refers to the 5th Northern General Hospital, Leicester, a Territorial Force hospital for 2,500 officers and other ranks. Betty Masson, Mary McLean, Edna Johnson, and Alice Houston were all from the Ottawa Nursing Division.

90 LAC, Voice of the Pioneer, 9861, acc. 1981–0111, Violet Wilson Interview, c. 1970.

91 Ibid.

92 Provincial Archives of Alberta (PAA), Agnes Wilson Teviotdale, MG 73.72, Interview, January 19, 1973.

93 Daisy Johnson Cook, "Who Am I?" in *A Review of the History of St. John Ambulance in Saskatchewan, 1911–1983*, ed. K.J. Quarry (Regina: St. John Ambulance, 1983), 34.

94 CNS, Sybil Johnson, Collection-201, file 2.01.013, Sybil Johnson to Mother, December 13, 1916.

95 CNS, Frances Cluett Fonds, Collection-174, file 2.02.001, Frances Cluett to Mother, November 24, 1916.

96 Ibid.

97 Newfoundland VADs now crossed the Atlantic on British military vessels from Halifax instead of on neutral American luxury liners. American military personnel crossed from their own naval ports.

98 Jeanette Coultas Wells, as told to Iris Power, "I Was a V.A.D.," *Atlantic Guardian* 11, no. 5 (July 1954): 27.

99 CNS, Frances Cluett Fonds, Collection-174, file 2.02.001, Frances Cluett to Mother, November 29, 1916. Vacated in 1919, Devonshire House was demolished in the 1920s because it was too costly to maintain.

100 CNS, Sybil Johnson, Collection-201, file 2.03.002, Sybil Johnson Diary, December 21, 1916.

101 Born in 1897, Princess Mary was the only daughter of King George V and Queen Mary, and sister of King Edward VIII and King George VI. After her marriage, she was known as the Princess Royal and Countess of Harewood.

102 LAC, Alice Bray fonds, MG 30, E572, vol. 1, Alice Bray to Mother, September 26 and 29, 1916.
103 Joint War Committee, *Reports by the Joint War Committee*, 196, 211–12.
104 Bruce, *Report on the Canadian Army Medical Service*, 24.
105 Joint War Committee, *Reports by the Joint War Committee*, 231–32.
106 "Annie Wynne-Roberts, Letter," in *Letters from the Front: Being a Record of the Part Played by Officers of the Bank in the Great War, 1914–1919*, ed. Charles Lyons Foster (Toronto: Southam Press, 1920), 2:161. There was another 1st Southern General Hospital in Selly Oak, Birmingham, and an affiliated auxiliary hospital for limbless men.
107 Adams, "Borrowed Buildings," 25–48; Isabel Morris, "Wandsworth Hospital: A Short Account of the Third London General Hospital, Wandsworth," *Newfoundland Quarterly* 16, no. 3 (December 1916): 14.
108 Wealtha A. Wilson and Ethel T. Raymond, "Canadian Women in the Great War," in *Canada and the Great War*, vol. 6, *Special Services, Heroic Deeds, Etc.* (Toronto: United Publishers of Canada, 1921), 176.
109 Ibid., 176–77.
110 National Archives (NA), Miscellaneous Files Relating to Army Nursing Staff and Nursing Establishment, 1914–18, WO 222/2134, E.M. McCarthy, "Report on the Work of the C.A.M.C. Nursing Service with the B.E.F. in France."
111 CRCNA, CRCS, *Bulletin* 27 (June 1917): 23.
112 Mary MacLeod Moore, "Canadian Women in the War Zone," *Saturday Night*, March 16, 1918, 17.
113 CRCNA, CRCS, *Bulletin* 27 (June 1917) 25.
114 Ibid. The report covered a period of six weeks ending April 28, 1917. Six Canadian VADs went to No. 1 Canadian General Hospital (CGH), Étaples, and four to No. 3 CGH, Boulogne. These hospitals relocated over the course of the war but remained in France. Mary MacLeod Moore, *The Maple Leaf's Red Cross: The War Story of the Canadian Red Cross Overseas* (London: Skeffington and Son, 1920), 183; National Archives (NA), Miscellaneous Files Relating to Army Nursing Staff and Nursing Establishment, 1914–18, WO 222/2134, E.M. McCarthy, "Report on the Work of the C.A.M.C. Nursing Service with the B.E.F. in France."
115 Moore, *The Maple Leaf's Red Cross*, 183.
116 LAC, Matron Margaret Macdonald fonds, MG 30, E45, "Westcliffe Eye and Ear Hospital, Folkestone," Matron Cameron-Smith's article. Aver was registered with SJAB Hamilton No. 16 Nursing Division and K. Baldwin with the Toronto Central No. 1 Nursing Division. Exactly how they were assigned their places at Westcliffe is unknown. It is possible that they acquired them via connections to CAMC personnel, or perhaps they were among the underqualified women whom Militia and Defence Minister Sam Hughes had approved.
117 Ibid. Privately funded by the Canadian War Contingent's Association and the Canada Lodge of Freemasons, the Queen's Canadian Military Hospital was established under the auspices of the Queen's Committee of the Order of St. John. The use of "Queen" in its name was by special permission of the Queen. See M.B., "The Queen's Canadian Military Hospital," *British Journal of Nursing* (October 24, 1914): 326–27.
118 CRCNA, "Annual Report, 1919," 36.
119 Moore, *The Maple Leaf's Red Cross*, 179–80; *Montreal Gazette*, July 25, 1918, 10.

120 Mann, *Margaret Macdonald*, 130–31.
121 Judge, *And We Knew How to Dance*. During her commentary in the Judge documentary, Eva Morgan referred to the Hôtel Juno rather than the Hôtel du Nord. Perhaps the rest home was known by this name following its conversion.
122 Moore, *The Maple Leaf's Red Cross*, 181.
123 As Susan Mann explains in her biography of Macdonald, the position of home sister was adapted from one invented by Florence Nightingale in the 1870s for her training school at St. Thomas Hospital. See Mann, *Margaret Macdonald*, 247–55.
124 LAC, Department of Militia and Defence, RG 9, III, B2, vol. 3453, file 7-2-0, Matron Macdonald to Chief Pay Master, CAMC, July 24, 1917; LAC, MG 30, E45, Matron Margaret Macdonald fonds, "Matron-in-Chief Macdonald's Article"; CRCNA, CRCS, *Bulletin* 4 (July 1915): 2.

CHAPTER 3: EVERY WOMAN IS A NURSE

1 Vera Brittain, *Testament of Youth: An Autobiographical Study of the Years 1900–1925* (1933, repr., London: Fontana, 1979), 17.
2 For Nightingale's imagery and legacy, see Sioban Nelson and Anne Marie Rafferty, eds., *Notes on Nightingale: The Influence and Legacy of a Nursing Icon* (Ithaca, NY: ILR Press, 2010); and Lynn McDonald, ed., *Florence Nightingale: The Crimean War*, Collected Works of Florence Nightingale Series Vol. 14 (Waterloo, ON: Wilfrid Laurier University Press, 2010). The VAD mythology is discussed in Deborah Gorham, *Vera Brittain: A Feminist Life* (Toronto: University of Toronto Press, 2000), 98. Beryl Oliver, *The British Red Cross in Action* (London: Faber and Faber, 1966), 239, states that British VAD nurses totalled twenty-three thousand and that there were forty-nine thousand Imperial VADs. The published experiences of British VADs include Enid Bagnold, *A Diary without Dates: Thoughts and Impressions of a VAD* (London: Heinemann, 1918); Olive Dent, *A V.A.D. in France* (London: Grant Richards, 1917); and Thekla Bowser, *The Story of British V.A.D. Work in the Great War* (London: Andrew Melrose, c. 1917). These sources are critically examined in Christine E. Hallett, "Portrayals of Suffering: Perceptions of Trauma in the Writings of First World War Nurses and Volunteers," *Canadian Bulletin of Medical History* 27, no. 1 (2010): 65–84.
3 Australians were also "colonial" VADs. See Patsy Adam-Smith, *Australian Women at War* (Ringwood, Australia: Penguin, 1996).
4 Anne Summers, *Angels and Citizens: British Women as Military Nurses, 1854–1914* (Newbury: Threshold Press, 2000), 270.
5 Lyn Macdonald, *The Roses of No Man's Land* (London: Penguin, 1993), xi; Janet S.K. Watson, "Wars in the Wards: The Social Construction of Medical Work in First World War Britain," *Journal of British Studies* 41, no. 4 (October 2002): 494.
6 Imperial War Museum (IWM), Women at Work Collection, BRCS 10.5/4, "Analysis of 200 Cases of Selected Members Taken at Random," November 28, 1916. In *Vera Brittain: A Feminist Life*, 101, Deborah Gorham also argues that the idealized upper-class VAD may be more image than reality.
7 The only published Canadian or Newfoundland VAD diaries or letters are those of teachers. Bill Rompkey and Bert Riggs, eds., *Your Daughter Fanny: The War Letters of Frances Cluett, VAD* (St. John's: Flanker Press, 2006); Margaret Conrad, Toni Laidlaw, and Donna

Smyth, "Elizabeth Hall," in *No Place Like Home: Diaries and Letters of Nova Scotia Women, 1771-1938*, ed. Margaret Conrad, Toni Laidlaw, and Donna Smyth (Halifax: Formac, 1988), 243–61.

8 Desmond Morton and Glenn Wright, *Winning the Second Battle: Canadian Veterans and the Return to Civilian Life, 1915-1930* (Toronto: University of Toronto Press, 1987), 20.

9 The many collections of First World War visual propaganda include Maurice F.V. Doll, *The Poster War: Allied Propaganda Art of the First World War* (Edmonton: Alberta Community Development, 1993); Australian War Memorial, *What Did You Do in the War Daddy? A Visual History of Propaganda Posters* (Melbourne: Oxford University Press, 1983); and Tonie Holt and Valmai Holt, *Till the Boys Come Home: The Picture Postcards of the First World War* (London: Macdonald and Jane's, 1977).

10 Bowser, *The Story of British V.A.D. Work*, 176.

11 Marjory Lang, *Women Who Made the News: Female Journalists in Canada, 1880-1945* (Montreal and Kingston: McGill-Queen's University Press, 1999), 189–215. Censorship regulations kept much of the details of VAD work and overseas travel out of the mainstream newspapers.

12 Mary MacLeod Moore, *The Maple Leaf's Red Cross: The War Story of the Canadian Red Cross Overseas* (London: Skeffington and Son, 1920), 69.

13 Mary MacLeod Moore, "Canadian Women in the War Zone," *Saturday Night*, March 16, 1918, 17.

14 Maude E. Seymour Abbott, "Lectures on the History of Nursing," *Canadian Nurse* 19, no. 2 (February 1923): 87.

15 Archibald K. Loyd, *The British Red Cross Society: The Country and Branches* (London: British Red Cross Society, 1917), 39.

16 John F. Hutchinson, *Champions of Charity: War and the Rise of the Red Cross* (Boulder: Westview, 1996), 253. Hutchinson argues that the BRCS was no more democratic than St. John, despite the lack of fees.

17 Charles Copp, "St. John's Ambulance Brigade," *Canadian Nurse* 14, no. 7 (July 1918): 1165.

18 Some eight to nine hundred of the two thousand women who qualified as either Canadian or Newfoundland VADs have been identified, as have the occupations of about 20 percent of their fathers. The occupations are taken primarily from Canadian city directories, 1913–19, plus a variety of news articles, personal documents of VADs, and the SJAA *First Aid Bulletin*. Of the two hundred identified occupations, at least twenty conform to the artisanal or skilled or unskilled labour category.

19 Janet Watson contends that VAD service equated to soldiering since both were voluntary and outside normal civilian roles, thus both gained status from war service. Janet S.K. Watson, *Fighting Different Wars: Experience, Memory, and the First World War in Britain* (Cambridge: Cambridge University Press, 2004), 86–94; Janet S.K. Watson, "Khaki Girls, VADs and Tommy's Sisters: Gender and Class in First World War Britain," *International History Review* 19, no. 1 (February 1997): 32–50.

20 Sara Z. Burke, *Seeking the Highest Good: Social Service and Gender at the University of Toronto, 1888-1937* (Toronto: University of Toronto Press, 1996), 48. Burke suggests that voluntary service was expected of educated men with leadership or administrative aspirations, but it was not yet a masculine career path.

21 The VADs represented diverse family backgrounds, from significant wealth and prominence to that of the respectable working class, although most fell into the broad category of

the middle class. Martha Allan trained as a VAD in England after her two sisters were lost on the *Lusitania*, and she served with a BRCS ambulance convoy in France. Daisy Offord, daughter of a horse clipper, worked as a VAD in Toronto and overseas. Jessie, daughter of caretaker John Hall, was a Toronto stenographer prior to serving overseas. Ethel Perley, daughter of Sir George Perley, Canada's wartime high commissioner to Britain, trained as a VAD in London. Lucy Bidwell's father was the bishop of Ontario, and Georgina Newnham's father was the bishop of Saskatchewan. Violet Copp, daughter of Charles Copp, served almost two years at King George Hospital, London.

22 Rompkey and Riggs, *Your Daughter Fanny*, xvi-xvii. Sybil and Jill were the daughters of George M. Johnson. See Centre for Newfoundland Studies, Memorial University Libraries (CNS), Sybil Johnson, Collection-201.

23 Library and Archives Canada (LAC), Great War and Canadian Society Project, Jean Marita Sears Interview, A1 9903–0008, July 23, 1974; G.W.L. Nicholson, *The White Cross in Canada: A History of St. John Ambulance* (Montreal: Harvest House, 1967), 41.

24 Jonathan F. Vance, *Death So Noble: Memory, Meaning, and the First World War* (Vancouver: UBC Press, 1997), 44. On Quebec, see Joseph Levitt, *Henri Bourassa on Imperialism and Bi-culturalism, 1900-1918* (Toronto: Copp Clark, 1970); and Patrice A. Dutil, "Against Isolationism: Napoléon Belcourt, French Canada, and 'La grande guerre,'" in *Canada and the First World War: Essays in Honour of Robert Craig Brown*, ed. David MacKenzie (Toronto: University of Toronto Press, 2005), 96–137.

25 Leslie A. Fiedler, "Images of the Nurse in Fiction and Popular Culture," in *Images of Nurses: Perspectives from History, Art and Literature*, ed. Anne Hudson Jones (Philadelphia: University of Pennsylvania Press, 1988), 103–4; Anne Summers, "Ministering Angels," *History Today* 39 (February 1989): 31. Fiedler and Summers discuss the wartime romanticization of Nightingale and Edith Cavell, who was executed for harbouring Allied soldiers in Belgium and assisting their escape. See also Alan R. Young, "'We Throw the Torch': Canadian Memorials of the Great War and the Mythology of Heroic Sacrifice," *Journal of Canadian Studies* 24, no. 4 (Winter 1989–90): 18; and Christina Bates, *A Cultural History of the Nurse's Uniform* (Gatineau: Canadian Museum of Civilization, 2012), 47.

26 Kathryn McPherson, "Carving Out a Past: The Canadian Nurses' Association War Memorial," *Histoire sociale* 29, no. 58 (November 1996): 417–29.

27 IWM, Women at Work Collection, BRCS 2/18, "Joint Women's VAD Department – Terms of Service" (March 15, 1917) 2 and (September 26, 1917).

28 Brittain, *Testament of Youth*, 180–81.

29 Lillian Brown's 1967 obituary states that she was forty-one when she began her overseas service, hinting at a discrepancy in her initial application for VAD work, which lists her age as thirty-eight. *Halifax Mail Star*, May 11, 1967, 67. Fanny Cluett was born on July 25, 1883. British Red Cross Society Museum and Archives (BRCS MA), Personnel Record Indexes.

30 Agatha Christie, *Agatha Christie: An Autobiography* (New York: Dodd, Mead, 1977), 217.

31 LAC, Great War and Canadian Society Project, Shirley Gordon Interview, A1 9903–0015, July 18, 1974.

32 LAC, Department of Militia and Defence, RG 9, III, B1, vol. 3419, N-5-47, Matron Macdonald to Col. Bridges, August 15, 1917.

33 Sally Mitchell, *The New Girl: Girls' Culture in England, 1880-1915* (New York: Columbia University Press, 1995), 3. Mitchell argues that this drive for new horizons was part of the

social discourse regarding young women of the era. Veronica Strong-Boag traces the postwar developments in Canada, in *The New Day Recalled: Lives of Girls and Women in English Canada, 1919-1939* (Toronto: Copp Clark Pitman, 1988). Aspects of the new woman movement in the United States are summarized in Catherine Lavender, "Notes on New Womanhood," prepared for students at the College of Staten Island/CUNY, 1998, https://csivc.csi.cuny.edu/history/files/lavender/386/newwoman.pdf.

34 Janet S.K. Watson explores this concept in her study of women's and men's roles in Britain during the war. See Watson, *Fighting Different Wars;* Watson, "Wars in the Wards"; and Watson, "Khaki Girls, VADs and Tommy's Sisters."

35 LAC, W.D. Lighthall fonds, MG 29, D93, vol. 14, clippings file, *Montreal Daily Witness,* January 22, n.d.

36 Margaret Gillett, *We Walked Very Warily: A History of Women at McGill* (Montreal: Eden, 1981), 94. Despite her mother's caution, Alice Lighthall did not marry.

37 LAC, Sir Andrew Macphail fonds, MG 30, D150, vol. 1, file Dorothy Macphail, 1915, Dorothy Macphail to My Darling Daddy, October 10, 1915.

38 Conrad, Laidlaw, and Smyth, *No Place Like Home,* 253.

39 Sandra Gwyn, *Tapestry of War: A Private View of Canadians in the Great War* (Toronto: Harper Collins, 1992), 445; Canadian War Museum (CWM), Grace MacPherson Records, 58A 1, Diary, August 7 to 9, 1916 (CWM, Grace MacPherson Diary, August 7 to 9, 1916); Laurie Mook, "Women at University: The Early Years," *Contents* 44, no. 1 (Winter 1996): 9–10.

40 In 1915, when the British War Office opened military hospitals to VADs, room and board plus twenty pounds per annum and one pound per quarter for "upkeep and uniform" were provided as the basic stipend. This was raised to thirty pounds a year by 1918. See Joint War Committee of the British Red Cross Society and the Order of St. John of Jerusalem in England, *Reports by the Joint War Committee* ... (London: H.M.S.O., 1921), 192, 197–98.

41 K.J. Quarry, ed., *A Review of the History of St. John Ambulance in Saskatchewan, 1911-1983* (Regina: St. John Ambulance Association, 1983).

42 For a comprehensive analysis of the DSCR, see Morton and Wright, *Winning the Second Battle,* Chapter 5. There were seventy Ottawa VADs as of November 1915, but no other data show their employment history. See City of Ottawa Archives, St. John Ambulance Association Records, Ottawa Nursing Division No. 32, 1910–27, MG26 D83, 26083, box 15, "Report of the Commandant," Ottawa Women's Voluntary Aid Detachment, November 8, 1915.

43 LAC, Voice of the Pioneer, 9861, acc. 1981–0111, Violet Wilson Interview, c. 1970.

44 Ibid.

45 Editorial, "The Roll of Honour," *Civilian* 12, no. 9 (August 1919): 347–48; Graham S. Lowe, "Women, Work and the Office: The Feminisation of Clerical Occupations in Canada, 1901-1931," in *Rethinking Canada: The Promise of Women's History,* ed. Veronica Strong-Boag and Anita Clair Fellman (Toronto: Oxford University Press, 1997), 263.

46 Letter from Muriel Wainwright to Miss Reynolds, October 4, 1918, *The Civilian* 12, no. 1 (December 1918): 39.

47 References from the *Civilian* are taken from various editions beginning vol. 11, no. 7 (July 1918) through vol. 13, no. 7 (June 1920). Additional material is from the *Ottawa City Directories,* 1914-30.

48 Amber Lloydlangston, "From Expendable to Indispensable: Women in Science in the Department of Agriculture during the First World War" (paper presented at the annual meeting of the Canadian Historical Association, March 13, 1998), 13; LAC, Department of Agriculture, RG 17, vol. 2789, file 242 743, "P.C. 2170 (October 12, 1916)," re: veterans' re-employment.

49 LAC, Department of Agriculture, RG 17, vol. 2796, file 251 115, G.H. Clark, Seed Commissioner, to J.H.Grisdale, Deputy Minister, April 28, 1919.

50 Lloydlangston, "From Expendable to Indispensable," 13.

51 LAC, Department of Agriculture, RG 17, vol. 2808, file 269 269, G.H. Clarke to Deputy Minister of Agriculture, June 25, 1919.

52 Charles Lyons Foster, ed., *Letters from the Front: Being a Record of the Part Played by Officers of the Bank in the Great War, 1914-1919* (Toronto: Southam Press, 1920), 2:160, 2:184, 2:213, 2:225, 2:493; Lowe, "Women, Work and the Office," 260. See also Brian Douglas Tennyson, *The Canadian Experience of the Great War: A Guide to Memoirs* (Lanham, MD: Scarecrow Press, 2013), 433. In his brief biographical outline, Tennyson notes that Wynne-Roberts attended Battersea Polytechnical College shortly before immigrating to Canada. She returned to the bank after the war but left in 1920 to become a social worker, eventually becoming Mrs. McCaul.

53 Regarding Anne Bredin, see LAC, G.W.L. Nicholson fonds, MG 31, G19, file White Cross: Saskatchewan, 1915–16, Dr. F.C. Middleton to Lt. Col. A.J. Hosie, October 12, 1916; and Gertrude Charters, "The Black Death at Drumheller," *Maclean's*, March 5, 1966, 20.

54 Alison Prentice, "The Feminization of Teaching," in *The Neglected Minority: Essays in Canadian Women's History*, ed. Susan Mann Trofimenkoff and Alison Prentice (Toronto: McClelland and Stewart, 1977), 1:49–65.

55 Geraldine Jonich Clifford, "Daughters into Teachers: Educational and Demographic Influences on the Transformation of Teaching into Women's Work in America," in *Women Who Taught: Perspectives on the History of Women and Teaching*, ed. Alison Prentice and Marjorie Theobald (Toronto: University of Toronto Press, 1991), 115–35.

56 Annie Wynne-Roberts, from First Southern General Military Hospital, Birmingham, England, to Staff, Canadian Bank of Commerce, in Foster, *Letters from the Front*, 2:160–61.

57 Prentice, "The Feminization of Teaching," 49–65. The recorded comments of supervising matrons regarding the performance and character of VADs do not mention any problems with teachers serving as VADs. Matrons' comments on the Personnel Record Indexes in the BRCS MA are subject to BRCS privacy restrictions.

58 SJH, St. John Ambulance Association, *First Aid Bulletin* 4, no. 8 (October 1923): 9; Strome Galloway, *The White Cross in Canada, 1883-1983: A History of St. John Ambulance, Centennial Edition* (Ottawa: St. John Priory, 1983).

59 SJH, World War I – World War II, Records: VAD Training, box X(b). Ethel Fraser of Montreal was overseas as a VAD in England and France. Isobel Stewart, also from Montreal, was a VAD masseuse at Sainte-Anne-de-Bellevue hospital.

60 Janet Lee, *War Girls: The First Aid Nursing Yeomanry in the First World War* (Manchester: Manchester University Press, 2005), 23, 122. The FANY also operated hospitals and casualty clearing stations. It was affiliated with, but not part of, the Territorial Forces and, when the RAMC refused a similar affiliation, drove ambulances for the French and Belgian armies.

61 Ibid., 2.

62 Moore, "Canadian Women in the War Zone," 17.

63 Helen Zenna Smith, *Not So Quiet ... Stepdaughters of War* (New York: Feminist Press, 1989), 59. The book is based on the (now) lost diaries of Winifred Young, possibly a Red Cross VAD driver. The title is a subtle reference to Erich Maria Remarque's 1929 novel *Im Westen nichts Neues* (All quiet on the Western Front) about the strain of the First World War on German soldiers.

64 IWM, Marjorie Starr Diary, December 12, 1915. Starr was describing ambulances operated by the Royaumont hospital, not the BRCS women's convoys that started in mid-1916.

65 Bowser, *The Story of British V.A.D. Work*, 232.

66 Gwyn, *Tapestry of War*, 443; Joint War Committee, *Reports by the Joint War Committee*, 200–1; IWM, Marjorie Starr Diary, December 2, 1915. By the end of the war, women were also driving ambulances throughout England and Italy.

67 Elsie Chatwin interview, in Maureen Judge, dir., *And We Knew How to Dance: Women in World War I* (Montreal: National Film Board of Canada, 1994). Chatwin (Mrs. R.P. Malone) was 101 when interviewed. Her father, James N. Chatwin, emigrated from England in 1883 to become a pioneer businessman and tailor for the North West Mounted Police in Regina. Obituary, *Regina Leader Post*, June 1, 1949.

68 IMW, Women at Work Collection, BRCS 12.8/4, The Étretat Convoy, April 1916 (Mrs. Graham Jones, O.C., April 1916-October 1916).

69 Gwyn, *Tapestry of War*, 444–48.

70 CWM, Grace MacPherson Diary, August 7 to 9, 1916.

71 As quoted in Gwyn, *Tapestry of War*, 448.

72 CWM, Grace MacPherson Diary, March 28, 1917.

73 Eleven Canadians and four Newfoundlanders have been identified as drivers, and there may be more. Colonial VAD drivers were greatly outnumbered by their nursing counterparts; most drivers were British.

74 The gender of technology in the industrial era is discussed in Joy Parr, *The Gender of Breadwinners: Women, Men and Change in Two Industrial Towns, 1880-1950* (Toronto: University of Toronto Press, 1990), 69.

75 British Red Cross, "British Red Cross Transport during the First World War," http://redcross.org.uk/WW1.

76 F. Tennyson Jesse, "A Night with a Convoy," in *The Vogue Bedside Book*, ed. Josephine Ross (London: Vermillion, 1984), 109. The essay became a chapter in Jesse's *The Sword of Deborah*, which details her experience as a journalist with British women working in France during the war. F. Tennyson Jesse, *The Sword of Deborah: First-Hand Impressions of the British Women's Army in France* (London: William Heinemann, 1919).

77 Jesse, "A Night with a Convoy," in Ross, *The Vogue Bedside Book*, 109.

78 CWM, Grace MacPherson Diary, April 26, 1917.

79 Ibid., April 13, 1917. See also Gwyn, *Tapestry of War*, 447–48, 451; Watson, *Fighting Different Wars*, 114–18; Jesse, "A Night with a Convoy," in Ross, *The Vogue Bedside Book*, 112.

80 Terry Bishop-Stirling, "'Such Sights One Will Never Forget': Newfoundland Women and Overseas Nursing in the First World War," in *Sisterhood of Suffering and Service: Women and Girls of Canada and Newfoundland during the First World War*, ed. Sarah Glassford and Amy Shaw (Vancouver: UBC Press, 2012), 132–33. Gilbert Gosling was a businessman and

mayor of St. John's after 1912. His wife, Armine Nutting Gosling, was the driving force in
Newfoundland's suffrage movement and sister of American nursing activist Adelaide
Nutting. See Duley, *Where Once Our Mothers Stood We Stand*, 69, 71, 117.

81 CWM, Grace MacPherson Records, 58A 1, "Draft for article published in *Gold Stripe*,"
1919. In addition to Annie Gosling, whose dates with the convoy are unclear, three Canadians
from Ontario had arrived at Étaples a month before MacPherson: Jean Harstone, Charlotte
Leitch, and Jessie McLaughlin.

82 Debbie Marshall, *Give Your Other Vote to the Sister: A Woman's Journey into the Great War*
(Calgary: University of Calgary Press, 2007), 173–201. In late 1917, four female journalists
were granted permission to accompany Roberta MacAdams, CAMC nursing sister and first
woman elected to the Alberta Legislature, on a tour behind the lines in France. They wanted
to chronicle the work of Canadian women, particularly in the hospitals and the CRCS.
They included Moore, Nasmyth, Elizabeth (Elsie) Montizambert, and Florence MacPhedran.

83 Bishop-Stirling, "Such Sights One Will Never Forget," 132–33; Moore, "Canadian Women
in the War Zone," 171; Beatrice Nasmyth, *Vancouver Daily Province*, January 14, 1918; E.
Montizambert, "Canadian Red Cross Work in France," *Lancet*, January 26, 1918, 159–60.

84 Beatrice Nasmyth, "Canadian Girls Drive Ambulances and Think It Fun," *Vancouver Daily
Province*, March 2, 1918, quoted in Marshall, *Give Your Other Vote to the Sister*, 190.

85 IWM, Women at Work Collection, BRCS 12.8/6 and 12.8/7, BRCS Convoy, Le Tréport,
August 1918-March 1919 (IWM, BRCS Convoy, Le Tréport).

86 The three CAMC nursing sisters who died were Katherine Macdonald of Bradford, Ontario,
Gladys Wake of Victoria, British Columbia, and Margaret Lowe of Winnipeg, Manitoba.

87 IWM, BRCS Convoy, Le Tréport.

88 IWM, Jean Emily Harstone Papers, DD, Misc. box 40, M.O. 540, "While the World Sleeps,
Étaples 1917," 2.

89 H.M. Usborne, ed., *Women's Work in Wartime: A Handbook of Employments* (London: T.
Werner Laurie, c. 1917), 81.

90 Watson, *Fighting Different Wars*, 19–20, 36, 40. A paramilitary women's auxiliary, the
WAAC was formed in 1917 under the auspices of the War Office.

91 McPherson observes that the uniform distinguished the trained nurse from underqualified, and unqualified, practical nurses, midwives, and casual aids. See Kathryn McPherson,
Bedside Matters: The Transformation of Canadian Nursing, 1900-1990 (Toronto: University
of Toronto Press, 2003), 43. The CAMC nurses were known as "bluebirds" because of
their distinctive dress.

92 For Canada, see Bates, *A Cultural History of the Nurse's Uniform;* and for Britain, see Diana
Condell and Jean Liddiard, *Working for Victory? Images of Women in the First World War,
1914-1918* (London: Routledge and Kegan Paul, 1987); and Summers, *Angels and Citizens*.

93 Stella Bingham, *Ministering Angels* (London: Osprey, 1979), 143.

94 *Nursing Times*, April 10, 1915, quoted in Ruth Adam, *A Woman's Place, 1910-1975* (London:
Chatto and Windus, 1975), 55. Anne Summers notes that one hospital matron tried un-
successfully to have VADs referred to as "Vadets." See Summers, *Angels and Citizens*, 262.

95 Nova Scotia Archives, McGregor-Miller Collection, MG1, vol. 661, no. 8, Bessie Hall to
Mother, October 2, 1918. Not all VAD nursing detachments used head scarfs. Variations
on the mob cap worn by Victorian housemaids were also popular.

96 CNS, Sybil Johnson, Collection-201, file 2.01.013, "Sybil to Daddy" [Judge George E.
Johnson], Christmas Day 1916.

97 LAC, Voice of the Pioneer, 9861, acc. 1981–0111, Violet Wilson Interview, c. 1970.
98 Ibid.
99 Katharine Furse, *Hearts and Pomegranates: The Story of Forty-Five Years, 1875 to 1920* (London: Peter Davies, 1940), 302.
100 Irene Schuessler Poplin, "Nursing Uniforms: Romantic Idea, Functional Attire, or Instrument of Social Change," *Nursing History Review* 2 (1994): 153.
101 Maude Wilkinson, "Four Score and Ten: Part I," *Canadian Nurse* 73, no. 10 (October 1977): 29; Maude Wilkinson, *Four Score and Ten: Memoirs of a Canadian Nurse* (Brampton, ON: M.M. Armstrong, c. 2003), 43–44.
102 Diana Souhani, *Edith Cavell* (London: Quercus, 2010); Katie Pickles, *Transnational Outrage: The Death and Commemoration of Edith Cavell* (New York: Palgrave Macmillan, 2007); Anne-Marie Claire Hughes, "War, Gender, and National Mourning: The Significance of the Death and Commemoration of Edith Cavell in Britain," *European Review of History* 12, no. 3 (2005): 425–44.
103 Jeffrey S. Reznik, *Healing the Nation: Soldiers and the Culture of Caregiving during the Great War* (Manchester: Manchester University Press, 2004), 56.
104 The visual representations of women's part in the First World War are analyzed in Condell and Liddiard, *Working for Victory?* 20–53.
105 Expatriate Canadian millionaire Sir Max Aitken (Lord Beaverbrook), elder brother of VAD Laura Aitken, established the Canadian War Records Office in London in 1916 to publicize and document Canada's war effort. In July 1917, the photographs of MacPherson appeared in a London exhibition of Canadian war images, and one was reprinted in the *Canadian Daily Record*, a wartime newsletter. Gwyn, *Tapestry of War*, 435–38; CWM, Grace MacPherson Diary, June 9, 1917.
106 Jesse, "A Night with a Convoy," in Ross, *The Vogue Bedside Book*, 112.
107 Contemporary perceptions of women as nurses during war are found in Francis Gribble, *Women in War* (New York: E.P. Dutton, 1917).
108 Hampden Gordon, *Our Girls in Wartime* (London: John Lane, Bodley Head, c. 1917), 17. The letters "D.V." may stand for *Deo volente* (God willing).
109 Holt and Holt, *Till the Boys Come Home*, 45, 144–50; *In Praise of Nurses*, postcard series (Shrewsbury, UK: Halcyon Cards, c. 1914–18).
110 Jeffrey A. Keshen, *Propaganda and Censorship during Canada's Great War* (Edmonton: University of Alberta Press, 1996), 161–62.
111 Sharon Ouditt, *Fighting Forces, Writing Women: Identity and Ideology in the First World War* (New York: Routledge, 1994), 19–20. For civilian nursing uniforms, see Bates, *A Cultural History of the Nurse's Uniform*, 47, 57.
112 Monica Salmond, *Bright Armour: Memories of Four Years of War* (London: Faber and Faber, 1935), 23.
113 Ian Hugh Maclean Miller, *Our Glory and Our Grief: Torontonians and the Great War* (Toronto: University of Toronto Press, 2002), 23, 183–84.

Chapter 4: No Time for Sentiment

1 Centre for Newfoundland Studies, Memorial University Libraries (CNS), Frances Cluett Fonds, Collection-174, file 2.02.001, Frances Cluett to Mother, May 7, 1917.

2 Kathryn McPherson, *Bedside Matters: The Transformation of Canadian Nursing, 1900-1990* (Toronto: University of Toronto Press, 2003), 95.

3 CNS, Sybil Johnson, Collection-201, file 2.03.002, Sybil Johnson Diary, December 21, 1916 (CNS, Sybil Johnson Diary).

4 Canadian War Museum (CWM), Grace MacPherson Records, 58A 1, "Draft for article published in *Gold Stripe*," 1919.

5 Nova Scotia Archives (NSA), McGregor-Miller Collection, Bessie Hall Correspondence, MG1, vol. 661, Bessie Hall to Mother, October 20 and November 2, 1918.

6 Margaret Conrad, Toni Laidlaw, and Donna Smyth, eds., *No Place Like Home: Diaries and Letters of Nova Scotia Women, 1771-1938* (Halifax: Formac, 1988), 253–55.

7 NSA, Bessie Hall Correspondence, Bessie to Mum (Weds. Evening) October, 1918. The letter is undated, but the envelope has a Halifax postmark for October 2, 1918.

8 Ibid. The letter appears to have been composed at intervals over several days.

9 "Bessie Hall, 1890-1969," in Conrad, Laidlaw, and Smyth, *No Place Like Home*, 257.

10 NSA, Bessie Hall Correspondence, Bessie Hall to Mother, October 2 and December 19, 1918, January 3 and 13, 1919.

11 NSA, McGregor-Miller Collection, Bessie Hall Correspondence, MG1, vol. 661, Bessie Hall to Mother, Jim, et al, January 26, 1919 (emphasis in original).

12 The comments refer to the summer and fall of 1918, when Gordon was a VAD. She was interviewed in July 1974 for the Great War and Canadian Society Project, under a Toronto Opportunities for Youth program. The many interviews were consolidated into Daphne Read, ed., *The Great War and Canadian Society: An Oral History* (Toronto: New Hogtown Press, 1978). Read published the excerpts from the Gordon interview under the pseudonym "Adrienne Stone" (on pages 183–84). The original interview is in Library and Archives Canada (LAC), Great War and Canadian Society Project, Shirley Gordon Interview, A1 9903–0015, July 18, 1974. Comments in the interview transcripts are identical to those published.

13 LAC, Great War and Canadian Society Project, Shirley Gordon interview

14 Ibid.

15 Ibid.

16 Ibid.

17 Ibid.

18 There were three waves of the epidemic, from spring 1918 through winter 1920. See Magda Fahrni and Esyllt W. Jones, "Introduction," in *Epidemic Encounters: Influenza, Society, and Culture in Canada, 1918-20,* ed. Magda Fahrni and Esyllt W. Jones (Vancouver: UBC Press, 2012), 3–4.

19 The substantive literature on the explosion includes John Griffin Armstrong, *The Halifax Explosion and the Royal Canadian Navy: Inquiry and Intrigue* (Vancouver: UBC Press, 2002); Alan Ruffman and Colin D. Howell, eds., *Ground Zero: A Reassessment of the 1917 Explosion in Halifax Harbour* (Halifax: Nimbus and Gorsebrook Research Institute, 1994); and Laura M. MacDonald, *Curse of the Narrows: The Halifax Explosion, 1917* (Toronto: Harper Collins, 2005).

20 Camp Hill Hospital had 280 beds, but it admitted 1,400 civilian and military casualties on December 6. See *Halifax Chronicle Herald*, June 26, 1958, 23; NSA, St. John Ambulance Brigade Overseas, *Report of the Chief Commissioner for Brigade Overseas, 1 October 1915 to 31 December 1917* (London: Chancery of the Order, 1918), 15 (NSA, *Report of the Chief*

Commissioner). and Andrew Macphail, *Official History of the Canadian Forces in the Great War, 1914-1919: The Medical Services* (Ottawa: F.A. Acland, 1925), 327–28.

21 Graham Metson, ed., *The Halifax Explosion, December 6, 1917* (Toronto: McGraw-Hill, Ryerson, 1978), 55–56, 171; T.J. Murray, "Medical Aspects of the Disaster: The Missing Report of Dr. Daniel Fraser Harris," in Ruffman and Howell, *Ground Zero*, 234–35, 241; NSA, Red Cross Collection, MG20, vol. 321, "Report of the Work of the Halifax Central Nursing Division of the St. John Ambulance Brigade Overseas, Following the Explosion of December 6th, 1917 until December 31st, 1917" (NSA, "Report of the Work").

22 NSA, "Report of the Work," 1.

23 Murray, "Medical Aspects of the Disaster," 234–35; James Cantlie, *British Red Cross Society Nursing Manual, No. 2* (London: Cassell, 1914).

24 Mary Ann Monnon, *Miracles and Mysteries: The Halifax Explosion, December 6, 1917* (Hantsport, NS: Lancelot Press, 1977), 99–100.

25 NSA, *Report of the Chief Commissioner*, 17. MacIntosh compiled an account of VAD work during the immediate aftermath of the explosion. It was included in the report under the heading "Report of the Lady Divisional Superintendent, Halifax Nursing Division, December 13th, 1917," 15–17.

26 NSA, *Report of the Chief Commissioner*, 14–15; NSA, "Report of the Work," 2; NSA, MG20, vol. 321, "A Brief Account of Relief Work Undertaken by Mrs. G.A. MacIntosh and Assistants at the City Hall," 3. Clara Harris MacIntosh was in her early thirties at the time of the disaster.

27 Kathryn McPherson, "Nurses and Nursing in Early 20th Century Halifax" (master's diss., Dalhousie University, 1982), 1, 87.

28 Editorial, *Canadian Nurse* 14, no. 1 (January 1918): 803.

29 NSA, *Report of the Chief Commissioner*, 15.

30 Letter from a nurse on duty at the Naval Hospital, Gottengen Street, Halifax. "The Halifax Disaster," *Canadian Nurse* 14, no. 1 (January 1918): 798.

31 Convenor on Public Health Nursing, "Public Health Nursing Department," *Canadian Nurse* 14, no. 12 (December 1918): 1477–78; NSA, *Report of the Chief Commissioner*, 14–17.

32 G.W.L. Nicholson, *The White Cross in Canada: A History of St. John Ambulance* (Montreal: Harvest House, 1967), 71–72; Christopher McCreery, *The Maple Leaf and the White Cross* (Toronto: Dundurn Press, 2008), 80–81; Eileen Pettigrew, *The Silent Enemy: Canada and the Deadly Flu of 1918* (Saskatoon: Western Producer Prairie Books, 1983), 17, 97.

33 LAC, Sir Andrew Macphail fonds, MG 30, D150, vol. 1/2/8, file Dorothy MacPhail, 1918, Dorothy Macphail to Andrew Macphail, October 13 and November 7, 1918. Andrew Macphail was also a McGill academic and military medical historian. See Macphail, *Official History of the Canadian Forces;* Max Braithwaite, "The Year of the Killer Flu," *Maclean's,* February 1, 1953, 43; J.T.H. Connor, *Doing Good: The Life of Toronto's General Hospital* (Toronto: University of Toronto Press, 2000); and Rhonda Keen-Payne, "We Must Have Nurses: Spanish Influenza in America, 1918-1919," *Nursing History Review* 8 (2000): 151–52.

34 "The Epidemic Workers," *Civilian* 12, no. 1 (December 1918): 39; Nicholson, *The White Cross in Canada,* 72; Archives of Ontario (AO), St. John Ambulance Association (SJAA): Administration Records, 1909–77, MU 6814, file "1917-1918 Secretary's Report, Ottawa Local Centre," 4.

35 Quoted in Pettigrew, *The Silent Enemy,* 100. Having learned from the lack of nursing resources and the high casualty rate during the epidemic, Mayor Fisher promoted the founding of the Ottawa Civic Hospital in 1920 despite criticism for its high cost of $2 million. See Valerie Knowles, *Capital Lives: 32 Profiles of Leading Ottawa Personalities* (Ottawa: Book Coach Press, 2005).

36 Gertrude [Murphy] Charters, "The Black Death at Drumheller," *Maclean's,* March 5, 1966, 20, 21.

37 John M. Barry, *The Great Influenza: The Epic Story of the Deadliest Plague in History* (New York: Viking, 2004), 319. "To special" means to give particular attention to patients who need extra care.

38 Gertrude [Murphy] Charters, "The Black Death at Drumheller," 29.

39 Gladys Morton, "The Pandemic Influenza of 1918," *Canadian Nurse* 72, no. 12 (December 1976): 32–37; Desmond Morton and Glenn Wright, *Winning the Second Battle: Canadian Veterans and the Return to Civilian Life, 1915-1930* (Toronto: University of Toronto Press, 1987), 91; Keen-Payne, "We Must Have Nurses," 150; Jean Gunn, "President's Address, C.N.A.T.N. Convention," *Canadian Nurse* 15, no. 8 (August 1919): 1920; Ian Hugh Maclean Miller, *Our Glory and Our Grief: Torontonians and the Great War* (Toronto: University of Toronto Press, 2002), 39.

40 Amelia Earhart, *The Fun of It: Random Records of My Own Flying and of Women in Aviation* (New York: Harcourt, Brace, 1975), 19–20.

41 For a discussion of these issues with regard to nursing during the influenza epidemic, see Nancy K. Bristow, "'You Can't Do Anything for Influenza': Doctors, Nurses and the Power of Gender during the Influenza Pandemic in the United States," in *The Spanish Flu Pandemic of 1918-1919: New Perspectives,* ed. Howard Phillips and David Killingray (London: Routledge, 2003), 58–69.

42 LAC, Great War and Canadian Society Project, Jean Marita Sears Interview, A1 9903–0008, July 23, 1974 (LAC, Jean Marita Sears Interview). Sears was posted to 2nd London General Hospital, in Chelsea.

43 Maureen Judge, dir., *And We Knew How to Dance: Women in World War I* (Montreal: National Film Board of Canada, 1994).

44 CNS, Frances Cluett Fonds, Collection-174, file 2.02.001, Frances Cluett to Mother, December 31, 1916.

45 McPherson, *Bedside Matters,* 29–47. McPherson notes that nursing probationers of the era were expected to demonstrate "intelligent subordination to the rules." Ibid., 33.

46 Viola Henderson, "V.A.D. Work in Montreal," *Canadian Nurse* 14, no. 8 (August 1918): 1244–48.

47 Elise Chenier, "Class, Gender, and the Social Standard: The Montreal Junior League, 1912-1939," *Canadian Historical Review* 90, no. 4 (December 2009): 690–92.

48 Charles Copp, "St. John's Ambulance Brigade," *Canadian Nurse* 14, no. 7 (July 1918): 1165–66.

49 "Annie Wynne-Roberts," in *Letters from the Front: Being a Record of the Part Played by Officers of the Bank in the Great War, 1914-1919,* ed. Charles Lyons Foster (Toronto: Southam Press, 1920), 2:161, 2:225.

50 CNS, Sybil Johnson Diary, January 3, 1917. Sybil and Jill were posted together to 1st Western General Hospital, Liverpool.

51 LAC, Voice of the Pioneer, 9861, acc. 1981–0111, Violet Wilson Interview, c. 1970 (LAC, Violet Wilson Interview).

52 Eileen Crofton, *The Women of Royaumont: A Scottish Woman's Hospital on the Western Front* (East Linton, UK: Tuckwell, 1997), 50; IWM, Marjorie Starr Diary, September 15, 1915.

53 CNS, Frances Cluett Fonds, Collection-174, file 2.02.001, Frances Cluett to Mother, December 31, 1916. According to the editors of Cluett's letters, she wrote in the idiomatic style of her Belleoram origins – her words were a "continuation of the chatter around the kitchen table." See Bill Rompkey and Bert Riggs, eds., *Your Daughter Fanny: The War Letters of Frances Cluett, VAD* (St. John's: Flanker Press, 2006), xxix.

54 CNS, Sybil Johnson, Collection-201, file 2.01.014, Sybil Johnson to Mother, January 10, 1917. A Bath chair is a high-backed wheeled chair made of wicker or rattan.

55 The term "Blighty" is a remnant of British imperialism; borrowed from Hindustani, it means "a country across the sea," in this instance Britain. It also referred to any wound that was sufficient to take a man out of active service without disabling him. Jeffrey A. Keshen, *Propaganda and Censorship during Canada's Great War* (Edmonton: University of Alberta Press, 1996), 143.

56 CNS, Frances Cluett Fonds, Collection-174, file 2.02.003, Frances Cluett to Mother, February 4, 1918. Hydrog Ammon Oil may have been Hydogen, and Red Lotion was a zinc-based salve for skin ulcerations. See Rompkey and Riggs, *Your Daughter Fanny*, 129.

57 IWM, Marjorie Starr Diary, October 1 and 4, 1915.

58 Ibid.

59 Ibid., September 28, 1915.

60 Ibid., January 7, 1916.

61 Ibid., October 8, 1915.

62 Ibid., September 15, 1915.

63 Henriette Donner, "Under the Cross: Why VADs Performed the Filthiest Tasks in the Dirtiest War: Red Cross Women Volunteers, 1914-1918," *Journal of Social History* 30, no. 3 (Spring 1997): 696–97.

64 Studies on shell shock in the First World War include Peter Leese, *Shell Shock: Traumatic Neurosis and the British Soldiers of the First World War* (Houndmills, UK: Palgrave Macmillan, 2002); Paul F. Lerner, *Hysterical Men: War, Psychiatry and the Politics of Trauma in Germany, 1890-1930* (Ithaca, NY: Cornell University Press, 2003); and Benjamin Shepard, *A War of Nerves: Soldiers and Psychiatrists, 1914-1918* (London: Jonathan Cape, 2000).

65 Terry Bishop-Stirling, "'Such Sights One Will Never Forget': Newfoundland Women and Overseas Nursing in the First World War," in *Sisterhood of Suffering and Service: Women and Girls of Canada and Newfoundland during the First World War*, ed. Sarah Glassford and Amy Shaw (Vancouver: UBC Press, 2012), 128. Sybil and Jill (Estelle) were aged thirty and twenty-eight respectively.

66 CNS, Frances Cluett Fonds, Collection-174, file 2.02.001, Frances Cluett to Mother, December 31, 1916. Cluett sailed with Bertha Bartlett, Henrietta Gallishaw, and Eda Clare Janes. A fifth VAD, Alice Hewitt, became ill and could not go to Lincoln.

67 LAC, Alice Bray fonds, MG 30, E572, vol. 1, Alice Bray to Mother, August 12, 1917.

68 IWM, Marjorie Starr Diary, December 2, 1915.

69 LAC, Jean Marita Sears Interview, July 23, 1974.

70 CWM, Grace MacPherson Records, 58A 1, Diary, May 13, 1917.

71 CWM, Grace MacPherson Records, "Draft for article published in *Gold Stripe*," 1919; Sandra Gwyn, *Tapestry of War: A Private View of Canadians in the Great War* (Toronto: Harper Collins, 1992), 451.

72 Carroll Smith-Rosenberg, "The Female World of Love and Ritual: Relations between Women in Nineteenth-Century America," in *Disorderly Conduct: Visions of Gender in Victorian America*, ed. Carroll Smith-Rosenberg (New York: Knopf, 1985), 67.

73 K.M. Barrow, "A 'V.A.D.' at the Base," in *Reminiscent Sketches: 1914-1918*, ed. Members of Her Majesty Queen Alexandra's Imperial Military Nursing Service (London: J. Bale, and Sons and Danielsson, 1922), 75.

74 Christine E. Hallett, *Containing Trauma: Nursing Work in the First World War* (Manchester: Manchester University Press, 2009), 85–92.

75 IWM, Marjorie Starr Diary, September 27, 1915.

76 Desmond Morton, *When Your Number's Up: The Canadian Soldier in the First World War* (Toronto: Random House, 1993), 191–92.

77 McPherson, *Bedside Matters*, 80.

78 CNS, Sybil Johnson Diary, August 13, 1917.

79 IWM, Marjorie Starr Diary, October 4, 1915. The rubber gloves were sent from Montreal by Starr's mother, as Royaumont had limited resources for extra supplies.

80 National Archives, Miscellaneous Files Relating to Army Nursing Staff and Nursing Establishment, 1914-18, WO 329/3254, "VADs – Much Illness and Debilitation," n.d.

81 CNS, Sybil Johnson Diary, April 27, May 2, and May 3, 1917. The sisters were posted to 1st Western General Hospital, Liverpool, from late 1916. Sybil returned to St. John's in July 1918. Jill remained until April 1919.

82 IWM, Marjorie Starr Diary, October 4, 1915; Crofton, *The Women of Royaumont*.

83 "Annie Wynne-Roberts," in Foster, *Letters from the Front*, 2:185–86.

84 CNS, Frances Cluett Fonds, Collection-174, file 2.02.001, Frances Cluett to Mother, October 26, 1917.

85 "Anne Wynne-Roberts," in Foster, *Letters from the Front*, 2:225.

86 CNS, Sybil Johnson Diary, July 4, 1917.

87 LAC, Violet Wilson Interview, c. 1970.

88 IWM, Marjorie Starr Diary, October 8, 1915.

89 Ibid., September 15 and October 10, 1915.

90 CNS, Frances Cluett Fonds, Collection-174, file 2.02.001, Frances Cluett to Mother, February 25, 1917.

91 IWM, Marjorie Starr Diary, September 15, 1915; CNS, Frances Cluett Fonds, Collection-174, file 2.02.001, Frances Cluett to Mother, February 25, September 28, and October 3, 1917; *Civilian* 11, no. 7 (July 1918): 150–51.

92 LAC, Jean Marita Sears Interview, July 23, 1974; CNS, Sybil Johnson Diary, June 12, 1917. Sears was posted to 2nd London General Hospital, Chelsea.

93 Canadian Red Cross Society, *What the Canadian Red Cross Society Is Doing in the Great War: Being an Outline of the Organization and Work of the Canadian Red Cross Society* (Toronto: Canadian Red Cross Society, 1918), 18.

94 IWM, Women at Work Collection, BRCS 25.3/10, "Women's Work in Relation to Sick and Wounded," 2, 18–20, n.d.

95 IWM, Marjorie Starr Diary, October 8, 1915; CNS, Sybil Johnson Diary, April 29, 1917.

96 IWM, Women at Work Collection, BRCS 1.1/40.

97 Enid Bagnold, *A Diary without Dates: Thoughts and Impressions of a VAD* (London: Heinemann, 1918); Anne Sebba, *Enid Bagnold: A Biography* (London: Weidenfeld and Nicholson, 1986), 61–62. Bagnold's VAD writing is also discussed in Christine E. Hallett, "Portrayals of Suffering: Perceptions of Trauma in the Writings of First World War Nurses and Volunteers," *Canadian Bulletin of Medical History* 27, no. 1 (2010): 65–84.

98 Diana Cooper, *The Rainbow Comes and Goes* (London: Hart-Davis, 1959), 126.

99 Editorial, "The Territorial Force Nursing Service," *Hospital*, December 18, 1920, 269.

100 Mary MacLeod Moore, *The Maple Leaf's Red Cross: The War Story of the Canadian Red Cross Overseas* (London: Skeffington and Son, 1920), 176; Keshen, *Propaganda and Censorship*, Chapter 5; Marjory Lang, *Women Who Made the News: Female Journalists in Canada, 1880–1945* (Montreal and Kingston: McGill-Queen's University Press, 1999), 59, 211, 274. A resident correspondent for *Saturday Night*, Moore contributed to other publications about Canadian women's wartime activities overseas.

101 Helen Kankitar, "'Real True Boys': Moulding the Cadets of Imperialism," in *Dislocating Masculinity: Comparative Ethnographies*, ed. Andrea Cornwall and Nancy Lindisfarne (New York: Routledge, 1994), 186–96.

102 Kate John Finzi, *Eighteen Months in the War Zone: A Record of a Woman's Work on the Western Front* (London: Cassell, 1916), 250; Mrs. (Elsa) Alphonse Courlander, "The V.A.D. Nurse," in *Women War Workers: Accounts Contributed by Representative Workers of the Work Done by Women in the More Important Branches of War Employment*, ed. Gilbert Stone (New York: Thomas Y. Crowell, 1917), 194.

103 Alan R. Young, "'We Throw the Torch': Canadian Memorials of the Great War and the Mythology of Heroic Sacrifice," *Journal of Canadian Studies* 24, no. 4 (Winter 1989–90): 7.

104 Ibid.

105 CNS, Frances Cluett Fonds, Collection-174, file 2.02.001, Frances Cluett to Mother, December 31, 1916.

106 CNS, Sybil Johnson, Collection-201, file 2.01.013, Sybil Johnson to Father, December 25, 1916, and January 15, 1917.

107 LAC, Jean Marita Sears Interview, July 23, 1974; LAC, Shirley Gordon Interview, July 18, 1974.

108 LAC, Alice Bray fonds, MG 30, E572, vol. 1, Alice Bray to Mother, October 5, 1916.

109 Quoted in Read, *The Great War and Canadian Society*, 125.

110 LAC, Alice Bray fonds, MG 30, E572, vol. 1, Alice Bray to Mother, October 21, 1916.

111 Ibid., April 1917.

112 LAC, Violet Wilson Interview, c. 1970.

113 Hallett, *Containing Trauma*, 127.

114 CNS, Frances Cluett Fonds, Collection-174, file 2.02.001, Fanny Cluett to Mother, October 26, 1917, Rouen.

115 IWM, Women at Work Collection, BRCS 10.4/10, "Stripes," n.d.

116 *Civilian* 11, no. 10 (September 1918): 254.

117 "Annie Wynne-Roberts," in Foster, *Letters from the Front*, 2:225. Due to censorship, it is unclear if this was in Calais, Le Havre, or Rouen.

118 Quoted in Crofton, *The Women of Royaumont*, 79–80.

119 Ibid.

120 IWM, Marjorie Starr Diary, November 14, 1915.

121 Lyn Macdonald, *The Roses of No Man's Land* (London: Penguin, 1993), 112.
122 CNS, Sybil Johnson Diary, January 14, 1917 (emphasis in original).
123 Ibid., June 16, 1917 (emphasis in original).
124 Ibid., July 17, 1917 (emphasis in original).
125 Ibid., February 3, 1918.
126 IWM, Marjorie Starr Diary, September 27, 1915.
127 CNS, Frances Cluett Fonds, Collection-174, file 2.02.001, Frances Cluett to Mother, February 17, 1918, September 1918, and October 26, 1917.
128 CNS, Sybil Johnson Diary, July 18, 1918.
129 "Annie Wynne-Roberts," in Foster, *Letters from the Front*, 2:184, 2:186.
130 Janet S.K. Watson, *Fighting Different Wars: Experience, Memory, and the First World War in Britain* (Cambridge: Cambridge University Press, 2004), 87.
131 Copp, "St. John's Ambulance Brigade," 1166; AO, A.K. Prentice Scrapbook, 1939-46, F823/MV6858, undated newspaper item, c. summer 1918.
132 St. John House Archives and Library (SJH), Canadian Branch of the St. John Ambulance Association, "His Excellency the Governor General Honours Young Ladies for Overseas Service," *First Aid Bulletin* (December 1923): 15; SJH, St. John Ambulance Association, "Service Medals, 1914-1918," *First Aid and the St. John Ambulance Gazette* (UK) 28, no. 325 (July 1921): 12. General Service Medals were for service in any overseas location, but Victory (or Allied) Medals were for service in a theatre of war. All were approved for men and women by the British War Office.
133 Quoted in Stella Bingham, *Ministering Angels* (London: Osprey, 1979), 130.
134 LAC, Jean Marita Sears Interview, July 23, 1974; CNS, Sybil Johnson Diary, July 8, 1917; LAC, Violet Wilson Interview, c. 1970. The Sears family published a small newspaper in Ontario. Sybil Johnson's father was a justice of the Supreme Court of Newfoundland in St. John's. Wilson was the daughter of an Edmonton physician.
135 IWM, Marjorie Starr Diary, September 28 and December 4, 1915.
136 CNS, Sybil Johnson Diary, March 30, 1917; Watson, *Fighting Different Wars*, 81–82, 92.
137 LAC, Violet Wilson Interview, c. 1970.
138 Ibid.; Janet S.K. Watson, "Active Service: Gender, Class and British Representations of the Great War" (PhD diss., Stanford University, 1996), 157–58; Watson, *Fighting Different Wars*, 81–82, 92.
139 CNS, Frances Cluett Fonds, Collection-174, file 2.02.001, Frances Cluett to Mother, March 29 and May 7, 1917; CNS, Frances Cluett Fonds, Collection-174, file 2.02.001, Frances Cluett to Lil, October 3 and 26, 1917.
140 Bishop-Stirling, "'Such Sights One Will Never Forget,'" 139.
141 Bagnold, *A Diary without Dates*, 81, 83.
142 LAC, Violet Wilson Interview, c. 1970.
143 Judge, *And We Knew How to Dance*.
144 LAC, Jean Marita Sears Interview, July 23, 1974.
145 Miller married Eric Ayre in Edinburgh in June 1915, and he was killed in action at Beaumont Hamel on July 1, 1916. In October 1918, Pinfold married Clarence Lawrence in England, who died of influenza on November 1. See CNS, Janet (Miller) Ayre Murray, Collection-158, file 106; information on Ruby Pinfold courtesy Randy Carey, independent researcher; "Daisy Johnson (Cook)," *Regina Leader Post*, June 9, 1983.

146 Eva Morgan's commentary, in Judge, *And We Knew How to Dance*. Referred to in the documentary by her married name, Eva Fraser Kingman was twenty-three when she joined the Canadian Imperial VADs. She married Douglas F. Morgan after the war.

147 LAC, Violet Wilson Interview, c. 1970.

148 Vera Brittain, *Testament of Youth: An Autobiographical Study of the Years 1900–1925* (1933, repr., London: Fontana, 1979), 165–66.

149 Sandra M. Gilbert, "Soldier's Heart: Literary Men, Literary Women, and the Great War," in *Behind the Lines: Gender and the Two World Wars*, ed. Margaret R. Higonnet et al. (New Haven: Yale University Press, 1987), 200, 211.

150 Deborah Gorham, *Vera Brittain: A Feminist Life* (Toronto: University of Toronto Press, 2000), 101, 117.

151 CNS, Frances Cluett Fonds, Collection-174, file 2.02.002, Frances Cluett to Mother, March 29, 1917.

152 CNS, Sybil Johnson Diary, January 25, 1917.

153 Ibid., February 12, 1917; CNS, Sybil Johnson, Collection-201, file 2.01.014, Sybil Johnson to Mother, January 29, 1917.

154 CNS, Frances Cluett Fonds, Collection-174, file 2.02.001, Frances Cluett to Mother, March 24 through April 1, 1917.

155 Lieutenant Allan Greery, CEF, in the autograph album of Beatrice Mack, Canadian Officers' Hospital, Crowborough, Sussex, April 25, 1917, Mack family papers, courtesy of Eric Wessman.

156 Nancy A. Nygaard, "'Too Awful for Words' ... Nursing Narratives of the Great War" (PhD diss., University of Wisconsin, 2002), 168–70. For underage soldiers, see Tim Cook, "'He Was Determined to Go': Underage Soldiers in the Canadian Expeditionary Force," *Histoire sociale* 41, no. 81 (May 2008): 41–47.

157 IWM, Marjorie Starr Diary, September 15, 1915.

158 Ibid., October 8, 1915.

159 CNS, Sybil Johnson Diary, August 13, 1917.

160 Ibid., April 20, 1917.

161 CNS, Frances Cluett Fonds, Collection-174, file 2.02.001, Frances Cluett to Mother, December 29, 1917; CNS, Sybil Johnson Diary, December 30, 1917.

CHAPTER 5: SAYING GOODBYE

1 Provincial Archives of Alberta (PAA), Agnes Wilson Teviotdale, MG 73.72, Interview, January 19, 1973

2 Janet S.K. Watson, *Fighting Different Wars: Experience, Memory, and the First World War in Britain* (Cambridge: Cambridge University Press, 2004), 263; Alison Light, *Forever England: Femininity, Literature, and Conservatism between the Wars* (London: Routledge, 1991), 19; Gail Braybon and Penny Summerfield, *Out of the Cage: Women's Experiences in Two World Wars* (London: Pandora, 1987), 64.

3 Gertrude [Murphy] Charters, "The Black Death at Drumheller," *Macleans*, March 5, 1966, 29.

4 John Ellis and Michael Cox, *World War I Databook: The Essential Facts and Figures for All Combatants* (London: Aurum Press, 2001); Magda Fahrni and Esyllt W. Jones,

"Introduction," in *Epidemic Encounters: Influenza, Society, and Culture in Canada, 1918-20*, ed. Magda Fahrni and Esyllt W. Jones (Vancouver: UBC Press, 2012), 4; Desmond Morton and Glenn Wright, *Winning the Second Battle: Canadian Veterans and the Return to Civilian Life, 1915-1930* (Toronto: University of Toronto Press, 1987), ix.

5 Doreen Gery's commentary, in Maureen Judge, dir., *And We Knew How to Dance: Women in World War I* (Montreal: National Film Board of Canada, 1994).

6 LAC, Alice Bray fonds, MG 30, E572, vol. 1, Alice Bray to Mother, November 18, 1918.

7 Ceta Ramkhalawansingh, "Women during the Great War," in *Women at Work: Ontario, 1850-1930*, ed. Janice Acton, Barbara Shepard, and Penny Goldsmith (Toronto: Canadian Women's Educational Press, 1974), 293, 296.

8 The female franchise in Newfoundland was passed into law on April 13, 1925. In October 1928, some fifty-two thousand Newfoundland and Labrador women voted for the first time in a general election.

9 LAC, Voice of the Pioneer, 9861, acc. 1981–0111, Violet Wilson Interview, c. 1970 (LAC, Violet Wilson Interview).

10 Sandra M. Gilbert, "Soldier's Heart: Literary Men, Literary Women, and the Great War," in *Behind the Lines: Gender and the Two World Wars*, ed. Margaret R. Higonnet et al. (New Haven: Yale University Press, 1987), 225.

11 Centre for Newfoundland Studies, Memorial University Libraries (CNS), Sybil Johnson, Collection-201, file 2.03.002, Sybil Johnson Diary, July 18, 1918 (CNS, Sybil Johnson Diary).

12 The princess was just twenty-one when the war ended.

13 Joint War Committee of the British Red Cross Society and the Order of St. John of Jerusalem in England, *Reports by the Joint War Committee ...* (London: H.M.S.O., 1921), 195–96. Three other imperial detachments were formed in addition to Lady Perley's VADs. They were led by Lady Robertson of Australia, Lady Gladstone of South Africa, and Miss Mackenzie of New Zealand.

14 Desmond Morton, *A Peculiar Kind of Politics: Canada's Overseas Ministry in the First World War* (Toronto: University of Toronto Press, 1982), 26–27, 104, 112; LAC, Sir George H. Perley fonds, MG 27 II, D12, vol. 15, 1918–1922; Mary MacLeod Moore, "Canadian Women War Workers Overseas," *Canadian Magazine* 52, no. 3 (January 1919): 743–44; Imperial War Museum (IWM), Women at Work Collection, BRCS 12.11/4, Lady Perley's report, "Canadian Imperial Voluntary Aid Detachment," July 10, 1919.

15 LAC, Sir George H. Perley fonds, MG 27, II, D12, vol. 14, file 1, Anne Merrill, "A New V.A.D. Organization Formed in England" (newspaper clipping, c. 1918).

16 Wealtha A. Wilson and Ethel T. Raymond, "Canadian Women in the Great War," in *Canada and the Great War*, vol. 6, *Special Services, Heroic Deeds, Etc.* (Toronto: United Publishers of Canada, 1921), 191. No explanation for the "R" has been found, but it may have stood for "Reserve," given that the Joint Women's VAD Committee at Devonshire House had authorized the creation of reserve detachments from Britain's colonies and dominions. Other Imperial VAD organizations created their own distinctive badges, including the Australians and the South Africans. See Merrill, "A New V.A.D. Organization."

17 National Archives (NA), Miscellaneous Files Relating to Army Nursing Staff and Nursing Establishment, 1914–18, WO 222/2134, E.M. McCarthy, "Report on the Work of the C.A.M.C. Nursing Service with the B.E.F. in France"; Serge Marc Durflinger, *Veterans with a Vision: Canada's War Blinded in Peace and War* (Vancouver: UBC Press, 2010),

Chapter 1; IWM, Women at Work Collection, BRCS 12.11/4, Lady Perley's report, "Canadian Imperial Voluntary Aid Detachment," July 10, 1919.

18 Archives of Ontario (AO), Sir George Perley Papers, MU 4113, file Canadian High Commissioner, 1918–1922, Draft Speech, April 15, 1922; Maude E. Seymour Abbott, "Lectures on the History of Nursing," *Canadian Nurse* 19, no. 5 (May 1923): 266–67. The Canadian Red Cross Nurses' Rest House was established in the former Hôtel du Nord, Boulogne. The Canadian Red Cross in Boulogne was headquartered in the former Hôtel Christol. These establishments were restored to their original purpose at the end of the war. See NA, War Diary, WO 95/3988–91, 256.

19 Canadian War Museum (CWM), Grace MacPherson Records, 58A 1, "Draft for article published in *Gold Stripe*," 1919.

20 Kathryn McPherson, *Bedside Matters: The Transformation of Canadian Nursing, 1900-1990* (Toronto: University of Toronto Press, 2003), 29–47.

21 Ruby Heap, "Training Women for a New 'Women's Profession': Physiotherapy Education at the University of Toronto, 1917–40," *History of Education Quarterly* 35, no. 2 (Summer 1995): 139; Judith Friedland, *Restoring the Spirit: The Beginnings of Occupational Therapy in Canada, 1890-1930* (Montreal and Kingston: McGill-Queen's University Press, 2011), 98–113; Morton and Wright, *Winning the Second Battle*, 41, 93.

22 LAC, Department of Militia and Defence CAMC Nursing Service Overseas, First World War, RG 9, III, B2, vol. 3459, file 10–1-7, four letters re Grace Jenkins application, February 1915 through May 1916. Jenkins was a qualified masseuse who had two years of nurses' training, but Macdonald refused her application. The Granville Special Hospital was relocated from the southeast coast to Buxton, Derbyshire in October 1917, due to air attacks. Macdonald initially referred massage applications to the St. John Ambulance and the British Red Cross, and later to the British Almeric Paget Corps, which supplied civilian masseuses to the Royal Army Medical Corps (RAMC) and the CAMC if needed.

23 Until 1976, "Overseas" referred to all colonial brigades; official direction came from the St. John Ambulance Association London office. Christopher McCreery, *The Maple Leaf and the White Cross* (Toronto: Dundurn Press, 2008), 145.

24 Heap, "Training Women," 139–40; Friedland, *Restoring the Spirit*, 114–17. Heap cites the twelve-month diploma course in massage and medical gymnastics that was established at McGill University School of Physical Education in 1916.

25 Some of the militarist terminology, such as "commandant," was also discarded for the nursing divisions, though local supervisors retained "lady superintendent" under the new WAD organization. See G.W.L. Nicholson, *The White Cross in Canada: A History of St. John Ambulance* (Montreal: Harvest House, 1967), 59.

26 LAC, Department of Militia and Defence, RG 9, III, B2, vol. 3459, file 10–1-7, Memorandum, Minister's Office, O.M.F.C., July 3, 1918; *Women's Aid Department (W.A.D.) - St. John Ambulance Brigade (Overseas) within the Dominion of Canada - Regulations* (Ottawa: King's Printer, 1918), 4–7. The new age limits varied slightly, with function trainers (FT) from twenty-one to fifty years, as compared to forty-eight years for Nursing Members. FTs were contracted for twelve-month terms, and VAD nurses continued with six-month contracts. There were other minor differences, but regulations and allowances were identical. Special service VADs were more limited, from twenty-two to thirty-eight years, with salary based on seniority and experience. All were required to obtain the two basic St. John Ambulance VAD certificates.

27 LAC, Department of Militia and Defence, RG 9, III, B2, vol. 3460, file 10–1-7, Memorandum, Minister's Office, O.M.F.C., July 3, 1918. The post of minister of overseas Military Forces was established in October 1916 and held by Sir George Perley until October 1917. He was succeeded by Sir Edward Kemp, who held the position until July 1920, when the ministry was dissolved.

28 Jean Gunn, "Canadian National Association of Trained Nurses' Convention, 1918," *Canadian Nurse* 14, no. 8 (August 1918): 1211.

29 LAC, Department of Militia and Defence, RG 9, B2, vol. 3460, file 10–1-7, Maj-Gen. G.L. Foster, D.M.S., to the Secretary, Hon. Minister, O.M.F.C., July 8, 1918.

30 LAC, Department of Militia and Defence, RG 9, B2, vol. 3460, file 10–1-7, Maj-Gen. Foster to Major E. Bristol, C.M.G., July 9, 1918.

31 LAC, Department of Militia and Defence, RG 9, B2, vol. 3460, file 10–1-7, Memo from Matron Macdonald, August 14, 1918.

32 LAC, Kemp fonds, MG 27 II, D9, vol. 106, Dr. Clarke to Prof. Mavor, February 16, 1917.

33 LAC, Kemp fonds, MG 27, II, D9, vol. 106, R.W. Turner, G.O.C./O.M.F.C., Cdn HQ, London, to General Foster, DMS, August 1, 1918; LAC, Department of Militia and Defence, RG 9, III, B2, vol. 3460, file 10–1-7, Memorandum from DDMS to DGMS, OMFC, August 20, 1918; LAC, Department of Militia and Defence, RG 9, III, B2, vol. 3588, file 22–7-10, O.C. No. 4 Canadian General Hospital, Basingstoke, to ADMS Canadians, October 27, 1918. Sir Richard Turner, general officer commanding the OMFC, summarized the opinions of Senators McLennan and White in a letter to General Foster, favouring the use of VADs over removing nursing sisters from regular duties. Dr. Lambert organized the Almeric Paget Corps prior to joining the RAMC in 1915 and believed that using nurses for massage was uneconomic, given that a laywoman could be trained as effectively, with a better knowledge of anatomy and physiology.

34 McPherson, *Bedside Matters*, 271n2. Census data show 5,600 nursing graduates in 1911, rising to 22,385 in 1921. See also Natalie Riegler, *Jean I. Gunn: Nursing Leader* (Toronto: A.M.S. and Fitzhenry and Whiteside, 1997), 83–84.

35 Margaret Stanley, "Report of Special Committee," *Canadian Nurse* 14, no. 8 (August 1918): 1232–33.

36 Jean Gunn, "Nursing: Address Given before National Council of Women," *Woman's Century* 6, no. 5 (August 1918): 11.

37 Ibid.

38 Charles Copp, "St. John's Ambulance Brigade," *Canadian Nurse* 14, no. 7 (July 1918): 1166; Stanley, "Report of Special Committee," 1235.

39 "Secretary's Report: Canadian National Association of Trained Nurses' Convention, 1918," *Canadian Nurse* 14, no. 8 (August 1918): 1226. Of the two thousand Canadian and Newfoundland VADs, no more than ten were found to have taken formal nurses' training in the postwar. The city directories identified fewer than ten who worked as casual nurses after the war.

40 "Canadian Association of Nurse Education: Summary of Convention Proceedings, Vancouver, 1919," *Canadian Nurse* 15, no. 9 (September 1919): 1989–90.

41 McPherson, *Bedside Matters*, 70n142; "The Second Annual Convention of the Saskatchewan Registered Nurses' Association," *Canadian Nurse* 15, no. 5 (May 1919): 1764.

42 Helen MacMurchy, "The Future of the Nursing Profession," *Canadian Nurse* 16, no. 2 (February 1920): 73.

43 Dianne Dodd, "Advice to Parents: The Blue Books, Helen MacMurchy, M.D., and the Federal Department of Health, 1920–1934," *Canadian Bulletin of Medical History* 8, no. 2 (1991): 203–30.

44 Gunn, "Canadian National Association," 1211.

45 As Susan Mann notes, calculations vary with the sources, but Macdonald counted 3,141 CAMC nurses in total. Their CAMC contracts terminated six months after the end of the war. See Susan Mann, *Margaret Macdonald: Imperial Daughter* (Montreal and Kingston: McGill-Queen's University Press, 2005), 148, 224n1; LAC, Macdonald fonds, MG 30, E45, file Correspondence 1923, Macdonald to W.R. London, May 19, 1922.

46 Jean Gunn, "President's Address C.N.A.T.N. Convention," *Canadian Nurse* 15, no. 8 (August 1919): 1920; Riegler, *Jean I. Gunn*, 84.

47 McPherson, *Bedside Matters*, 67–68.

48 St. John House Archives and Library (SJH), St. John Ambulance Association (SJAA), "Eleventh Annual Report, 1920," 30.

49 Christine Smith, "The Trained Attendant," *Canadian Nurse* 17, no. 2 (February 1921): 70.

50 Gunn, "President's Address," 1922.

51 CNS, Sybil Johnson Diary, July 18, 1918.

52 Daisy Johnson Cook, "Who Am I?" in *A Review of the History of St. John Ambulance in Saskatchewan, 1911–1983*, ed. K.J. Quarry (Regina: St. John Ambulance, 1983), 34–35.

53 IWM, Women at Work Collection, BRCS 12.2/2, Rachel Crowdy, Principal Commandant V.A.D.s, France and Belgium, 1914–19, "Report of Work of V.A.D. Department, France."

54 LAC, Violet Wilson Interview, c. 1970.

55 Ibid.

56 Ibid.

57 CNS, Frances Cluett Papers, Collection-174, files 2.02.004, 2.02.005, and 2.02.003, Frances Cluett to Mother, December 4, 1919, November 21, 1919, and March 13, 1918.

58 CWM, MacPherson "Draft for article published in Gold Stripe," 1919; Sandra Gwyn, *Tapestry of War: A Private View of Canadians in the Great War* (Toronto: Harper Collins, 1992), 459.

59 LAC, Great War and Canadian Society Project, Jean Marita Sears Interview, A1 9903–0008, July 23, 1974 (LAC, Jean Marita Sears Interview).

60 Nova Scotia Archives (NSA), McGregor-Miller Collection, MG1, vol. 661, no. 8, Bessie Hall to Mother, December 19, 1918, and April 28, 1919.

61 Jean Gunn, "The Services of Canadian Nurses and Voluntary Aids during the War," *Canadian Nurse* 15, no. 9 (1919): 1978.

62 Canadian Red Cross National Archive (CRCNA), Canadian Red Cross Society, Executive Committee Minute Book 6, February 1 and February 14, 1924. The nature of Geraldine Sewell's health issues is not recorded in any of the documents.

63 Joint War Committee, *Reports by the Joint War Committee*, 202–3; SJH, *First Aid*, "The Journal of the Order of the Hospital of St. John of Jerusalem in England," 363 (September 1924): 56–57; SJH, *First Aid and the St. John Ambulance Gazette* (UK) 28, no. 355 (May 1922): 177–78.

64 IWM, Women at Work Collection, BRCS 25.5.4/26, "Memorial Service for Nurses Who Have Fallen in the War," April 10, 1918; Beryl Oliver, *The British Red Cross in Action* (London: Faber and Faber, 1966), 244.

65 The memorial remains today just beyond the forecourt of the Hotel Newfoundland, al-
    though it has been relocated to the edge of a parking area. Bert Riggs, "What's All the
    Fuss about Ethel Dickinson?" *St. John's Gazette,* July 6, 1995, 12; St. John's Local Council
    of Women, *Remarkable Women of Newfoundland and Labrador* (St. John's: Valhalla Press,
    1976), 17.

66 Dorothy Pearson Twist emigrated from England in her mid-twenties, working as a secretary
    in the Victoria branch of the Canadian Imperial Bank. A clerical volunteer with the Red
    Cross in Switzerland early in the war, she returned home due to ill health and joined the
    Victoria Central Nursing Division No. 34. In mid-1918, she worked as a VAD in the
    Frensham Hill Military Hospital. See British Red Cross Society Museum and Archives,
    Personnel Record Indexes; and *Cowichan Leader,* October 3, 1918. Other details courtesy
    Tom Paterson and John Orr.

67 SJH, SJAA, "Eighteenth Annual Report, 1924, " 37.

68 SJH, World War I – World War II: Records: VAD Training (Records: Training), box X(b),
    Register and Record Sheets: Sainte-Anne-de-Bellevue, No. 4 Military Hospital (1918–19).
    As of April 1, 1919, fifty-two VADs were registered at the hospital; twenty-eight were
    nurses and twenty-four were massage or general service workers.

69 McGill's diploma course in massage and medical gymnastics was founded in 1916. Heap,
    "Training Women," 139. Eugenie Marjorie Ross served at Gifford House, London, until
    mid-1917 (prior to Violet Wilson). She married Eric B. Finley on July 5, 1919. See
    Montreal Daily Star, March 24, 1945; and G. Gower-Rees, Department of Veterans' Affairs,
    to Mrs. M. Ross Finley, March 10, 1953, courtesy the late E.G. Finley, Ottawa. Ross's
    sister-in-law, Enid Finley, was a pioneer in the development of medical physiotherapy in
    Canada. See Suzanne Evans, "Love amid the Ruins," *Canada's History,* February-March
    2013, 28–33.

70 Dorothy Chown was a VAD at Rugeley Camp Hospital from October 1918 to May 1919.
    LAC, Department of Militia and Defence, RG 9, III, B1, vol. 3419, file N-5–47, ADMS
    Folkestone to E.H. Jackes, March 24, 1917; LAC, Great War and Canadian Society Project,
    Shirley Gordon Interview, A1 9903–0015, July 18, 1974.

71 Joyce Nevitt, *White Caps and Black Bands: Nursing in Newfoundland to 1934* (St. John's:
    Jesperson, 1978), 104, 108–9, 112.

72 AO, "Report of Ontario Provincial", 2; *Ottawa City Directory,* 1927 and 1930. Ellen Scobie
    was employed by the British American (later Canadian) Bank Note Company, Ottawa.
    Hazel Todd was with the federal Board of Pension Commissioners.

73 SJH, SJAA, "Eleventh Annual Report, 1920, " 41–42, 50. Marion Magee earned two red
    efficiency stripes after three years of VAD service in England and France.

74 Thomas married Edward Bliss Day in 1924. Her father, Arnold Thomas, was an execu-
    tive with Copp Clark Publishing, Dr. Charles Copp was related to the publishing family.
    Toronto Mail, June 5, 1926; *The Times* (London), June 21, 1919.

75 Ruby Pinfold married Lieutenant Clarence Lawrence, both of St. Thomas, Ontario, in
    October 1918. He died on November 1, 1918. Courtesy Randy Carey, St. Thomas, Ontario.

76 LAC, Violet Wilson Interview, c. 1970.

77 Ibid.; *Edmonton Journal,* July 27, 1974, 14.

78 Provincial Archives of Alberta (PAA), Agnes Wilson Teviotdale Interview, July 19, 1983.
    City of Edmonton Archives (CEA), file David and Agnes Teviotdale. Agnes Kathleen
    Wilson (no relation to Violet Wilson) married David S. Teviotdale in 1922.

79 Charters, "The Black Death at Drumheller," 20–21, 27, 29; *Grande Prairie Herald-Tribune*, February 3, 1975. Under Gertrude's watch, the paper was called the *Prairie Herald-Tribune*.

80 Saskatchewan Archives Board, Cullum Family Papers, news clippings; LAC, Jean Marita Sears Interview, July 23, 1974; Museum of the Order of St John (MOSJ), Canada File, Tribute to Dr. Charles J. Copp, December 1938; Cook, "Who Am I?" 35; Ruby Pinfold Lawrence material, courtesy Randy Carey.

81 Gwyn, *Tapestry of War*, 459–60; CWM, Grace MacPherson Photo Archives, 52A, "Grace Leading New Recruits in Exercises" (c. 1942).

82 Bill Rompkey and Bert Riggs, eds., *Your Daughter Fanny: The War Letters of Frances Cluett, VAD* (St. John's: Flanker Press, 2006), xxxi; *St. John's Gazette*, December 2, 1993.

83 Sybil married lawyer Brian E.S. Dunfield in 1918 and raised three children. She became Lady Dunfield in 1949, when her husband was knighted prior to Newfoundland's entry into Confederation. See CNS, Sybil Johnson, Collection-201, Johnson Family Biography, n.d.; and Bert Riggs, "Remembering Another Group of War Volunteers," *St. John's Gazette*, November 13, 1977, 12.

84 Marian Frances White, ed., *The Finest Kind: Voices of Newfoundland and Labrador Women* (St. John's: Creative, 1992), 9. The observation was made by Janet Miller, niece of Janet Miller Ayre Murray, during an interview with the author.

85 Janet (Miller) Ayre Murray lost her husband, Eric Ayre, her brother-in-law, and two cousins on July 1, 1916, at Beaumont Hamel. Her brother also died of pneumonia contracted in the trenches in 1917. She went overseas in 1915 with Ruby Ayre, Mary Rendell, and Nell Job, all members of the St. John's elite, well educated and much travelled. Mary joined the First Aid Nursing Yeomanry (FANY) as an ambulance driver in France. Nell married in 1917. Janet remarried following the war, to Alexander Murray of St. John's. See CNS, Ruby Edith Ayre, M/F 210; CNS, Janet (Miller) Ayre Murray, Collection-158; and Joint War Committee, *Reports by the Joint War Committee*, 199.

86 CNS, Janet (Miller) Ayre Murray, Collection-158, file 1.06, "Biographical Outline: Janet Morison Miller," n.d.

87 Margot I. Duley, "'The Radius of Her Influence for Good': The Rise and Triumph of the Women's Suffrage Movement in Newfoundland, 1909–1925," in *Pursuing Equality: Historical Perspectives on Women in Newfoundland and Labrador*, ed. L. Kealey (St. John's: Institute for Social and Economic Research, Memorial University, 1993), 43–44.

88 Duley, "'The Radius of Her Influence,'" 38–39, 43–44; Margot I. Duley, *Where Once Our Mothers Stood We Stand: Women's Suffrage in Newfoundland, 1890-1925* (Charlottetown: Gynergy Books, 1993), 74.

89 LAC, Jean Marita Sears Interview, July 23, 1974; IWM, Marjorie Starr Diary, December 2, 1915.

90 In December 1931, Toronto VAD veterans commissioned a portrait of Dr. Charles Copp in recognition of his work as the VAD commissioner, which they presented to him at the Art Gallery of Ontario. "Portrait Given of Dr. C. Copp," *Toronto Globe*, December 28, 1931.

91 Nicholson, *The White Cross in Canada*, 73; *Civilian* 11, no. 11 (October 1918): 310; SJH, SJAA, "Sixteenth Annual Report, 1925," 38. From 1918 to 1925, nursing divisions decreased from forty-eight to twenty-three, whereas ambulance divisions increased from eleven to twenty-four.

92 Jay Winter, *Sites of Memory, Sites of Mourning: The Great War in European Cultural History* (Cambridge: Cambridge University Press, 1995), 29–30.
93 Morton and Wright, *Winning the Second Battle*, 24–25; Cynthia R. Comacchio, *Nations Are Built of Babies: Saving Ontario's Mothers and Children, 1900-1940* (Montreal and Kingston: McGill-Queen's University Press, 1993), 3.
94 SJH, SJAA, "Eleventh Annual Report, 1920," 11, 51.
95 V.A. Macdonald, "Nursing in Disasters," *Canadian Nurse* 18, no. 1 (January 1922): 9–10; Deanna Toxopeus, "Women in the St. John Ambulance Brigade, 1916-1990: A Study of Change in a Conservative Organisation" (unpublished paper, Carleton University, Ottawa, 1994), 35.
96 SJH, SJAA, "Canadian First Aid" (May 1929): 7. Note that the *First Aid Bulletin* changed format in January 1927, adopting a new name and dispensing with volume and issue numbers. The British American Bank Note Company became the Canadian Bank Note Company in 1923.
97 Anne Summers, *Angels and Citizens: British Women as Military Nurses, 1854-1914* (Newbury: Threshold Press, 2000), 288–89.
98 A delegation of twenty-two VADs from Canada, including Hazel Todd, attended the SJAA 1931 Empire Competition in First Aid in London, but participation was sparse during the Depression. The VAD program was revived in 1942, but training was much more rigorous, requiring 80–240 hours of hospital work depending on whether the VAD was designated as a nursing assistant, ambulance driver, or physiotherapist. During the Second World War, 221 VADs were sent overseas, none before 1944. McCreery, *The Maple Leaf and the White Cross*, 120–24; City of Ottawa Archives, St. John Ambulance Association Records, MG42–18–181, box 2, Photograph: *At Grand Central Hotel – Empire Competitions in First Aid*, London, England, 1931.
99 The acronym "VAD" was often used by patients and by VADs themselves, in humorous puns. This one is courtesy of the late E.G. Finley, son of VAD Eugenie Marjorie Ross.
100 LAC, Alice Bray fonds, MG 30, E572, vol. 1, Alice Bray to Mother, February 2, 1919.

BIBLIOGRAPHY

Archival Sources

Archives of Manitoba, Winnipeg
Augustus Nanton Papers, MG14, C85.

Archives of Ontario, Toronto (AO)
Sir George Perley Papers, MU 4113.
St. John Ambulance Association, Administration Records, MU 6814/MU 6858/MU 6860.

British Red Cross Society Museum and Archives, London (BRCS MA)
Personnel Record Indexes.

Calgary Public Library, Calgary
Local History Collection.

Canadian Red Cross National Archive, Ottawa (CRCNA)
Annual Reports, 1919–23.
Bulletin, 1915–20.
Divisional Annual Reports, 1919–29.
Executive Committee Minute Books, 1911–27.

Canadian War Museum, Ottawa (CWM)
Beaverbrook Collection of War Art.
Grace MacPherson Records, 58A 1.
Photo Archives 52A.

Centre for Newfoundland Studies, Memorial University Libraries, St. John's (CNS)
Ruby Edith Ayre, M/F 210.
Janet (Miller) Ayre Murray, Collection-158.
Frances Cluett, Collection-174.
Sybil Johnson, Collection-201.

City of Edmonton Archives, Edmonton (CEA)
Addie E. Geach, audio file.
David and Agnes Teviotdale file.

City of Ottawa Archives, Ottawa (COA)
St. John Ambulance Association Records,
    Ottawa Nursing Division No. 32, 1910–27, MG26 D83.

Glenbow Museum and Archives, Calgary
Vernon Parslow fonds.

Imperial War Museum, London (IWM) Department of Documents (DD)
Jean Emily Harstone Papers, 9348.
Marjorie Starr (Manson) Diary, 4572.
Women at Work Collection.

Library and Archives Canada, Ottawa (LAC)
Alice H. Bray fonds, MG 30, E572.
Canada Census, 1911.
Department of Agriculture, RG 17.
Department of Militia and Defence, RG 9.
Great War and Canadian Society Project, audio files, A1 9903.
    Shirley Gordon, A1 9903–0015.
    Jean Marita Sears, A1 9903-0008.
Imperial Order Daughters of the Empire, MG 28, G19.
Sir Edward Kemp fonds, MG 27, II, D9.
W.D. Lighthall fonds, MG 29, D93.
Margaret C. Macdonald fonds, MG 30, E45.
Sir Andrew Macphail fonds, MG 30, D150.
G.W.L. Nicholson fonds, MG 31, G19.
Sir George H. Perley fonds, MG 27, II, D12.
Voice of the Pioneer, audio files: Violet Wilson, 9861, acc. 1981–0111.

Museum of the Order of St. John, London (MOSJ)
Canada File.
World War I: Joint Committee and VAD.

Nanaimo Community Archives, Nanaimo
Alice and Arthur Leighton Collection.

National Archives, Kew, England (NA)
Miscellaneous Files Relating to Army Nursing Staff and Nursing Establishment,
    1914–18.

Nova Scotia Archives, Halifax (NSA)
Local Council of Women, MG20, vol. 535.
McGregor-Miller Collection, MG1, vol. 661.
Red Cross Collection, MG20, vol. 321.
"Report of the Chief Commissioner for Brigade Overseas, St. John Ambulance,
    October 1, 1915, to December 31, 1917." London: Chancery of the Order, 1918.

Provincial Archives of Alberta, Edmonton (PAA)
Agnes Wilson Teviotdale, audio file.

Provincial Archives of Saskatchewan, Saskatoon (PAS)
Cullum Family Papers.

St. John House Archives and Library, Ottawa (SJH)
Canadian Branch of the St. John Ambulance Association, *First Aid Bulletins*, 1916–32.
First Aid and the St. John Ambulance Gazette (UK), 1920–31.
St. John Ambulance Association Canadian Branch, Annual Reports, 1920–29.
World War I – World War II Records: VAD Training.

Toronto Reference Library, Toronto
City of Toronto Biographical Index.

PRIVATELY HELD MATERIAL

Mack, Beatrice. Collection held by Eric Wessman, Ottawa, Ontario.
Pinfold, Ruby. Collection held by Randy Carey, St. Thomas, Ontario.
Powys, Gwen. Collection held by Frances Powys MacNeil, Marjorie A. Cunliffe North, and Debra B. North.
Ross, Eugenie Marjorie. Collection held by the family of the late E.G. Finley, Ottawa, Ontario.

OTHER SOURCES

Abbott, Maude E. Seymour. "Lectures on the History of Nursing." *Canadian Nurse* 19, no. 2 (February 1923): 84–87.
–. "Lectures on the History of Nursing." *Canadian Nurse* 19, no. 3 (March 1923): 147–51.
–. "Lectures on the History of Nursing." *Canadian Nurse* 19, no. 4 (April 1923): 208–10.
–. "Lectures on the History of Nursing." *Canadian Nurse* 19, no. 5 (May 1923): 266–69.
Adam, Ruth. *A Woman's Place, 1910–1975*. London: Chatto and Windus, 1975.
Adams, Annmarie. "Borrowed Buildings: Canada's Temporary Hospitals during World War I." *Canadian Bulletin of Medical History* 16, no. 1 (1999): 25–48.
Adam-Smith, Patsy. *Australian Women at War*. Ringwood, Australia: Penguin, 1996.
Adie, Kate. *Corsets to Camouflage: Women and War*. London: Hodder and Stoughton, 2003.
Anon. "Halifax Disaster and Relief Work Performed." *Canadian Nurse* 14, no. 11 (November 1918): 1404–6.
Archibald, Edith J. (Mrs. Charles). *Nova Scotia Red Cross during the Great War: Nineteen Fourteen-Eighteen*. Halifax: Nova Scotia Provincial Branch, Canadian Red Cross Society, c. 1920.
Armstrong, John Griffin. *The Halifax Explosion and the Royal Canadian Navy: Inquiry and Intrigue*. Vancouver: UBC Press, 2002.
Australian War Memorial. *What Did You Do in the War Daddy? A Visual History of Propaganda Posters*. Melbourne: Oxford University Press, 1983.
Bagnold, Enid. *A Diary without Dates: Thoughts and Impressions of a VAD*. London: Heinemann, 1918.

Barrow, K.M. "A 'V.A.D.' at the Base." In *Reminiscent Sketches: 1914-1918*, ed. Members of Her Majesty Queen Alexandra's Imperial Military Nursing Service, 71–79. London: J. Bale, and Sons and Danielsson, 1922.

Barry, John M. *The Great Influenza: The Epic Story of the Deadliest Plague in History*. New York: Viking, 2004.

Bassett, Jan. *Guns and Brooches: Australian Army Nursing from the Boer War to the Gulf War*. New York: Oxford University Press, 1992.

Bates, Christina. *A Cultural History of the Nurse's Uniform*. Gatineau: Canadian Museum of Civilization, 2012.

Bates, Christina, Dianne Dodd, and Nicole Rousseau, eds. *On All Frontiers: Four Centuries of Canadian Nursing*. Ottawa: University of Ottawa/Canadian Museum of Civilization, 2005.

Bingham, Stella. *Ministering Angels*. London: Osprey, 1979.

Bishop, Alan, ed. *Chronicle of Youth: Vera Brittain's War Diary, 1913–1917*. London: Victor Gollancz, 1981.

Bishop, Alan, and Mark Bostridge, eds. *Letters from a Lost Generation: First World War Letters of Vera Brittain and Four Friends*. London: Abacus/Little Brown, 1999.

Bishop-Stirling, Terry. "'Such Sights One Will Never Forget': Newfoundland Women and Overseas Nursing in the First World War." In *Sisterhood of Suffering and Service: Women and Girls of Canada and Newfoundland during the First World War*, ed. Sarah Glassford and Amy Shaw, 126–47. Vancouver: UBC Press, 2012.

Blanchard, Jim. *Winnipeg's Great War: A City Comes of Age*. Winnipeg: University of Manitoba Press, 2010.

Bostridge, Mark. *Florence Nightingale: The Making of an Icon*. New York: Farrar, Strauss and Giroux, 2008.

Bowser, Thekla. *The Story of British V.A.D. Work in the Great War*. London: Andrew Melrose, c. 1917. Reprint, Imperial War Museum, 2003.

Braithwaite, Max. "The Year of the Killer Flu." *Maclean's*, February 1, 1953, 10–11, 43–44.

Brandt, Gail Cuthbert, Naomi Black, Paula Bourne, and Magda Fahrni. *Canadian Women: A History*. 3rd ed. Toronto: Nelson Education, 2010.

Braybon, Gail, and Penny Summerfield. *Out of the Cage: Women's Experiences in Two World Wars*. London: Pandora, 1987.

Bristow, Nancy K. "'You Can't Do Anything for Influenza': Doctors, Nurses and the Power of Gender during the Influenza Pandemic in the United States." In *The Spanish Flu Pandemic of 1918–1919: New Perspectives*, ed. Howard Phillips and David Killingray, 58–69. London: Routledge, 2003.

British Army. *Scheme for the Organization of Voluntary Aid in England and Wales*. London: H.M.S.O., 1909.

Brittain, Vera. *Testament of Youth: An Autobiographical Study of the Years 1900–1925*. 1933. Reprint, London: Fontana, 1979.

Brown, Cassie. *Death on the Ice: The Great Newfoundland Sealing Disaster of 1914*. Toronto: Doubleday, 1972.

Bruce, Herbert A. *Politics and the Canadian Army Medical Corps*. Toronto: William Briggs, 1919.

–. *Report on the Canadian Army Medical Service*. London: HMSO, 1916.

Burke, Sara Z. *Seeking the Highest Good: Social Service and Gender at the University of Toronto, 1888–1937.* Toronto: University of Toronto Press, 1996.

Burr, Mary. "The English Voluntary Aid Detachments." *American Journal of Nursing* 15, no. 6 (March 1915): 461–67.

"Canadian Association of Nurse Education: Summary of Convention Proceedings, Vancouver, 1919." *Canadian Nurse* 15, no. 9 (September 1919): 1987–90.

Canadian Red Cross Society. *What the Canadian Red Cross Society Is Doing in the Great War: Being an Outline of the Organization and Work of the Canadian Red Cross Society.* Toronto: Canadian Red Cross Society, 1918.

Cantlie, James. *British Red Cross Society Nursing Manual, No. 2.* London: Cassell, 1914.

—. *First Aid to the Injured.* London: St. John Ambulance Association, 1914.

Charters, Gertrude. "The Black Death at Drumheller." *Maclean's,* March 5, 1966, 20–21, 27, 29.

Chenier, Elise. "Class, Gender, and the Social Standard: The Montreal Junior League, 1912-1939." *Canadian Historical Review* 90, no. 4 (December 2009): 671–710. http://dx.doi.org/10.3138/chr.90.4.671.

Christie, Agatha. *Agatha Christie: An Autobiography.* New York: Dodd, Mead, 1977.

Clifford, Geraldine Jonich. "Daughters into Teachers: Educational and Demographic Influences on the Transformation of Teaching into Women's Work in America." In *Women Who Taught: Perspectives on the History of Women and Teaching,* ed. Alison Prentice and Marjorie Theobald, 115–35. Toronto: University of Toronto Press, 1991.

Coates, Colin M., and Cecilia L. Morgan. *Heroines and History: Representations of Madeleine de Verchères and Laura Secord.* Toronto: University of Toronto Press, 2002.

Coburn, David. "The Development of Canadian Nursing: Professionalization and Proletarianization." *International Journal of Health Services* 18, no. 3 (1988): 437–56. http://dx.doi.org/10.2190/1BDV-P7FN-9NWF-VKVR.

Coburn, David, et al., eds. *Health and Canadian Society: Sociological Perspectives.* Toronto: Fitzhenry and Whiteside, 1981.

Coburn, Judi. "'I See and I Am Silent': A Short History of Nursing in Ontario." In *Women at Work: Ontario, 1850–1930,* ed. Janice Acton, Barbara Shepard, and Penny Goldsmith, 127–63. Toronto: Canadian Women's Educational Press, 1974.

Comacchio, Cynthia R. *The Infinite Bonds of Family: Domesticity in Canada, 1850–1940.* Toronto: University of Toronto Press, 1999.

—. *Nations Are Built of Babies: Saving Ontario's Mothers and Children, 1900–1940.* Montreal and Kingston: McGill-Queen's University Press, 1993.

Condell, Diana, and Jean Liddiard. *Working for Victory? Images of Women in the First World War, 1914–1918.* London: Routledge and Kegan Paul, 1987.

Connor, J.T.H. *Doing Good: The Life of Toronto's General Hospital.* Toronto: University of Toronto Press, 2000.

Conrad, Margaret, Toni Laidlaw, and Donna Smyth, eds. *No Place Like Home: Diaries and Letters of Nova Scotia Women, 1771–1938.* Halifax: Formac, 1988.

Convenor on Public Health Nursing. "Public Health Nursing Department." *Canadian Nurse* 14, no. 12 (December 1918): 1477–78.

Cook, Daisy Johnson. "Who Am I?" In *A Review of the History of St. John Ambulance in Saskatchewan, 1911–1983,* ed. K.J. Quarry, 34–35. Regina: St. John Ambulance, 1983.

Cook, Tim. *At the Sharp End: Canadians Fighting the Great War, 1914–1916.* Vol. 1. Toronto: Penguin Canada, 2009.

—. "'He Was Determined to Go': Underage Soldiers in the Canadian Expeditionary Force." *Histoire sociale* 41, no. 81 (May 2008): 41–74. http://dx.doi.org/10.1353/his.0.0009.

—. *No Place to Run: The Canadian Corps and Gas Warfare in the First World War.* Vancouver: UBC Press, 1999.

Cooper, Diana. *The Rainbow Comes and Goes.* London: Hart-Davis, 1959.

Copp, Charles "St. John's Ambulance Brigade." *Canadian Nurse* 14, no. 7 (July 1918): 1162–66.

Cott, Nancy. *The Bonds of Womanhood: "Woman's Sphere" in New England, 1780–1835.* New Haven: Yale University Press, 1977.

Courlander, Mrs. (Elsa) Alphonse. "The V.A.D. Nurse." In *Women War Workers: Accounts Contributed by Representative Workers of the Work Done by Women in the More Important Branches of War Employment,* ed. Gilbert Stone, 194–213. New York: Thomas Y. Crowell, 1917.

Crofton, Eileen. *The Women of Royaumont: A Scottish Women's Hospital on the Western Front.* East Linton, UK: Tuckwell, 1997.

Darrow, Margaret. "French Volunteer Nursing and the Myth of War Experience in World War I." *American Historical Review* 101, no. 1 (February 1996): 80–106. http://dx.doi.org/10.2307/2169224.

—. *French Women and the First World War: War Stories of the Home Front.* Oxford: Berg, 2000.

Davies, Celia. *Rewriting Nursing History.* London: Croom Helm, 1989.

Dent, Olive. "How Women Rallied to the Call." In *The War Illustrated: A Pictorial Record of the Conflict of the Nations.* Vol. 9, ed. J.A. Hammerton, 111. London: Amalgamated Press, 1918.

—. "On Home Service." In *The War Illustrated: A Pictorial Record of the Conflict of the Nations.* Vol. 9, ed. J.A. Hammerton, 175. London: Amalgamated Press, 1918.

—. *A V.A.D. in France.* London: Grant Richards, 1917.

Dickens, Charles. *Martin Chuzzlewit.* First published 1843. http://dx.doi.org/10.1093/oseo/instance.00121330.

Director General, St. John Ambulance Association. Letter to the editor. *Ottawa Journal,* c. January 1922. Reprinted in St. John Ambulance Association, *First Aid Bulletin* 3, no. 2 (February 1922): 3.

Dodd, Dianne. "Advice to Parents: The Blue Books, Helen MacMurchy, M.D., and the Federal Department of Health, 1920-1934." *Canadian Bulletin of Medical History* 8, no. 2 (1991): 203–30.

Doll, Maurice F.V. *The Poster War: Allied Propaganda Art of the First World War.* Edmonton: Alberta Community Development, 1993.

Donahue, Patricia. "Reflections on the Changing Image of Nurses in Wartime." *Caduceus: A Humanities Journal for Medicine and the Health Sciences* 11, no. 1 (1995): 53–58.

Donner, Henriette. "Under the Cross: Why VADs Performed the Filthiest Tasks in the Dirtiest War: Red Cross Women Volunteers, 1914-1918." *Journal of Social History* 30, no. 3 (Spring 1997): 687–704. http://dx.doi.org/10.1353/jsh/30.3.687.

Drombrowski, Nicole Ann, ed. *Women and War in the Twentieth Century: Enlisted with or without Consent.* New York: Garland Press, 1999.

Duley, Margot I. "'The Radius of Her Influence for Good': The Rise and Triumph of the Women's Suffrage Movement in Newfoundland, 1909–1925." In *Pursuing Equality: Historical Perspectives on Women in Newfoundland and Labrador*, ed. L. Kealey, 14–65. St. John's: Institute for Social and Economic Research, Memorial University, 1993.

—. "The Unquiet Knitters of Newfoundland: From Mothers of the Regiment to Mothers of the Nation." In *A Sisterhood of Suffering and Service: Women and Girls of Canada and Newfoundland during the First World War*, ed. Sarah Glassford and Amy Shaw, 5–74. Vancouver: UBC Press, 2012.

—. *Where Once Our Mothers Stood We Stand: Women's Suffrage in Newfoundland, 1890–1925*. Charlottetown: Gynergy Books, 1993.

Durflinger, Serge Marc. *Veterans with a Vision: Canada's War Blinded in Peace and War*. Vancouver: UBC Press, 2010.

Dutil, Patrice A. "Against Isolationism: Napoléon Belcourt, French Canada, and 'La grande guerre.'" In *Canada and the First World War: Essays in Honour of Robert Craig Brown*, ed. David MacKenzie, 96–137. Toronto: University of Toronto Press, 2005.

Earhart, Amelia. *The Fun of It: Random Records of My Own Flying and of Women in Aviation*. New York: Harcourt, Brace, 1975. First published in 1932.

Editorial. "The Territorial Force Nursing Service." *Hospital*, December 18, 1920, 269.

Elliott, Jayne. "Keeping the Flag Flying: Medical Outposts and the Red Cross in Northern Ontario, 1922-1984." PhD diss., Queen's University, 2004.

Elliott, Jayne, Meryn Stuart, and Cynthia Toman, eds. *Place and Practice in Canadian Nursing History*. Vancouver: UBC Press, 2008.

Ellis, John, and Michael Cox. *World War I Databook: The Essential Facts and Figures for All Combatants*. London: Aurum Press, 2001.

Elshtain, Jean Bethke. *Women and War*. New York: Basic Books, 1987.

Enloe, Cynthia. *Does Khaki Become You? The Militarization of Women's Lives*. London: Southland Press, 1983.

—. *Maneuvers: The International Politics of Militarizing Women's Lives*. Berkeley: University of California Press, 2000.

Evans, Suzanne. "Love amid the Ruins." *Canada's History*, February-March 2013: 27–33.

Fahrni, Magda, and Esyllt W. Jones, eds. *Epidemic Encounters: Influenza, Society, and Culture in Canada, 1918–20*. Vancouver: UBC Press, 2012.

Fallis, Donna. "World War I Knitting." *Alberta Museums Review*, Fall 1984: 8–10.

Fiedler, Leslie A. "Images of the Nurse in Fiction and Popular Culture." In *Images of Nurses: Perspectives from History, Art and Literature*, ed. Anne Hudson Jones, 100–12. Philadelphia: University of Pennsylvania Press, 1988.

Fingard, Judith. "College, Career and Community: Dalhousie Co-eds, 1881-1921." In *Youth, University and Canadian Society: Essays in the Social History of Higher Education*, ed. Paul Axelrod and John G. Reid, 26–50. Montreal and Kingston: McGill-Queen's University Press, 1989.

Finzi, Kate John. *Eighteen Months in the War Zone: A Record of a Woman's Work on the Western Front*. London: Cassell, 1916.

Fisher, Susan R. *Boys and Girls in No Man's Land: English Canadian Children and the First World War*. Toronto: University of Toronto Press, 2011.

Foster, Charles Lyons, ed. *Letters from the Front: Being a Record of the Part Played by Officers of the Bank in the Great War, 1914–1919*. Vol. 1 and 2. Toronto: Southam Press, 1920.

Friedland, Judith. *Restoring the Spirit: The Beginnings of Occupational Therapy in Canada, 1890–1930.* Montreal and Kingston: McGill-Queen's University Press, 2011.

Furse, Katharine. *Hearts and Pomegranates: The Story of Forty-Five Years, 1875 to 1920.* London: Peter Davies, 1940.

Galloway, Strome. *The White Cross in Canada, 1883–1983: A History of St. John Ambulance, Centennial Edition.* Ottawa: St. John Priory, 1983.

Gilbert, Sandra M. "Soldier's Heart: Literary Men, Literary Women, and the Great War." In *Behind the Lines: Gender and the Two World Wars,* ed. Margaret R. Higonnet, Jane Jenson, Sonya Michel, and Margaret Collins Weitz, 197–226. New Haven: Yale University Press, 1987.

Gillett, Margaret. *We Walked Very Warily: A History of Women at McGill.* Montreal: Eden, 1981.

Glassford, Sarah Carlene. "'The Greatest Mother in the World': Carework and the Discourse of Mothering in the Canadian Red Cross Society during the First World War." *Journal of the Association for Research on Mothering* 10, no. 1 (2008): 219–32.

Glassford, Sarah, and Amy Shaw, eds. *A Sisterhood of Suffering and Service: Women and Girls of Canada and Newfoundland during the First World War.* Vancouver: UBC Press, 2012.

Goldie, Sue M., ed. *"I Have Done My Duty": Florence Nightingale in the Crimean War, 1854–1856.* Manchester: Manchester University Press, 1987.

Gordon, Hampden. *Our Girls in Wartime.* London: John Lane, Bodley Head, c. 1917.

Gorham, Deborah. *Vera Brittain: A Feminist Life.* Toronto: University of Toronto Press, 2000.

Government of Canada. *Canada's War Effort, 1914–1918.* Ottawa: Government Printer, 1918.

–. *The Organization of Voluntary Medical Aid in Canada.* Ottawa: Government Printing Bureau, 1914.

–. *Women's Aid Department (W.A.D.) - St. John Ambulance Brigade (Overseas) within the Dominion of Canada – Regulations.* Ottawa: King's Printer, 1918.

Graf, Mercedes. *On the Field of Mercy: Women Medical Volunteers from the Civil War to the First World War.* Amherst, NY: Humanity Books, 2010.

Gray, Sheila. *The South African War, 1899–1902: Service Records of British and Colonial Women.* Auckland, NZ: self-published, 1993.

Grayzel, Susan R. *Women's Identities at War: Gender, Motherhood and Politics in Britain and France during the First World War.* Chapel Hill: University of North Carolina Press, 1999.

Gregor, Frances M. "Mapping the Demise of the St. John Ambulance Home Nursing Program in Nova Scotia, 1950-1975." *Canadian Bulletin of Medical History* 21, no. 2 (2004): 351–75.

Gribble, Francis. *Women in War.* New York: E.P. Dutton, 1917.

Gunn, Jean. "Canadian National Association of Trained Nurses' Convention, 1918." *Canadian Nurse* 14, no. 8 (August 1918): 1210–13.

–. "Nursing: Address Given before National Council of Women." *Woman's Century* 6, no. 5 (August 1918): 11.

–. "President's Address, C.N.A.T.N. Convention." *Canadian Nurse* 15, no. 8 (August 1919): 1919–24.

—. "The Services of Canadian Nurses and Voluntary Aids during the War." *Canadian Nurse* 15, no. 5 (May 1919): 1975–79.

Gwyn, Sandra. *Tapestry of War: A Private View of Canadians in the Great War.* Toronto: Harper Collins, 1992.

Hallett, Christine E. *Containing Trauma: Nursing Work in the First World War.* Manchester: Manchester University Press, 2009.

—. "'Emotional Nursing': Involvement, Engagement and Detachment in the Writings of First World War Nurses and VADs." In *First World War Nursing: New Perspectives,* ed. Christine E. Hallett and Alison Fell. New York: Routledge, 2013.

—. *Nurse Writers of the Great War.* Manchester: Manchester University Press, 2016.

—. "Portrayals of Suffering: Perceptions of Trauma in the Writings of First World War Nurses and Volunteers." *Canadian Bulletin of Medical History* 27, no. 1 (2010): 65–84.

—. *Veiled Warriors: Allied Nurses of the First World War.* Oxford: Oxford University Press, 2014.

Hallett, Christine E., and Alison Fell, eds. *First World War Nursing: New Perspectives.* New York: Routledge, 2013.

Hammerton, J.A., ed. *The War Illustrated: A Pictorial Record of the Conflict of the Nations.* Vol. 9. London: Amalgamated Press, 1918.

Harding, Robert J. "Glorious Tragedy: Newfoundland's Cultural Memory of the Attack at Beaumont Hamel, 1916-1925." *Newfoundland and Labrador Studies* 21, no. 1 (2006): 3–40.

Heap, Ruby. "Physiotherapy's Quest for Professional Status in Ontario, 1950-1980." *Canadian Bulletin of Medical History* 12, no. 1 (1995): 69–99.

—. "Training Women for a New 'Women's Profession': Physiotherapy Education at the University of Toronto, 1917–40." *History of Education Quarterly* 35, no. 2 (Summer 1995): 135–58. http://dx.doi.org/10.2307/369630.

Heap, Ruby, Wyn Millar, and Elizabeth Smyth, eds. *Learning to Practise: Professional Education in Historical and Contemporary Perspective.* Ottawa: University of Ottawa Press, 2005.

Heap, Ruby, and Meryn Stuart. "Nurses and Physiotherapists: Issues in the Professionalization of Health Occupations during and after World War I." *Health and Canadian Society* 3, no. 1–2 (1995): 179–93.

Henderson, Viola. "V.A.D. Work in Montreal." *Canadian Nurse* 14, no. 8 (August 1918): 1244–48.

Higonnet, Margaret R., Jane Jenson, Sonya Michel, and Margaret Collins Weitz, eds. *Behind the Lines: Gender and the Two World Wars.* New Haven: Yale University Press, 1987.

Holman, Andrew C. *A Sense of Their Duty: Middle-Class Formation in Victorian Ontario Towns.* Montreal and Kingston: McGill-Queen's University Press, 2000.

Holt, Tonie, and Valmai Holt. *Till the Boys Come Home: The Picture Postcards of the First World War.* London: Macdonald and Jane's, 1977.

Hopkins, J. Castell. *The Canadian Annual Review of Public Affairs.* Toronto: Canadian Annual Review, 1915-17.

—. *The Province of Ontario in the War: A Record of Government and People.* Toronto: Warwick Bros. and Rutter, 1919.

Hughes, Anne-Marie Claire. "War, Gender, and National Mourning: The Significance of the Death and Commemoration of Edith Cavell in Britain." *European Review of History* 12, no. 3 (2005): 425–44. http://dx.doi.org/10.1080/13507480500428938.

Hutchinson, John F. *Champions of Charity: War and the Rise of the Red Cross*. Boulder: Westview, 1996.

Jardine, Pauline. "An Urban Middle-Class Calling: Women and the Emergence of Modern Nursing Education at the Toronto General Hospital, 1881-1914." *Urban History Review* 17, no. 3 (February 1989): 176–90. http://dx.doi.org/10.7202/1017630ar.

Jesse, F. Tennyson. "A Night with a Convoy." In *The Vogue Bedside Book*, ed. Josephine Ross, 108–12. London: Vermillion, 1984. Essay first published c. 1918.

–. *The Sword of Deborah: First-Hand Impressions of the British Women's Army in France*. London: William Heinemann, 1919.

Joint War Committee of the British Red Cross Society and the Order of St. John of Jerusalem in England. *Reports by the Joint War Committee and the Joint War Finance Committee of the British Red Cross Society and the Order of St. John of Jerusalem in England on Voluntary Aid Rendered to the Sick and Wounded at Home and Abroad and to British Prisoners of War, 1914–1919, with appendices*. London: H.M.S.O., 1921.

Judge, Maureen, dir. *And We Knew How to Dance: Women in World War I*. Montreal: National Film Board of Canada, 1994.

Kahn, Richard J. "Women and Men at Sea: Gender Debate aboard the Hospital Ship Maine during the Boer War, 1899-1900." *Journal of the History of Medicine and Allied Sciences* 56, no. 2 (April 2001): 111–39. http://dx.doi.org/10.1093/jhmas/56.2.111.

Kankitar, Helen. "'Real True Boys': Moulding the Cadets of Imperialism." In *Dislocating Masculinity: Comparative Ethnographies*, ed. Andrea Cornwall and Nancy Lindisfarne, 184–96. New York: Routledge, 1994.

Kealey, Linda. *Enlisting for the Cause: Women, Labour and the Left in Canada, 1890–1920*. Toronto: University of Toronto Press, 1998.

–, ed. *A Not Unreasonable Claim: Women and Reform in Canada, 1880s–1920s*. Toronto: Canadian Women's Educational Press, 1979.

Keen-Payne, Rhonda. "We Must Have Nurses: Spanish Influenza in America, 1918-1919." *Nursing History Review* 8 (2000): 143–56.

Kerr, Janet Ross. "Professionalization in Canadian Nursing." In *Canadian Nursing: Issues and Perspectives*, ed. Janet Ross Kerr and Jannetta MacPhail, 24–31. St. Louis: Mosby, 1991.

Keshen, Jeffrey A. *Propaganda and Censorship during Canada's Great War*. Edmonton: University of Alberta Press, 1996.

Knowles, Valerie. *Capital Lives: 32 Profiles of Leading Ottawa Personalities*. Ottawa: Book Coach Press, 2005.

Koven, Seth, and Sonya Michel, eds. *Mothers of a New World: Maternalist Politics and the Origins of Welfare States*. New York: Routledge, 1993.

Ladd, Molly-Taylor. *Mother-Work: Women, Child Welfare, and the State, 1890–1930*. Urbana: University of Illinois Press, 1994.

Landells, E.A., ed. *The Military Nurses of Canada: Recollections of Canadian Military Nurses*. Vol. 1. White Rock, BC: Co-publishing, 1995.

Lang, Marjory. *Women Who Made the News: Female Journalists in Canada, 1880–1945*. Montreal and Kingston: McGill-Queen's University Press, 1999.

Lee, Janet. *War Girls: The First Aid Nursing Yeomanry in the First World War*. Manchester: Manchester University Press, 2005.

Leese, Peter. *Shell Shock: Traumatic Neurosis and the British Soldiers of the First World War*. Houndmills, UK: Palgrave Macmillan, 2002. http://dx.doi.org/10.1057/9780230287921.

Lerner, Paul F. *Hysterical Men: War, Psychiatry and the Politics of Trauma in Germany, 1890–1930*. Ithaca, NY: Cornell University Press, 2003.

Levitt, Joseph. *Henri Bourassa on Imperialism and Bi-culturalism, 1900–1918*. Toronto: Copp Clark, 1970.

Lewis, Jane. *Women and Social Action in Victorian and Edwardian England*. Aldershot, UK: Edward Elgar, 1991.

Light, Alison. *Forever England: Femininity, Literature, and Conservatism between the Wars*. London: Routledge, 1991.

Lloydlangston, Amber. "From Expendable to Indispensable: Women in Science in the Department of Agriculture during the First World War." Paper presented at the annual meeting of the Canadian Historical Association, Ottawa, March 13, 1998.

Lowe, Graham S. "Women, Work and the Office: The Feminisation of Clerical Occupations in Canada, 1901-1931." In *Rethinking Canada: The Promise of Women's History*, ed. Veronica Strong-Boag and Anita Clair Fellman, 253–70. Toronto: Oxford University Press, 1997.

Loyd, Archibald K. *The British Red Cross Society: The Country and Branches*. London: British Red Cross Society, 1917.

MacDermot, Hugh E. *History of the School for Nurses of the Montreal General Hospital*. Montreal: Alumnae Association, 1940.

MacDonald, Laura M. *Curse of the Narrows: The Halifax Explosion, 1917*. Toronto: Harper Collins, 2005.

Macdonald, Lyn. *The Roses of No Man's Land*. London: Penguin, 1993. First published 1980.

Macdonald, V.A. "Nursing in Disasters." *Canadian Nurse* 18, no. 1 (January 1922): 9–10.

MacKenzie, David. "Eastern Approaches: Maritime Canada and Newfoundland." In *Canada and the First World War: Essays in Honour of Robert Craig Brown*, ed. David MacKenzie, 350–76. Toronto: University of Toronto Press, 2005.

MacMurchy, Helen. "The Future of the Nursing Profession." *Canadian Nurse* 16, no. 2 (February 1920): 69–74.

Macphail, Andrew. *Official History of the Canadian Forces in the Great War, 1914–1919: The Medical Services*. Ottawa: F.A. Acland, 1925.

Mangan, J.A., and James Walvin, eds. *Manliness and Morality: Middle-Class Masculinity in Britain and America, 1800–1940*. New York: St. Martin's Press, 1987.

Mann, Susan. *Margaret Macdonald: Imperial Daughter*. Montreal and Kingston: McGill-Queen's University Press, 2005.

–, ed. *The War Diary of Clare Gass, 1915–1918*. Montreal and Kingston: McGill-Queen's University Press, 2000.

Marshall, Debbie. *Give Your Other Vote to the Sister: A Woman's Journey into the Great War*. Calgary: University of Calgary Press, 2007.

McCreery, Christopher. *The Maple Leaf and the White Cross: A History of St. John Ambulance and the Most Venerable Order of the Hospital of St. John of Jerusalem in Canada*. Toronto: Dundurn Press, 2008.

McDonald, Lynn, ed. *Florence Nightingale: The Crimean War*. Collected Works of Florence Nightingale Series. Vol. 14. Waterloo, ON: Wilfrid Laurier University Press, 2010.

–. "Florence Nightingale a Hundred Years On: Who She Was and What She Was Not." *Women's History Review* 19, no. 5 (November 2010): 721–40. http://dx.doi.org/10.108 0/09612025.2010.509934.

McKenzie, Andrea, ed. *War-Torn Exchanges: The Lives and Letters of Nursing Sisters Laura Holland and Mildred Forbes*. Vancouver: UBC Press, 2016.

McPherson, Kathryn. *Bedside Matters: The Transformation of Canadian Nursing, 1900–1990*. Toronto: University of Toronto Press, 2003.

–. "Carving Out a Past: The Canadian Nurses' Association War Memorial." *Histoire sociale* 29, no. 58 (November 1996): 417–29.

–. "Nurses and Nursing in Early 20th Century Halifax." Master's diss., Dalhousie University, 1982.

Melman, Billie, ed. *Borderlines: Gender and Identities in War and Peace, 1870–1930*. New York: Routledge, 1998.

Melosh, Barbara. *"The Physician's Hand": Work Culture and Conflict in American Nursing*. Philadelphia: Temple University Press, 1982.

Metson, Graham, ed. *The Halifax Explosion, December 6, 1917*. Toronto: McGraw-Hill, Ryerson, 1978.

Miller, Ian Hugh Maclean. *Our Glory and Our Grief: Torontonians and the Great War*. Toronto: University of Toronto Press, 2002.

Mitchell, Sally. *The New Girl: Girls' Culture in England, 1880–1915*. New York: Columbia University Press, 1995.

Monnon, Mary Ann. *Miracles and Mysteries: The Halifax Explosion, December 6, 1917*. Hantsport, NS: Lancelot Press, 1977.

Montizambert, E. "Canadian Red Cross Work in France." *Lancet* 191, no. 4926 (January 26, 1918): 159–61. http://dx.doi.org/10.1016/S0140-6736(01)23218-8.

Mook, Laurie. "Women at University: The Early Years." *Contents* 44, no. 1 (Winter 1996): 9–10.

Moore, Mary MacLeod. "Canadian Women in the War Zone." *Saturday Night*, March 16, 1918, 17.

–. "Canadian Women War Workers Overseas." *Canadian Magazine* 52, no. 3 (January 1919): 737–51.

–. *The Maple Leaf's Red Cross: The War Story of the Canadian Red Cross Overseas*. London: Skeffington and Son, 1920.

Morris, Isabel. "Wandsworth Hospital: A Short Account of the Third London General Hospital, Wandsworth." *Newfoundland Quarterly* 16, no. 3 (December 1916): 14–15.

Morton, Desmond. *Fight or Pay: Soldiers' Families in the Great War*. Vancouver: UBC Press, 2004.

–. *A Military History of Canada: From Champlain to the Gulf War*. Toronto: McClelland and Stewart, 1992.

–. *A Peculiar Kind of Politics: Canada's Overseas Ministry in the First World War*. Toronto: University of Toronto Press, 1982.

–. *When Your Number's Up: The Canadian Soldier in the First World War*. Toronto: Random House, 1993.

Morton, Desmond, and J.L. Granatstein. *Marching to Armageddon: Canadians and the Great War, 1914–1919*. Toronto: Lester and Orpen Denys, 1989.

Morton, Desmond, and Glenn Wright. *Winning the Second Battle: Canadian Veterans and the Return to Civilian Life, 1915–1930*. Toronto: University of Toronto Press, 1987.

Morton, Gladys. "The Pandemic Influenza of 1918." *Canadian Nurse* 72, no. 12 (December 1976): 32–37.

Moss, Mark L. *Manliness and Militarism: Educating Young Boys in Ontario for War.* Don Mills, ON: Oxford University Press, 2001.

Murray, T.J. "Medical Aspects of the Disaster: The Missing Report of Dr. Daniel Fraser Harris." In *Ground Zero: A Reassessment of the 1917 Explosion in Halifax Harbour,* ed. Alan Ruffman and Colin D. Howell, 229–44. Halifax: Nimbus and Gorsebrook Research Institute, 1994.

Nelson, Sioban. *Say Little, Do Much: Nurses, Nuns, and Hospitals in the Nineteenth Century.* Philadelphia: University of Pennsylvania Press, 2001. http://dx.doi.org/10.9783/9780812202908.

Nelson, Sioban, and Anne Marie Rafferty, eds. *Notes on Nightingale: The Influence and Legacy of a Nursing Icon.* Ithaca, NY: ILR Press, 2010.

Nevitt, Joyce. *White Caps and Black Bands: Nursing in Newfoundland to 1934.* St. John's: Jesperson, 1978.

Nicholson, G.W.L. *Canada's Nursing Sisters.* Toronto: Samuel Stevens Hakkert, 1975.

–. *The Fighting Newfoundlander: A History of the Royal Newfoundland Regiment.* St. John's: Government of Newfoundland, 1964.

–. *The White Cross in Canada: A History of St. John Ambulance.* Montreal: Harvest House, 1967.

Nursing Sister, C.A.M.C. "Military Nursing." *Canadian Nurse* 13, no. 8 (August 1917): 482–84.

Nygaard, Nancy A. "'Too Awful for Words' ... Nursing Narratives of the Great War." PhD diss., University of Wisconsin, 2002.

Oliver, Beryl. *The British Red Cross in Action.* London: Faber and Faber, 1966.

Ouditt, Sharon. *Fighting Forces, Writing Women: Identity and Ideology in the First World War.* New York: Routledge, 1994. http://dx.doi.org/10.4324/9780203359167.

Parr, Joy. *The Gender of Breadwinners: Women, Men and Change in Two Industrial Towns, 1880–1950.* Toronto: University of Toronto Press, 1990.

Parsons, W. David. "Newfoundland in the Great War." In *Canada and the Great War: Western Front Association Papers,* ed. Briton C. Busch, 147–60. Montreal and Kingston: McGill-Queen's University Press, 2003.

Penner, Louise. *Victorian Medicine and Social Reform: Florence Nightingale among the Novelists.* New York: Palgrave Macmillan, 2010. http://dx.doi.org/10.1057/9780230106598.

Pettigrew, Eileen. *The Silent Enemy: Canada and the Deadly Flu of 1918.* Saskatoon: Western Producer Prairie Books, 1983.

Pickles, Katie. *Female Imperialism and National Identity: Imperial Order Daughters of the Empire.* Manchester: Manchester University Press, 2002. http://dx.doi.org/10.7228/manchester/9780719063909.001.0001.

–. *Transnational Outrage: The Death and Commemoration of Edith Cavell.* New York: Palgrave Macmillan, 2007.

Pierson, Ruth Roach. *"They're Still Women After All": The Second World War and Canadian Womanhood.* Toronto: McClelland and Stewart, 1986.

Pitsula, James M. *For All We Have and Are: Regina and the Experience of the Great War.* Winnipeg: University of Manitoba Press, 2008.

Poplin, Irene Schuessler. "Nursing Uniforms: Romantic Idea, Functional Attire, or Instrument of Social Change." *Nursing History Review* 2 (1994): 153–67.

Power, Iris. "I Was a V.A.D." *Atlantic Guardian* 11, no. 5 (July 1954): 26–30.

Prentice, Alison. "The Feminization of Teaching." In *The Neglected Minority: Essays in Canadian Women's History.* Vol. 1, ed. Susan Mann Trofimenkoff and Alison Prentice, 49–65. Toronto: McClelland and Stewart, 1977.

Quarry, K.J., ed. *A Review of the History of St. John Ambulance in Saskatchewan, 1911–1983.* Regina: St. John Ambulance Association, 1983.

Quiney, Linda J. "'Bravely and Loyally They Answered the Call': St. John Ambulance, the Red Cross, and the Patriotic Service of Canadian Women during the Great War." *History of Intellectual Culture* 5, no. 1 (2005). http://www.ucalgary.ca/hic/.

–. "'We Must Not Neglect Our Duty': Enlisting Women Undergraduates for the Red Cross during the Great War." In *Cultures, Communities and Conflict: Histories of Canadian Universities and War,* ed. Paul Stortz and E. Lisa Panayotidis, 71–94. Toronto: University of Toronto Press, 2012.

Ramkhalawansingh, Ceta. "Women during the Great War." In *Women at Work: Ontario, 1850–1930,* ed. Janice Acton, Barbara Shepard, and Penny Goldsmith, 261–307. Toronto: Canadian Women's Educational Press, 1974.

Read, Daphne, ed. *The Great War and Canadian Society: An Oral History.* Toronto: New Hogtown Press, 1978.

Rémillard, François, and Brian Merrett. *Mansions of the Golden Square Mile, Montreal, 1850–1930.* Translated by Joshua Wolfe. Montreal: Meridian Press, 1987.

Reverby, Susan M. *Ordered to Care: The Dilemma of American Nursing, 1850–1945.* Cambridge: Cambridge University Press, 1987.

Reznik, Jeffrey S. *Healing the Nation: Soldiers and the Culture of Caregiving during the Great War.* Manchester: Manchester University Press, 2004.

Riegler, Natalie. *Jean I. Gunn: Nursing Leader.* Toronto: A.M.S. and Fitzhenry and Whiteside, 1997.

–. "Sphagnum Moss in World War I: The Making of Surgical Dressings by Volunteers in Toronto, Canada, 1917-1918." *Canadian Bulletin of Medical History* 6, no. 1 (1989): 27–43.

–. "The Work and Networks of Jean I. Gunn, Superintendent of Nurses, Toronto General Hospital, 1913-1941: A Presentation of Some Issues in Nursing during Her Lifetime, 1882-1941." PhD diss., University of Toronto, 1992.

Roberts, Barbara. *"Why Do Women Do Nothing to End the War?" Canadian Feminist-Pacifists and the Great War.* CRIAW Paper No. 13. Ottawa: Canadian Research Institute for the Advancement of Women, 1985.

Roberts, Julia. "British Nurses at War, 1914-1918: Ancillary Personnel and the Battle for Registration." *Nursing Research* 45, no. 3 (May-June 1996): 167–72. http://dx.doi.org/10.1097/00006199-199605000-00008.

Rode, Mary W. "The Nursing Pin: Symbol of 1,000 Years of Service." *Nursing Forum* 24, no. 1 (January 1989): 15–17. http://dx.doi.org/10.1111/j.1744-6198.1989.tb00813.x.

Rogers, Anna. *While You Are Away: New Zealand Nurses at War, 1899–1948.* Auckland, NZ: Auckland University Press, 2003.

Rompkey, Bill, and Bert Riggs, eds. *Your Daughter Fanny: The War Letters of Frances Cluett, VAD.* St. John's: Flanker Press, 2006.

Ruckman, JoAnn. "'Knit, Knit, and Then Knit': The Women of Pocatello and the War Effort of 1917–1918." *Idaho Yesterdays* 26 (Spring 1982): 26–36.

Ruffman, Alan, and Colin D. Howell, eds. *Ground Zero: A Reassessment of the 1917 Explosion in Halifax Harbour.* Halifax: Nimbus and Gorsebrook Research Institute, 1994.

Rutherdale, Robert Allen. *Hometown Horizons: Local Responses to Canada's Great War.* Vancouver: UBC Press, 2004.

Salmond, Monica. *Bright Armour: Memories of Four Years of War.* London: Faber and Faber, 1935.

Sangster, Joan. "Mobilizing Women for War." In *Canada and the First World War: Essays in Honour of Robert Craig Brown,* ed. David MacKenzie, 157–93. Toronto: University of Toronto Press, 2005.

Sarnecky, Mary T. *A History of the U.S. Army Nurse Corps.* Philadelphia: University of Pennsylvania Press, 1999.

Saskatchewan Registered Nurses' Association. "The Second Annual Convention of the Saskatchewan Registered Nurses' Association." *Canadian Nurse* 15, no. 5 (May 1919): 1764–65.

Scott, Joan Wallach. *Gender and the Politics of History.* New York: Columbia University Press, 1999.

Sebba, Anne. *Enid Bagnold: A Biography.* London: Weidenfeld and Nicholson, 1986.

"Secretary's Report: Canadian National Association of Trained Nurses' Convention, 1918." *Canadian Nurse* 14, no. 8 (August 1918): 1213–15.

Shepard, Benjamin. *A War of Nerves: Soldiers and Psychiatrists, 1914–1918.* London: Jonathan Cape, 2000.

Skocpol, Theda. *Protesting Soldiers and Mothers: The Political Origins of Social Policy in the United States.* Cambridge, MA: Harvard University Press, 1999.

Smallwood, Joseph R., and Robert D.W. Pitt, eds. *Encyclopaedia of Newfoundland and Labrador.* St. John's: Newfoundland Book Publishers, 1981.

Smith, Angela K. *The Second Battlefield: Women, Modernism and the First World War.* Manchester: Manchester University Press, 2000.

Smith, Christine. "The Trained Attendant." *Canadian Nurse* 17, no. 2 (February 1921): 69–74.

Smith, Helen Zenna. *Not So Quiet ... Stepdaughters of War.* New York: Feminist Press, 1988. First published 1930.

Smith, Nathan. "Comrades and Citizens: Great War Veterans in Toronto, 1915-1919." PhD diss., University of Toronto, 2012.

Smith-Rosenberg, Carroll. "The Female World of Love and Ritual: Relations between Women in Nineteenth-Century America." In *Disorderly Conduct: Visions of Gender in Victorian America,* ed. Carroll Smith-Rosenberg. New York: Knopf, 1985.

Souhani, Diana. *Edith Cavell.* London: Quercus, 2010.

St. John's Local Council of Women. *Remarkable Women of Newfoundland and Labrador.* St. John's: Valhalla Press, 1976.

Stanley, Margaret. "Report of Special Committee." *Canadian Nurse* 14, no. 8 (August 1918): 1231–35.

Staton, Patricia A. *It Was Their War Too: Canadian Women and World War I.* Toronto: Green Dragon Press, 2006.

Stewart, Jean Cantlie. *The Quality of Mercy: The Lives of Sir James and Lady Cantlie.* London: George Allen and Unwin, 1983.

Stortz, Paul, and E. Lisa Panayotidis, eds. *Cultures, Communities and Conflict: Histories of Canadian Universities and War*. Toronto: University of Toronto Press, 2012.

Strong-Boag, Veronica J. *The New Day Recalled: Lives of Girls and Women in English Canada, 1919–1939*. Toronto: Copp Clark Pitman, 1988.

–. *The Parliament of Women: The National Council of Women of Canada, 1893–1929*. Ottawa: National Museums of Canada, 1976.

Strong-Boag, Veronica, and Anita Clair Fellman, eds. *Rethinking Canada: The Promise of Women's History*. Toronto: Oxford University Press, 1997.

Stuart, Meryn. "Shifting Professional Boundaries: Gender Conflict in Public Health, 1920-1925." In *Caring and Curing: Historical Perspectives on Women and Healing in Canada*, ed. Dianne Dodd and Deborah Gorham. Ottawa: University of Ottawa Press, 1994.

–. "War and Peace: Professional Identities and Nurses' Training, 1914-1930." In *Challenging Professions: Historical and Contemporary Perspectives on Women's Professional Work*, ed. Elizabeth Smyth, Sandra Acker, Paula Bourne, and Alison Prentice, 171–93. Toronto: University of Toronto Press, 1999.

Summers, Anne. *Angels and Citizens: British Women as Military Nurses, 1854–1914*. Newbury, Berks: Threshold Press, 2000.

–. "Ministering Angels." *History Today* 39 (February 1989): 31–37.

Szychter, Gwen. "The War Work of Women in Rural British Columbia, 1914-1919." *British Columbia Historical News* 27, no. 4 (Fall 1994): 5–9.

Taschereau, Marie. "Home Nursing of Value to Women." *First Aid Bulletin* (Canadian Branch of the St. John Ambulance Association) 2, 7 (May 1921): 2–3.

Tennyson, Brian Douglas. *Canada's Great War, 1914-1918: How Canada Helped Save the British Empire and Become a North American Nation*. Lanham, MD: Rowman and Littlefield, 2015.

–. *The Canadian Experience of the Great War: A Guide to Memoirs*. Lanham, MD: Scarecrow Press, 2013.

Theobald, Andrew. *Bitter Harvest of War: New Brunswick and the Conscription Crisis of 1917*. Fredericton, NB: Goose Lane Editions, New Brunswick Military History Project, 2008.

Tilly, Louise A., and Joan W. Scott. *Women, Work and Family*. New York: Routledge, 1987.

The Times History of the War. Vol. 4. London: The Times, 1915.

Toman, Cynthia. "A Loyal Body of Empire Citizens: Military Nurses and Identity at Lemnos and Salonika, 1915-1917." In *Place and Practice in Canadian Nursing History*, ed. Jayne Elliott, Meryn Stuart, and Cynthia Toman, 8–24. Vancouver: UBC Press, 2008.

–. *An Officer and a Lady: Canadian Military Nursing and the Second World War*. Vancouver: UBC Press, 2007.

–. *Sister Soldiers of the Great War: The Nurses of the Canadian Army Medical Corps*. Vancouver: UBC Press, 2016.

Toxopeus, Deanna. "Women in the St. John Ambulance Brigade, 1916-1990: A Study of Change in a Conservative Organisation." Unpublished paper, Carleton University, Ottawa, 1994.

Usborne, H.M., ed. *Women's Work in Wartime: A Handbook of Employments*. London: T. Werner Laurie, c. 1917.

Valverde, Mariana. *The Age of Light, Soap, and Water: Moral Reform in English Canada, 1885–1925*. Toronto: McClelland and Stewart, 1991.

Vance, Jonathan F. *Death So Noble: Memory, Meaning, and the First World War*. Vancouver: UBC Press, 1997.

Vining, Margaret, and Barton C. Hacker. "From Camp Follower to Lady in Uniform: Women, Social Class and Military Institutions before 1920." *Contemporary European History* 10, no. 3 (2001): 353–73. http://dx.doi.org/10.1017/S0960777301003022.

Warren, Gale Denise. "The Patriotic Association of the Women of Newfoundland, 1914-1918." *Aspects* 33, no. 2 (Summer 1998): 23–32.

Watson, Janet S.K. "Active Service: Gender, Class and British Representations of the Great War." PhD diss., Stanford University, 1996.

—. *Fighting Different Wars: Experience, Memory, and the First World War in Britain*. Cambridge: Cambridge University Press, 2004.

—. "Khaki Girls, VADs and Tommy's Sisters: Gender and Class in First World War Britain." *International History Review* 19, no. 1 (February 1997): 32–51. http://dx.doi.org/10.1080/07075332.1997.9640773.

—. "Wars in the Wards: The Social Construction of Medical Work in First World War Britain." *Journal of British Studies* 41, no. 4 (October 2002): 484–510. http://dx.doi.org/10.1086/341439.

Weeks, Clara S. *Textbook of Nursing*. New York: Garland, 1986. First published New York: Appleton, c. 1885.

White, Marian Frances, ed. *The Finest Kind: Voices of Newfoundland and Labrador Women*. St. John's: Creative, 1992.

Whittaker, JoAnn. "The Search for Legitimacy: Nurses' Registration in British Columbia, 1913-1935." In *Not Just Pin Money: Selected Essays on the History of Women's Work in British Columbia*, ed. B.K. Latham and R. Pazdro, 315–26. Victoria: Camosun College, 1984.

Wilde, Terry. "Freshettes, Farmerettes, and Feminine Fortitude at the University of Toronto during the First World War." In *A Sisterhood of Suffering and Service: Women and Girls of Canada and Newfoundland during the First World War*, ed. Sarah Glassford and Amy Shaw, 75–97. Vancouver: UBC Press, 2012.

Wilkinson, Maude. *Four Score and Ten: Memoirs of a Canadian Nurse*. Brampton, ON: M.M. Armstrong, c. 2003.

—. "Four Score and Ten: Part I." *Canadian Nurse* 73, no. 10 (October 1977): 26–29.

Wills, Gale. *A Marriage of Convenience: Business and Social Work in Toronto, 1918–1957*. Toronto: University of Toronto Press, 1995.

Wilson, Barbara M., ed. *Ontario and the First World War: A Collection of Documents*. Toronto: University of Toronto Press, 1977.

Wilson, Wealtha A., and Ethel T. Raymond. "Canadian Women in the Great War." In *Canada in the Great War*. Vol. 6, *Special Services, Heroic Deeds, Etc.*, 176–218. Toronto: United Publishers of Canada, 1921.

Winter, Jay. *Sites of Memory, Sites of Mourning: The Great War in European Cultural History*. Cambridge: Cambridge University Press, 1995.

Wood, James. *Militia Myths: Ideas of the Canadian Citizen Soldier, 1896–1921*. Vancouver: UBC Press, 2010.

Young, Alan R. "'We Throw the Torch': Canadian Memorials of the Great War and the Mythology of Heroic Sacrifice." *Journal of Canadian Studies* 24, no. 4 (Winter 1989–90): 5–28.

INDEX

Note: "t" after a page number refers to a table, "f" to a figure.

Abbott, Maude, 82–83
Abernethy, Flora Edna, 90t
age: of British VADs, 85, 86, 87; of
    Canadian/Newfoundland VADs, 46,
    53, 85–87; for function trainers (FT),
    229n26; for home service, 85; of
    Imperials, 166; for overseas service,
    58, 85–86
Aitken, Florence, 54t
Aitken, Laura Katherine, 90t; Beaver-
    brook as brother, 219n105
Aitken, Sir Max (Lord Beaverbrook),
    219n105
Alberta: nursing divisions, 52t; VAD
    program, 51, 53; VADs serving over-
    seas, 50t
Allan, Martha Marguerite, 100t, 214n21
Almeric Paget Corps, 229n22, 230n33
ambulance divisions: first aid course and,
    35; gender and employment in, 23; in
    Manitoba, 51; numbers ready at out-
    break of war, compared to nursing
    divisions, 19; in "Organization of
    Voluntary Medical Aid in Canada," 18;
    postwar increase in numbers vs nursing

divisions, 186; in Quebec, 47; social
    class and membership, 26; training of
    men in, 26
ambulance drivers/driving: and battle-
    fields, 99; bombardment along French
    coast and, 106–7; BRCS, 97, 99, 101,
    108–9, 137–38; British vs Canadian/
    Newfoundland, 104, 107; Canadian/
    Newfoundland VADs and, 99, 100–1t,
    101; and clearing stations, 99; conditions
    in France, 98; families of, 98–99; fem-
    ininity and, 97–98, 103, 104; fiction, 98;
    first aid course and, 101; gender norms
    and, 102–3; glamour of, 97; MacPherson
    and, 91, 137–38, 163; Newfoundland
    VADs as, 58; numbers of, 99; numbers
    of British compared to colonial, 217n73;
    Rendell as, 233n85; requirements for,
    107; at Royaumont, 99; social class and,
    104, 137–38; through England/Italy,
    217n66; uniforms, 97, 102–3, 109; VADs
    as, 14; vehicle maintenance/mechanics,
    98, 101; V. Wilson and, 107, 132
American Military Hospital, London, 177
Anzacs, 72

Archibald, Edith, 48–49
archives, 10–12
armistice: ambivalence regarding, 161, 189; celebrations, 161, 162; and changes, 162; and continuation of work, 163; costs of, 162; and dismantling of military hospitals, 175; and reluctance to leave VAD careers, 175, 177–78; and return to civilian life, 14; and women's employment, 162. *See also* employment, postwar; repatriation of soldiers
Atwill, Mabel, 90t
auxiliary home hospitals, 62, 63
Aver, Mrs., 76
Ayre, Eric, 186, 226n145
Ayre, Ruby, 233n85

bacteria, 36, 139
Bagnold, Enid, 144, 156
Baker, Phyllis, 100t
Baldwin, K., 76
Barrow, K.M., 138
Barry, John, 127
Bartlett, Bertha, 178t
Bates, Christina, 115
Beatty, Betty Maude, 90t
Beaumont Hamel, battle of, 185–86, 208n56, 226n145, 233n85
Bedside Matters (McPherson), 5–6
Bennett, George, 68
Bennett, R.B., 68
Bidwell, Lucy Frances Dorothea, 90t, 214n21
Bingham, Stella, 153
Birch, Ruth, 178t
Birmingham, 1st Southern General Hospital: F. Aitken at, 54t; Bray at, 47, 65, 137, 146, 147; Humphrys at, 137; Wynne-Roberts at, 33–34, 72, 74, 132, 147
Bishop-Stirling, Terry, 104
Blaylock, H.W., 77
Bleasdell, Isabelle Marjorie, 90t
Bolton, Grace Errol, 90t, 178t
bombardment: along French coast, 77–78, 106–7; and ambulance drivers, 106–7;

and London/south coast hospitals, 142; and shell shock, 142
Borden, Robert, 44, 59, 78
Boulogne: bombing raids, 77; Canadian Red Cross headquarters in, 177, 229n18; CRCS Nurses' Rest House, 77–78, 157–58, 166, 167f; Hôtel Christol (*see under* Canadian Red Cross Society [CRCS]); Hôtel du Nord (*see under* Canadian Red Cross Society [CRCS]); influenza epidemic in, 176; No. 3 Canadian General Hospital (CGH), 75, 211n114
Boy Scouts, 28, 30
Bray, Alice, 29f; at 1st Southern General Hospital, Birmingham, 47–48, 65, 137, 146, 147; on armistice celebrations, 162; class perceptions of, 137; at Devonshire House, 72; on dismissal of VAD, 147; on leaving VAD life behind, 189; on military rule in hospital, 146; overseas service, 67, 68; and preference of Montreal VADs for France, 68; at Royal Herbert Hospital, London, 137
Bredin, Anne, 95
British Columbia: influenza epidemic in, 125; nursing divisions, 52t; VADs serving overseas, 50t
British military hospitals: auxiliary home hospitals, 62, 63; BRCS deployment of VADs to, 21; Bruce report and, 72; component institutions, 72; dependence on VADs, 64; expansion of beds in, 64; Joint Women's VAD Committee as recruiting for all, 72; matrons, 122; RAMC and, 61; uniforms/dress code, 122
British military nurses: dependence on VADs, 65; diminishing supply of, 148; uniforms, 108
British nurse-Canadian/Newfoundland VAD relationship: colonial status in, 145; compared to Canadian equivalent, 146; discipline in, 147; S. Johnson and, 145–46, 150–51, 174; matrons in, 146, 147, 150; in overseas service, 147–50; Sears on, 146–47; ward sisters in, 146–47; V. Wilson on, 147

British Red Cross Society (BRCS): and ambulance drivers/driving, 97, 99, 101, 108–9, 137–38; Canadian/Newfoundland women training with, 64; and deployment of VADs to military hospitals, 21; direct enlistment with, 58; division of responsibilities with St. John, 31; and free VAD training, 83; MacPherson as ambulance driver, 137–38; majority of VADs remaining under, 21; Miller as VAD/motor driver, 186; Museum and Archives archival holdings, 11; records in Joint Women's VAD Committee records, 12; recruitment of Newfoundland VADs through, 36–37; relationship with British St. John Ambulance, 20–21, 31; VAD recruitment poster, 62f; VAD "Terms of Service," 8; VAD uniform, 108

British Red Cross Society Nursing Manual (Cantlie), 26, 47

British St. John Ambulance: division of responsibilities with BRCS, 31; fees for VAD training, 83; relationship with BRCS, 20–21, 31; response from middle-class women as nursing members, 16; VADs and South African War, 5

British ties: of Canadian/Newfoundland VADs, 84–85; and choice of Canadian candidates, 17; of Newfoundland women, 59; and St. John Ambulance in Canada, 84; of VADs, 84–85; Westerners and, 53

British VAD program/scheme: establishment of, 16; General Service Division, 8; as integral to RAMC convalescent hospitals, 61–62; Joint Women's Committee, 20; middle-class women and, 16, 17; nursing activists and, 39–40; nursing divisions lacking novelty/glamour of, 19; and nursing registration, 39–40; women's interest in, 17

British VADs: age of, 85, 86, 87; Canadian/Newfoundland VADs compared to, as models of nursing volunteer, 81; collection of interviews in Imperial War Museum, 10; commemoration in York Minster, 179; educational levels, 80; employed women as, 80; journalism on work in military hospitals, 51; memorial service for, 179; military hospitals' dependence on, 39, 64; numbers of, 132, 209n78, 212n2; nurse-training credit for overseas service, 173; Personnel Record Indexes, 11; pre-war employment, 81; qualifications as, 64; scholarships for training in health-related occupations, 179; social class vs of qualified nurses, 80; social class and, 150; stipends, 64; training camps, 30; upper classes and, 80; as working-class women, 81

Brittain, Vera: acceptance of application, 87; age on starting as VAD, 86; diary, 3; first reaction to war, 80; privileged upbringing, 80; *Testament of Youth*, 3; VAD experience as awakening sexuality, 158

Brown, Lillian, 87

Browning, Adeline, 20, 22, 37

Bruce, Amy Augusta, 180t

Bruce, Herbert, 61–63, 72

Burden, Dr., 27–28

Burns, Mary Gladys, 90t

Burr, Mary, 39

Butcher, Arthur, "Second Aid," 114, 115f

Butler, Norine, 90t, 100t

Calgary: General Hospital, 126–27; influenza epidemic in, 126–27

Camberwell Hospital, London, 86

Cameron-Smith, Matron, 76–77

Camp Hill Military Convalescent Hospital, Halifax, 120, 123, 124, 220n20

Campbell, Lilian Mary, 90t

Canadian Army Medical Corps (CAMC): Bruce report on, 61–63; Imperials working in non-nursing capacity with, 166; A. Macphail with, 125; and massage therapy, 168; MHC relations with, 44, 128; non-nursing VADs with, 78; Lady Perley and, 166; political turmoil in, 63; records, 12; resistance to VADs in hospitals, 8–9, 61, 65, 74, 168; and return of soldiers to field, 168; VADs as nursing assistants in hospitals, 36. *See also* military convalescent hospitals

Canadian Army Medical Corps (CAMC) nurses: candidates for overseas placement outnumbering opportunities, 66–67; capitalization on legacy for professional recognition, 173; choice of qualified nurses vs volunteers as, 59–60; deaths in bombardment, 106; first overseas contingent, 6; Hughes's appointment of underqualified women as, 78; and massage therapy, 170–71; numbers of, 209n66, 231n45; and public health nursing, 173–74; qualifications, 61; relations with VAD workers, 76–77; in scholarship, 4; uniforms, 108; VADs applying as, 8–9, 61, 63, 65. *See also* military nurses

Canadian Association of Nurse Education, 172

Canadian Bank of Commerce, 94–95

Canadian Expeditionary Force (CEF), 31

Canadian First Aid, 187–88

Canadian Imperial Voluntary Aid Detachment ("Imperials"): about, 164–65, 166; age and, 166; cross-section of volunteers, 166; formation of, 164; numbers of members, 165; postings, 166–67; social class and, 165, 166; uniforms, 166

Canadian National Association of Trained Nurses (CNATN): and *Canadian Nurse*, 46; Copp on VADs and, 152; and government VAD service extension as solution to nursing shortages, 172; inception of, 6; and Militia Dept. approval of underqualified volunteers, 59–60; and National Nursing Service Corps, 124; and permanent use of VAD nurses/masseuses in veterans' hospitals, 171–73; and public health nursing, 173–74, 188; and university-level training standards, 188; on usefulness of VADs to war effort, 172; on VAD insertion into training schools as probationers, 173; and

VAD threat to qualified nurses' jobs, 188; and VADs' admission to CAMC hospitals, 167–68; and VADs' lack of intention to continue with nursing, 174; and VADs' patriotic motivations, 172. *See also* Gunn, Jean

Canadian National Committee for Mental Hygiene, 39

Canadian Nurse, 46, 124

Canadian Red Cross Society (CRCS): and compensation for health problems, 179; headquarters in Boulogne, 177, 229n18; and National Relief Committee, 17; and non-nursing VADs, 74; Nurses' Rest House, Boulogne, 77–78, 157–58, 166, 167; outreach nursing programs, 174; Perley and, 166; and postwar VAD program, 178–79; and public health/social services, 187; records, 12; rest homes for Imperial nurses, 143; Ryerson and, 15; and South African War, 15; St. John Ambulance Canada relationship with, 21

Canadian Stationary Hospital (CSH), No. 8, 65

Canadian VADs: achievement, 41; community service, 6–7; economic value as unremunerated volunteers, 169; as either nursing members or function trainers (FTs), 169; ideal requirements for, 17–18; in middle ground between qualified nurses and amateur practitioners, 36; narratives/personal writings, 9–10; as nursing candidates, 36; and patriotism, 152; postwar continuation in nursing, 174, 175; qualified career nurses vs, 5; rationale for training, 18; as role models, 26; society's view of, 13, 49; sources/records, 10–12; as volunteer workers vs military nurses, 7

Canadian War Records Office, 112

"Canadian Women in the War Zone" (Moore), 82

Canadian/Newfoundland VADs: age of, 85–87; as ambulance drivers, 99, 100–11, 101; British ties, 84–85; British VADs compared to, as models of nursing volunteer, 81; colonialism and, 137–38, 147; database of, 12; independently travelling overseas, 64–65; lack of official memorialization of work, 179; as "new women," 81, 88; numbers, compared to British VADs, 132; and patriotism, 6–7, 129, 186–87; in Personnel Record Indexes, 11; serving overseas, 50t; social class, 81, 83–84, 88; socioeconomics, compared to military nurses, 81; varied roles, 13–14. *See also* Newfoundland VADs

Cantlie, James: *British Red Cross Society Nursing Manual*, 26, 47; *First Aid to the Injured/Premiers soins aux blessés*, 47; and role of VAD nurse, 36

caregiving: definition of "nurse" and, 162; femininity and, 78; postwar redirection of women to, 187

Carleton-Jones, Guy, 62–63

Carlyle, Margaret Mackay, 90t

casualties: among families of VADs, 51, 53, 67, 185–86; Cluett and, 134; from French coast bombardment, 106–7; growth in numbers, 43–44; and patriotism, 61; projection of number, 28; Starr and, 134–36; in summer 1918, 128; VAD adjustment to, 134; VADs' working conditions and, 143; and workload, 134. *See also* deaths; illness/infection; wounds/injuries/disabilities

Cavell, Edith, 111, 153

censorship: and concealment of work/travel details from newspapers, 213n11; and lack of information about hospitals, 145; of letters, 144; self-, 9; and VADs' letters, 9; Wynne-Roberts's letters and, 34, 95

Chatwin, Elsie: as ambulance driver, 100t, 101, 156; in documentary, 10; and Portuguese patients, 156

Chatwin, James N. (father of Elsie), 217n67

Chelsea, 2nd London General Hospital, Sears at, 137, 146–47, 224n92

Chenier, Elise, 131

Chown, Dorothy: about, 232n70; as dietitian, 182

Christianity: Anglican Church and St. John Ambulance, 85; iconography in uniform, 111; and propaganda, 85; spirituality in illustrations/photographs, 111; VADs as Protestant, 7, 26, 46, 84

Christie, Agatha, 16, 87

Church, Tommy, 128

City of Marseilles (convoy ship), 71

Civil Service Association (CSA), 92–94

Civilian (CSA), 92–94, 148

Clarke, C.K., 39, 170

Cluett, Frances (Fanny), 23f; at 4th Northern General Hospital, Lincoln, 37, 130, 133, 134, 136–37, 155, 158; about, 21–22; age, 87; as Belleoram schoolteacher, 84; birth date, 214n29; Browning and, 204n72; at Constantinople RAMC base, 177; at Devonshire House, 71; on fainting "dead away," 145; family background/social class, 84; on health, 142; humour, 134; and Janes, 22; length of overseas service, 136; on length of shifts, 130; letters, 151; maternal identity, in relationships with patients, 159; on night duty, 117–18, 156–57; nursing POWs, 155, 156–57; on nursing supervisors, 151; postwar career, 185; at Queen Mary's Hospital, 37; on rationing of bread/sugar, 142; return to Canada, 177; in Rouen, 117–18, 142, 148, 151, 155, 156–57, 160, 177; routine/duties, 133; secondment to France, 134; and stress of work, 141; temperament, 130, 134, 151; training, 22, 27–28, 31, 33, 204n72; on VADs' relationships with patients, 158; on voyage, 70

Cobble Hill, BC, Twist's name on cenotaph, 180

Code, Dorothy Leslie, 90t

College Nursing Division, Toronto: and overseas service, 58, 66; recruitment of undergraduates from University of Toronto, 45; on salaries for VADs, 152

colonialism, and Canadian/Newfoundland VADs, 137–38, 147
community service: Halifax explosion and, 122–24; and patriotic work, 6; social class and, 6, 13; VADs and, 6–7
Connaught, Duke of, 21
convalescent hospitals. *See* military convalescent hospitals
Cook, Felicia Hannah (Nan), 90t
Cook, Harry, 157
Coon, Eva, 90t
Coonan, Mary, 100t
Copp, Charles: in charge of SJAB VAD program, 38; and CNATN on VADs endangering qualified nurses, 172; and conversion of VADs into qualified nursing reserve, 171; daughter, 214n21; family, 232n74; portrait, 233n90; on quality of VAD program, 131; on RAMC living allowance, 209n80; on social class of VAD applicants, 83; on VADs' lack of hospital experience, 38; on VADs' motivation as pure patriotism, 59, 152
Copp, Violet, 214n21
Coultas, Jeanette, 37, 70–71
CRCS Red Cross Nurses' Rest Home, 77–78, 229n18
Creelman, Louise Ashmore, 90t
Crimean War, 5
Crowdy, Elsie, 100t

Dalhousie University: female enrollment, 207n51; Hall's graduation from, 50
Davisville Military Orthopaedic Hospital, Toronto: about, 203n58; duties at, 120–21; Gordon at, 120–21, 146; opening of, 210n85; Sears at, 146; Wynne-Roberts at, 132
Day, Edward Bliss (husband of Thomas), 232n74
Dearden, Beth, 126
deaths: of CAMC nurses in Étaples bombardment, 106; from influenza, 128–29; during influenza crisis, 127; numbers of Canadian service personnel, 161–62; of

nurses from enemy action, 143; of VADs, 129, 178t, 179; and women's marital status, 162
Deauville officers' convalescent home, 154, 175
Dent, Olive, 7
Department of Agriculture, 94
Department of Immigration and Colonization, 92
Department of Militia/Militia and Defence: and costs of rehabilitation, 168; and diversification of VAD organization, 168–69; and National Relief Committee, 17; records, 12; and salary for VADs, 152; underqualified volunteers' use of contacts for approval by, 59; and WAD, 169
Department of Soldiers' Civil Re-establishment (DSCR): about, 91–92; demobilized VADs employed at, 91–92; and Geach as federal employee, 94; and MacPherson, 185
Devonshire House, London: call for colonial VADs, 58, 65; demolition of, 210n99; direct enlistment at, 58; Joint Women's VAD Committee headquartered at, 12; limited human resources, 71–72; MacPherson and, 101–2; screening of reserve of volunteer nurses for British military hospitals, 64; VADs' first impressions of, 71–72; V. Wilson posted to, 132
diaries, 9–10
Dickens, Charles, 5
Dickinson, Ethel G., 178t, 181f; death from influenza, 180; memorial to, 180; as teacher, 179; as university graduate, 90t
dietitians, 14, 182
disabilities. *See* wounds/injuries/disabilities
Donnelly, Madeline, 201n27
Donner, Henriette, 136
"Don'ts for V.A.Ds," 143–44
Douglass, Ellen, 26–27
Doull, Marion, 48–49

Drumheller, influenza epidemic in, 127
Duchess of Connaught Canadian Red
　Cross Hospital, Cliveden, 112f
Dufour, Georgette, 93
Dunfield, Brian E.S., 233n83
duties. *See* routine/duties

Earhart, Amelia, 56–57, 128
Earhart, Edwin, 207n48
Edmonton, VAD training in, 51, 53
educational levels: of British VADs, 80; of
　Canadian/Newfoundland VADs, 26,
　88–91; and marital status, 89; and post-
　war careers/lives, 162; of Toronto-area
　VADs, 57
Edward, Prince of Wales, 31, 157–58
elites/upper classes: and ambulance driv-
　ing, 103, 104, 138; and British pre-war
　VADs, 80, 81; and British VADs, 80,
　153; and Canadian/Newfoundland
　VADs, 88, 131; and educational level,
　88–89; and Imperials, 165, 167; Johnson
　sisters as, 70; and Montreal VADs, 46–
　47, 130, 131, 153; as nursing volunteers
　in South African War, 8; occupations
　of, 6, 16; and Order of St. John vs Red
　Cross, 21, 31; and overseas service,
　130–31
Emerson, Jean, 201n27
employment: gendered expectations and,
　6; marital status and, 87–88, 91, 93, 94;
　social class and, 6; war, and opportun-
　ities for working-class women, 16
employment, postwar: about, 162; in banks,
　94–95; and continuation with nursing,
　174, 175, 186–87; dental nursing, 183;
　with federal/provincial governments,
　91–92, 93, 94, 183, 184; first aid room
　nursing, 183; former occupations and,
　91–92, 94–95, 162; gender and, 94, 162;
　Hall, 91; health-related, 182–84, 186;
　lack of interest in nursing careers, 9,
　152, 172, 186–87; in military hospitals,
　95; Newfoundland VADs, 185–86; non-
　health related, 183–85, 186; nursing, 163;
　overseas, 184; private duty nursing, 183;

re-employment of male veterans, 94;
　repatriation of soldiers and, 94, 183,
　187; salaried nursing work, 162; with
　St. John Ambulance, 183, 185, 186–87;
　teaching, 95, 162, 183–84, 185; Thomas,
　183; veteran status and, 91
employment, pre-war: British VADs and,
　80, 81; Canadian middle-class women
　and, 16; Canadian/Newfoundland
　VADs' occupations, 88, 89t; colonial
　VADs and, 81; with federal/provincial
　governments, 91, 92–94; Joint Women's
　VAD Committee survey of British
　VADs regarding, 81; MacPherson, 91;
　overseas service, and relinquishment of,
　91; of PEI VADs, 53; in private sector,
　94–95; social class and, 80, 81; in teach-
　ing, 91, 95–96
Esquimalt Military Convalescent Hospital,
　55
Étaples: motor convoy, 101, 103, 106,
　113f; No. 1 Canadian General Hospital
　(CGH), 211n114
ethnicity: British heritage and choice of
　candidates, 17; and choice of VADs,
　7–8; and patient-nurse relationship,
　156–57; of VADs in Khaki Homes, 53
Étretat, male ambulance unit at, 99

families of VADs: ambivalence of, 42–43;
　ambulance drivers, 98–99; Anglican
　Church and, 85; Bidwell, 214n21; British
　ties, 46; casualties among, 51, 53, 67,
　185–86; Cluett, 155; Earhart, 57; and
　educational levels vs marital status,
　89; Gosling, 104; B. Hall, 91; J. Hall,
　214n21; illustrations/photographs and,
　113; influence, and selection for over-
　seas service, 130–31; Johnson sisters, 84,
　132, 226n134; Lighthall, 89; Macphail,
　89, 125–26; MacPherson, 101; and mar-
　riages vs liaisons, 157; and nursing of
　POWs, 155; patriotism of, 42–43; Sears,
　85, 177, 226n134; social class of, 81, 83–
　84, 153, 214n21; St. John Ambulance
　connections, 46, 130; V. Wilson, 67, 177,

226n134; and work in war zone, 153. *See also* social class

Farrar, Kathleen, 100t

federal government: female employees filling positions vacated by men departing for war, 92–93; postwar employment with, 91–92, 93; pre-war employment with, 92–94; veteran status and employment with, 92

femininity: and ambulance drivers, 97–98, 103, 104; and caregiving, 78; and choice for VAD program, 17; illustrations/photographs and, 111, 112; and non-nursing VADs as social convenors/hostesses, 82; and nursing practice, 167; and patriotism, 82; propaganda and, 49; and uniforms, 18, 42. *See also* motherhood

feminism: Canadian/Newfoundland VADs and, 88, 91; scholarship on VADs, 3–4. *See also* suffrage

Finley, E.G. (son of Ross), 234n99

Finley, Eric B. (husband of Ross), 232n69

First Aid Bulletin, 234n96

first aid course: about, 26; and ambulance drivers/driving, 101; and ambulance service, 35; certificate, 29f; gendered expectations and, 35; introduction by St. John Ambulance, 16; numbers of lectures in, 32; numbers receiving, 23; in St. John's (NL) nursing division, 20; WAD and, 169

First Aid Nursing Yeomanry (FANY), 97, 99, 101, 102, 233n85

First Aid to the Injured/Premiers soins aux blessés (Cantlie), 47

First World War: attitude of Canadians toward possibility of, 16; duration of, 28; outbreak of, 16; preparation for, 28, 30

Fisher, Harold, 126, 127–28

Fleming Hospital, Ottawa, 45, 47, 48

Foringer, A.E., *The Greatest Mother in the World*, 85, 86f

Foster, Gilbert L., 170, 230n34

France: ambulance driving conditions in, 98; Bray on, 47; dismantling of military hospitals in, 175; Montreal VADs sent to, 47, 67–68, 209n77; Service Automobile Sanitaire, 99, 101; structure of hospitals in, 148; VAD deployment to, 130; V. Wilson et al. travelling in, 175–76

franchise. *See* suffrage

francophones: and bilingualism, 46–47; St. John Ambulance Canada and, 85

Fredericton Nursing Division, 66

Frensham Hill Military Hospital, 180

function trainers (FTs), 169, 181, 229n26

Furse, Dame Katharine: as founder/commandant of Joint Women's VAD Committee, 12; personal message from, 144; on uniform, 110

Gamp, Sarah (fictional character), 5, 61

gas warfare, 36, 61

Geach, Adine, 94

gender norms: and ambulance driving, 102–3; and employment in ambulance divisions, 22–23; and first aid/home nursing courses, 35; illustrations/photographs and, 114; and marital status, 88; and middle-class women's patriotism, 57; in postwar careers, 162; and postwar employment, 94; social class and appropriate activities, 107; and unmarried women as nurses during influenza epidemic, 129; and VAD uniform, 7; and volunteer nursing, 43; and V. Wilson et al. travelling in France, 176; and women's paid wartime labour, 6

General Service Medal, 153

George V, King, 107

Gery, Doreen: on bayoneted soldier, 129–30; brother, 61; in documentary, 10; duties, 133; and patriotism, 61; on war losses, and fatigue, 162

Gifford House convalescent hospital, London: Ross at, 232n69; V. Wilson at, 132, 142, 147, 154, 156, 184

Gilbert, Sandra, 158, 162, 163

Gillespie, Nellie, 54t

Glassford, Sarah, *A Sisterhood of Suffering and Service*, 4

Gordon, Mary W.M., 180t

Gordon, Shirley: age, 87; on convalescent hospitals, 45; at Davisville Hospital, 120–21, 146; on emergency bandaging techniques, 33; marital status as reason for becoming VAD, 87–88; on necessity of volunteers, 44; and nursing staff, 121, 122; relationship with nursing supervisor, 146; on uniform, 121; as university graduate, 90t; in University of Toronto VAD program, 33, 120

Gordon-Brown, Ethel: and CRCS Nurses' Rest House, Boulogne, 77, 166, 167f; as Imperial, 166

Gordon-Brown, Evelyn, as ambulance driver, 100t

Gorham, Deborah, 158

Gosling, Armine Nutting (mother of Harriet), 218n80

Gosling, Gilbert (father of Harriet), 217–18n80

Gosling, Harriet Armine (Annie), 105f; as ambulance driver, 101t, 104

graduate nurses. *See* qualified/trained nurses

Granville Special Hospital, 168, 170

The Greatest Mother in the World (Foringer), 85, 86f

Grenadier Guards Emergency Hospital, 125–26

Grey Nuns' Convalescent Home, Montreal, 67

Grey Nuns' Hospital, Regina, 185

Gunn, Jean: and CAMC nurses' postwar careers, 173; and capitalization on CAMC nurses' legacy for professional recognition/employment security, 173; complaint to Borden, 59, 78; on conversion of VADs' certification into civilian nursing jobs, 39; and Hughes/Militia Dept. approval of underqualified women, 59, 78; on lowering of nursing standards, 39, 170; meeting with Copp, 171–72; on no middle ground between amateur and professional, 36; as president of CNATN, 36; and public health nursing, 173–74; on training of VAD student nurses, 171–72; on usefulness of VADs to war effort, 172; on VAD work in veterans' hospitals, 173; on VADs as nursing candidates, 36; on VADs deserving recognition for war work, 178; and VADs' patriotic motivations, 172; and VADs undermining value/security of nursing work, 169–70

Gwyn, Sandra, 185

Halifax: Camp Hill Military Convalescent Hospital, 120, 123, 124, 220n20; creation of Voluntary Aid Detachment (VAD), 24; explosion, 13, 50, 70, 118–19, 122–24; Infants' Home, 120; influenza epidemic in, 124–25; military convalescent hospitals in, 48–49; Naval Hospital, 124; Pine Hill Military Convalescent Hospital, 49, 119, 120; Red Cross, 124; St. John Ambulance founding in, 199n3; VAD propaganda in, 49; Victoria General Hospital, 119

Halifax Nursing Division: about, 48–49; establishment of, 50–51; and Halifax explosion, 122–24; numbers sent overseas, 66

Hall, Elizabeth (Bessie), 119f; at Camp Hill Military Convalescent Hospital, 120; duration of service, 123; family of, 91; as graduate student, 120; and Halifax explosion, 123; hope for overseas posting, 30, 50–51, 65; at Infants' Home, 120; and influenza epidemic, 124; letters, 119–20; nursing staff and, 119, 120; in pediatric ward, 119–20; at Pine Hill Hospital, 120; postwar career, 91, 95; reluctance to leave VAD experience, 177–78; as teacher, 91, 95; on uniform, 109, 110; as university graduate, 50, 89, 90t, 91, 119; at Victoria General Hospital, Halifax, 119–20

Hall, Jessie, 214n21

Hallett, Christine, 138

Harris, Reginald V., 124

Harstone, Jean: as ambulance driver, 100t, 106–7; at Étaples, 218n81; as university graduate, 90t

hemorrhage, 34–35

Henderson, Viola: and acceptance of vs resistance to VADs, 48; and Bray/ Humphrys, 137; as lady superintendent of Montreal St. John Ambulance, 46; and Montreal VAD numbers/experience, 48; and Montreal VADs sent overseas, 67–68, 89, 130; recruitment by St. John, 97; on suitability vs unsuitability of recruits, 47; on VADs, 46; on VADs in Khaki Homes being equivalent to probationers, 53

Henshaw, Isabel, 178t

Hodgetts, Charles A., 77

home nursing course: about, 26–27; certificate, 29f; content of, 35; as core of training program, 34–36; domestic rationale for, 18; gendered expectations and, 35; infection/disinfection, 35–36; and influenza epidemic, 125; introduction by St. John Ambulance, 16; numbers of lectures in, 32; numbers taking, 23; postwar decline of interest in, 187; in St. John's (NL) nursing division, 20; WAD and, 169

home sisters, 78

home-front service: about, 118; age for, 85; demobilization from, 177–79; duties/ tasks in, 118; overseas service compared, 118; VADs in, 118–29

Hope, Helen Christine, 90t

Horrocks, Sister, 151

hospital experience/training: Bray and, 48; as not guaranteed for VADs, 36; nursing supervisors vs VADs and, 130; of Ottawa vs Montreal VADs, 47; in qualifications in call for colonial VADs, 65; in Toronto, 56; VADs and, 36, 37–39, 40. *See also* training, nursing; training, VAD

hospital hierarchy: nursing probationers and, 8; teachers and, 96; VAD cognizance of position within, 150; VADs

and, 8; VADs in, 121; volunteer nurses in, 96

hospital ships, 48, 50–51, 119

hospitals: increasing numbers of female volunteers in, 13–14; student nurses as primary workforce of, 38; Territorial Forces, 204n75. *See also* military convalescent hospitals; *and names of individual hospitals*

Hôtel Christol, Boulogne. *See under* Canadian Red Cross Society (CRCS)

Hôtel du Nord, Boulogne. *See under* Canadian Red Cross Society (CRCS)

Houston, Alice Sophia, 180t; at 4th Northern General Hospital, Lincoln, 68; hospital training, and overseas service, 48; as Mentioned-in-Dispatches, 93, 96; postwar return to post office, 93

Hudson's Bay Company, 44

Hughes, Sam, 59, 78, 102

Humphrys, Gladys: at 1st Southern General Hospital, Birmingham, 47, 48, 137; at Royal Herbert Hospital, London, 137

Hutchinson, John, 4, 21

hygiene/infection control: about, 138–40; casualties from lack of, 139; infection/ disinfection, 35–36; in Royaumont, 138–39; VAD casualties and, 140; and workload, 139–40

illness/infection, 13, 139, 140

illustrations/photographs: deviant/less savoury images in, 112–15; and families of VADs/nurses, 113; femininity in, 111, 112; and ideal image, 107, 111–12; patient-nurse relationship in, 111–12, 113–14, 115; postcards, 114, 115

Imperial Order Daughters of the Empire (IODE), 19, 42, 44, 187

Imperial War Museum: British VAD interviews collection, 10; Women at Work Collection, 12

"Imperials." *See* Canadian Imperial Voluntary Aid Detachment ("Imperials")

infection. *See* hygiene/infection control; illness/infection

influenza epidemic: about, 124–29; in
Boulogne, 176; in British Columbia, 125;
in Calgary, 126–27; deaths from, 128–
29, 161, 183–84; Dickinson and, 179–80;
in Drumheller, 127; Earhart and, 128;
in Halifax, 124–25; Hall and, 120, 178;
and health of VADs/nurses, 143; home
nursing course and, 125; impact of, 118–
19; Macphail and, 89, 125–26; mentioned,
13; and military convalescent hospitals,
122, 128; in Montreal, 125–26; Murphy
and, 127, 163; in New Brunswick, 125;
in Ontario, 125; in Ottawa, 126; and
public health, 187; and register of VADs/
volunteers, 187; three waves of, 220n18;
Twist and, 180–81; and University of
Toronto, 120; and unmarried women as
nurses, 129; and value of VAD scheme,
122; and women's marital status, 162
injuries. *See* wounds/injuries/disabilities
International Red Cross Society (IRCS):
creation of, 4; St. John Ambulance
compared, 15
Ivens, Frances, 135, 148–49

Janes, Clare: Cluett as friend of, 22; train-
ing, 22, 27–28, 31, 33
Jenkins, Grace, 229n22
Jesse, F. Tennyson, 102–3, 104, 112
Job, Nell, 233n85
Johnson, Daisy (later Cook): and Cook,
157; delayed return to Canada, 175; at
King George Hospital, London, 175;
marriage, 175; nursing repatriated POWs,
175; postwar resumption of pre-war
career, 91, 185; on voyage, 69–70
Johnson, Edna: at 4th Northern General
Hospital, Lincoln, 68; hospital training,
48
Johnson, George M. (father of Sybil and
Jill), 214n22
Johnson, Jill (Marie Estelle), 141f; at 1st
Western General Hospital, Liverpool,
132, 136, 150; consciousness of amateur
status, 150; family background, 84, 132;
infection of thumbs, 140; relationships

with patients, 155; return to St. John's,
224n81; social class, 84, 132; training, 37;
on voyage, 70
Johnson, Sybil, 38f; at 1st Western General
Hospital, Liverpool, 37, 132, 136, 141–42,
150–51; about, 36; on British nurses, 145–
46, 150; and Christmas, 160; Cluett's
temperament compared to, 151–52; at
Devonshire House, 71; diaries, 9–10;
doubts/misgivings, 36–37; family
background, 84, 132; father, 226n134;
and hemorrhage, 35; humour used by,
143; on infection, 140; on maternal role
with patients, 158–59; and military
nurses' relationship with VADs, 118,
151–52; on night duty, 141–42; on nursing profession, 174; on nursing supervisors, 150, 151; on patients, 154, 158–59,
174; postwar marriage and life, 175, 185,
233n83; probationer's training, 132, 145–
46; reflections on experience, 174–75;
return to St. John's, 175, 224n81; routine/
duties, 132, 133; social class, 84, 132, 174;
on social class of patients, 153; summary
of experience as VAD, 163–64; on uniform, 109–10; on up-patients, 159–60;
on VAD resignations, 151; on voyage,
70; on workload, 139
Joint War Committee: and embarkation
of Canadian St. John VADs, 64; and
Imperial detachments, 164; management of RAMC auxiliary home hospitals, 61–62; War Office initiation of, 21
Joint Women's VAD Committee: about,
12; and age of British VAD applicants,
85; Devonshire House as headquarters,
71; Furse as founder/first commandant,
12; and Imperial VADs, 164–65; Princess
Mary and, 107; ranking system devised
by, 148; records in Imperial War
Museum's Women at Work Collection,
12; as recruitment for all British military
hospitals, 72; and reserve detachments,
164; and Scottish Women's Hospital
(Abbaye de Royaumont), 132; survey of
VADs' previous employment, 81; and

VAD marriages, 88; VAD Personnel Record Indexes, 11

journalism: about VADs' work, 82; British VADs in military hospitals, 51; censorship and, 213n11; and lack of information about hospitals, 145; limited access to military hospitals, 82; on non-nursing VADs, 75; and propaganda, 82. *See also* illustrations/photographs; Moore, Mary MacLeod

Kemp, Sir Edward, 169
Kenilworth Castle (convoy ship), 71
Kennedy, May, 186
Keogh, Sir Alfred, 72
Keshen, Jeffrey, 114
Khaki League/Homes, Montreal, 44, 46, 47, 53, 67, 130
Kilmer, Margaret Helen, 90t
Kilpatrick, Elizabeth Margaret Ritchie (Bessie), 90t
King George Hospital, London, 175, 206n30, 214n21
Kingman, Eva Fraser. *See* Morgan, Eva
Kipling, Rudyard, 145

Lady Roberts' Convalescent Hospital, Ascot, 136
lady superintendents, 32, 122, 229n25
Lambert, Barrie, 170–71
Laurier, Sir Wilfrid, 205n3
Lawrence, Clarence, 226n145, 232n75
Le Messurier, Isobel, 201n27
Le Tréport convoy, 106–7
Lee, Janet, 97
Leitch, Charlotte: as ambulance driver, 100t; at Étaples, 218n81
Leitch, Marion St. Clair, 90t
Lighthall, Alice, 89
Lighthall, William Doux, 89
Lincoln, 4th Northern General Hospital: Cluett at, 37, 130, 133, 134, 136–37, 155, 158; Houston at, 68; Johnson at, 68; Newfoundland VADs at, 136–37
Liverpool, 1st Western General Hospital: infection/injuries of VAD/nursing

personnel at, 140; J. Johnson at, 150; S. Johnson at, 37, 132, 133, 141–42, 150–51; Johnson sisters at, 132, 136, 140; Macmillan at, 54t; Nicholson at, 54t; night duty at, 141–42; VAD resignations from, 151
living allowances. *See* stipends/living allowances
Local Councils of Women, 19
Lowe, Margaret, 218n86
Loyd, Archie, 31
Luck, Amy Eliza Haydon, 180t

MacAdams, Roberta, 218n82
Macdonald, Katherine, 218n86
Macdonald, Lyn, 80, 150
Macdonald, Margaret: Bruce report and, 63; creation of special class of work for nurses' residences, 78; and employment of VADs as masseuses, 170; and Hughes's approval of underqualified women, 59; and integrity of nursing service, 59–60; and married nurses, 88; and masseuses, 168; and military nurses trained in massage at Granville Hospital, 170; and Nurses' Rest House in London, 77; records of, 12; resistance to VADs, 8–9, 40, 61, 65, 74, 168; and untrained nursing volunteers, 8; and VADs as undermining status of military nurses, 40; and VADs in CAMC hospitals, 8–9, 61, 65, 74, 168
MacIntosh, Clara, 122–24, 123, 124
MacIntosh, George A., 122
Mack, Beatrice, 159
MacKeen, Anna Mary, 90t
Macmillan, Belle, 54t
MacMurchy, Helen, 172–73
Macphail, Dorothy: about, 89; and influenza epidemic, 125–26
Macphail, Sir Andrew, 89, 125
MacPherson, Alex, 101
MacPherson, Grace, 105f, 113f; as ambulance driver, 91, 100t, 101–2, 103–4, 106, 112, 137–38, 163; application to Hughes, 102; characteristics/temperament,

137–38; as clerk in Canadian Pay and Records Office, London, 102; delayed return to Canada for "decompression," 177; as driver for American Military Hospital in London, 177; with DSCR in Vancouver, 185; family, 101; marriage, 185; as Lady Perley's secretary, 167, 177; persistence in getting to England, 101–2; personality, 104; photographs for War Records Office, 112; pre-war occupation, 91; relationship with military nurses, 118; return to Vancouver, 177; as St. John Ambulance volunteer in Second World War, 185; supporting self in London, 91

Magee, Marion, 183

Manitoba: ambulance division, 51; numbers of VADs overseas, 51; nursing divisions, 51, 52t; VADs serving overseas, 50t

Mann, Susan, 59, 209n66, 209n76, 212n123, 231n45

Manners, Diana, 144–45

Marine Department, 94

marital status: of Canadian Imperial Voluntary Aid Detachment members, 166; casualties and, 162, 183–84; double day during emergencies for unmarried women, 126; and employment, 93; gender norms and, 88; Gordon, 87–88; and government employment, 94; higher education and, 89; influenza epidemic and, 162, 183–84; D. Johnson, 175; S. Johnson, 175, 185; MacPherson, 185; marriages to patients, 157; Miller, 186; Newfoundland VADs, 185–86; and postwar careers, 183–84; and qualified nurses, 88; records of VAD marriages, 88; and re-employment of male veterans, 94; and teaching careers, 95; unmarried women as nurse volunteers during influenza epidemic, 129; of VADs, 46; widowhood, 157, 186; A. Wilson, 185; and women's employment, 87–88

Maritimes: military convalescent hospitals in, 48–51; numbers of VADs serving

abroad, 50. *See also* New Brunswick; Nova Scotia; Prince Edward Island

Mary, Princess, Countess of Harewood, 72, 107, 108f, 165

Mary, Queen, 157

massage therapy, 168–69, 170–71, 181–82. *See also* physical therapy

Masson, Betty, 48, 68

matrons: Bray and, 147; and "colonial class" of VAD, 147; dominance of, 122, 146; S. Johnson on, 151; Sears and, 146; Starr and, 150. *See also* nursing supervisors

May Court Club, Ottawa, 131

McArthur, Annie Alexandrina, 100t

McCarthy, E.M., 74, 75

McCord, Nora Young, 178t

McGill University: Lighthall as student, 89; Macphail as student, 89; massage program, 181; School of Physical Education, 229n24

McLaughlin, Jessie, 100t; at Étaples, 218n81

McLean, Marion, 48

McLean, Mary, 68

McPherson, Kathryn, 7–8, 36, 139, 173; *Bedside Matters*, 5–6

Medical Relief Committee, Halifax, 122

Merrill, Anne, 166

Michelangelo, *Pietà*, 85

middle classes: and ambulance driving, 14; and British VAD program, 17; and Canadian VADs as, 16, 46, 53, 57; and employment, 16; and image of "nurse," 4–5; in nursing division membership, 26; as readership of women's journalism, 82; and university attendance, 88–89; volunteers in wartime nursing, 5; women's patriotism in, 57, 78. *See also* social class

military convalescent hospitals: armistice, and winding down, 163; British (*see* British military hospitals); CAMC vs MHC over, 128; CNATN defence against permanent use of VAD nurses/masseuses in, 171–73; construction of

network of, 28; conversion of buildings for, 45; Department of Militia and salary for VADs in, 152; diet kitchens in, 182; dismantling following armistice, 175; establishment of, 44; in France, 148; growing need for space, 45; in Halifax, 48–49; increase in, 44; increasing staffing needs, 40; infection control in, 36; influenza epidemic and, 122, 128; limited access of journalists to, 82; majority of VADs working in, 11; in Maritimes, 48–51; MHC and, 44, 128; in Montreal, 46–47, 48; nursing in, 17; opposition/resistance to VADs in, 38–39, 40, 48–49, 171–73; in Ottawa, 25, 45, 47–48; patient-nurse relationship in, 111–12; physical therapists in, 169; postwar part-time work in, 95; regular VAD service in, 63–64; and rehabilitation of disabled, 117; resistance to VADs in, 38–39, 40, 48–49, 171–73; and return of soldiers to field, 117; Sainte-Anne-de-Bellevue, 181; schools compared to, 138; scientific management and, 111; social class in system of, 154; in Toronto, 32–33; undergraduate VADs in, 58; VAD physical therapists in, 170; VAD work as temporary in, 173; VADs as fixtures in, 56; VADs as maids-of-all-work in, 120; VADs as probationers in, 45; VADs in, 40, 44; VADs in expanding network of, 13; VADs setting up emergency, 40; in Victoria, 53, 55; volunteer women in, 170. *See also* military nurses
military honours: Mentioned-in-Dispatches, 93, 179, 180t, 183; as rare for women, 93; for VAD nurses/drivers for "active service," 152–53; Victory Medal, 153; War Service Badges, 179, 181
Military Hospitals Commission (MHC): acceptance of VADs, 78; CAMC relations with, 44, 128; and convalescent hospital in Victoria, 55; DSCR and, 92; mandate, 44; and repatriated sick/wounded soldiers, 44

military nurses: attitudes toward VADs, 118; elite women as nursing volunteers vs, 8; image of, 5; and massage therapy, 170–71; memorial in St. John's, NL, 180; MHC hospitals and, 44; in North West Rebellion, 5; qualifications, 61; social class and, 5; socio-economic background of VADs compared to, 81; in South African War, 5; training, 5; uniforms, 42, 110–11, 115; and wartime nursing, 37. *See also* British military nurses; Canadian Army Medical Corps (CAMC) nurses; qualified/trained nurses
military nurse-VAD relationship: Cameron-Smith on, 76–77; close monitoring in, 121; in France, 148; Gordon and, 121; S. Johnson and, 118, 151–52; supplementary role of VAD in, 44, 172; VADs as assistants in, 36, 145; VADs as undermining status of military nurses, 40; VADs as volunteer workers vs military nurses, 7; war zone lessening of friction/cultural discrimination in, 147–48. *See also* qualified nurse-VAD relationship
military nursing: history of, 4–5; and professional recognition for nursing, 39; professionalization of, 6; regularization of, 6
Military School of Orthopaedic Surgery and Physiotherapy, University of Toronto, 168, 169, 181
Militia, Canadian, 5
Militia Council, "Organization of Voluntary Medical Aid in Canada," 18, 22, 30–31
Miller, Ian, 116
Miller, Janet (later Ayre; Murray): marriage and widowhood, 157, 186; postwar remarriage and career, 186, 233n85; as university graduate, 90t
Moffat, Ruth Isobel, 90t
Mont-Blanc (SS), 118
Montreal: creation of Voluntary Aid Detachment (VAD), 24; Grey Nuns' Convalescent Home, 67; influenza

epidemic in, 125–26; Junior League, 131; Khaki League/Homes, 44, 46, 47, 53, 67, 130; military convalescent hospitals in, 44, 46–47, 48; numbers of VADs, 48; VADs in overseas service, 47, 67–68, 89, 130–31, 209n77

Moore, Mary MacLeod: on air raids and CRCS Nurses' Rest House, 78; on ambulance drivers, 97–98, 104; "Canadian Women in the War Zone," 82; on censorship, 145; on development of maternal instinct during war, 82; on Hôtel du Nord's transformation to CRCS Nurses' Rest House, 77; on "motherly" influence of VADs, 76; vignettes of VADs in recreation huts, 75, 76

Morgan, Douglas F. (husband of Eva), 227n146

Morgan, Eva: on Boulogne bombing raids, 77; dancing with Prince of Wales, 157–58; in documentary, 10

Morton, Desmond, 128, 139

motherhood: Moore on, 76; in VADs' relationships with patients, 158–59; and war service, 82. *See also* femininity

motor vehicle driving: Étaples convoy, 101, 103, 106, 113f; and FANY, 97; in general service convoys, 99; Miller as BRCS driver at driver-testing school, 186; social class and, 101; Wilson and mechanics course, 67, 132. *See also* ambulance drivers/driving

Mulvaugh, Laura, 94

Munro, Colonel, 65

Murphy, Gertrude (later Charters): on armistice, 161; and influenza epidemic, 126–27, 161, 163; postwar marriage and career, 185

Murray, Alexander (Miller's husband), 233n85

Nanton, Sir Augustus and Lady, 206n33

Nasmyth, Beatrice, 104

National Council of Trained Nurses, 39

National Council of Women of Canada, 42

National Nursing Service Corps, 124

National Relief Committee, 17, 21, 61

"Nesta the VAD," 113, 114f

New Brunswick: influenza epidemic in, 125; Magee as travelling secretary to St. John Ambulance Branch, 183; nursing divisions, 52t; VAD program, 50; VADs and influenza epidemic, 125; VADs serving overseas, 50t

"new woman": about term, 199n39; VADs as, 13, 81, 88

Newfoundland: British ties in, 59; dental nursing in, 183; franchise/vote in, 162; influenza epidemic in, 179–80; nursing divisions, 52t; patriotism in, 59; Red Cross-St. John sharing of training/organization in, 58; St. John Ambulance in, 15, 19–20; suffrage movement in, 186, 218n80

Newfoundland (SS), 20

Newfoundland General Hospital, St. John's, 37

Newfoundland Regiment, 59, 72, 185–86

Newfoundland VADs: at 4th Northern General Hospital, Lincoln, 136–37; memorial in St. John's, NL, 180; numbers of, 20; ocean crossing, 70–71; overseas service, 50t, 58–59; postwar careers, 185–86; at Queen Mary's Convalescent Auxiliary Hospital, 204n73; sent overseas earlier than Canadians, 22; social class, 84. *See also* Canadian/Newfoundland VADs

Newnham, Georgina, 214n21

Nicholson, Emma, 54t

night duty: Cluett on, 117; difficulties adjusting to, 136; Earhart and, 128; S. Johnson and, 141–42; Starr and, 136, 142

Nightingale, Florence, 5, 61, 80, 111, 212n123

non-nursing VADs: as auxiliary personnel, 74–75; Canadian Red Cross and, 74; clerical support in hospitals, 76–77; as home sisters, 78; Imperials with CAMC as, 166; journalism on, 75; in nurses' residences operation, 78; in Nurses' Rest House, Boulogne, 77–78; as social convenors in recreation huts, 74, 82; uniforms, 75

North West Rebellion, 5

Not So Quiet (Smith), 98

Nova Scotia: nursing divisions, 52t; nursing registration in, 208n62; VAD program in, 50; VADs serving overseas, 50t

"nurse"/nurses: Cavell's execution and idealization of, 111; definition of, 162; designation as loosely defined, 97; identity of, 5, 6, 115; lack of legal restrictions on employment as, 60; middle-class womanhood and image of, 4–5; Nightingale schools and, 5. *See also* military nurses; qualified/trained nurses

Nurses' Rest House, London, 77

nursing: feminine respectability and, 7–8; importance in wartime, 4–5; lowering of standards of, 39, 170; professionalization of, 5–6; as purview of all women in times of need/crisis, 126; as unskilled women's work, 39; VADs as candidates for, 36; as work any woman could do, 6. *See also* professionalization of nursing; training, nursing

nursing community: British VAD abundance/popularity and, 40; and British VAD program/scheme, 39–40; and distinction between nurse and VAD, 59; and government eagerness to embrace VAD wartime nursing, 39; and growing numbers/role of volunteer nurses in convalescent hospitals, 40; Henderson and disapproval lf VAD scheme, 46; and inferior representation of nurses, 60–61; and overseas service–training credits for VADs, 172–73; and professional vs amateur nurses, 36; and provincial registration, 9; and "quality"/elitism of VADs, 83; and underqualified women as CAMC nurses, 59–60; and university-level training, 9; and VAD certification vs graduate nursing qualifications, 36; and VAD training, 36, 39;

on VADs' contribution to war effort, 172; and VADs in veterans' hospitals, 163; and VADs vs nursing professionalization, 40–41. *See also* Canadian National Association of Trained Nurses (CNATN)

nursing divisions: establishment of, 17–18; lacking novelty/glamour of British VAD program, 19; middle class in, 26; numbers of, 24; numbers of individuals certified to join, 23–24; numbers ready at outbreak of war, compared to ambulance divisions, 19; at outbreak of war, 18–19; postwar decline in numbers, vs ambulance divisions, 186–87; pre-war activities, 18; by province, 52t; rationale for establishment of, 18; uniform, 18. *See also names of individual divisions; and* nursing divisions *under names of cities and provinces*

nursing education. *See* training, nursing

nursing reserves: and Canadian Imperial VADs, 164–65; depletion of qualified RAMC, 65; detachments (*see also* Canadian Imperial Voluntary Aid Detachment); Devonshire House screening of volunteer nurses for British military hospitals, 64; Joint Women's VAD Committee and, 164–65; nursing shortages and conversion of VADs into qualified, 171–72

nursing shortages: conversion of VADs into qualified nurse reserve and, 171–72; demand for convalescent nursing and, 171; government extension of VAD service as alleviation of, 172; military/territorial nursing opportunities and, 39–40; physical therapists and, 169; postwar, 171–72; pre-war, 39–40; VADs and, 163; and VADs in civilian nursing jobs, 39; women's other employment opportunities and, 40, 171

nursing supervisors: Cluett and, 151; S. Johnson on, 150–51; and patient-nurse relationships, 155–56; and probationers, 222n45; Starr on, 151; VADs and, 130. *See also* matrons

Nursing Times, on VAD uniforms, 110
nursing volunteers. *See* volunteer nurses/
 nursing
Nutting, Adelaide, 218n80
Nygaard, Nancy, 159

officers: CAMC nurses' commissioned
 ranks, 59, 108; convalescence in England
 vs France, 154–55; different care for, vs
 other ranks, in military hospital system,
 154; medical, 157; nursing of other ranks
 vs, 153; relationships with VADs, 155,
 157, 158; up-patient posing as, 160
Offord, Daisy, 214n21
Ontario: Emergency Volunteer Health
 Auxiliary, 125; influenza epidemic in,
 125; numbers of SJAA branches in,
 207n44; nursing divisions, 52t, 55–58;
 nursing registration in, 208n62; proportion of VAD personnel, 48; VADs serving overseas, 50t
Order of St. John: as ambulance association, 4; and military nursing, 4; postwar
 scholarships/supports, 179; and War
 Service Badges, 179; and women as
 auxiliary nurses in event of war, 19. *See
 also* British St. John Ambulance; St.
 John Ambulance
orderlies: J. Johnson and, 155; lack of, at
 Royaumont, 140; in Liverpool hospital,
 141–42; night duty and, 141–42, 155;
 Pellatt's request for, 201n24; recreation
 huts, and release for active service, 74;
 up-patients as, 159–60
"Organization of Voluntary Medical Aid
 in Canada" (Militia Council), 18, 22,
 30–31
Otis, Alfred G., 207n48
Ottawa: creation of Voluntary Aid Detachment (VAD), 24; Fleming Hospital, 45,
 47, 48; influenza epidemic in, 126; military convalescent hospitals, 25, 45, 47–
 48; Todd as secretary of Social Hygiene
 Council, 183
Ottawa Nursing Division: basic nursing
 tasks/duties, 28; federal employees

among, 91; numbers enrolled, 24, 25;
 numbers of members, 45; organizational
 framework, 24–25; and Ottawa convalescent hospital, 45; Todd as commandant, 183; training within, 24–25
Ouditt, Sharon, 115
Our Girls in Wartime, 113
outreach nursing programs, 174
overseas service: age for, 58, 85–86;
 arrival in London, 71–74; British nurse-
 VAD relationship in, 147–50; choice of
 qualified nurses vs volunteers for, 59–
 60; and *Citizen*, 94; College Nursing
 Division and, 58, 66; direct enlistment
 at Devonshire House, 58; federal government attitude toward employees in,
 92–93; home-front service compared,
 118; independent applications/travel
 for, 51, 64–65; length of tenure in, 130,
 136; living allowance, 64–65; Montreal
 VADs and, 67–68, 89; Newfoundland
 VADs in, 22, 58–59; as not guaranteed,
 51; numbers of VADs in, 50t; and nursing school credit offered to VADs for,
 172–73; and patriotism, 129; PEI VADs
 in, 53, 54t; postings by month, 131f;
 postwar return from, 174–77; postwar
 return to, 184; and pre-war employment,
 91; qualifications for, 64; Regina VADs
 in British military hospitals, 55; schooldays compared to, 138; during Second
 World War, 234n98; social class and,
 130–31; St. John Ambulance absorption
 of men into military medical services
 for, 22–23; St. John Ambulance VAD
 contingents selected, 66t; support systems vs isolation in, 136–37; teachers
 as ideal for, 95–96; Toronto Central
 Nursing Division and, 66; Toronto-
 area women advantages in, 57–58;
 travel costs, 64–65; voyages to, 68–71.
 See also France

patient-VAD/nurse relationship: admiration of patients, 153; Bagnold and, 156;
 Chatwin and, 156; at Christmas, 160;

Cluett and, 159, 160; ethnicity and, 156–57; gratitude of patients, 143; in illustrations/photographs, 111–12, 113–14, 115; S. Johnson on, 153, 154, 159–60; and marriages, 157; maternal images/role in, 158–60; nursing supervisors and, 155–56; romantic attachments in, 155–56; Sears and, 153; and sharing food, 142; sick/wounded men as giving meaning to work, 152; social class and, 153, 154; Starr and, 153–54, 159; suffering of patients in, 143; up-patients as orderlies, 159–60; and VAD sexuality, 158; V. Wilson on, 153, 154

patriotism: of Canadian soldiers, 53; casualties and, 61; femininity and, 82; middle-class women and, 6–7, 42–43, 57, 78; and militarist rhetoric, 7; in Newfoundland, 59; and nursing as accepted task, 78; nursing wounded vs sick and, 154; and objections to VAD scheme, 39; overseas service and, 129; and propaganda, 55; Sears and, 85; teachers and, 96; as VAD motivation, 13, 59, 129, 152, 172, 186–87; working classes and, 84

Patterson, Margaret: adaptation of classes to influenza pandemic, 125; and College Nursing Division, 45; establishment of own nursing division, 26–27; nursing program at University of Toronto, 32–34, 58; recruitment of undergraduates from University of Toronto, 57; and Sisters of Service (SOS), 125

peace. *See* armistice

Pellatt, Sir Henry, 67, 201n24

Perley, Ethel, 214n21

Perley, Milly, Lady, 165, 166, 167, 177

Perley, Sir George, 165, 166, 214n21, 230n27

Peterkin, Ruby Gordon, 60f

physical therapy/therapists, 14, 168–69, 185. *See also* massage therapy

Pietà (Michelangelo), 85

Pine Hill Military Convalescent Hospital, Halifax, 49, 119, 120

Pinfold, Ruby (later Lawrence): marriage and widowhood, 157, 183–84, 232n75;

remarriage and postwar career, 185; return to teaching, 183–84

postwar careers. *See* employment, postwar

Powys, Gwen, 43f

Price, Evadne, 98

Prince Edward Island: nursing divisions, 52t; VAD program in, 50, 53; VADs serving overseas, 50t, 53, 54t

prisoners-of-war: Cluett and nursing of German, 155, 156–57; repatriation of Allied, 175

probationers, nursing: educational levels, 26; and hospital protocol/hierarchy, 8; S. Johnson as, 132, 145–46; nursing supervisors and, 222n45; VADs as, 25, 40, 45, 53, 58, 63, 118; VADs compared to, 39; VADs in hospital-training schools as, 173; VADs training alongside, 131

professional nurses. *See* qualified/trained nurses

professionalization of nursing: about, 60–61; capitalization on legacy of CAMC nurses for, 173; CNATN and, 6, 173; of military nursing, 6; military nursing as stage for, 39; nursing activists, and VADs vs, 40–41; nursing schools and, 167; rise of VAD movement and, 6; struggle for, 5–6; underqualified women as "nurses" vs, 60–61. *See also* registration, nursing

propaganda: Christianity and, 85; empire and, 55; illustrations/photographs, 111, 115; imagery in, 145; journalism about women's war work as, 82; and non-nursing VADs, 74–75; patriotism and, 55; Pine Hill Hospital VADs used in, 49; reality of nursing work vs, 129, 145; soldiers in, 114; and uniforms, 111. *See also* journalism

public health: influenza epidemic and, 187; need for infrastructure, 187; repatriation of soldiers and, 187; role for Halifax Red Cross, 124. *See also* hygiene/infection control

public health nurses/nursing: CAMC veterans and, 173–74; CNATN and,

173–74, 188; Halifax explosion and, 123, 124; qualified nurses and, 187

Pyke, Edith, 48–49

qualifications: as British VADs, 64; in call for Canadian VADs, 65; of CAMC nurses, 59–60, 61; earned by VADs postwar, 162; for overseas service, 64; and postwar push for nursing registration, 173; rigour of standard for nursing, 61; standardization of nursing, 6; of VADs vs nurses, 59–61. *See also* professionalization of nursing; registration, nursing

qualified nurse-VAD relationship: Gordon and, 122; Hall and, 119, 120; on home front, 146; Macphail and, 125–26; nurses as superiors to VADs in, 143; and promotion of VADs, 148–49; VAD adjustment to, 143. *See also* military nurse-VAD relationship

qualified/trained nurses: Bruce report on VADs as indistinguishable from, 63; choice for CAMC nursing sisters, 59; conversion of VADs into reserve of, 171; denial of admission to VAD ranks, 97; Halifax explosion and VADs substituting for, 123; lowering of standards and, 170; marital status and, 88; Newfoundland VADs under guidance of British, 58; and postwar public health, 187; social class vs of British VADs, 80; teacher VADs as little threat to future job security of, 96; training of VADs as disruption for, 49; uniforms of, 108; VAD threat to postwar career prospects, 168, 172, 188; VADs vs, 5, 13, 31–32. *See also* Canadian Army Medical Corps (CAMC) nurses; military nurses

Quebec: creation of Quebec City VAD, 24; nursing divisions, 52t; proportion of VAD personnel, 48; Sainte-Anne-de-Bellevue military hospital, 48; St. John Ambulance Provincial Council, 47; VADs serving overseas, 50t

Queen Alexandra's Imperial Military Nursing Service (QAIMNS), 108

Queen Mary's Convalescent Auxiliary Hospital, London, 37

Queen's Canadian Military Hospital, Shorncliffe, 77

railway rest stations, 40, 175

ranking system, 148

Raymond, Ethel, 74

Reading, 1st War Military Hospital, 54t

reality of nursing work. *See* working conditions

recreation huts, 74–76, 82, 175

Reeves, William, 22, 27

Regina: Grey Nuns' Hospital, 185; Nursing Division, 66; St. Chad's convalescent hospital, 55, 95, 101; VADs serving in British military hospitals, 55

registration, nursing: in Britain, 39–40; Canada-wide, 188, 208n62; history of, 6, 60; in Nova Scotia, 208n62; nursing activists and, 9; postwar push for, 173; provincial legislation, 173. *See also* professionalization of nursing

rehabilitation: CAMC vs MHC and, 44; costs of, 169; massage therapy and, 169; military hospitals and, 117; physical therapy and, 168; and Toronto convalescent homes, 56; VADs as dietitians/physical therapists and, 14. *See also* return of soldiers to field

Rendell, Mary, 101t, 233n85

repatriation of invalided soldiers: and community convalescent hospitals, 45; escorting, 177–78; to Halifax, 48; increasing numbers of, 43–44; influenza pandemic vs, 118–19; Military Hospitals Commission and, 44; and propaganda, 55

repatriation of soldiers: and federal government employment, 183; prisoners-of-war, 175; and public health, 187; and women's employment, 94, 183, 187 return of soldiers to field: French vs English convalescence and, 154–55; military hospitals and, 117; physical therapy and, 168–69. *See also* rehabilitation

Reznik, Jeffrey, 111

Robinson, Christobel, 90t, 180t

Ross, Eugenie Marjorie (later Finley): about, 232n69; postwar marriage and career, 181–82, 185

Rouen: Cluett in, 117–18, 142, 148, 151, 155, 156–57, 160, 177; No. 5 General Hospital, 89

routine/duties: Cluett and, 130, 133; Earhart on, 56; Gery and, 129–30, 133; in home-front service, 118; hygiene/ infection control and, 139–40; J. Johnson and, 132; S. Johnson and, 132, 133, 139; night duty (*see* night duty); Somme casualties and, 140–41; Starr and, 132–33, 134–36, 139–40; in war zones, 134; V. Wilson and, 132; Wynne-Roberts and, 132. *See also* working conditions

Royal Army Medical Corps (RAMC): 1st Southern General Hospital, Birmingham, 33–34; auxiliary home hospitals, 62, 63; compensation for health problems, 179; Constantinople base, 177; demand for colonial VADs, 64; Joint Women's VAD Committee and recruitment/deployment of VADs to, 12; living allowance provision, 64–65; VADs as integral to convalescent hospitals, 61–62

Royal Herbert Hospital, London: Bagnold at, 144; Bray at, 137; Humphrys at, 137

Royal Patriotic School, 72, 73f

Royal Red Cross Medal, 183

Royal Victoria Hospital, Netley, Hampshire, 206n30

Royaumont, Abbaye de. *See* Scottish Women's Hospital (Abbaye de Royaumont)

Rugeley Camp Hospital, 232n70

Rutherdale, Robert, 55, 57

Ryerson, George Sterling, 15

Saint John: creation of Voluntary Aid Detachment (VAD), 24; VADs, and influenza epidemic, 125; VADs from, 123

Sainte-Anne-de-Bellevue military hospital (QC), 48, 97, 181–82

Salaberry, Louise de, 60f

Saskatchewan: nursing divisions, 52t, 55; Saskatoon Nursing Division, 66; VADs serving overseas, 50t, 58

Scobie, Ellen Beatrice, 180t; *Canadian First Aid* article on, 187–88; as Mentioned-in-Dispatches, 96–97; pre- and postwar employment, 96, 183

Scott, Madelaine, 48–49

Scottish Women's Hospital (Abbaye de Royaumont): ambulance service, 99; back injuries at, 140; bilingualism at, 46–47; and Creil clearing station, 99; fleas in, 142; hygiene regimen, 138–39; night duty in, 142; nurse-VAD relationships in, 150; promotion of VADs in, 148–49; raising status of VADs/ volunteers, 148–49; social class of patients, 153–54; social class of VADs in, 137, 149–50; Starr at, 34–35, 46–47, 99, 132–33, 134–36, 137, 138–40, 150, 153–54, 186; suffragists at, 186

Sears, Jean: at 2nd London General Hospital, Chelsea, 137, 146–47, 224n92; armistice, and sense of dislocation, 177; on British ward sisters, 146–47; at Davisville Hospital, 146; family, 42–43, 85, 226n134; on friction between British nurses and VADs, 146; on matrons, 146, 147; and patriotism, 85; persistent sore throat, 143; on privilege of overseas service, 129; on relationships with patients, 157; return to Canada, 177; and Romanian soldiers, 157; on social class of patients, 153; as social convenor for Toronto Nursing Division, 185; on unimaginable tasks, 129; on women's vote, 186

"Second Aid" (Butcher), 114, 115f

Second World War: MacPherson and, 185; physiotherapy for veterans, 182; revival of VAD program during, 234n98

Sewell, Geraldine Wickstead: father's petition to CRCS to cover health expenses, 178–79; as university graduate, 90t

sexuality, 158

Shaw, Amy, *A Sisterhood of Suffering and Service*, 4

Sheppard, Anne, 207n43

shifts, length of, 130

Shrum, Daisy, 123

A Sisterhood of Suffering and Service (Glassford; Shaw), 4

Sisters of Service (SOS), 125

Smethurst, Sophie, 65

Smith, Helen Zenna (pseud. of Evadne Price), *Not So Quiet*, 98

Smith-Rosenberg, Carroll, 138

social class: in ambulance division membership, 26; and ambulance drivers, 104, 137–38; Bray and, 137; and BRCS vs Order of St. John, 21; and British VADs, 150; of British VADs vs qualified nurses, 80; and Canadian Imperials, 166; and Canadian VAD program, 17–18; of Canadian/Newfoundland VADs, 81, 83–84, 88; and community service, 6, 13; in defining VADs, 7–8, 17–18; of families of VADs, 81, 83–84, 153; and gender appropriate activities, 107; illustrations/photographs and, 114; and image of nurse, 4–5; and Imperial VADs, 165; Johnson sisters, 84, 132; and MacPherson, 137–38; medical officers and, 157; in military hospital system, 154; and military nurses, 5; and motor vehicle driving, 101; of Newfoundland VADs, 84; and non-nursing VADs as social convenors/hostesses, 82; and nursing of other ranks vs officers, 153; and overseas service, 130–31; and patient-nurse relationship, 153, 154; and postwar careers/lives, 162; and pre-war employment, 80, 81; propaganda and,

49; in Scottish Women's Hospital, 137, 149–50, 153–54; Starr and, 153; and suffrage movement, 7; and volunteer nursing, 43; of women chosen for VAD work, 82–83; and women's paid wartime labour, 6; and work in war zone, 153. *See also* elites/upper classes; families of VADs; middle classes; working classes

Somme, battles of, 59, 140–41. *See also* Beaumont Hamel, battle of

South African War: military nurses in, 5; nursing volunteers vs military nurses in, 8, 36; and reorganization of volunteer medical military aid, 20; Ryerson in, 15

Spadina Military Hospital, Toronto, 56–57

Sparling, V., 90t

St. Chad's convalescent hospital, Regina, 55, 95, 101

St. John Ambulance: and absorption of men into military medical services overseas, 22–23; and Anglican Church, 85; archives/records, 11–12; British ties, 84; CNATN proposal for conversion of VADs into qualified nursing reserve and, 171–72; CRCS relationship with, 21; establishment in Canada, 15–16; first aid course established, 16 (*see also* first aid course); founding in Halifax, 199n3; and francophones, 85; home nursing course established, 16 (*see also* home nursing course); IRCS compared, at outbreak of war, 15; lack of interest by civilian men at home, 22–23; lack of interest in VAD nursing organization, 16; launch of VAD program (*see* Voluntary Aid Detachment [VAD] program/ scheme); list of VAD nursing members, 11; and massage therapy, 168–69; membership in, VAD overseas service, 130; and National Relief Committee, 17; in Newfoundland, 15; nursing divisions (*see* nursing divisions); nursing proposal, on outbreak of war, 16–17; postwar careers with, 183, 185, 186–87; in postwar decade, 187–88; postwar ending women's dominance in, 187; postwar nursing activities, 187–88; postwar outreach nursing programs, 174; and public health/social services, 187; Quebec Provincial Council, 47; role in training and organizing VADs, 17, 21; VADs' connections with members of, 46; women's role in early, 15–16. *See also* British St. John Ambulance; Order of St. John

St. John's: memorial to Newfoundland military nurses/VADs, 180; Newfoundland General Hospital, 37; nursing division, 20

St. Mary's Hostel for Nurses, London, 37

Starr, Marjorie: on ambulance journey to fetch wounded, 99; bilingualism of, 46–47; designation as "orderly," 132; diaries, 9–10; on duties, 132–33; on expediency vs scientific hygiene/infection practice, 139–40; experience as differing from expectations/endurance, 163; and fleas, 142; frustration with personal problems, 143; on hemorrhage, 34–35; insomnia, 134, 135; isolation at Royaumont, 136; and lack of baths, 142; length of overseas service, 136; on lifting/carrying stretcher patients, 140; and matron, 150; on night duty, 142; on nurse-VAD relationship, 150; on nursing supervisors, 151; in operating room, 135; on *poilu* patients, 159; reassignment to kitchen duties, 135–36; routine/duties, 134–36; at Royaumont, 46–47, 132–33, 134–36, 137, 138–40, 142, 150, 153–54, 186; sewing by, 136; and social class, 137; on social class of patients, 153–54; on suffragist movement, 186; temperament, 134, 135

stipends/living allowances, 64–65, 91, 209n80, 215n40

Stourbridge, 1st Southern General Hospital annex, Gillespie at, 54t

suffrage: in Canada, 186; movement, 7; in Newfoundland, 162, 186, 218n80; VADs and, 91

Suffrage War Auxiliary, 6

Summers, Anne, 23, 30, 80, 81, 188, 209n78, 218n94

Sydney, NS, home for repatriated wounded soldiers, 44

Taylor, Margaret, 90t

Taylor, Phyllis Madeline, 180t

teachers: Hall as, 91; and hospital hierarchy, 96; as ideal candidates for overseas service, 95–96; and patriotism, 96; pre-war as employment, 95–96; undergraduate VADs as, 88; A. Wilson, 91

Territorial Forces: FANY and, 216n60; hospitals, 204n75

Testament of Youth (Brittain), 3

Teviotdale, David S. (husband of A. Wilson), 232n78

Thistle, Blanche, 182–83

Thomas, Arnold, 232n74

Thomas, Mary Maud Isobel (later Day), 180t; marriage, 232n74; postwar career, 183; as university graduate, 90t

Todd, Hazel, 24–25, 28, 32, 183, 234n98

Toman, Cynthia, 65

Toronto: Central Nursing Division, 18, 19f, 66; military convalescent hospitals in, 32–33, 45; Military Orthopaedic Hospital, 203n58; nursing divisions, 55–58; Spadina Military Hospital, 56–57; veterans' orthopaedic hospital in North Toronto, 33 (*see also* Davisville Military Orthopaedic Hospital)

trained nurses. *See* qualified/trained nurses

training: of ambulance division men, 26; level of, and difference between VAD and nurse, 13; in massage therapy, 168–69

training, nursing: CNATN and, 173, 188; history in Canada, 209n68; history of, 5; military nurses and, 5; Nightingale schools, 5; numbers of Canadian/Newfoundland VADs taking postwar, 230n39; nursing schools and conversion of VADs into qualified nursing reserve, 171–72; nursing schools and credit offered to VADs for overseas service, 172–73; standardization of, 61, 167; student nurses as primary workforce of hospitals, 38; university-level, 6, 9, 188; VAD awareness of lacking, 13; VADs as ideal candidates for, 83. *See also* hospital experience/training; probationers, nursing

training, VAD: with BRCS, 64, 83; British camps, 30; British criticism of, 39; British St. John Ambulance fees for, 83; Canadian, 26–28; Cluett's account of, 22; as disruption for qualified nursing staff, 49; emergency bandaging techniques, 33; and emergency nursing situations, 40; goal of, 31–32; infection/disinfection, 35–36; length of/time spent, 7, 31–32; manuals/syllabuses, 32; numbers of students completing, 58; nursing activists on, 39; nursing community on, 36; in Ottawa Nursing Division, 24–25; Patterson's program at University of Toronto, 32–34; during Second World War, 234n98; St. John rationale for, 18; standardization of, 26; Wynne-Roberts and, 33. *See also* first aid course; home nursing course; hospital experience/training

Turner, Sir Richard, 230n34

Twist, Dorothy Pearson, 178t, 181f, 182f; about, 232n66; death from influenza, 180; name mistakenly included among deaths of CAMC nurses on active service, 179, 180

undergraduates: Canadian/Newfoundland VADs as, 88–89; enrollment of, 58; later service in military convalescent hospitals, 58; male as soldiers, 58; as VADs, 45, 57

uniforms: of ambulance drivers, 97, 102–3, 109; badges, 228n16; British military nursing services, 108; of CAMC military nurses, 60, 108; and caregiving, 78; charge for, 83; Christian iconography in, 111; commissioned officers,

108; dress, 110–11; in English military hospitals, 122; femininity and, 18, 42; gender norms and, 7; Gordon on, 121; of graduate nurses, 108; Imperial VADs, 166; of military nurses, 42, 110–11, 115; military style of VAD, 7; of non-nursing VADs, 75; and nursing identity, 115; propaganda and, 111; of QAIMNS, 108; Red Cross VADs, 108; similarity of St. John's VAD to CAMC nurses, 60; St. John Ambulance VADs, 3, 108; Toronto Central Nursing Division No. 1, 18; VAD as similar to military nurses', 42; VAD reactions to, 109–11; of VAD student nurses in nursing schools, 171–72; of volunteer vs qualified nurses, 109; WAAC, 107; V. Wilson on, 68–69

university graduates: Hall as, 89, 90t, 91; VADs as, 90t; A. Wilson, 91

University of Toronto: influenza epidemic and, 120; Military School of Orthopaedic Surgery and Physiotherapy, 168, 169, 181; Patterson's nursing program at, 32–34; Patterson's undergraduate VAD classes at, 58; undergraduates as VADs, 45, 57; Women's University Association, 58

upper classes. *See* elites/upper classes

Vandyk, Navana, 108f

veteran status, 91, 92, 184

veterans' hospitals. *See* military convalescent hospitals

Victoria: Central Nursing Division No. 34, 232n66; creation of St. John Voluntary Aid Detachment (VAD), 24; naval hospital, 55; nursing division, 53, 55

Victoria General Hospital, Halifax, 119–20

Voluntary Aid Detachment nurses (VADs). *See* British VADs; Canadian VADs; Canadian/Newfoundland VADs; Newfoundland VADs

Voluntary Aid Detachment (VAD) program/scheme: Canadian middle-class women and, 16; CRCS and, 178–79;

demobilization of, 175, 187; ethnicity and, 17; femininity and, 17; framework of detachments, 30–31; Halifax explosion and value of, 122–23, 124; and identity of nurse, 6; influenza epidemic and, 122; launch by St. John Ambulance in Canada, 12–13; as mirroring health/social welfare projects, 19; numbers of detachments, 24; revised as WAD, 32; Second World War revival of, 234n98; service as equivalent to soldiering, 213n19; social class and, 17–18; St. John Ambulance concentration on training and organizing detachments, 17, 21; St. John Ambulance interest in, 16–17; transferred to St. John Ambulance Brigade (Overseas), 168. *See also* ambulance divisions; British VAD program/scheme; nursing divisions

Voluntary Medical Aid Scheme, 21

volunteer nurses/nursing: gender and, 43; image of ideal, 107; as lowest rank in British hospital nursing, 96; military nurses vs, in South African War, 8; popular approval of, 39; postwar lapse of interest in, 186–87; reasons for commitment of, 55; social class and, 43

vote. *See* suffrage

Wainwright, Muriel, 149f; and food rationing, 142; in Italian RAMC military hospital, 94, 148; letters in *Civilian*, 94; promotion to senior VAD, 148

Wake, Gladys, 218n86

Walwyn, Frances Marion, 90t

Wandsworth Hospital (3rd London General Hospital), 72, 73f

War Office: and British VADs, 5; and enrollment of British VADs, 64; and Joint War Committee, 21; MacPherson's applications to, 101; and Order of St. John, 31; recognition of VADs, 153; and War Service Badges, 179, 181

Watson, Janet, 7, 80–81, 107, 152, 154, 213n19

Westcliffe Eye and Ear Hospital, Folkestone, 76, 209n67

Wilkinson, Maude, 110–11

Wilson, Agnes Kathleen (later Teviotdale): marriage, 185, 232n78; overseas service, 91, 96; postwar career, 184–85; as teacher, 91, 96; as university graduate, 90t; on VAD experience, 161; on voyage, 69

Wilson, Charles (Charlie; brother of Violet), 53, 67, 154, 210n86

Wilson, Herbert C., 199n7

Wilson, Violet: about, 66–67; and ambulance driving, 107, 132; brother, 154; at Deauville Officers' Home, 154, 175; on English nursing sisters/matron, 147; father, 199n7, 226n134; at Gifford House hospital, 132, 142, 147, 154, 156, 184; as housekeeper for Red Cross HQ at Hôtel Christol, 177; and marriage, 184; motor mechanics course, 67, 132; move to Toronto nursing division, 66–67; Pellatt and, 67; posting to Devonshire House, 132; postwar careers/travels, 92, 163, 175–76, 184; on postwar homecoming, 163; on pre-war atmosphere, 16; relationship with officer, 158; return to Canada, 177; as risk-taker, 156; on social class of patients, 153; training in Edmonton, 51, 53; on uniform, 68–69, 110; at VAD headquarters in Boulogne, 176; on voyage, 68–69; at Wimereux demobilization camp, 158, 176–77, 184

Wilson, Wealtha, 74

Wimereux demobilization camp, 158, 176–77, 184

Windeler, Cecile, 201n27

Winnipeg: military convalescent hospitals, 44; Tuxedo Military Hospital, 206n33

Winter, Jay, 187

Women's Aid Department (WAD): CNATN and, 171; and multiple roles for VADs, 181; VAD program revised as, 32, 169

Women's Army Auxiliary Corps (WAAC), 107

Index

Women's Patriotic Association, 6, 20
working classes: British VADs as, 81;
Canadian/Newfoundland VADs from,
88, 96–97; and employment of women,
16; General Service Division and, 8;
and patriotism, 84; and WAAC, 107.
See also social class
working conditions: casualties, and workload, 134; Cluett on, 141; food rationing,
142; Gery on bayoneted soldier, 129–30;
Gery on war losses, and fatigue, 162;
hospital vermin and, 141; ideal vs, 117;
and illness/infection, 140; and injuries/
disabilities, 140–41, 142–43; isolation
and support systems for VADs, 136–
37; S. Johnson on workload, 139;
MacPherson and stress of ambulance
work, 163; need for discretion in, 144–
45; as not depicted in publications, 115–
16; preconceptions vs, 117; propaganda
vs, 129, 145; scientific hygiene/infection
practice and, 138–40; Starr on, 134, 135,
136, 142, 163; workload, and illness/
injury, 142–43; Wynne-Roberts on,
140–41, 145. *See also* routine/duties

Worsley, Annie, 201n27
wounds/injuries/disabilities: Earhart on,
56; from Halifax explosion, 122–23;
numbers of Canadian service personnel, 161–62; from VAD workload, 140–
41, 142–43
Wright, Glenn, 128
Wynne-Roberts, Annie (later McCaul):
at 1st Southern General Hospital,
Birmingham, 72, 74, 132, 147; at
Battersea Polytechnical College,
216n52; in Birmingham, 132; in
Canadian Bank of Commerce, 95;
on Canadian soldiers marching to conflict, 152; at Davisville, 132; letters, 34,
95; as "night duty nurse," 148; on patients, 96; postwar re-employment by
bank, 95; routine/duties, 132; as social
worker, 216n52; training, 33; transfer to
France, 132, 148; as university graduate,
90t; on vermin in hospitals, 141; on
working conditions, 140–41, 145

Young Women's Christian Association, 19
Ypres, Second Battle of, 61